The Music of Béla Bartók

The Music of
Béla Bartók

A Study of Tonality and Progression
in Twentieth-Century Music

Elliott Antokoletz

UNIVERSITY OF CALIFORNIA PRESS

BERKELEY LOS ANGELES LONDON

University of California Press
Berkeley and Los Angeles, California

University of California Press, Ltd.
London, England

© 1984 by
The Regents of the University of California

First Paperback Printing 1989

Library of Congress Cataloging in Publication Data

Antokoletz, Elliott.
The music of Béla Bartók.

Includes bibliographical references and indexes.
1. Bartók, Béla, 1881–1945. Works.   2. Tonality.
3. Musical intervals and scales.   I. Title.
ML410.B26A8   1984   780'.92' 4   82-17352
ISBN 0-520-06747-9

This publication has been supported by subventions
from the American Musicological Society, the
National Endowment for the Humanities, and The
University of Texas at Austin.

Some of the material in this book originally
appeared in "Principles of Pitch Organization in
Bartók's Fourth String Quartet," *In Theory Only*
3/6 (September 1977): 3–22. Copyright 1978 by
the Michigan Music Theory Society. Used by
permission.

Other material originally appeared in "The Musical
Language of Bartók's 14 Bagatelles for Piano,"
Tempo 137 (June 1981): 8–16. Used by permission
of Boosey and Hawkes Music Publishers Ltd.

Printed in the United States of America

To my parents, Jack and Esther
To my wife, Juana
To my son, Eric

Contents

Illustrations

(following page 77)

Abbreviations used above and in holograph captions:
FSS = Full Score Sketch
NYBA = New York Bartók Archive
PS = Piano Sketch
Vo PS = Vocal-Piano Sketch

Preface

The significance of the evolution of Béla Bartók's musical language from the folk modes to a highly systematic and integrated use of abstract melodic and harmonic formations lies in the growth toward a new kind of tonal system and a new means of progression. Although most of Bartók's works form an important part of the standard repertoire, the basic principles of progression and the means by which a sense of tonality is established in his music remain problematical to many theorists. The underlying principles that govern his musical structures have been given diverse and often contradictory interpretations: there are almost as many theories as there are essays on the subject. In this wealth of essays are many meaningful contributions to our understanding of the music, but such insights are generally limited to isolated instances and do not encompass the broad spectrum of his musical language. Since both the harmonic and the melodic constructions in Bartók's music include practically every possible combination of intervallic relations, which have varying functions within the different contextual settings, such isolated insights into some single excerpt bring with them the danger of oversimplification and distortion. For example, to discover that chromaticism is produced by polymodal combination in one passage or work is not to establish a universal principle for the chromatic relations in his music; in many of his compositions, chromaticism is so far removed from any modal source that it can only be considered on its own abstract terms.

Part of the problem that has existed in determining the basic means of pitch organization in Bartók's music is that there has been no theory, comparable to that of the traditional tonal system, to draw together all pitch formations in his music under one unified set of principles. Yet, one senses in Bartók's total output an all-encompassing system of pitch relations. The present study is intended to demonstrate that Bartók's music is indeed based on such a system. Certain fundamental principles are related to a larger system that has been referred to by George Perle as "twelve-tone tonality."[1] In contrast to the traditional tonal system, in which the octave was divided into *unequal* parts (the fundamental division being derived from the perfect fifth, which served as the basis of harmonic root function and as the primary structural interval of major and minor triads), pitch relations in Bartók's music are primarily based on the principle of *equal subdivision* of the octave into the total complex of interval cycles.[2] The fundamental concept underlying this equal-division system is that of *symmetry*.[3] The functions and interactions of symmetrical pitch collections are significant both in the generation of the interval cycles in a given composition and in the establishment of central tonal or sonic areas. Although Bartók's music is permeated by nonsymmetrical pitch collections (including the traditional major and minor triads) as well as symmetrical ones, properties of the former in the organic growth of a work can generally be understood as having latent symmetrical possibilities; that is, nonsymmetrical collections often emerge in the course of a composition as segments of larger symmetrical formations. The means by which various nonsymmetrical pitch collections (both traditional and nontraditional) are symmetrized in Bartók's music constitute an important part of this study.

The theory set forth in the present study is based on both in-depth and brief analyses of Bartók's musical compositions. The selections have been chosen both for their relevance and comprehensiveness in illustrating the basic principles and tools of the musical language and to represent the various genres—solo works, chamber music, solo with orchestra, large orchestral works with contrasting instrumentation, solo voice with piano, and solo voices with orchestra or chorus and orchestra. These studies include the *Fourteen Bagatelles for Piano*, Op. 6 (1908), *Eight Improvisations on Hungarian Peasant Songs for Piano*, Op. 20 (1920), pieces from the *Mikrokosmos* (1926–1939), the *First, Second, Fourth, Fifth*, and *Sixth String Quartets* (respectively completed in 1909, 1917, 1928, 1934, and 1939), the *Third Piano Concerto* (1945), *Music for Strings, Percussion, and Celesta* (1936), *Concerto for Orchestra* (1943), *Eight Hungarian Folk Songs* for solo voice and

1 George Perle, the author of *Serial Composition and Atonality* (5th ed., rev. Berkeley and Los Angeles: University of California Press, 1981), is also the author of *Twelve-Tone Tonality* (Berkeley and Los Angeles: University of California Press, 1977).
2 An *interval cycle* is a series based on a single recurrent interval, the sequence of which is completed by the return of the initial pitch class at the octave. The entire set of uni-intervallic cycles is illustrated in Example 70.
3 A collection of pitches is *symmetrical* if the intervallic structure of one-half of it can be mapped into the other half through mirroring, i.e., literal inversion. The properties of symmetrical inversion are discussed in depth in Chapter IV.

piano (1907–1917), the opera *Duke Bluebeard's Castle* (1911), and *Cantata Profana* for tenor and baritone solos with mixed chorus and orchestra (1930). In order to reflect as fully as possible the historical evolution of Bartók's musical language, the discussions of these selected works are organized chronologically within each chapter.

Studies of other primary source materials, including Bartók's essays and lectures[4] and his preliminary musical sketches, which are for the most part stored in the New York Bartók Archive (the small percentage remaining are in the Budapest Bartók Archívum), have yielded important evidence regarding the development of his musical language. I have had the opportunity to study at length the New York Archive materials and to survey the holdings of the Budapest Archivum. Although Bartók said little, if anything, directly regarding his compositional processes and the interrelations of the sonorities that govern his musical structures, his numerous references to the sources and properties of his compositional tools have been invaluable in illuminating the present theoretical interpretations. Furthermore, studies of the sketches in conjunction with the final versions of the music have, in many cases, demonstrated that Bartók explicitly proceeded from basic structures of the system to more subtle and interesting stages of the artistic creation, in the way that a painter may first sketch the essential forms and then superimpose, alter, and elaborate upon them with integrative details and colors.

Comparisons of the sketches with the final versions have also illuminated an issue of more general significance with regard to the evolution of Bartók's musical language. We often find in such comparisons that diatonic folk modes in the sketches are systematically transformed into symmetrical and other abstract formations in the final versions. Such correspondences between folk music and the abstract pitch relations of the equal-division system have historical and philosophical significance in Bartók's creative development; Bartók often spoke of his desire to derive much of his musical language from the music of the peasants. This brings us to a basic organizational feature of the consecutive chapters—the transformation in Bartók's works from folk-music material and other traditional sources to the new system of pitch relations. While the discussions of the works within each

4 The main collected edition of Bartók's essays and lectures, in English, is *Béla Bartók Essays*, ed. Benjamin Suchoff (New York: St. Martin's Press, 1976), 567 pp. Included are Bartók's writings on the investigation of musical folklore, book reviews and polemics, discussions of the relation between folk and art music, autobiographical statements, brief analyses of his own music, and discussions of other music and musicians. The original source materials used by Suchoff for purposes of translating or editing are noted when they are referred to in the present study. Those sources that appear in print for the first time in Suchoff's edition are noted accordingly.

Another substantial collection of Bartók's writings, in Hungarian, is *Bartók Béla összzegyűjtött írásai*, ed. András Szőllősy (Budapest: Zeneműkiadó Vállalat, 1966). A thorough listing of numerous smaller collected editions in various languages, mostly Hungarian, appears in *Bartók Essays*.

chapter are chronologically ordered, chapters are categorized according to principles moving from traditional (folk) characteristics through increasingly abstract pitch formations. Although this organization does not perfectly reflect the historical evolution of Bartók's musical language—since traditional and nontraditional features are joined in most of his compositions—it does accord with his musical emphases and his integration of diverse materials. The successive chapters are organized according to this tendency. Rhythmic and metric structural relations are discussed whenever they elucidate the functions of pitch constructions in the overall musical design.

A fundamental consideration is the approach to be chosen in investigating pitch relations in Bartók's music. On the one hand, one could deal with the separate dimensions of melody and harmony and show how they are interrelated. On the other hand, one could explore groups of pitch classes regardless of their relations to the two contextual dimensions. While the former problem is considered to some extent in the present study, the primary approach is the latter. In works using the major-minor scale system, the first approach seems more relevant, since harmonic structures are usually distinguished from linear or thematic formations; while triads in the major-minor system contain the fundamental elements of harmonic and melodic construction, the intervals of the triad on the melodic level (in contrast to the harmonic level) are often filled in by step. In many of Bartók's works, the melodic and harmonic dimensions appear to be undifferentiated in terms of pitch formation; pitch collections of divergent intervallic content are equally exploited on both contextual levels.

New systems of pitch relations usually require new terms and labels, since traditional terminology inevitably carries with it the conceptual implications of the traditional system, which may no longer be relevant to the new one. Where traditional terms (e.g., *diatonic, half-step, whole step*) can be applied without seriously distorting the nontraditional concepts, they will be retained for the sake of familiarity. We have a special decision to make with regard to the traditional alphabetical nomenclature of pitch classes. In traditional triadic music, the notes C and C♯ in the key of A, as one instance, are diatonic inflections of one another, since the two tones have an analogous function as the third degree of the tonic (major or minor) triad. In Bartók's music, where the twelve tones are undifferentiated in terms of traditional tonal functions (*even* where triads exist), C and C♯ are independent and equal entities. Yet, the common nomenclature of "C" suggests an inherent connection between these two otherwise independent integers of the chromatic continuum. Such traditional nomenclature, therefore, may inadvertently give rise to misconceptions regarding a progression or pitch-class function, especially in the difficult area of enharmonicism. While certain theorists of contemporary music have entirely substituted numerical notation for the alphabetic names of pitch classes (numbers 0 through 11 being assigned to the twelve pitch classes, with the octave designated by either 0 or 12),[5] I have chosen to retain the traditional alphabetic nomenclature where possible, primarily for the sake of familiarity. However, for those concepts that cannot be meaningfully expressed by the traditional labels or terms, numerical notation will be used. Bartók himself anticipated the necessity of a new notational system:

> It would be desirable to have at one's disposal a notation with twelve similar symbols, where each of the twelve tones would have a comparably equivalent symbol, in order to avoid the necessity of notating certain tones exclusively as alterations of others. Meanwhile, however, this invention awaits its inventor.[6]

I should like to allay any fears that the reader may have regarding a prerequisite knowledge of higher mathematics; the use of numbers to express theoretical and analytical concepts related to Bartók's music is no more mathematical than is use of Roman and Arabic numerals for triads and their inversions in the music of the preceding centuries. No more than a knowledge of simple arithmetic addition and subtraction is necessary. Complexities that may be encountered in the course of this study are primarily musical and can be worked out almost exclusively in those terms. In order for the reader to derive maximum benefit from the study of these musical complexities, it is advisable to supplement the illustrative musical examples within the text by keeping in hand the musical score of the work under discussion.

Finally, a statement must be made regarding occasional discrepancies between different published versions of the score, and between score and parts. Such discrepancies can generally be resolved, on the one hand, by a comparative study of primary sources (Bartók's sketches and their related documentation) and, on the other, by an in-depth analytical understanding of Bartók's compositional methodology. As one instance, in the last movement of the *Fifth String Quartet* (m. 825), a discrepancy between the cello part of the current edition (U.E. 10.736, 10.737d; U.E.W.Ph.V.167/EMB Z.9008, printed in Hungary, as well as in a set of parts bearing the U.E. plate No. 10.737d, printed in the U.S.A.) and that of previous editions (Vienna U.E. 10.736 and the London B&H 9044 Pocket Score No. 78) was brought to my attention by George Perle. I, in turn, requested Dr. Benjamin Suchoff to make a comparative study of the *Quartet* drafts and related material at the New York Bartók Archive. Except for the first (that is, sketch) draft, in which mm. 821-28 (end) are completely different, all other versions composed (and proofread) by Bartók himself show the cello double-stop D-F (not D-F♯) in apposition to the viola F♯-D at m. 825. Analysis of the resultant D-F/F♯-D

5 See Perle, *Twelve-Tone Tonality*, p. xi.
6 *Bartók Essays*, p. 459. The original publication of this essay is "Das Problem der neuen Musik," *Melos* (Berlin) 1/5 (April, 1920): 107–10.

sonority provides additional evidence that this construction, and not the D-F♯/F♯-D change in the currently reprinted editions, is the logical culmination of the pitch relations of the preceding measures (see Chapter VI, below, end of discussion of the *Fifth String Quartet*). As another instance, discrepancies are also found in the metronome markings between editions of the score and the parts for the first two string quartets. With regard to the *Second String Quartet*, for example, the metronome indications in the original U.E. score (1920) were subsequently revised by Bartók; the list of corrections was sent to André Gertler in 1935 and published, with the latter's permission, by István Barna, "Bartók II. vonósnégyesének módosított metronóm jelzései" [The altered Metronome Indications in Bartók's Second Quartet], *Zenei Szemle* (Budapest, 1948).

Acknowledgments

With gratitude, I should like first to acknowledge my teacher, colleague, and friend, George Perle, for his confidence in and support of my work, and for his suggestions and keen criticisms in the reading of the final manuscript. His profound musical knowledge has been a source of inspiration in the development of my own musical thinking. I am also grateful to my colleague and friend, Benjamin Suchoff (Trustee of the Estate of Béla Bartók and Head of the New York Bartók Archive), for our many discussions of Bartók, and for his help in researching the primary source materials at the Archive. Special thanks are also due to him for his permission to reproduce a number of facsimiles of Bartók's musical sketches.

To László Somfai (Head of the Budapest Bartók Archívum). I am indebted for permission to survey the materials at the Budapest Archívum. I am pleased to have this opportunity to thank the National Endowment for the Humanities for a fellowship supporting my research in 1980—without it this book might never have been completed. Their kindness has been extended by a grant in 1982 to aid in publishing the book. I am also grateful to the American Musicological Society for their generous subvention also in 1982, and to the University Research Institute of The University of Texas at Austin for a grant in the same year to aid in publication. For the skillful preparation of the musical examples and drawings reproduced here, I should like to thank Irwin Rabinowitz at Akrit Music Service in New York City. I must also thank the Editorial Committee of the University of California Press for their confidence in accepting this, my first book, for publication. I want to express special appreciation to Alain Hénon, Associate Editor, for his expert advice throughout the long period of preparing the manuscript for publication, and to Jane-Ellen Long, whose intelligent, thorough, and meticulous editing of the final draft improved its readability. I am indeed grateful to both of them. Finally, but not least of all, my deepest appreciation and affection must go to my wife, Juana, and my son, Eric, for their interest in my work and their patience during the many hours each day I spent on research and writing.

For permission to reprint copyrighted material, acknowledgment is gratefully made to the following:

Belmont Music Publishers, Los Angeles, California, for excerpts from Schoenberg: Opus 11, No. 1.

Boosey and Hawkes, Inc., New York, N.Y., for excerpts from Bartók: *String Quartets*, Nos. 2, 4, 5, 6; *Fourteen Bagatelles*, Op. 6; *Eight Hungarian Folk Songs; Improvisations*, Op. 20; *Piano Concerto No. 3; Cantata Profana; Mikrokosmos; Concerto for Orchestra; Bluebeard's Castle;* and *Music for Strings, Percussion, and Celesta;* R. Strauss: *Elektra;* Stravinsky: *The Rite of Spring; Symphony of Psalms.*

C. F. Peters Corporation, New York, N.Y., for excerpts from Liszt: *Sonnetto 104 del Petrarca.*

European American Music Distributors Corp., Totowa, N.J., for excerpts from R. Strauss: *Elektra.*

International Music Company, New York, N.Y., for excerpts from Scriabin: *Prelude, Op. 74, No. 3, for piano.*

McGraw-Hill Book Company, New York, N.Y., for material from Salzer-Schachter: *Counterpoint in Composition.*

Dr. Benjamin Suchoff, Successor-Trustee of the Estate of Béla Bartók, Cedarhurst, N.Y., for: frontispiece photo of Bartók (Photo Kata Kálmán, 1936); excerpts from *Fourteen Bagatelles*, Op. 6, prepared from Vol. 1 of the Archive Edition, *Piano Music of Béla Bartók*, ed. Benjamin Suchoff (New York: Dover, 1981); excerpts from *First String Quartet*, Op. 7, prepared from Vol. 3 of the Archive Edition, *Chamber Music of Béla Bartók*, ed. Benjamin Suchoff (New York: Dover, in preparation); MS facsimile excerpts from Bartók's sketches.

Theodore Presser Company, Bryn Mawr, Pa., for excerpt from Debussy: *Voiles.*

Universal-Edition, A.G., Vienna, for excerpts from Kodály: *Sonate*, Op. 4; Webern: *String Quartet Bagatelle*, Op. 9, No. 5; and Berg: *Lyric Suite.*

Universal Edition (London), Ltd., for excerpts from Bartók: *String Quartets*, Nos. 2, 4, 5; *Eight Hungarian Folk Songs; Improvisations*, Op. 20; *Cantata Profana; Bluebeard's Castle;* and *Music for Strings, Percussion, and Celesta.*

CHAPTER I

The Musical Language of Bartók: Historical Backgrounds

Folk- and Art-Music Sources

Bartók's musical language may be approached from either of two points of view—one in which the concepts and terminology are derived from folk-music sources, and the other in which the concepts and analytical tools are derived from certain currents in contemporary art music. This study is intended to demonstrate that the assumptions underlying *both* approaches are essential in understanding the evolution of Bartók's musical language and that fundamental relationships exist between the diatonic folk modes and various abstract pitch formations commonly found in contemporary compositions.

Bartók's early masterpieces, which were written shortly after his first investigations, with Kodály, of Hungarian folk music, bear the first important evidence of his ability to synthesize folk and art music. Among these early works, the *Fourteen Bagatelles for Piano*, Op. 6 (1908) had juxtaposed, transformed, and to some extent synthesized many of the elements that were to be basic to his musical language throughout his compositional evolution. The fusion of all these elements in his mature works was to result in a highly complex and systematic network of divergent chords and scales. Bartók's comments regarding the *means* by which he derived his harmonies from modal folk melodies suggest a link between the folk-music sources and certain procedures associated with serial composition.[1] (The term *series*

---

1 *Béla Bartók Essays*, ed. Benjamin Suchoff (New York: St. Martin's Press, 1976), p. 335. The original publication is in "The Folk Songs of Hungary," *Pro Musica* (1928): 28–35.

denotes a succession of elements, such as the Schoenbergian twelve-tone set, that have a fixed order. Although Bartók's music is based on unordered non–twelve-tone sets, that is, those that have fixed intervallic content but not ordering, the means by which he establishes connections between the melodic and harmonic levels are closely related to those found in serial compositions.)[2] Bartók described his transformation of folk elements into unordered abstract pitch sets as follows:

> Through inversion, and by placing these [modal] chords in juxtaposition one above the other, many different chords are obtained and with them the freest melodic and harmonic treatment of the twelve tones of our present day harmonic system. . . . Of course, many other (foreign) composers, who do not lean upon folk music, have met with similar results at about the same time—only in an intuitive or speculative way, which, evidently, is a procedure equally justifiable. The difference is that we created through Nature.[3]

Bartók was evidently aware that, with the dissolution of traditional tonal functions in the early part of the present century, composers of divergent stylistic backgrounds and influences were evolving a new concept of the relations contained in the chromatic continuum. The trend toward equalization of the twelve tones led to a tonally acentric system that underwent developments primarily in the works of the Viennese composers Schoenberg, Berg, and Webern, and also to a body of musical compositions that were deeply rooted in a sense of tonal centricity. These compositions, which have some connection with certain works of the Viennese composers, are significantly represented by the works of Bartók and other non-Germanic composers.

Orientation toward French, Russian, and Folk-Music Sources: Nonfunctional Bases in Pentatonic, Modal, and Whole-Tone Constructions

While the atonal and twelve-tone works of the Viennese composers and certain works of Bartók have a common origin in the extended chromatic tonal relations of late Romantic music, Bartók's music also has origins in sources that are largely removed from the Germanic tradition of the atonalists. Reaction against the ultra-chromaticism of the Wagner-Strauss period led Bartók in two new directions. With an increased demand for a national Hungarian art, Bartók turned to the exploration of authentic folk music from Eastern Europe. At the same time, as Hungarian cultural life, after a long tradition of Germanic influences, was becoming reoriented toward that of France, Bartók found a new source for his musical language in the works of Debussy.[4]

2 George Perle, *Serial Composition and Atonality* (5th ed., rev., Berkeley and Los Angeles: University of California Press, 1981), p. 40.
3 *Bartók Essays*, p. 338. The original publication appears in n. 1, above.
4 Béla Bartók, "Témoignage (sur Ravel)," *Revue Musicale* 19/2 (December, 1938): 436.

Bartók's appointment in 1907 as a teacher of piano at the Academy of Music in Budapest was important for his development in both areas, permitting him both to settle in Hungary and continue his investigations of folk music, and at the instigation of Kodály, who was appointed as composition teacher there at the same time, to study the music of Debussy thoroughly. According to evidence obtained from invoices and the contents of Bartók's library now in the Bartók Archivum in Budapest,[5] Bartók purchased in Budapest copies of several works by Debussy, including the *String Quartet* (in October, 1907) and, between 1907 and 1911, a number of the piano works such as *Pour le piano, L'isle joyeuse, Images I* and *II*, and *Préludes I*. Bartók's own *Quatre nénies*, Op. 9a[6] (written in Budapest in 1910) reveal significant connections with the Debussy works, not only in the use of a French title but also in the prominent use of pentatonic formations, as in the *Andante* movement.[7] More extensive similarities between the musical languages of these two composers may be seen in the use of modal and whole-tone formations, for example, in Bartók's *First String Quartet* (1908/9) and his opera, *Duke Bluebeard's Castle* (1911), the pentatonic opening of which is strikingly similar to that of the *Andante* from the *Quatre nénies*.

Bartók was surprised to find in Debussy's work "pentatonic phrases" similar to those in Hungarian peasant music. He attributed this to influences of folk music from Eastern Europe, particularly Russia, and felt that similar Russian folk influences could be traced in the works of Stravinsky.[8] Bartók's suggestion that the development of his own works sprang from sources similar to those of Debussy and Stravinsky (although they developed largely independently of one another) brings to our attention a larger historical framework within which his personal musical language emerged. Mussorgsky is a major forerunner of this tendency toward assimilation of folk music, and there is evidence that Debussy acquired certain features of folk music primarily from Mussorgsky. Similarly, in works by Stravinsky such as *Le sacre du printemps*, we find an extension of those Russian folk elements that had already appeared in the works of the Russian nationalists.[9] Thus, in the music of the Russian nationalists, French impressionists, and Hungarian composers (Kodály as well as Bartók), there is a common

5 Anthony Cross, "Debussy and Bartók," *Musical Times* 108 (1967): 126.

6 This is incorrectly designated as Op. 8b in the edition; see Halsey Stevens, *The Life and Music of Béla Bartók* (New York: Oxford University Press, 1954, rev. 1964), p. 327.

7 I am indebted to Benjamin Suchoff, Head of the New York Bartók Archive, for bringing to my attention the unusual employment by Bartók of a French title and also for pointing out to me certain Debussyian characteristics of this work.

8 *Bartók Essays*, p. 410. Bartók's "Selbstbiographie" originally appeared in several versions in: *Musikblätter des Anbruch* (Vienna) 3/5 (March, 1921): 87–90; *Magyar Írás* (Budapest) 1/2 (May, 1921): 33–36; *Az Est Hármaskönyve* (Az Est Lapkiadó RT Kiadása, Budapest, 1923), cols. 77–84; *Sovremennya Muzyka* (Moscow) 2/7 (1925): 1–6; and *Színházi Élet* (Budapest) 17/51 (December, 1927): 49–51.

9 Ibid., p. 325. The original publication is "The Relation of Folk Song to the Development of the Art Music of Our Time," *The Sackbut* 2/1 (June, 1921): 5–11. This essay was also published in *Muzyka* (Warsaw) 2/6 (June, 1925): 230–33, and 4/6 (June, 1927): 256–59.

bond in the inclination toward the pentatonic and modal constructions of folk music, such constructions forming a nonfunctional basis on which a new kind of tonality (or sense of pitch-class priority) is established. The basic principles underlying these historical developments were stated by Bartók:

> The early researches . . . into the youngest of the sciences, namely musical folklore, drew the attention of certain musicians to the genuine peasant music, and with astonishment they found that they had come upon a natural treasure-store of surpassing abundance.
>
> This exploration . . . seems to have been the inevitable result of a reaction against the ultra-chromaticism of the Wagner-Strauss period. The genuine folk music of Eastern Europe is almost completely diatonic and in some parts, such as Hungary, even pentatonic. Curiously enough, at the same time an apparently opposite tendency became apparent, a tendency towards the emancipation of the twelve sounds comprised within our octave from any system of tonality. (This has nothing to do with the ultra-chromaticism referred to, for there chromatic notes are only chromatic in so far as they are based upon the underlying diatonic scale.) The diatonic element in Eastern European folk music does not in any way conflict with the tendency to equalize the value of semitones. This tendency can be realized in melody as well as harmony; whether the foundation of the folk melodies is diatonic or even pentatonic, there is still plenty of room in the harmonization for equalizing the value of the semitones.[10]

Use of Symmetrical Pitch Collections by Russian, French, and Hungarian Composers

Concomitant with the tendency to equalize the twelve tones, in the latter part of the nineteenth century symmetrical pitch collections[11] began to appear as textural devices or local structural elements. While symmetrical formations contributed to the dissolution of traditional tonal functions, they also contributed to the establishment of a new means of progression. Furthermore, the specific means by which Bartók employed symmetries on all levels of his music led to a new sense of pitch-class priority. The growth toward this new system of establishing tonal priority was already apparent in the Russian nationalists' and, subsequently, French and Hungarian composers' operations on symmetrical pitch constructions.

Russian Nationalists: Symmetrical Properties of the Dominant-Ninth Chord

Works of the Russian nationalist and impressionist composers contain prominent examples of pitch symmetry.[12] The excerpt in Example 1a, the

---

10 Ibid., pp. 323–24. See ibid. for original publication.
11 See Preface, n. 3, above, for a definition of *symmetry*.
12 The symmetrical relations in Exx. 1–5, by Mussorgsky and Debussy, have been dis-

opening of the Clock Scene at the end of Act II of Mussorgsky's *Boris Godunov* (1871),[13] is entirely based on symmetrical pitch constructions and progressions. The accompaniment alternates two transpositions of a dominant-ninth chord [B-D♯-( )-A-C♯ and E♯-A-( )-D♯-Fx][14] a tritone apart. While the dominant-ninth chord is a traditional tertian construction, it is its symmetrical intervallic properties that are exploited in this passage. The primary connection between these two symmetrical dominant-ninth transpositions is their common tritone, D♯-A, which is held as an ostinato in the bass and reiterated in the voice. This tritone (D♯-A), which serves as a common pivot in the progression, also symmetrically encompasses the implied axes (F♯ and C, respectively) of the two chords (Ex. 1b). While these axes are only implied, each dominant-ninth symmetrically progresses to the axis of the other transposition, that is, C♯-B of the first [B-D♯-(F♯)-A-C♯] moves to axis C-C of the second [( )-A-C-D♯-( )], while Fx-E♯ of the second [E♯-A-(C)-D♯-Fx] moves to axis F♯-F♯ of the first [( )-D♯-F♯-A-( )]. Thus, the invariant segment (axial tritone D♯-A) functions as a common pivot in the progression between the two transpositions of the "set." This procedure, employed by Rimsky-Korsakov as early as 1867, foreshadowed the concept of invariant set-segments in serial compositions and also served as a new means of establishing pitch-class priority (i.e., based on an axis of symmetry).

1   Mussorgsky, *Boris Godunov*, Act II, Clock Scene (p. 155)

(a)

(b)

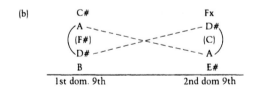

---

cussed by George Perle in "Symmetrical Formations in the String Quartets of Béla Bartók," *Music Review* 16 (November, 1955): 301.

13 The piano-vocal score published by J. and W. Chester, London, which reproduces the copy Mussorgsky possessed on the day of the first complete stage performance, January 24, 1874, is used here.

14 Where a note is missing from a given pitch formation, parentheses ( ) will be used.

Russian Nationalists, Debussy, and Stravinsky:
Symmetrical Properties of Nontraditional as Well as Traditional
(Pentatonic and Modal) Pitch Constructions

Other types of symmetrical formations that are outside of the spectrum of traditional tonal music are locally employed by the Russian composers. In the introduction to the Clock Scene of *Boris Godunov*, the original "hallucination" motive (Ex. 2a) is transformed into a symmetrical formation (Ex. 2b). While this eighth-note figure at the Rallentando sempre symmetrically expands from its axis, G♯, by an alignment of inversionally related chromatic lines, the G♯-G♯ axis is also held as a tremolo in the bass. This is immediately followed by Boris's words, "Phew, give me air! this suffocates my soul! I felt the blood rush surging upward to my face, then down again like a torrent." A strikingly similar passage is later found in movement V of Bartók's *Fifth String Quartet* (see Ex. 199).

2 Mussorgsky, *Boris Godunov*

(a)

(b)

The whole-tone scale, which appears as early as 1842 in Glinka's second opera, *Russlan and Ludmilla*, as part of a traditional harmonic progression, was employed by Debussy as the basis of most of the symmetrical material in his second prelude for piano, *Voiles* (1910). The opening whole-tone descent is registrally bounded by the octave G♯-G♯, which, together with its tritone, D, at the midpoint of this symmetrical scale, forms the dual axis (any symmetrical formation has two points of intersection separated by the tritone, in this case, G♯-G♯ and D-D). The first prominent cadential point (m. 5) (Ex. 3) on C-E, further establishes the priority of the D-D axis. A B♭-pedal, which disrupts the opening symmetry, is immediately absorbed into the second thematic idea (mm. 7ff.) as the new axis of symmetry, or secondary "key" area (Ex. 4). At m. 15, the simultaneous statement of the two themes vertically juxtaposes the two axes. Theme 1 is then expanded (mm.

17–21) by an ascent back to the initial octave position of G♯, after which the axis D-D is for the first time expressly stated as a primary foreground event. At mm. 31ff. the D-D axis appears as the octave boundary of the sixteenth-note figure, both primary axial pitch classes, D and A♭ (m. 41), prominently ending the first large whole-tone section. The six-measure middle section shifts to a new symmetrical formation, the pentatonic scale E♭-G♭-A♭-B♭-D♭ (Ex. 5), which retains the original axis of symmetry, G♯-G♯, of theme 1. The modified recapitulation (mm. 48ff.), which brings back the two whole-tone themes in reversed order to produce an overall symmetrical three-part form, correspondingly progresses in reversed order from the secondary axis of symmetry (B♭-B♭) through a passing-axis, C-C, to the primary one, D-D (or G♯-G♯), at m. 58. (The passing-axis, C-C, originally connected the basic ones in the first section, at mm. 11–12, lower staff.) After some alternation between the primary and secondary axes (D-D and B♭-B♭), the final cadence

3 Debussy, *Voiles*, mm. 1–5, main theme

4 Debussy, *Voiles*, mm. 7ff., second theme

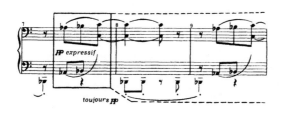

5 Debussy, *Voiles*, mm. 42ff.

on C-E establishes the priority of the primary axis. Thus, the work is exclusively based on two unordered non–twelve-tone sets (the whole-tone and pentatonic scales), linked by a common axis of symmetry. Axes of symmetry were already exploited by Bartók two years earlier (1908) in the second of the *Fourteen Bagatelles for Piano*, Op. 6 (see Ex. 163, 164, 165, below).

In the early years of the present century, the most important foreign composers associated with the international cultural scene in Paris were Russians. The interaction of non-Western folk elements (significantly stemming from the music of the Russian nationalists) with the new harmonic vocabulary of Debussy laid the groundwork for a tonal-modal musical language that was to have a profound influence on the works of Stravinsky as well as Bartók. Stravinsky's first important works were created under the influence of Rimsky-Korsakov, with whom he studied (mostly orchestration) privately in St. Petersburg from 1903 to 1906.[15] Although Stravinsky lived in French Switzerland for a large part of the time between 1910 and 1920, he was in close proximity to the artistic developments of Paris during those years, and it was during that time that his friendship with Debussy had its origin.[16] The styles of the two composers differ—the colorful, exotic sonorities of Debussy's scores are absorbed and transformed in the violent rhythmic-accentual idiom of Stravinsky's *Le sacre du printemps* (1912)— but Debussy's transformations of traditional modal and pentatonic structures into symmetrical formations within his static isolated sound patterns can be traced in Stravinsky's mosaic forms throughout his career. In *Le sacre*, which was written in association with Diaghilev's Ballets Russes, symmetrical pitch formations are frequent in the melodic and harmonic fabric of the local forms. A special use of symmetry appears in the "Mystic Circles of the Young Girls," in which the primary (tonic) chord in B major-minor and the main pentatonically derived melody in viola I (based on B-C♯-E-F♯) have a common axis of symmetry (D-D♯). This four-note symmetry (B-C♯-E-F♯) also forms the exclusive pitch content of the ostinato pattern in the celli and bassi (Ex. 6). At m. 6, one of the axial tones (D) is added to the four-note symmetry in the horn line, and at m. 7, the other axial tone (D♯) is explicitly added to the four-note symmetry in the main thematic line of viola I. The basic chords within the larger harmonic progression of the six violas support the linear four-note symmetry. Under each occurrence of the dominant degree (F♯) in the vaI melody, the upper three violas play a B-minor triad against which the lower three violas play three variant B triads: B-D♯-F♯; B♯-D-F♯; and B♯-D♯-F♯. The first vertical combination— (1) B-D♯-F♯/B-D-F♯—forms a major-minor symmetry (B-D-D♯-F♯) with the

15 Igor Stravinsky and Robert Craft, *Conversations with Igor Stravinsky* (Berkeley and Los Angeles: University of California Press, 1980), p. 39.
16 See letters from Debussy, ibid., pp. 48–56.

6   Stravinsky, *Le sacre du printemps*, "Mystic Circles of the Young Girls," first eight measures

same axis (D-D♯) as the modal tune (B-C♯-E-F♯). The priority of this vertical harmonic combination is established by the rhythmic structure of the passage;[17] both occurrences of (1) (Ex. 7) support principal melodic statements of F♯, the first before the E-neighbor tone (m. 1), the other after the E-neighbor tone (m. 3), while the two occurrences of each of the other two variants—(2) B♯-D-F♯/B-D-F♯, and (3) B♯-D♯-F♯/B-D-F♯—support one prin-

17 This metric and rhythmic analysis is given by Boulez, "Stravinsky Remains," *Notes of an Apprenticeship*, pp. 75–79 in trans. Herbert Weinstock (New York: Alfred A. Knopf, 1968).

7 Stravinsky, *Le sacre du printemps*, "Mystic Circle of the Adolescents"

cipal melodic statement of F♯ and one appoggiatura F♯ statement. Furthermore, the relative positions of these three bitonal combinations (123132) form a symmetrical scheme in which (1) is primary. With the exception of the present example, the concept of an axis of symmetry does not appear to be significant in *Le sacre;* that is, although interval cycles and other symmetrical formations are prominent throughout the work, strict inversionally complementary relations that define a single axis are not.[18]

Russian Nationalists, Scriabin, and Kodály: Symmetrical Partitions of the Octatonic Scale

As early as 1867, an eight-note symmetrical scale based on alternating whole and half-steps—this is known as an *octatonic* scale[19]—was employed by Rimsky-Korsakov in his symphonic poem *Sadko*, Op. 5. The descending form of the scale at the beginning of the *Allegro* 3/4 depicts Sadko's fall into the sea and his being dragged to the depths by the Sea King. This use of the scale is reminiscent of Glinka's use of a descending whole-tone scale at the moment when Ludmilla is spirited away by Chernomor in Act I of *Russlan and Ludmilla*.[20] The octatonic scale, which plays an important role in many of Rimsky-Korsakov's compositions, is also extensively employed by Stravinsky, Scriabin, Kodály, Bartók, and others. Scriabin's *Prelude for Piano*, Op. 74, No. 3 (1914) is exclusively based on a single octatonic set (A♯-B♯-C♯-D♯-E-F♯-G-A), in which one chromatic passing-tone (e.g., G♯ in m. 1)

---

18 George Perle, "Berg's Master Array of the Interval Cycles," *Musical Quarterly* 63/1 (January, 1977): 13.

19 See Chapter IV, n. 14, below.

20 Nicolai Rimsky-Korsakov, *My Musical Life*, ed. Carl Van Vechten, trans. Judah A. Joffe (New York: Alfred A. Knopf, 1923), p. 72.

occurs in each of the two-measure thematic statements (Ex. 8). In the opening section (mm. 1–8), the accompaniment is linearly partitioned into two equivalent symmetrical subcollections: the alto and tenor lines each unfold one of the two diminished-seventh chords (A♯-C♯-E-G) of the octatonic set, while the bass unfolds the other (B♯-D♯-F♯-A). The latter further appears partitioned into its two tritones (B♯-F♯ and D♯-A). Example 9 illustrates the symmetrical partitioning of the octatonic scale into these equivalent subcollections. Since the tritone complement of each note is present in the octatonic set (producing four tritones altogether) and in each of the symmetrical subcollections, the exact return of the first two sections (mm. 1–8 and 9–12) at the tritone transposition (mm. 13–20 and 21–24) permits total invariance both of the set and of each of its segments. (This is due to the principle of *tritone equivalence*, that is, the tritone remains invariant at its own transposition or in its complementary inversion.) Thus, the concept of invariance among transpositions of the set (or its segments), in terms of both intervallic and pitch content, establishes a new means of thematic association and progression within this limited symmetrical context. In the basic nondodecaphonic set (seven-note segment of the octatonic scale) of Scriabin's *Seventh Sonata* (1911/12), invariant set-segments function in a more

8 Scriabin, *Prelude for Piano*, Op. 74, No. 3, mm. 1–2

9 Scriabin, *Prelude*, Op. 74, No. 3, symmetrical partitioning of the octatonic set into equivalent subcollections

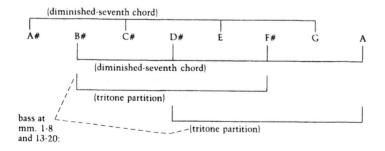

complex manner, as pivotal elements among the various transpositions of the set.[21]

Another possibility of symmetrically partitioning the octatonic scale occurs in Movement II of Kodály's *Sonata for Violoncello and Piano*, Op. 4 (1910).[22] At mm. 52ff., the octatonic scale, Db-Eb-E-Gb-G-A-Bb-C, is a focal point for the development and interaction of two equivalent symmetrical partitions, Db-G-Gb-C and Bb-E-Eb-A, each of which is based on two tritones a perfect fourth (or minor second) apart. The two tritones (Db-G and Gb-C) of the former partition first appear together (m. 24) as unobtrusive boundaries of two gapped whole-tone chords [Db-Eb-( )-G and Gb-Ab-( )-C] (Ex. 10). At the cadence (mm. 31–33, piano part), a partial statement of this

10 Kodály, *Sonata for Violoncello and Piano*, Op. 4, movement II, mm. 18–36

21 See Perle, *Serial Composition*, pp. 41–42. According to Perle, Scriabin had systematically exploited unordered non–twelve-tone sets as a means of compensating for the loss of traditional tonal functions.

22 See Linda Brewer, "Progressions among Non–Twelve-Tone Sets in Kodály's *Sonata for Violoncello and Piano*, Op. 4" (D.M.A. treatise, University of Texas at Austin, 1978).

11 Kodály, *Sonata for Violoncello and Piano,* Op. 4, movement II,
symmetrical partitioning of octatonic scale

Db   Eb   E   Gb   G   A   Bb   C

octatonic subcollection (D♭-G♭-( )-C) now emerges as a more prominent
foreground event against a partial statement (cello part) of the second octatonic subcollection [B♭-E♭-( )-( )]. The latter appears complete at mm. 35–36,
where its two tritones are linearly interlocked (B♭-E♭-E-A), while a tritone
(F♯-C) from the initial partition is vertically stated against the latter partition, giving us six notes of the larger octatonic set [( )-E♭-E-F♯-( )-A-B♭-C].
The symmetrical relations between these equivalent double-tritone partitions of the octatonic set are shown in Example 11. Furthermore, tritone
G♭-C from the initial partition serves as a common link between this octatonic set and the diatonic theme at mm. 18–23, first eighth-note (see
Ex. 10). The single tritone contained in this diatonic collection is G♭-C,
which expressly appears also as the boundary of the accompanying gapped
whole-tone chord, G♭-( )-B♭-C. [An inversion, G♭-A♭-( )-C, of the latter
chord appears at m. 24 of the next thematic statement, in juxtaposition with
its inversion, D♭-E♭-( )-G, the two tritone boundaries together implying the
presence of the initial octatonic partition, D♭-G-G♭-C.] Thus, as early as
1910 we find in Kodály's music complex procedures based on invariant segments common to octatonic, diatonic, and partial whole-tone sets. Similar
relations among these set forms had appeared two years earlier in some of
Bartók's *Bagatelles* for piano (see Chapter VII).

*Late Nineteenth- and Early Twentieth-Century
Germanic Influences: Symmetrical Organization
of Chromatically Related Keys*

Despite the reaction against the prevailing Germanic influences in Budapest
at the turn of the century and the search for new sources of artistic inspiration, many of Bartók's compositions continued to manifest certain characteristics prevalent in the Germanic musical tradition. Fundamental features
of this tradition were to be absorbed into his compositions and synthesized
along with those of the peasant melodies and French-Russian musical
sources. The Brahmsian style of Bartók's music from the early years in Poz-
sony (1890s) was transformed during his student days at the Academy of
Music in Budapest (1899–1903) by his intensive studies of the chromatic
scores of Wagner (particularly the *Ring* cycle, *Tristan und Isolde,* and *Die
Meistersinger*). However, according to Bartók, it was a performance of Rich-

ard Strauss's symphonic poem, *Also sprach Zarathustra*, by the Philharmonic Orchestra on February 2, 1902, that led him out of a period of stagnation: the Strauss work contained "the seeds of a new life."[23]

Bartók's study of the Straussian idiom led him to create a new type of chromatic melody, exemplified in movement I of his *First String Quartet* (1908–1909). While this melodic line evokes the romantic restlessness expressed in the musical thread of Wagner's *Tristan*, Bartók's freer tonality (largely achieved by sudden major-minor mixtures) and an almost continuously dissonant texture (based on pervasive use of appoggiaturas and sevenths) may be primarily associated with the more daring harmonic fabric of such works as Richard Strauss's *Elektra* (1906–1908).[24] While the Bartók quartet and Strauss opera are still based on the assumptions of triadic harmony, the constantly shifting tonalities in both works frequently result in polytonal relations.

These similarities are even more striking when we consider that the chromatically related tonalities in both works are set within a large-scale symmetrical scheme, each key being locally established as a point of departure or convergence for the tonally ambiguous contrapuntal lines. This symmetrical tonal scheme in Bartók's *First String Quartet*, in which the basic tonality of A is axial in the background-level unfolding of three prominent tonal areas, F, A, and C♯, is discussed in depth in Chapter VI, below. In *Elektra*, the basic tonality of D serves as the axis of the series of tonalities associated with the seven main character presentations of the opera (Ex. 12). In the Introduction, the opening statement of the Agamemnon motive establishes the priority of D minor. At the point at which Elektra "darts back, like an animal to its lair" (mm. 12–15), her motive alternates two first-inversion triads (B-minor and F-minor) a tritone apart (Ex. 13). This local harmonic progression based on B and F offers the first suggestion of a symmetrical root relation to the axial D tonality (B-D-F). In Elektra's first monologue (section 1, at No. 36, mm. 6ff.), B♭ is established as the tonality associated with Agamemnon, while F♯ is established (in section 3, No. 130, mm. 3ff.) as the tonality associated with Klytemnestra. The tonalities (B♭ and F♯) of the two parents are symmetrically polarized on either side of the B-F motive of the child (Elektra) and, ultimately, the D axis. At the first words of Orestes (in section 5, No. 123a), "Here must I tarry," these two tonalities (B♭ and, in enharmonic spelling, G♭) are locally juxtaposed with D as the roots of three solemn chords (Ex. 14). In the recognition scene (section 6, No. 148a, mm. 9ff.), the only tender music of Elektra in the entire opera is exclusively

23 *Béla Bartók Essays*, ed. Benjamin Suchoff (New York: St. Martin's Press, 1976), p. 409. The citation of original publication appears in n. 8 of this chapter.

24 This should not be construed to mean that the quartet is influenced by Strauss's opera but, rather, that they demonstrate parallel developments. While the general impact of Strauss's idiom on Bartók was decisive, Bartók expressed a specific dislike for *Elektra* in an essay written in 1910; see ibid., p. 446. The original publication is "Strauss: Elektra," *A Zene* (Budapest) 2/4 (April, 1910): 57–58.

12 Symmetrical scheme of tonalities in Richard Strauss, *Elektra*

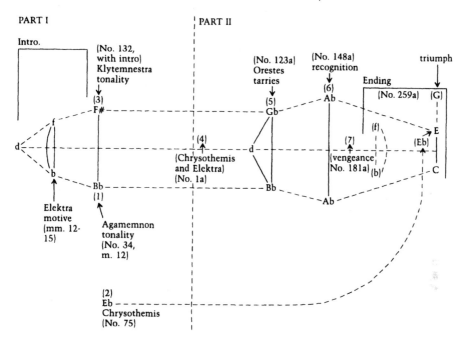

13 Strauss, *Elektra*, Introduction, mm. 12–15

14 Strauss, *Elektra*, No. 123a

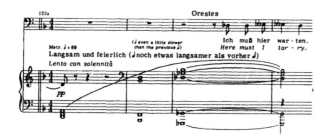

expressed in A♭ major. The latter is the tritone of the original D tonality and, with D, represents the dual axis of the symmetrical scheme (see Ex. 12). The opera ends in C major, which is associated with Elektra's triumph. We may consider the sudden and prominent appearance, in the last four measures, of the major-third degree (E) of the C-major tonic triad as part of an implied frame (C-E) for the D axis. Although the concept of symmetry has little meaning on the local harmonic levels of the opera, it appears to be the primary organizing factor in the large-scale scheme of chromatic key relations.

The Schoenberg School: Symmetrical Formations as the Basis of Progression in Free-Atonal Compositions

Strauss's *Elektra* and Bartók's *First String Quartet*, which epitomize late Romantic music on the threshold of a new chromatic idiom, are still set within the limits of tonality. While the expressionistic quality and certain nontonal aspects of *Elektra* pre-date the free-atonal idiom of Schoenberg's *Erwartung* (1909) and Berg's *Wozzeck* (1914–1922), Strauss never crossed that threshold, and after *Elektra*, in *Der Rosenkavalier* and *Ariadne auf Naxos* (1911–1912), he reverted to classical techniques and forms. Bartók's works of this period, however, were only the beginning of his new chromaticism, which may in special ways be more closely associated with certain works of the Viennese composers Schoenberg, Berg, and Webern than is commonly acknowledged. Bartók's works are stylistically removed from those of the Schoenberg school,[25] but his exploitation of pitch sets forms a direct link with them.

Although Bartók first became acquainted with Schoenberg's music only in 1912,[26] his *Eighth Bagatelle for Piano*, Op. 6, written in 1908, reveals important similarities *both* in style and method to the first of Schoenberg's *Three Piano Pieces*, Op. 11, which it preceded by about a year. Both the *Eighth Bagatelle* and Schoenberg's Opus 11, No. 1, employ "pitch cells,"[27] which replace the traditional triad as the basic harmonic premise. In both works a nonsymmetrical three-note cell is ultimately transformed, by means of intervallic expansion and literal inversion, into a four-note symmetry. A comparison of Example 15 with Example 85 illustrates that the latter for-

---

25 Bartók fuses the dense chromatic counterpoint and dissonant atonality of Schoenberg with the modal material of peasant tunes and the transparent textures of Debussy; Schoenberg's own music is tonally and rhythmically free from the influences of the latter sources.

26 *Bartók Essays*, p. 467. The original publication is "Arnold Schönbergs Musik in Ungarn," *Musikblätter des Anbruch* (Vienna) 2/20 (December, 1920): 647–48.

27 A *cell* is defined by Perle (in *Serial Composition*, p. 9) as a group of pitches that "may operate as a kind of microcosmic set of fixed intervallic content, statable either as a chord or as a melodic figure or as a combination of both." Its components, however, are not fixed with regard to order in Bartók's works or the early free-atonal works of Schoenberg.

15 Schoenberg, *Three Piano Pieces*, Op. 11, No. 1

(a)

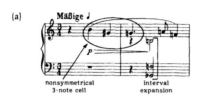

nonsymmetrical   interval
3-note cell   expansion

(b)

(c)

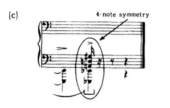

mation, based on two tritones a minor second or perfect fourth apart, is identical in the two works. More significant, however, is the use of symmetrical pitch constructions in both works for transposition of themes (or cells) away from and back to their original pitch-levels. In the *Eighth Bagatelle*, the (symmetrical) diminished triad G♯-B-D is outlined on the background level as the basis for transposing the primary cell by minor thirds. (For a fuller discussion of this work see Chapter V, below.) In Opus 11, No. 1, the (symmetrical) augmented triad (employed earlier by composers such as Wagner as a means of progression) functions on the local level as a primary thematic pivot. The augmented triad D-F♯-A♯, which first occurs at mm. 4–5, lower staff, as an unobtrusive structural element in the second theme (Ex. 16a), returns as a local foreground detail in the recapitulation (at mm. 51–54, left hand) in three successive rotations (F♯-B♭-D, A♯-D-F♯, and D-F♯-A♯), the last of which restores the second theme to its original pitch-level (Ex. 16b).[28]

In the fifth of Webern's *Six Bagatelles for String Quartet*, Op. 6 (1911/13), symmetrical pitch relations form the basis of the overall structure. In this regard, this piece, together with Debussy's *Voiles* and Bartók's *Second*

28 See ibid., p. 15.

16   Schoenberg, *Three Piano Pieces*, Op. 11, No. 1

(a) mm. 4–5 (opening of theme 2)

augmented triad (D-F♯-A♯)

(b) mm. 51–54 (recap. of theme 2, preceded by closing material)

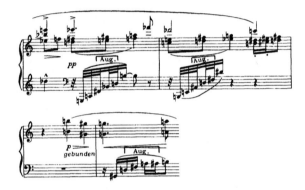

Bagatelle, exemplifies the early developments toward a new concept of content in its relationship to form. In all three of these works, which represent divergent stylistic tendencies, the symmetrical form is commonly determined in large part by the organic growth of material around a primary axis of symmetry.[29] The opening section (A) of the Webern piece symmetrically unfolds from the initial chord C-C♯-D♯-E, which is based on an implied axis of D.[30] Three new notes (B-D-F) are added at the opening of the second phrase (mm. 2–3, vnI and va) (Ex. 17), symmetrically expanding the pitch content to B-C-C♯-D-E♭-E-F. In the last two measures of this phrase (mm. 4–5), vnI further expands this symmetry by the addition of its double-stop, B♭-G♭. In the final phrase of this section (mm. 6–7), the latter interval (in enharmonic spelling, F♯-B♭) is now chromatically filled by the remaining tones, giving us the symmetry F♯-G-A♭-A-B♭ around the dual-axis A♭; that is, D-D and

29 A less systematic use of local symmetries is explored by Bruce Archibald in "Some Thoughts on Symmetry in Early Webern: Op. 5, No. 2," *Perspectives of New Music* 10/2 (Spring–Summer, 1972): 159ff.

30 The rounded binary form of this piece is primarily determined by the following: (1) the symmetrical scheme of dynamics (section A, mm. 1–7) *ppp-pp-ppp*, (section B, mm. 8–10) *pp-pp*, (section A', mm. 11–13) *ppp-pp-ppp*; (2) corresponding subdivisions of these three large sections, according to complete rests or cadences, into 3, 2, and 3 smaller sections, respectively; and (3) the departure from and return to a primary axis of symmetry.

17 Webern, *Fifth Bagatelle for String Quartet*, Op. 9

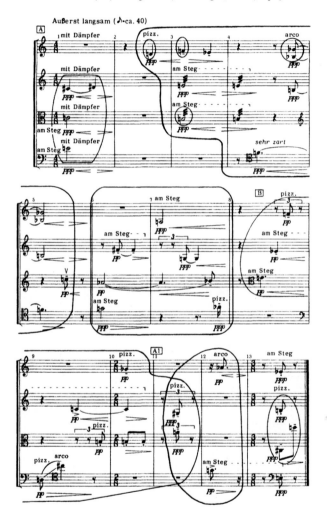

its tritone, A♭-A♭, represent the two intersections of the same symmetry (Ex. 18).[31] In the middle section, B (mm. 8–10), the entire pitch content, which is based on a chromatic filling of B-G♭, produces a "modulation" to a new set of symmetrical relations with a dual axis of D-E♭ or G♯-A (Ex. 19).

31 For a fuller explanation of this principle, see Chapter IV, Examples 77–79 and the corresponding discussion.

18 Webern, *Fifth Bagatelle*, Op 9, inversional symmetry based on axial intersections D-D and A♭-A♭

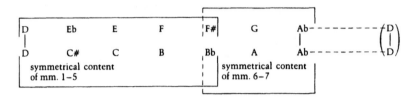

19 Webern, *Fifth Bagatelle*, Op. 9, shift to new axis (D-E♭ or G♯-A) in section B (mm. 8–10)

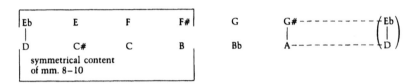

The modified return (A') at m. 11 is initiated by dyad G♯-A, which, while maintaining the preceding axis, also serves as a pivot back to the original axis (D-D or A♭-A♭); this dyad, with the following one (G-A♭), forms a four-note symmetry, G-A♭/G♯-A, based on the original A♭-A♭ axis. The final chord of the piece (B-C♯-D-E♭-E), though nonsymmetrical, appears to function as part of a long-range symmetrical relation. Three of its notes (B-C♯-D), played pizzicato, are a literal intervallic inversion of the first three pizzicato notes of the piece (D-E♭-F) in vnI. Together, these two pizzicato segments form a long-range symmetry (B-C♯-D/D-E♭-F) around the primary D-D axis. (Such long-range inversional relationships are also significant in Bartók's *Fourth String Quartet*; see Ex. 187, below.)

Berg and Webern:
Total Systematization of the Concepts of the Interval Cycle
and Inversional Symmetry in Dodecaphonic Serial Compositions

Due to the outbreak of World War I, Bartók had to give up much of his ethnomusicological fieldwork after 1914. As a result, he devoted more of his time to the systematic arrangement of the large quantities of folk material he had accumulated. This new stage in work with the folk material and the greater amount of time that he was able to spend in composing partly account for the developments in his compositional creativity. The works of this period, especially his *Second String Quartet* (1915/17), reveal a greater fusion of those diverse sources found in his earlier compositions, with a tendency toward more pervasive manifestations of the folk-music sources. After the signing of the Treaty of Trianon in 1920, Hungary had lost much of her prewar territory to surrounding nations, including Rumania, Czechoslovakia, and the Kingdom of Serbs, Croats, and Slovenes (now Yugoslavia). This severely interrupted Bartók's collecting of folk music, causing him to shift his activities during this period toward composition and an intensive concert career.

The significance of this change in activities can be seen in Bartók's increased contact with international composers and their works. In his two *Sonatas for Violin and Piano* (1921 and 1922), Bartók came closer than in any of his other works to the extreme atonal chromaticism and harmonic serialization found in the expressionistic works of the Schoenberg school.[32] (At about the same time, Schoenberg was producing his first completely serial twelve-tone works.) In Bartók's wealth of piano music written in the mid-1920s and in his *Fourth String Quartet* (1928), the transformation of his musical language into further abstractions (or at least fusions) of the modal elements of folk music may have been given some direction toward extreme systematization by his contact with other contemporary works. In 1922, Bartók participated with members of the Schoenberg school, Stravinsky, Milhaud, and others, in the formation of the International Society for Contemporary Music (ISCM). At the ISCM concert in Baden-Baden on 26 July 1927, Bartók performed his own *Piano Sonata* on the same program as Berg's *Lyric Suite* for string quartet. Shortly afterward, Bartók completed his *Third* and *Fourth String Quartets* (September 1927 and September 1928, respectively). Although the Bartók works show little stylistic resemblance to the lush romantic textures of the *Lyric Suite*, we may observe a superficial yet striking similarity in their common use of exotic instrumental colors (compare the *Allegro misterioso* movement of the *Lyric Suite* with the Coda of the *Third Quartet* and movement II of the *Fourth*, which are based on light rapid textures including such devices as sul ponticello, glissando, pizzicato, and the use of mutes in the *Lyric Suite* and *Fourth Quartet*). Certain common assumptions underlying the pitch relations in the latter two works may also be observed—the concepts of the interval cycle and of strict inversional symmetry. The latter comparison is not meant to suggest that Bartók was influenced by Berg's use of these concepts but, rather, that the two works reveal parallel historical developments; Bartók had already exploited properties of the interval cycles and strict inversional symmetry in certain of his *Bagatelles for Piano*, Op. 6, in 1908.

The basic twelve-tone row of movement I of the *Lyric Suite* (Ex. 20a)

32 Bartók commented that he "wanted to show Schoenberg that one can use all twelve tones and still remain tonal": Yehudi Menuhin, *Unfinished Journey* (New York: Alfred A. Knopf, 1977), p. 165.

can be referred to as a *cyclic set*,[33] its alternate tones outlining inversionally related segments of the cycle of fifths (or fourths). These complementary cyclic segments within each of the two hexachordal partitions generate a complete succession of symmetrically related dyads (F-E, C-A, G-D/Ab-Db, Eb-Gb, Bb-B) that intersect at the dual axis (E-F and Bb-B) a tritone apart (Ex. 20b). At mm. 33–36 (closing theme and opening of the recapitulation), the cello part successively unfolds two new twelve-tone rows (Ex. 21). Both are derived from the basic row, in that the original hexachordal pitch content is maintained, though in a revised ordering. Due to the cyclic intervallic properties, the elements within each of the hexachords appear symmetrically reorganized around the original axial dyads (E-F and Bb-B), respectively (Ex. 22). (The third row unfolds the hexachords explicitly in their cyclic ordering of consecutive perfect fifths.)

In the nondodecaphonic context of Bartók's *Fourth Quartet*, movement I opens with the same axis, E-F (or Bb-B), and symmetrically related dyads as in the *Lyric Suite*. This axis is established at primary structural points throughout the movement: in the first measure of each of the opening four phrases; in a passage (mm. 54ff.) near the opening of the development section, which unfolds around a nucleus (D♯-E-E♯-F♯) in vnII and va; and in the Coda (mm. 134ff.), which begins with an E-F ostinato in the inner voices. (These symmetrical relations are discussed in depth in Chapter VI,

20 Berg, *Lyric Suite*, movement I, mm. 2–4, vnI

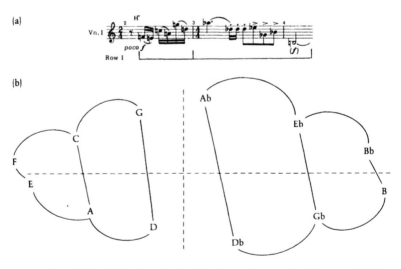

33 George Perle, *Twelve-Tone Tonality* (Berkeley and Los Angeles: University of California Press, 1977), p. 19.

21   Berg, *Lyric Suite*, movement I, mm. 33–36, vc

22   Berg, *Lyric Suite*, movement I, three related cyclic sets

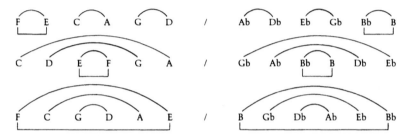

below.)[34] A comparison of the structural properties of the opening phrase of Bartók's quartet with the opening statement of the row in Berg's quartet suggests other hidden connections between the two works. In the Bartók excerpt (Ex. 23a), the initial chord, C-E-F, is intervallically mirrored by the cadential chord, B♭-B-E♭. The same two symmetrically related axial dyads (E-F and B♭-B) that temporally encompass Berg's row (Ex. 23b) are contained in these two Bartók chords. Furthermore, in Berg's row, dyads C-A and E♭-G♭, which are adjacent to the two axial dyads (E-F and B♭-B), respectively, are both partially represented by the remaining notes (C and E♭) within the two Bartók chords, the complete dyad (C-A) appearing in the cello part. These similarities are more meaningful when we realize that the symmetrical placement in Berg's row of two intervallically equivalent symmetrical tetrachords—one implied by the axial dyads E-F and B♭-B (which subsequently appear together in rotations of the row), the other appearing as the central four notes of the row (D♭-D-G-A♭)—forms the two main transpositions of the most important pitch cell in Bartók's quartet (see Ex. 181, below).

34 The discussions of Bartók's *Fourth String Quartet* in the present book are derived from Elliott Antokoletz, "Principles of Pitch Organization in Bartók's *Fourth String Quartet*" (Ph.D. dissertation, City University of New York, 1975), an extract of which was published in the University of Michigan Journal, *In Theory Only* 3/6 (September, 1977). Material from this extract is incorporated into the following chapters with kind permission from the editor of that journal.

23 Comparison of opening passage of Bartók's *Fourth String Quartet* (mm. 1–2) with that of Berg's *Lyric Suite* (basic twelve-tone row)

(a) *Fourth Quartet*

(b) *Lyric Suite*

Whereas these cell transpositions define the symmetrical properties of the larger twelve-tone series in Berg's work, they function as independent unordered four-note sets in Bartók's work. In the last movement of the *Fourth Quartet*, a new transposition of this four-note symmetry is essential in generating the entire cycle of fifths in two partitions, each stemming from one of the perfect-fifth (or perfect-fourth) dyads of this cell (see Chapter VIII, below).[35]

Symmetrical pitch relations in Webern's Opus 9, No. 5 (discussed above) foreshadow systematic exploitation of strict inversional symmetry in some of his twelve-tone serial compositions. In movement I of both his *Symphony*, Op. 21 (1928) and *Saxophone Quartet*, Op. 22 (1930) and in movement II of the *Variations for Piano*, Op. 27 (1936), contrapuntal alignments of prime (P) and inverted (I) forms of the twelve-tone row (i.e., successive pairings of inversionally related set-forms) strictly maintain a common axis of symmetry throughout. In movement II of the *Variations*, for instance, the four successive P/I pairings all have a common axis, A-A or E♭-E♭, the sym-

---

35 Similar relations between this cell and the interval cycles in Berg's *Lulu* are discussed by Douglas Jarman in "Dr. Schön's Five-Strophe Aria: Some Notes on Tonality and Pitch Association in Berg's *Lulu*," *Perspectives of New Music* 8/2 (Spring-Summer, 1970): pp. 33–35. This material also appears in Jarman's *The Music of Alban Berg* (Berkeley and Los Angeles: University of California Press, 1979), pp. 95ff.

24 Webern, *Variations for Piano*, Op. 27, movement II

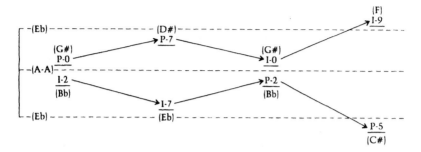

metrical relations of which are illustrated in Example 24.[36] (These P and I components of each pair are transposed in opposite directions by an equivalent number of semitones in relation to the preceding pair.)

The tendency toward equalization of the twelve tones, which was significantly manifested in the local textural uses of symmetrical formations in the late nineteenth century, led in many twentieth-century compositions to pervasive use of symmetrical formations as the primary means of integrating the large-scale structure. While symmetrical properties were to a large extent commonly derived (e.g., by Russian and French composers) from the pentatonic and modal materials of Eastern-European folk music, the concept of symmetry emerged in the works of others (e.g., German and Viennese composers) from the chromatic tonality of late nineteenth-century Romantic music. Certain types of symmetrical pitch collections became associated with certain composers: a few instances are the pentatonic and modal scales of Debussy and Stravinsky, the whole-tone scale of Debussy, the octatonic scale of Rimsky-Korsakov, Scriabin, and Stravinsky, and the use of strict inversionally symmetrical procedures in the atonal works of the Viennese composers. Bartók's works (and, to a lesser extent, Kodály's) can be considered an historical focal point for all these musical sources, since in the course of his compositional evolution he comprehensively absorbed and integrated all these formations (both traditional and nontraditional) into an all-encompassing system of symmetrical relations.

36 See Peter Westergaard, "Webern and 'Total Organization,'" *Perspectives of New Music* I/2 (Spring, 1963): 109.

CHAPTER II

Harmonization of Authentic Folk Tunes

A study of Bartók's harmonic evolution may well begin with the early works based on harmonic settings of authentic Eastern-European folk melodies. In December, 1906, after Bartók's first expedition with Kodály to collect and study Hungarian peasant music, the two composers jointly arranged and published *Twenty Hungarian Folksongs* for voice and piano (*Magyar népdalok*). Already the modalities of the tunes show evidence of a weakening of traditional dominant-tonic relations. For instance, the bass progression of the triads in the first phrase of No. 6 outlines a minor-seventh chord. The latter is a substructure of the pentatonic scale (C-E♭-F-G-B♭), which is prevalent in the C-Aeolian modal folk tune. Tonal staticism is also produced to some degree by sustaining a single third or fourth, as in the harmonization of No. 3. For Bartók, there followed many settings of authentic folk melodies—for piano alone, for voice and piano, for two violins, and for chorus. His detailed studies of the melodic and rhythmic characteristics of these monodic peasant tunes led him to new sources for the formation of his musical language. In his autobiography Bartók discussed the influence of these sources:

> The outcome of these studies was of decisive influence upon my work, because it freed me from the tyrannical rule of the major and minor keys. The greater part of the collected treasure, and the more valuable part, was in old ecclesiastical or old Greek modes, or based on more primitive (pentatonic) scales, and the melodies were full of most free and varied rhythmic phrases and changes of tempi, played both *rubato* and *giusto*. It became clear to me that the old modes, which had been forgotten in our music, had lost nothing of their vigor. Their

new employment made new rhythmic combinations possible. This new way of using the diatonic scale brought freedom from the rigid use of the major and minor keys, and eventually led to a new conception of the chromatic scale, every tone of which came to be considered of equal value and could be used freely and independently.[1]

In his desire to move away from traditional Western influences, Bartók had to find a means for deriving new pitch structures to harmonize both authentic folk melodies of Eastern origin and his own original inventions, which might include imitations of folk melodies. The folk tunes themselves showed Bartók new ways of harmonization. In his early explorations into the sources of Hungarian peasant music, certain musical styles became apparent. He found that the peasants, in their oral musical tradition, naturally tended to transform the elements of their music, giving rise to numerous variants of one or another melody.[2] Some peasant groups who had been minimally exposed to outside cultural influences (as with a segment of the Rumanian population) tended to preserve their old traditions without change. Other peasant groups who had intercommunication with surrounding tribes and with the towns tended to absorb foreign elements into their existing music, creating a new style that had probably begun to develop only in the second half of the nineteenth century. Thus, Bartók found older and newer styles present alongside one another in some nations (e.g., the Moravians and the Slovaks), while a single homogeneous style several centuries old was preserved in other nations. Of the diversely collected folk melodies, Bartók distinguished three categories: (1) melodies in the old Hungarian peasant-music style; (2) a group of melodies exhibiting no unity of style; and (3) melodies in the new Hungarian peasant-music style.[3] Among the fundamental characteristics of the old style is a pentatonic scalar basis for the melodies, with occasional transformations of the latter into the Dorian, Phrygian, or Aeolian mode. Among the fundamental characteristics of the new style is a heptatonic modal basis for the melodies, including Dorian and Aeolian scales with strong pentatonic inflections, and Mixolydian, Phrygian, and even major scales sometimes strongly felt. The Lydian mode, which is strongly characteristic of certain Slovak melodies, is never found in these old Hungarian melodies.[4]

From the pentatonic scale, the basis of the oldest of the Hungarian peasant tunes, Bartók derived special limited possibilities for harmonization. These included two triads (one major, the other minor), the minor-seventh

---

1 *Béla Bartók Essays*, ed. Benjamin Suchoff (New York: St. Martin's Press, 1976), p. 410. The original publication appears in n. 8 of Chapter I.
2 Ibid., p. 81. The original publication is "Hungarian Peasant Music," *Musical Quarterly* 19/3 (July, 1933): 267–89.
3 Ibid., p. 84. See ibid. for original publication.
4 Ibid., p. 66. The original publication is "La musique populaire hongroise," *Revue Musicale* 2/1 (November, 1921): 8–22.

chord, and the inversions of these chordal structures. Bartók traced the consonant use of the minor-seventh chord to the old pentatonic melodies, where the seventh appears as an interval of equal importance with the third and fifth. Since these intervals were frequently heard as of equal value in the linear succession, it seemed natural to make them sound of equal importance when used simultaneously. Also, the frequent use of fourth intervals in the pentatonic melodies suggested the use of fourth chords.[5] In the new modal folk tunes the underlying linear structure is often pentatonic, so Bartók gave priority to pentatonically derived harmonies here also. Such heptatonic modal melodies did, however, expand the number of harmonic possibilities:

> The simpler the melody the more complex and strange may be the harmonization and accompaniment that go well with it. . . . It is obvious that we are much freer in the invention of an accompaniment than in the case of a melody of a more complex character. These primitive melodies, moreover, show no trace of the stereotyped joining of triads. . . . It allows us to bring out the melody most clearly by building round it harmonies of the widest range varying along different keynotes. I might also say that the traces of polytonality in modern Hungarian music and in Stravinsky's music are to be explained by this possibility.[6]

Thus, chords were freely used to harmonize melody notes that do not belong to them. This led to the use of traditionally dissonant intervals as consonances even within cadential chords.

The harmonizations of authentic folk tunes in the fourth and fifth of the *Fourteen Bagatelles for Piano*, Op. 6 (1908), are a significant point of departure for the development of Bartók's individual harmonic language. In *Bagatelle No. IV* the harmonic fabric is determined primarily by means other than those of the traditional major-minor scale system.[7] This harmonized folk tune is in the D-Aeolian mode, or D minor. Since there is no major-seventh degree, or leading tone (C♯), in this mode, the triad built on the fifth degree (A-C-E) does not play the same tonality-defining role here that it did in traditional tonal music. Instead, the function of the modal minor-seventh degree (C) appears to be static since, without an adjacent

---

5 Each of these pentatonic derivations is discussed by Bartók in ibid., pp. 334–36. The original publication is given in n. 1 of Chapter I.

6 Ibid., p. 342. The original publication is "A parasztzene hatása az újabb műzenére" ("The Influence of Peasant Music on Modern Music"), *Új Idők* (Budapest) 37/23 (May, 1931): 718–19. Versions of this essay also appeared in: *Magyar Minerva* (Bratislava) 2/8 (October, 1931): 225–28; *Mitteilungen der Österreichischen Musiklehrerschaft* (Vienna) No. 2 (March–April, 1932): 8–10, and No. 3 (May–June, 1932): 5–8; *Revista Fundatiilor* (Bucharest) 1/6 (June, 1934): 114–18; and *Ankara Halkevi* (Turkey) No. 8 (1936): 18–23.

7 The tune is an old Hungarian folksong that Bartók collected in 1907 in Felsőiregh, Tolna, a district west of the Danube. The present discussion of *Bagatelle No. IV* as well as the discussions of some of the others in subsequent chapters (specifically, *Bagatelle Nos. I, II, VIII, IX,* and *X*) are based on my article, "The Musical Language of Bartók's *14 Bagatelles* for Piano," *Tempo* 137 (June, 1981): 8–16. (The latter is incorporated into the present book with the kind permission of Malcolm MacDonald, editor of *Tempo*.)

25 *Bagatelle No. IV*, mm. 1–4

semitone, it does not have a strong tendency toward another tone. In the first two phrases of the melody (Ex. 25), the minor-seventh degree occurs as one of four principal tones, D-F-A-C, the sixth degree (B♭) and fourth degree (G) of the mode having passing functions and the second degree (E) being omitted altogether. While the first phrase is simply harmonized by triads, the second phrase adds a seventh degree to each of the original triads, so that in all but two of the chords (ninth chords on F and C) the minor-seventh chord outline of the melody is vertically projected.

A special property of the minor-seventh chord is its symmetrical intervallic construction—half of the chord intervallically mirrors the other half—which tends to weaken traditional tonal functions by imparting a static quality.[8] The parallel motion of these root-position chords contributes to the equalization of the chordal tones, by eliminating the necessity for logical preparation or resolution of any of the tones in terms of traditional voice-leading. The bass line, or root progression, supporting these parallel chords is also a manifestation of the minor-seventh-chord outline, the bass-note G functioning as a passing-tone. This note (G), together with the minor-seventh-chord outline (D-F-A-C), symmetrically expands the four notes to a pentatonic substructure (D-F-G-A-C) of the D-Aeolian melody.[9] This exclusively pentatonic bass line, which contains no semitone adjacencies, contributes to a weakening of the tonal motion. The harmonic fabric seems, therefore, simply to exist within the D-Aeolian framework rather than functionally participating, in the traditional sense, in the establishment of D as a tonal priority. Whereas traditional tonal centers are established by certain hierarchical relations inherent in the structure of major and minor scales, the priority of pitch-class D is established here by other

8 George Perle states in *Serial Composition and Atonality* (5th ed., rev., Berkeley and Los Angeles: University of California Press, 1981), p. 26, that "Because of its self-evident structure such a chord tends to have a somewhat stable character."

9 According to *Bartók Essays*, pp. 371f., four of the five notes of the pentatonic scale, that is, those outlining the minor-seventh chord, are almost equal in weight, the remaining fourth degree usually occurring as a passing-tone. Only extracts of the MSS. of four of Bartók's Harvard Lectures, given during February, 1943, were published in John Vinton, "Bartók on his own Music," *Journal of the American Musicological Society* 19/2 (Summer, 1966): 232–43.

means. Within three of the four melodic phrases (the fifth and sixth phrases are exact reiterations of the third and fourth), D prominently appears in the melodic contour as the highest and lowest note, is exposed temporally as the last note of all the phrases and is repeated in the final measure, and is the only tone that appears melodically in more than one octave position. Its priority is further supported by the prominence of the tonic triad.

The pentatonic-bass and minor-seventh-chord outlines also emerge in the third and fourth melodic phrases as primary foreground material (Ex. 26). These melodic phrases are exclusively based on this pentatonic formation, but the four tones of the minor-seventh chord now appear, in the third phrase, in linear adjacency. In the latter phrase, the supporting bass progression is then derived from four of five notes of another pentatonic substructure [G-B♭-C-D-( )] of the Aeolian tune. Although the melody retains the cadential focus on D, a sense of modulation is suggested by the new bass and the cadential major-seventh chord on B♭.

26 *Bagatelle No. IV*, third and fourth phrases

In his harmonization Bartók projects the prominent melodic perfect fourth (or its harmonic inversion, the perfect fifth) both vertically and into the bass line.[10] While the vertical projection retains a fundamental association with traditional tonal music (as the boundary of the triad), this association is more apparent than real, since the perfect fifth of each triad in the first phrase is registrally isolated in the two lower lines and presented in parallel motion. Consecutive fifths (e.g., in the eighth-note groups of the first phrase—F-C, G-D, and A-E—which outline a symmetrical six-note segment of the cycle of fifths) suggest a symmetrical, cyclic reordering of the intervals of the modal folk tune. The projection of this melodic interval, either singly or compounded to form a larger symmetry, occurs even more prominently and still more removed from functional roles in other bagatelles. Thus, Bartók's folk-tune harmonization establishes a new concept of sonic unification.

10 Ibid., p. 336. The original publication is given in n. 1 of Chapter I.

27 *Bagatelle No. V*, mm. 1–15

In *Bagatelle No. V*, the opening statement of the folk tune (mm. 1–27) is harmonized by a minor-seventh chord, G-B♭-D-F, which is built up from the tonic degree of the G-Dorian mode.[11] This chord, which appears in an eighth-note ostinato pattern, returns (mm. 65ff.) in the consequent phrase of the final folk-tune statement and as the final chord of the work. The employment of a single (implicitly symmetrical) chord as the basis of large sections of the work tends to produce even greater tonal staticism than in *Bagatelle No. IV*. Bartók's choice of the first inversion (B♭-D-F-G) appears to be primarily determined by the contour of the melody (Ex. 27). The antecedent melodic phrase (mm. 5–11) is initiated by the tonic and seventh modal degrees, G-F. This dyadic segment occurs prominently three times in the first three measures of this melody, as a sort of nucleus. The prominence of G-F is further established at mm. 12–15, where it initiates each of the two subdivisions of the consequent phrase. By employing the inverted position (B♭-D-F-G) of the minor-seventh chord, G and F are brought into vertical proximity as the upper two notes of the chord, thereby harmonically reflecting this prominent melodic interval. The vertical order of the two remaining tones (D and B♭) of the chord reflects the descending melodic pattern of the principal modal tones (see Ex. 27).

After the first piano interlude (mm. 20–27), in which textural variety and tonal motion are achieved through successive statements of this chord in all its inversions, a new chord is established (m. 28) at the opening of the second statement of the folk tune. This tune, now in the right hand, appears an octave higher than before, so that the initial melodic dyad, G-F, occupies the registral position it had in the opening inverted tonic sonority, B♭-D-F-G (Ex. 28). The new chord, C-E-( )-B♭, outlines a dominant-seventh on the

11 This tune is a Slovakian folksong from the province of Gömör.

28   *Bagatelle No. V, mm. 28–45*

fourth modal degree. This chord is also inverted, so the whole tone, in this case C-B♭, is retained in the upper two notes of the chord. At m. 40, C-B♭ ends the first melodic segment of the consequent phrase, analogous to the point in the antecedent phrase occupied by G-F.

The derivation of this vertical (harmonic) ordering from the melodic contour foreshadows basic concepts and procedures of serial music. Such vertical projections of basic melodic features are the main criteria for establishing connections between the harmonic and melodic levels. However, *Bagatelle No. V* may be considered transitional, since a sense of tonality is partly determined by a reminiscence of traditional tertian harmony and by the specific melodic organization of the diatonic mode. (In connection with the latter, tonality is established by a melodic motion from the initial G to a semi-cadence on the fifth degree, D, at the end of the antecedent phrase, and back to G at the end of the consequent phrase. The priority of G is also asserted by its prominent registral and temporal position within the melodic contour.) Consequently, while this accompanying minor-seventh chord retains some association with traditional chords, it appears as a collection of equal pitches.

The tunes of four of the *Eight Hungarian Folk Songs*[12] for solo voice and piano are exclusively pentatonic, and pentatonic segments are prominent in

12 Most of the tunes are from the Csík District in Transylvania.

the vocal lines of two songs that are otherwise modally heptatonic.[13] In many cases, the linear pentatonic properties are projected into the harmonic structure, where they serve as the framework for chromatic unfolding of triads and seventh chords that produce expanded modal pitch collections.

In the *First Song* ("Black Is the Earth"), the E-pentatonic pitch-content of the folk tune is projected into the bass line, where it forms part of a complete statement of the E-Phrygian mode (Ex. 29). The contrapuntal alignment of the E-Phrygian bass against the E-pentatonic vocal line serves to establish the exclusive tonal priority of E throughout the song: in the first section, the bass line moves from the tonic (E) to an upper-neighbor sixth (C)

29 *First Song,* contrapuntal alignment of E-Phrygian bass line against E-pentatonic vocal line

13 In addition to the folk tunes of nos. I, II, IV, and V, which are exclusively E-pentatonic, those of nos. III (in E♭-Aeolian) and VIII (in D-Aeolian) are cadentially based on pentatonic melodic segments. In contrast, the vocal cadences in nos. VI (in E-Dorian) and VII (in F-Phrygian) are unambiguously defined in terms of their respective heptatonic modes. The songs will be discussed in this order.

30 *First Song, mm. 3–8*

at the first cadence (m. 6) and back to the E tonic at the second cadence (m. 8); in the second section (mm. 9ff.), the bass line moves from the fifth degree (B) through the passing fourth degree (A) at the first cadence (m. 13) to the final E-Phrygian descent (G-F-E). The E-pentatonic collection, established in the introduction as a scale figure (E-G-A-B-D) that alternates with its arpeggiated tonic minor-seventh chord (E-G-B-D), forms the harmonic basis (at mm. 3 and 8) of the first and last notes of the tune (seventh degree, D, and tonic, E). While the overall harmonic root-progression is determined by the E-Phrygian bass outline, the local harmonic progression between these two pentatonic points expands the E-pentatonic pitch-content to larger E-modal collections (Ex. 30). At m. 3, the second-inversion seventh chord, E-G-A-C♯, contains the first chromatic element (C♯) outside the E-pentatonic scale, expanding the latter to an incomplete E-Dorian collection (E-(-)-G-A-B-C♯-D). At the beginning of m. 4, the Dorian III65 (B-D-F♯-G) supplies the missing second degree (F♯) to complete the mode (E-F♯-G-A-B-C♯-D). At the cadence of the first phrase (mm. 5–6), a local progression (V65/VI to VI), which microtonicizes the upper-neighbor bass note, C, presents two new notes, F and C. The latter, a chromatic lowering of the second and sixth degrees (F♯ and C♯) of the preceding E-Dorian collection, contribute to the establishment of the E-Phrygian mode (E-F-G-A-B-C-D). (While the local harmonic progres-

sion suggests the C-major permutation of this diatonic collection, the larger
linear unfolding in the bass line and voice suggest the E-Phrygian permutation; see Ex. 29.)

The significance of this harmonic juxtaposition of the E-Dorian and E-
Phrygian collections is that together they symmetrically expand around the
common E-pentatonic nucleus (Ex. 31).[14] At m. 8, the second phrase returns
to the exclusive E-pentatonic pitch content following a partial restatement
(at m. 7, beats 3–4) of the E-Dorian mode (E-( )-G-A-B-C♯-D). (The latter E-
Dorian interpretation is supported by an earlier draft of the song, in which
the entire mode pervades these cadential measures; see Ex. 32.)[15] Thus, the
pentatonic structure of the folk tune is employed in this triadic context as a
new means of harmonic and melodic unification, i.e., it serves as a common
symmetrical segment between two larger heptatonic modal sets.

In the second statement of the tune (mm. 11–16), these modal areas
are redistributed in the accompaniment. The initial phrase (m. 11 through
m. 13, first arpeggiation) is now primarily harmonized by the basic E-
pentatonic scale, thereby establishing its priority. In correspondence with

31   *First Song*, mm. 3–6

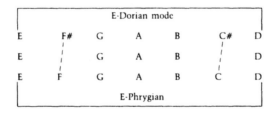

32   *First Song*, early draft of mm. 7–8 (see Illustration 1)

14 The concept of symmetry in this context, which is still based on traditional tertian
harmony, is less systematic than in Bartók's later works, in that pitch-class duplication and
register do not play a symmetry-defining role. However, these modal relations are an early development that foreshadows a new concept of symmetrically filling in musical space.

15 All quoted sketches or autograph manuscripts of Bartók's music in the present book
are held at the New York Bartók Archive.

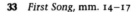

33 *First Song,* mm. 14–17

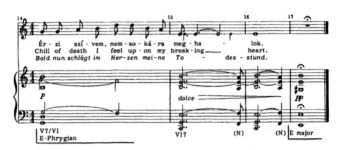

the text, "hogy még megsem siratott" ("Is it so true lovers part?"), the E-pentatonic arpeggiation shifts to the A-major triad at the cadential point (m. 13). The latter chord, with the E-pentatonic scale, reestablishes the original E-Dorian segment (E-( )-G-A-B-C♯-D). Then, at mm. 14–16 the consequent phrase is exclusively harmonized in E-Phrygian,[16] the original cadential V7–I progression in the microtonicized key of C (mm. 5–6) now unambiguously functioning as a V7/VI–VI7 progression in the E-Phrygian mode (Ex. 33). The cadential F-major-seventh chord serves as an incomplete neighbor to the final major-tonic triad.

In the *Second Song* ("Coldly Runs the River"), as in the *First,* the E-pentatonic pitch-content of the folk tune serves as a common symmetrical referent around which larger heptatonic modes are chromatically balanced. The contour of the introductory E-pentatonic scale foreshadows that of the accompanying bass line in the opening statement of the tune (mm. 4–14). The descending bass expands the introductory E-pentatonic scale to a complete E-Aeolian statement, which exclusively establishes E as the tonal priority (Ex. 34); i.e., the introductory scale moves from the high note, E, to a half-cadence on the fifth degree (B), while the modally expanded bass moves from the fifth degree (B) back to the E tonic at the beginning and ending of the second phrase (mm. 9, 13). The pitch content of the first two vocal phrases (mm. 4–8), which is exclusively based on the central three notes (G-A-B) of the basic E-pentatonic collection (E-G-A-B-D) (Ex. 35a), serves as a nucleus for the unfolding of chromatic chords above the E-Aeolian bass. Against the vocal line of the first phrase, the accompaniment linearly unfolds this segment (G-A-B) in retrograde, the additional note, F♯, at the first cadence expanding the three pentatonic notes to four notes (F♯-G-A-B) of the E-Aeolian mode. At the opening of the second phrase (m. 6), the new note, C, the sixth degree of the latter mode, now symmetrically expands the segment to F♯-G-A-B-C in the combined chord and vocal part (Ex. 35b).

16 The one nonmodal pitch class (E♭) of this song, which has appeared in the first statement of the tune (m. 7), is omitted from the second statement.

34 *Second Song*, mm. 1–14, contrapuntal alignment of E-Aeolian bass
against pentatonic vocal segment

35 *Second Song*, mm. 1–14, polymodal balance around
E-pentatonic referent

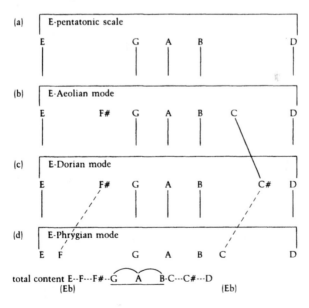

The remainder of the harmonic progression in the second phrase (upbeat to m. 7 through m. 8) introduces a modal conflict between the chromatic sixth degrees (C and C♯) of E-Aeolian and E-Dorian, which produces an asymmetrical chromatic imbalance above the pentatonic referent, G-A-B (Ex. 35c). Within the final passage of this section, the chromatic conflict between the C and C♯ sixth degrees (at mm. 10–11) is then symmetrically balanced around the pentatonic collection by another modal conflict between the chromatic second degrees (F♯ and F) of the E-Aeolian (or Dorian) and E-Phrygian modes (Ex. 35b, c, d). At the repeat of the tune after the interlude, the E-Aeolian root-progression serves as the basis for a greater chordal chromaticism. Thus, the pentatonic folk tune forms a symmetrical framework around which unfolds a balanced combination of modes on E.

In the *Fourth Song* ("Sad My Heart and Weary with Pain"), the second phrase of the E-pentatonic vocal line (mm. 4–6) contains a segment, D-B-A-E, that is linearly projected into the accompaniment as the structural basis of a larger chromatically descending thread.[17] Each of these four notes is consecutively presented as a component of one of the four cadential chords (mm. 3, 6, 9, 11) (Ex. 36). This background-level unfolding of the referential E-pentatonic segment significantly contributes to the establishment of E as the tonal priority. The nontraditional progression of triads and seventh chords built around this cantus firmus unfolds larger modal and then polymodally chromatic pitch collections. In the first phrase (mm. 1–3), both the

36 *Fourth Song*, contrapuntal alignment of E-pentatonic voice with a chromatic cantus firmus that prolongs a vocal pentatonic segment (D-B-A-E)

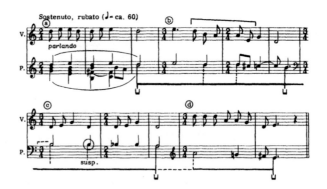

17 The hidden linear unfolding of this chromatically embellished pentatonic segment is reminiscent of sixteenth-century works in which a head motive generates a larger *cantus firmus* distributed among various voices. This slower-moving chromatic manifestation of the vocal segment may perhaps be interpreted as a reflection of the text, "Any-nyi bánat az szüvemen, Kétrét hajlott az egeken" ("Skies above are heavy with rain, sad my heart and weary with pain").

37   *Fourth Song*, early draft of mm. 7–8 (see Illustration 2)

initial and cadential chords are exclusively based on the E-pentatonic pitch-content, which serves as a frame of reference for the symmetrical expansion to the larger E-Aeolian collection (E-F♯-G-A-B-C-D) (the same relation occurs at the opening of the *Second Song*; see Ex. 35a, b). At mm. 5–6 of the second phrase, a conflict is introduced in the chromatically descending cantus-firmus line between the sixth degree (C♯ and C) of the E-Dorian and of the E-Aeolian mode. The successive building of E modes from the basic E-pentatonic set is also seen in the motion from the exclusively E-pentatonic opening chord of this phrase (m. 4, beats 1–2) to the cadential E-Aeolian "dominant" (m. 6). The third phrase opens (at m. 7) with a continuation of the E-Aeolian mode. (In an early draft of this song [Ex. 37], F♮ appears in place of F♯ in the accompaniment; thus in Bartók's earlier idea the same symmetrical balance, around the E-pentatonic referent, would have been maintained as in the first two songs.) At mm. 8–9, the remaining chromatic voice-leading then establishes an incomplete cadence in the remote key of Bb (i.e., a tritone away from the E tonic).[18] The latter progression supplies all but one of the remaining chromatic tones in a context that moves out of the E-modal spectrum. At the opening of the fourth phrase (m. 10), the bass moves from the cadential F to F♯, and this new chord, B-D♯-F♯-A (the dominant-seventh of E), anticipates the return to the E-modal context at the cadence (m. 11) and E-pentatonic mode at the strophic repeat (m. 12). Thus, while the E-pentatonic pitch-content remains invariant between the larger diatonic modal sets, the background unfolding of the pentatonic vocal segment (D-B-A-E) establishes the latter also as a framework for the unfolding of the larger chromatic cantus firmus. Significantly, these invariant functions of the pentatonic pitch collection are related to the "serial procedures" in other post-tonal works based on pitch sets.[19]

In the *Fifth Song* ("If I Climb Yonder Hill"), the E-pentatonic pitch-content of the tune is expanded beyond the limits of the polymodal chromaticism of the preceding songs. The E-pentatonic collection is harmon-

---

18 This appears to reflect the textual meaning in the strophic return of the song (mm. 18ff.): "Tőllem több panaszt nem hallasz" ("Home and homestead I must leave too").
19 Also see *Bagatelle No. V* (Ex. 27).

38 *Fifth Song*, mm. 1–5, beat 1

ically expanded to larger E modes at points, and pentatonic properties also serve as a frame of reference for the chromatic unfolding of triads and seventh chords that produce larger nondiatonic symmetrical structures. The E-pentatonic collection is vertically established at the opening (mm. 1–4, beat 2) as two alternating triads which together form the tonic minor-seventh chord, E-G-B-D, while at the main vocal cadence (m. 10), it is linearly stated as a complete pentatonic scale. At the first cadential point (m. 4, last two beats), two new chords together form another pentatonic construction (minor-seventh chord A-C-E-G), expanding the basic E-pentatonic pitch-content to a partial E-Aeolian collection (E-( )-G-A-B-C-D). The first chord of the next phrase symmetrically completes the latter mode (E-F♯-G-A-B-C-D), (Ex. 38).

The chordal progression accompanying the second phrase (m. 5, beat 2, through m. 7) marks a radical departure from the opening pentatonic and modal context.[20] The whole-tone progression of parallel root-position triads in the left hand linearly establishes both whole-tone scales—the bass unfolds one of the whole-tone scales (E-D-C-B♭-A♭-F♯), and the upper two lines of this triadic succession separately unfolds the other in parallel minor-sixths (B-A-G-F-E♭-C♯ and G-F-E♭-D♭-C♭-( )) (Ex. 39). These two mutually exclusive whole-tone scales may be considered cyclic extensions of the two whole-tone segments (E-D and B-A-G) that form the basic E-pentatonic scale, which simultaneously initiate the two lower lines of this progression. Furthermore, the perfect fifths of the triads registrally isolated in the two lower lines systematically form the cycle of fifths (B-E, A-D, G-C, F-B♭, E♭-A♭, C♯-F♯). The first five notes of this series (B-E-A-D-G), which give us the perfect-fifth ordering of the basic E-pentatonic collection, are explicitly manifested in the next phrase (mm. 8–9, right hand) as two perfect-fifth,

20 This departure appears to correspond with the words of the fickle lover: "Találok én szeretőre kettőre. Ej, baj, baj, baj, de Nagy baj" ("Sure I'll find a sweetheart waiting, maybe two. Ah me, love's free, will not stay").

or -fourth, segments (A-E-B, D-G). (The most significant differences between an early draft and the final version of the song are based on the transformation of modal material into the symmetrical cyclic lines, i.e., whole-tone scales and cycle of fifths, which are produced by the parallel progression of triads: compare these measures of the early draft in Ex. 40.)

Against the latter pentatonic segment the supporting root-progression of the final two phrases (mm. 7–10) contracts the preceding whole tones to semitones, this chordal progression moving far from the cadential E-tonic of the voice. The bitonal implication at this cadential point is resolved at m. 11: the F-major six-four chord, harmonically set against the E-pentatonic scale, moves down a half-step to the E-tonic six-four chord. The opening of the interlude (Più allegro) establishes the latter conflict entirely within the E-Phrygian mode (m. 10, beat 3, through m. 12, beat 2) (Ex. 41). For the remainder of the interlude, the E-pentatonic pitch-content serves as an invariant symmetrical construction both in the larger E-Phrygian/E-Dorian progression (mm. 11–13, beat 3) and in the exclusively E-Aeolian melodic line.[21]

39 *Fifth Song,* mm. 5–7

40 *Fifth Song* (originally the *Third*), an early draft of mm. 5–8
(see Illustration 3)

21 The tonal priority of E is established at the final cadence of the postlude (m. 34) when the tonic triad is added to the original cadence of the interlude.

41   *Fifth Song,* interlude (Piú allegro)

At the same time, the pentatonic E-minor-seventh chord (m. 13, beat 2) initiates the return of the earlier whole-tone progression in a chromatic progression of triads. Thus, the E-pentatonic pitch-content of the folk tune serves not only as an invariant symmetrical structure within a polymodal chromaticism (E-Phrygian, E-Dorian, and E-Aeolian) but also as a point of departure for the generation of a larger set of interval cycles (two whole-tone scales and the cycle of fifths). This significantly foreshadows a new means of progression in Bartók's later works.

The *Third Song* ("Wives, Let Me Be One of Your Company") is the first in a mode other than E-pentatonic. While the pitch content of the tune is modally ambiguous, implying either E♭-Aeolian or E♭-Phrygian (E♭-(-)-G♭-A♭-B♭-C♭-D♭), the former is explicitly established in the linear bass progression that supports the entire first strain (Ex. 42). The pitch-class content of this complete E♭-Aeolian linear statement (E♭-F-G♭-A♭-B♭-C♭-D♭) is a symmetrical expansion of the underlying E♭-pentatonic substructure (E♭-G♭-A♭-B♭-D♭), which is explicitly presented as a melodic segment at each of the four cadential points of the tune. The significance of the latter is harmonically established in the final strain of the tune, mm. 28–35, where the accompaniment is exclusively based on the symmetrical E♭ minor-seventh chord, E♭-G♭-B♭-D♭.

In the first strain (mm. 3–10), the tune and the triadic harmonies together unfold a set of E♭ modes that chromatically fill in the common E♭-pentatonic substructure.[22] At m. 3, the first modal conflict is produced by the juxtaposition in voice and accompaniment of the chromatic sixth degrees, C and C♭. This forms an imbalance (E♭-G♭-A♭-B♭-C♭-C-D♭) in the upper part of the E♭-pentatonic referent (represented by the E♭ minor-seventh chord at the first cadence, m. 4). In the second phrase (mm. 5–6), the two sixth degrees are juxtaposed in the accompaniment, the E♭ minor-seventh chord again serving as a focal point at the cadence. In the final two phrases (mm. 7–10), the inclusion of both the major-second and minor-second degrees, F and F♭, chromatically fills in the lower part of the E♭-pentatonic referent to form a large polymodal symmetry (E♭-F♭-F-G♭-A♭-B♭-C♭-C-D♭). Thus, the pentatonic collection once again serves as the invariant nucleus for coordination of the Aeolian, Dorian, and Phrygian modes.

The second strain (mm. 14–21) is based on revised polymodal relations which, despite the enharmonic respelling, remain within the original

42 *Third Song*, mm. 1–13, contrapuntal alignment of Eb-Aeolian bass against the folk tune

22 This polymodal procedure is analogous to those in the E-pentatonic songs discussed above.

43 *Third Song*, mm. 13–15

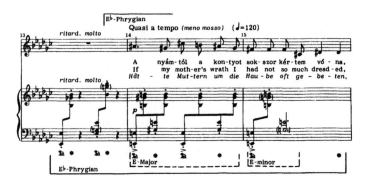

E♭-tonal spectrum. Furthermore, the original E♭-pentatonic pitch-content is retained as the invariant substructure. The alternating E♭-minor and E♭-major triads of the interlude (mm. 11–13), which supplies one new chromatic tone, G, introduce the new strain. In the first phrase (mm. 14–15), the initial impression suggests a bitonal relation between the D♯ (i.e., E♭) tonality of the tune and the now-transposed alternations between E-major and E-minor triads. However, if we maintain that the preceding G is still chromatic with respect to the present statement of the tune, the remaining pitch-content can be defined within the spectrum of the E♭-Phrygian mode (Ex. 43)—the harmonic predominance of the E-major (in enharmonic spelling, F♭-major) triad strongly contributes to the E♭-Phrygian modal quality. This interpretation is expressly confirmed by the final descending bass line (mm. 19–21). At the return (m. 18) to the original E♭-modal spelling, the chords and tune together form the E♭-Phrygian collection with lowered fifth degree (B♭♭). (The latter chromatically altered tone appears to be a carry-over of the A from the preceding cadence, m. 18, where it belonged to E major in the bitonal conflict of E and E♭ tonalities.) The entire pitch content of this strain thus establishes the E♭-Phrygian mode with two chromatic tones (G, and B♭♭—in enharmonic spelling, A), giving us a chromaticized E♭-Phrygian pitch collection, E♭-F♭-G♭-G-A♭-B♭♭-B♭-C♭-D♭. Thus, the one structure that remains invariant in all the polymodally chromatic relations of the entire song is the basic E♭-pentatonic pitch content, E♭-G♭-A♭-B♭-D♭.

In the *Eighth Song* ("Snow Is Melting"), too, melodic and harmonic pentatonic segments serve as a frame of reference for larger polymodal chromatic relations. The folk tune, like that of the *Third Song*, is modally ambiguous. The second degree was missing from the *Third Song*; the sixth degree is missing from the *Eighth*, implying either D-Aeolian or D-Dorian (D-E-F-G-A-( )-C). The pentatonic implications in this incomplete modal scale are manifested in certain melodic segments of phrase a[23] (Ex. 44), the pentatonic segments of which are also harmonically projected at prominent structural points. The opening measures (1–3) and first cadence (m. 6) are exclusively based on the pitch content of the tonic minor-seventh chord (D-F-A-C), a segment (D-C-A) of which is implied in the first measure of the melody. Also, the final measure of the song is an harmonic projection of the linear cadential pentatonic segment, D-F-G-A-( ), the note G functioning as a prominent embellishing tone in both cases. The bass line (at m. 4) supplies one new note (B♭), which expands the entire pitch collection of phrase a to the complete D-Aeolian mode (D-E-F-G-A-B♭-C) (Ex. 44). The initial D-pentatonic segment (i.e., minor-seventh chord, D-F-A-C), which unfolded in mm. 1–3, is a symmetrical substructure of the larger modal pitch collection.

The supporting bass line in phrase a unfolds a secondary pentatonic collection, D-F-G-B♭-C, from the larger D-Aeolian mode. Although pitch-class D is established as the tonal priority of this secondary pentatonic formation

44   *Eighth Song,* mm. 1–6

23 The song consists of two differentiated four-measure phrases (a and b), which unfold according to the formal outline a a b a. (The fifth and sixth phrases are exact textual and musical repetitions of the third and fourth, b and a.) The harmonizations for the three basic phrase-a statements differ from one another, so that we can more specifically refer to the phrasal statements in the formal outline as a a′ b a″ (and repeated b a″).

(by its temporal position as the first and last note of the bass progression and by its repetition in the introduction), the continuation of the latter progression into the opening of phrase a' (m. 7), with the prominent metric position of B♭ on the downbeat, produces a shift of tonal priority to B♭. The establishment of this tonality is confirmed by the V–I progression first in B♭ minor (mm. 8–9), then in B♭ major at the cadence (mm. 9–10). It is significant that the one note (sixth degree, B♭) that is missing from the D-Aeolian folk tune is established as the basic tonality of the second phrase-a statement.

At mm. 10–13, the supporting bass line, which overlaps the end of phrase a' and the first three measures of phrase b, unfolds a third pentatonic collection (E-G-A-C-D) from the larger D-Aeolian mode. The secondary pentatonic collection (D-F-G-B♭-C) included the sixth degree (B♭) and omitted the second (E), but this new pentatonic partition (E-G-A-C-D) of the larger mode includes the second degree while omitting the sixth; the note E is now prominent in the vocal phrase also. Above this pentatonic bass, the harmonic progression introduces the first significant chromatic conflict, i.e., between the sixth degrees (B and B♭) of the D-Dorian and D-Aeolian modes. These sixth degrees produce an asymmetrical imbalance within this D-modal complex.

At the cadential point of phrase b (m. 14), the B♭ bass abruptly returns in tritone juxtaposition with the preceding E, the B♭ now serving as the root of the dominant-seventh chord (B♭-D-F-A♭) in the key of E♭ major. The tonic E♭-major triad then initiates the fourth phrase (a''). The resulting bitonal conflict between the E♭ triad and D-Aeolian tune produces a larger bimodal conflict between the D-Aeolian melody and D-Phrygian harmonization (Ex. 45). Thus, the new local chromatic conflict between the second degrees (E♭ and E) in this modal complex reestablishes the symmetrical balance that was momentarily disturbed by the preceding juxtaposition of the sixth de-

45   *Eighth Song*, mm. 15–16

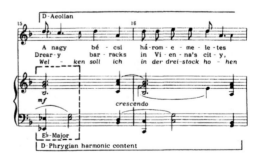

grees, B and B♭. The tonal priority of D is harmonically reaffirmed (mm. 17–18) by the cadential V7-i progression.

The *Sixth Song* ("They're Mending the Great Forest Highway") is the first of two examples in this collection in which the folk tune appears as a complete diatonic mode (E-Dorian). Whereas the polymodal harmonization in each of the foregoing songs was seen as a balanced expansion around the symmetrical pentatonic structure (or substructure) of a given folk tune, the polymodal design in the present song seems to unfold around the entire pitch-content of the E-Dorian referent. The two strains of the tune are harmonized differently, the modal harmonic content of the second strain (mm. 16–27) generally complementing that of the first in this design. The tune is presented in four phrases, the first two (mm. 3–7) focusing on the upper content (A-B-C♯-D-E) of the E-Dorian mode, the last two phrases (mm. 8–14) on the lower content (E-F♯-G-A-B-( )-D). These modal partitions exclude the second (F♯) and sixth (C♯) degrees, respectively, permitting a certain freedom in harmonic alteration or omission of one or the other of these two tones throughout the song.

The complete E-Dorian pitch content (E-F♯-G-A-B-C♯-D) is exclusively established in the first phrase (mm. 3–4) as a point of departure for this complex of E modes.[24] (In this phrase, the harmonic pitch content of the i6–ii7 progression modally completes that of the tune.) In the second phrase (mm. 5–7), the modally ambiguous melodic line is supported by a chromatic bass progression in which the second modal degree, F♯, descends to a chromatic passing note, F. The latter suggests an E-Phrygian tendency in conflict with the now incomplete E-Dorian collection (E-F-F♯-( )-A-B-C♯-D). At the downbeat of the next phrase, the E minor-seventh chord serves as a focal point (i.e., symmetrical frame of reference) for this nonsymmetrical chromatic filling-in of the lower modal area. In the third phrase (mm. 8–10), only the Dorian second (F♯) remains, and the sixth degree is omitted altogether. This omission, which permits further emphasis on the chromatic filling of the lower modal area, also produces a modal ambiguity between the implied modes of basic E-Dorian and E-Aeolian (E-F♯-G-A-B-( )-D). (The latter mode is explicitly realized [mm. 21–23] at the return of this phrase in the second strain, where the focus shifts to the filling-in of the upper part of the E-modal spectrum.) The Dorian sixth, C♯, is reestablished at the opening of the fourth phrase (m. 11).

In the second strain, in which all the remaining chromatic tones are

24 The priority of E in this polymodal context is primarily established by the linear voice-leading motions in nontraditional progressions of seventh chords, which serve as prolongations between statements of the tonic chord. For example the opening weak first-inversion tonic triad linearly moves through a succession of root-position and inverted-seventh chords to the E minor-seventh chord (m. 8) that opens the third phrase, the chromatic bass descent (G-F♯-F-E) having a strong tonality-defining function. The only other statement of the tonic chord occurs in the final measure as a focal point for the linear motion of the harmonic accompaniment.

46 *Sixth Song, mm. 16–24*

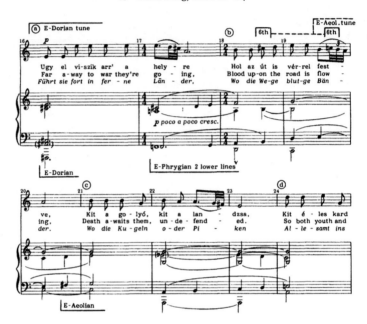

eventually unfolded, a large-scale complementary balance of E modes can be discerned in the linear voice-leading of the harmonic structure. Against the vocal line, which introduces a bimodal conflict between the Dorian and Aeolian sixth degrees (C♯ and C) in the folk tune itself, the accompanying counterpoint linearly unfolds both the chromatic sixth degrees (C♯ and C) and chromatic second degrees (F♯ and F) (Ex. 46). From the second measure of the first phrase through the opening of the last (m. 24), the two lower lines exclusively unfold both the E-Phrygian and E-Aeolian modes (E-F-F♯-G-A-B-C-D). While these lines primarily focus on the chromatic filling (F♯-F) of the lower E-bimodal area, the upper lines primarily focus on the chromatic filling (C♯-C) of the upper area. (Chromatic embellishing tones E♭ and A♯ in the last two phrases, at mm. 22–25, extend the chromatic continuum to eleven notes, and the final E-major-tonic triad supplies the twelfth note, G♯.) Thus, the basic E-Dorian pitch-content of the folk tune in the voice and first measure (16) of the piano part serves as a frame of reference for the chromatic unfolding of the polymodal complex on E.

The *Seventh Song* ("Up to Now My Work Was Ploughing in the Spring") is the second of two examples in this collection in which the folk tune appears as a complete diatonic mode (F-Phrygian). The harmonic realization is

unique in this song, in that it prominently serves as both a contrapuntal and
an harmonic elaboration of a single modal interval (tritone) rather than as a
balanced polymodal expansion around the basic mode or its pentatonic substructure. The tonal priority of the folk tune remains ambiguous until the
main cadence (mm. 18–20) of the first strain, but the descending bass outline of the complete F-Phrygian mode (from the fifth degree, middle C, to
the F tonic, an octave and a fifth below, at m. 20) serves to establish the priority of F. Certain focal points within the bass line tend to produce linear
modal partitions encompassed by the F-Phrygian tritone, C-G♭ (Ex. 47). At
mm. 1–5, the bass descends from C to G♭, both notes held (m. 5) as the
boundary of the piano part in support of the vocal entry. This basic tritone
(G♭-C) is further made prominent by the contrary chromatic motion at the
first cadential point (mm. 6–7). (The contrapuntal resolution to the new F-
D♭ boundary completes the F-Phrygian pitch content within this opening
passage.) At the opening of the fourth phrase (mm. 16–17), we get the first
disruption of the descending F-Phrygian scale. G♭ ends the large-scale descent initiated by C, the G♭ being emphasized by its appearance at the midpoint of the crescendo-decrescendo marking and by the interruption of a
perfect-fifth leap away from it to a nonmodal tone, C♭. Thus, the basic
modal tritone serves both as a registral (m. 5) and a temporal boundary (mm.
1–16) in the accompaniment of this strain.

47 *Seventh Song*, contrapuntal alignment of F-Phrygian bass against the
folk tune of vocal line, mm. 1–20

48   *Seventh Song*, mm. 16–20

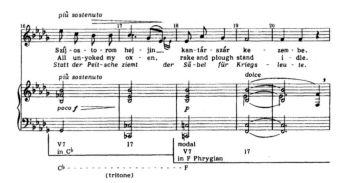

In the closing phrase (mm. 16–20), this disruptive harmonic progression, which is a chromatic deviation from the F-Phrygian pitch-content, contains another tritone relationship. The chordal structures built on the bass notes—Gᵇ-Cᵇ and C-F, respectively—unfold the progressions V7–I7 in Cᵇ and the modal V7-i7 in F-Phrygian (Ex. 48), thereby juxtaposing a microtonicized Cᵇ with the basic tonic F. The bass line, Gᵇ-Cᵇ-C-F, which supports these local modal-harmonic progressions, linearly interlocks the basic tritone (Gᵇ-C) with the chromatically extended one (F-Cᵇ); this double-tritone relation plays a significant nontraditional harmonic as well as melodic role in many of Bartók's later works.[25] The revised harmonization of the second strain supplies all but one of the remaining twelve tones, in a polymodal context containing prominent vertical statements of tritones (e.g., mm. 32ff.).

25 See Chapter IV, Examples 74 and 75, where the symmetrical properties of this four-note construction are fundamental to a larger set of pitch relations.

CHAPTER III

Symmetrical Transformations
of the Folk Modes

The frequent melodic skips of a perfect fourth in the old Hungarian folk melodies were a significant source for Bartók's melodic and harmonic inventions: "The frequent repetition of this remarkable skip occasioned the construction of the simplest fourth-chord."[1] This procedure transforms the diatonic modes into symmetrical pitch constructions. Any diatonic mode— e.g., the white-key collection of the piano (C-D-E-F-G-A-B, or any of its modal permutations)—can be reordered as a seven-note segment (F-C-G-D-A-E-B) of the cycle of fifths, or fourths. When presented in six of its seven modal permutations, this diatonic collection appears to be nonsymmetrical, since the two diatonic semitones (E-F and B-C) are not equidistant from a central point within the scale; a diatonic scale can only be shown to be symmetrical when its notes are permuted to form either the Dorian mode (D-E-F-G-A-B-C-D) or a seven-note segment of the cycle of fifths (F-C-G-D-A-E-B).[2]

Bartók discusses the pentatonic derivation of the fourth (or fifth) chord A-E-B, which pervades both the melodic and harmonic levels throughout the final measures of the *First String Quartet*.[3] Such fourth (or fifth) chords more explicitly appear as symmetrical reorderings of diatonic thematic ma-

---

1 *Béla Bartók Essays*, ed. Benjamin Suchoff (New York: St. Martin's Press, 1976), p. 336. The original publication is given in n. 1 of Chapter I.

2 The axis of a symmetrical formation is always two notes, either expressed or implied (see Ex. 80, the sum-4 column, in reference to the axis of the present symmetries); that is, the D-Dorian and perfect-fifth orderings have the same axis of symmetry, D-D (or G♯-G♯). Axial functions will be discussed in Chapter IV.

3 *Bartók Essays*, p. 336. The original publication is given in n. 1 of Chapter I.

terial in many of his other works, among them the *Fourth String Quartet*. In Movement III, m. 10, through the first beat of m. 12, the cello unfolds a diatonic ("white-key") melody that is simultaneously reordered in the accented "Magyar" figures (accented short-long rhythm) as perfect-fifth segments G-C-F, G-C-D, and E-A-B; the last two are harmonically inverted. Together, these three segments give us a seven-note segment of the cycle of fifths (F-C-G-D-A-E-B) (see Ex. 357a and b, the latter of which expressly gives these perfect-fifth segments in their root positions). The same diatonic collection, which appears in vnII and va at mm. 50–51 in scalar order (see Ex. 190), is reordered in Movement V (in vc and va at mm. 45–68) in terms of its perfect-fifth properties. At mm. 323–40, this diatonic collection is vertically projected as an incomplete six-note chord (F-C-G-D-A-E-(⟩)) on fifths. Such reorderings can also be demonstrated with the pentatonic scale. At mm. 47–52 of Movement III, vnI and vc play a pentatonic ("black-key") ostinato pattern that can be understood as a five-note segment (G♭-D♭-A♭-E♭-B♭) of the cycle of fifths. Bartók has grouped these five notes into two symmetrical four-note chords, an inverted minor-seventh chord, G♭-B♭-D♭-E♭ (in root position, E♭-G♭-B♭-D♭), and a perfect-fifth chord, G♭-D♭-A♭-E♭, both types of which were discussed in Chapter II in connection with folk-derived material.

In *Music for Strings, Percussion, and Celesta*, both scalar and perfect-fifth orderings of the A-Lydian mode (A-B-C♯-D♯-E-F♯-G♯ and A-E-B-F♯-C♯-G♯-D♯) are explicitly manifested. The main thematic material that initiates the last movement in Lydian-scale order unfolds on the background level of the opening fugue movement in its perfect-fifth ordering (see Ex. 209, 210).

As early as *Bagatelle No. I*, symmetrical melodic formations emerge as primary foreground events through intervallic reordering of the opening modal material. (Bartók combines two lines of distinctly different modes— one with four sharps, the other with four flats; the chromatic synthesis produces a "Phrygian-coloured C major."[4] The upper melodic line ambiguously begins in either C♯-Aeolian or E major, and the lower line unfolds modal fragments in C-Phrygian and F-Aeolian. However, at almost all the cadential points, both lines metrically focus on the C-major tonic chord as the primary vertical sonority.) In the upper melodic line (mm. 1–4), the perfect-fifth C♯-G♯ appears as the boundary of the C♯-minor triadic outline (Ex. 49). In the consequent phrase (mm. 5–8) of the same line, the perfect fifth (or its harmonic inversion, the perfect fourth) appears with increasing frequency as a melodic detail. The last two measures (mm. 7–8) of the consequent phrase outline three intervallically equivalent segments (Ex. 50).[5] While B-F♯-E and

---

4 Ibid., p. 433. The source is "Introduction to *Béla Bartók Masterpieces for the Piano*," the MS. of which was drafted in January, 1945.

5 The interval numbers in Example 50 are calculated in semitones: the major second is designated as interval 2; the perfect fourth, interval 5; and the perfect fifth, interval 7.

49 *Bagatelle No. I*, mm. 1–5

50 *Bagatelle No. I*, mm. 7–8

51 *Bagatelle No. I*, mm. 9–15

A-B-E are implied segments of the cycle of fifths (E-B-F♯ and A-E-B), F♯-C♯-G♯ is explicitly ordered as a cyclic segment.[6] At m. 14 of the second section, the pitch content of each of the latter two segments is conversely reordered so that the presence of perfect fifths in the ordering of C♯-F♯-G♯ is implied, while the ordering of A-E-B presents the perfect fifths in linear adjacency.

The upper line in the opening of the second section (mm. 9–11) is exclusively pentatonic (Ex. 51). The pitch content (E-B-F♯-C♯-G♯), which still belongs to the opening mode of C♯-Aeolian (or E major), only implies the presence of a symmetrical five-note segment of the cycle of fifths. The consequent phrase is initiated (m. 12) by another pentatonic formation (E-A-B-C♯-F♯) that also remains within this modal spectrum. This pentatonic formation is now bounded by two perfect fourths, E-A and C♯-F♯, the five

6 The pentatonic derivation of these intervallically equivalent perfect-fifth figures is mentioned by Halsey Stevens in *The Life and Music of Béla Bartók* (New York: Oxford University Press, 1953, rev. 1964), p. 42. Also see *Bartók Essays*, p. 336. The original publication is given in n. 1 of Chapter I.

notes explicitly appearing in a symmetrical ordering. The following measure unfolds a six-note segment (E-B-F♯-C♯-G♯-D♯) of the cycle of fifths, explicitly ordered in terms of both its symmetrical and cyclic properties. Consequently, the entire upper melodic line of the piece, which is exclusively based on the diatonic pitch-content of the C♯-Aeolian or E-major mode, can be understood as a seven-note segment (A-E-B-F♯-C♯-G♯-D♯) of the cycle of fifths. This is largely confirmed by the explicit six-note ordering (m. 13) of successive fifths (or fourths) in the consequent phrase.

One note, A, of this transformed modal melody does not appear in its cyclic position (( )-E-B-F♯-C♯-G♯-D♯-(A)). Instead, it occurs after the six-note cyclic segment, on the downbeat of m. 14, where it interrupts the succession of fifths by forming a tritone (D♯-A) with the last component. The notes A and D♯, which together (as first and last notes) define the boundary of the seven-note cyclic ordering (A-E-B-F♯-C♯-G♯-D♯), are brought into melodic proximity by this displacement of the A. (This is the only melodic occurrence of a tritone in the piece.) The tritone, therefore, which served as the key-defining interval in the traditional major-minor scale system, appears here as the boundary of a symmetrical formation. Thus, while the polymodal context (i.e., the upper melodic line in either C♯-Aeolian or E major, the lower ostinato figures defining segments of the C-Phrygian and F-Aeolian modes) retains some harmonic association with traditional tonality (i.e., C-major harmonic assertions at prominent cadential points), the intervallic reordering of the upper modal melody produces new (symmetrical) melodic pitch formations.

Bagatelle No. VII is also based on symmetrical reorderings of the melodic modal material into segments of the cycle of fifths. The stepwise and arpeggiated thematic material in the left hand (mm. 1–8) asserts the priority of D♯.[7] It also implies the presence of a gapped segment (A♯-D♯-( )-C♯-F♯-( )-E) of the cycle of fourths, which (mm. 6–8) is explicitly reordered (mm. 9–15) as perfect fourths, giving us A♯-D♯-G♯-C♯-F♯-( )-E, the new note, G♯, filling one of the gaps (Ex. 52). Although a seven-note diatonic collection is implied, Bartók never presents more than five notes outlining adjacent fourths. This establishes a pentatonic quality for the melodic segment. One prominent example (mm. 49–70) explicitly unfolds the pentatonic collection A♯-D♯-G♯-C♯-F♯, and another (mm. 79–83) unfolds C♯-F♯-B-E-A. Against the opening cyclic segment, A♯-D♯-G♯-C♯-F♯-( )-E, the right hand (through m. 25) is exclusively based on the complementary diatonic segment, F-C-G-D-A-E-B. Together, these segments produce the entire cycle of fifths, or all twelve tones.

---

7 While there are no harmonic suggestions of the triad, Bartók has designated that this piece is in D♯ minor, which is asserted at local cadential points (e.g., mm. 4–5, left hand, and at the end of the work). However, he points out that various methods cross one another. Sometimes a mode is implied in only one bar or even one note (e.g., mm. 4ff.), with each note treated separately: see *Bartók Essays*, p. 370. The source is given in n. 9 of Chapter II.

52   *Bagatelle No. VII*, mm. 6ff.

53   *Bagatelle No. XII*, mm. 39–40

In *Bagatelle No. XII* there is some reference to diatonic folk sources, though the triadic progressions tend to produce a sense of tonality in a chromatic idiom.[8] Traditional tonal functions are obscured by mixed progressions of minor-seventh, whole-tone, perfect-fourth, and major-minor chords (e.g., at mm. 6–7, above the F♯-major triadic outline in the bass). Furthermore, traditional diatonic material is obscured by its harmonic ordering into fourth chords. As one instance (mm. 39–40), following a succession of triads primarily asserting B minor, the pitch content of F♯ major largely appears as perfect fourths ((F♯)-B♭-E♭, D♯-G♯-C♯, and C♯-F♯-B) (Ex. 53) outlining a six-note segment of the cycle of fourths (in enharmonic spelling, ( )-A♯-D♯-G♯-C♯-F♯-B). These perfect fourths, together with whole-tone occurrences (e.g., the voice-leading of the upper lines of the latter chords, the whole-tone scales in the bass line at m. 3), reveal the local importance of symmetrical formations within the diversity of diatonic and chromatic material.

In the first of the *Eight Improvisations for Piano*, Op. 20, symmetrical harmonic formations are derived from a reordering of certain properties of

8 Stevens, *Life and Music of Béla Bartók*, p. 112, suggests a non-Western derivation for this work: the repeated A in rubato, which reminds one of *Music for Strings, Percussion, and Celesta*, Movement III, produces an atmosphere like that of some Indonesian gamelan music and possibly "a relation . . . to the music of the [Hungarian] cimbalom."

54 *First Improvisation*, mm. 1–4

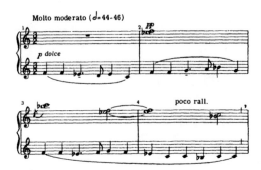

55 *First Improvisation*, mm. 5–8

the modal folk tune.[9] The melody, which is repeated complete three times, is in the C-Dorian mode. The Dorian mode is the only permutation of the diatonic scale that has a symmetrical construction: in its scalar order (C-D-Eb-F-G-A-Bb-C), it can be partitioned into two equivalent tetrachords (C-D-Eb-F and G-A-Bb-C) a perfect fifth apart. Strain 1 (mm. 1–4) of the tune is exclusively accompanied by two whole-tone dyads, Eb-F and Bb-C (Ex. 54), which are verticalizations of the corresponding upper segments of the two tetrachords. In strain 2 (mm. 5–8), these whole-tone dyads are reordered in the initial two grace-note figures to form perfect-fifth dyads (F-C and Eb-Bb) (Ex. 55).

These perfect-fifth ornaments play a dual role in this strain. They are linked to traditional harmony in that they serve as the boundary intervals of the vertically stated major and minor triads, but at the same time they sys-

9 Collected in 1907 in Felsőiregh, Tolna.

tematically generate a series of fifths in the successive grace-note figures—a significant step in the symmetrical reorganization of the modal intervals.

The series of fifths in each of the four phrase-segments forms part of a larger, balanced progression in the strain (Ex. 56).[10] The first three phrase-segments are each initiated by dyad F-C, which serves as a nucleus for the symmetrical unfolding of the other dyads. This procedure establishes the priority of F-C, which melodically appears as the boundary interval of the lower C-Dorian tetrachord and also forms one of the two perfect fifths (F-C and E♭-B♭) implied in the whole-tone accompaniment of strain 1. The cadential phrase-segment (m. 8) disrupts the symmetrical pattern and establishes the other dyad (E♭-B♭) as its initial ornament. Thus far, the grace notes have jointly unfolded a symmetrical six-note segment (E♭-B♭-F-C-G-D) of the cycle of fifths. Strain 3 opens (Ex. 57: m. 9) with two rolled chords, the two lower notes of each of which (D-A and A♭-E♭) are aurally perceived as continuations of the preceding perfect-fifth grace notes. Together, these dyads symmetrically extend the six-note cyclic segment to A♭-E♭-B♭-F-C-

56 *First Improvisation,* strain 2 phrase-segments:

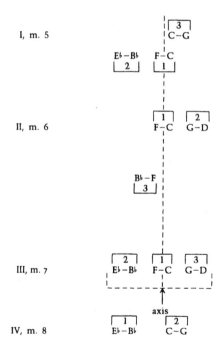

10 The number in each bracket represents the order of entry of a given perfect-fifth dyad.

57   *First Improvisation*, m. 9

58   Pitch content of *First* and *Fifth Improvisations*

(a) *First Improvisation*, properties of the folk mode

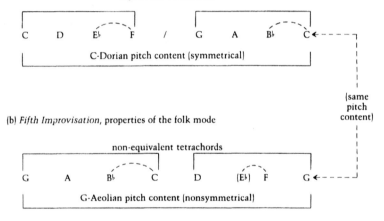

G-D-A.[11] Thus, the intervallic structure of the C-Dorian folk tune is symmetrically reordered as a segment of the cycle of fifths.

A special relationship exists between the *Fifth* and *First Improvisations* in the symmetrical reordering of their modal intervals. The pitch content of the G-Aeolian folk tune [12] of the *Fifth* is identical with that of the C-Dorian tune of the *First* (Ex. 58). However, while the C-Dorian mode is symmetrical, the G-Aeolian permutation of it is not. In the *First*, the four-note symmetrical segment Eb-Bb-F-C, which first unfolds in the accompaniment of

---

11   The chromatic note, Ab, implies a modal shift, the combination of both new dyads (A-D/Eb-Ab) forming a nondiatonic symmetry. Since the latter partially lies outside the pitch content of the C-Dorian folk tune, its significance is beyond the scope of the present discussion (see Chapter VII).

12   From the Hottó Collection, Zala. Although the sixth degree (Eb or E) is omitted from the tune, the modal ambiguity is immediately resolved (m. 13) by the Eb grace-note, which initiates strain 2.

strain 1 as a pair of whole-tone dyads and then at the opening of strain 2 as perfect-fifth ornaments, is derived from the upper corresponding parts of the two equivalent C-Dorian tetrachords (see the slur markings in Ex. 58a). In the *Fifth*, the same four-note symmetry, which is unfolded in the succession of initial ornamental pitches of strain 2 (Ex. 59), is derived from noncorresponding parts of the two nonequivalent G-Aeolian tetrachords (see the slur markings in Ex. 58b). Thus, a long-range relationship between the contrasting modes of the *Fifth* and *First Improvisation* is established by the derivation of a common four-note symmetry, Eb-Bb-F-C.

A basic property of the G-Aeolian tune [13] in the *Fifth Improvisation* is its pentatonic substructure (G-Bb-C-D-F), which exclusively forms the first phrase (mm 5–8). (The modal second degree, A, appears in the second phrase as a passing tone and the sixth degree, Eb, is omitted altogether.) Episode 1 (Ex. 60: mm. 21–26) unfolds a succession of 5/7 dyads, the initial pair, G-D and Bb-F, symmetrically forming the minor-seventh-chord outline, G-Bb-D-F, of this primary pentatonic substructure, G-Bb-C-D-F. The reordering into perfect fourths explicitly establishes their symmetrical property. The next

59   *Fifth Improvisation*, strain 2, mm. 13–20

60   *Fifth Improvisation*, Episode 1, mm. 21–26

13 The tune remains unchanged in each of the five strains, while the accompaniments and ornamentation are varied.

pair of dyads, A-D and F-C (m. 23), similarly form a minor-seventh chord, D-F-A-C, which represents a symmetrical reordering of another, secondary segment of the main (G-Aeolian) mode. Thus, this initial succession of 5/7 dyads (mm. 21–23), which forms the first half of the episode, gives us a symmetrical reordering of the entire six-note pitch collection of the diatonic folk tune, G-A-B♭-C-D-F.[14]

In the *Third Improvisation*, the first thematic statement (mm. 3–15, right hand) is in the mixed mode of D major-minor. By comparing this modal construction (Ex. 61a) with the original folk tune as Bartók presented it in the preface to his sketches of the *Improvisations*, Op. 20 (Ex. 61b), we see that he chose the raised third degree in the *Third Improvisation*.[15] The new hybrid modal construction now gives us major and minor (lower and upper) tetrachords, D-E-F♯-G and A-B♭-C-D, which together form a symmetrical scale. A basic symmetrical property (augmented triad, D-F♯-A♯) of this hybrid modal tune emerges as an important foreground event in Episode 2 (the quintuplet upbeat to m. 26 through m. 30). The quintuplet figure is initiated by the augmented triad (D-F♯-A♯), which is reiterated throughout the passage. (As shown by the whole notes in Ex. 61a, this chord is basic to the symmetrical structure of the theme in strain 1, where it is encompassed by the octave boundary D-D. Pitch-class D, the tonality of this modal tune,

14 These perfect-fifth dyads are then cyclically extended in the remaining part of the episode, producing a sense of modulation by moving out of the diatonic spectrum of the tune. The accompaniments of the remaining strains are then primarily based on fifths (rather than on the semitones of the first two strains); the significance of this is beyond the scope of the present discussion.

15 László Somfai, Head of the Budapest Bartók Archívum, has kindly brought to my attention that the key signature of two flats in the preface to the sketches is an error. This appears to be confirmed by a comparison of this version of the tune with another version (No. 40) in Béla Bartók, *The Hungarian Folk Song*, ed. Benjamin Suchoff, trans. M. D. Calvocoressi (Albany: State University of New York Press, 1981), p. 229, in which B♭ does not appear in the key signature. Suchoff, Head of the New York Bartók Archive, has suggested to me that in the preface version the engraver for the first edition may have entered the flat sign into the key signature because he assumed it was an error to have only an E♭.

Suchoff, however, also directed me to Bartók's discussion in reference to this tune on p. 18 of *The Hungarian Folk Song*, which suggests another reason for the difference between the two versions: "Another kind of alteration of the pentatonic scale (G-B♭-C-D-F) crops up now and then. . . . It is the sharpening of the third degree. At times this sharpening is less than a semitone, and the result is a neutral third . . . at other times it is a full semitone. But even then the pentatonic structure remains so obvious that the origin of all such scales is unmistakable (Nos. . . . 40)" He also states (n. 3) that the third is sometimes raised and lowered in the course of one tune.

I am also grateful to Vera Lampert-Deák, who worked at the Budapest Bartók Archívum from 1969 to 1978, for mentioning certain markings in Bartók's transcriptions in connection with nontempered alterations of tones. Vertical arrows designating these alterations (as in No. 40 of *The Hungarian Folk Song*) were cancelled after 1934 and a footnote was added, so that, as one instance, even the second modal degree, A, appeared as a neutral tone. Thus, there are several ways that the second and third modal degrees could be performed: A and B, A♭ and B♭, A and B♭, or A♭ and B. The basic, and most prominent, way is with raised second and third— hence the hybrid modal form Bartók used in the *Third Improvisation*. I am also indebted to Lampert-Deák for informing me that it was Ákos Garay rather than Bartók who collected this tune at Kórógy, Szerém.

61 *Third Improvisation*

(a) Scalar structure of Strain 1, mm. 3–15, right hand

(b) Original Aeolian folk tune

62 *Third Improvisation*, Episode 2, mm. 25–30

also functions, as does an implied G♯-G♯, as its axis of symmetry.) Through-out Episode 2, this augmented triad appears in all three of its harmonic positions (Ex. 62). These permutations produce a rotating motion around the registrally stable (or invariant) axis tone, D, further establishing the symmetrical connection of this chord with the D major-minor scale of strain 1.

The augmented triad D-F♯-A♯ is anticipated in the accompaniment of the first phrase of strain 2 (Ex. 63, mm. 19–21). The succession of major thirds exclusively outlines a five-note segment (D-E-F♯-G♯-A♯) of one of the whole-tone cycles. The pitch content of the latter is symmetrically constructed around D-F♯-A♯, which is produced by the adjacency as a local foreground event, for the first time, of the two major thirds, F♯-A♯ and D-F♯. At

63 *Third Improvisation*, mm. 18–21

64 *Third Improvisation*, strain 2, mm. 18–25

the quintuplet figure (m. 25) that initiates Episode 2, the whole-tone segment (D-E-F♯-G♯-A♯) is explicitly partitioned into the primary augmented triad (D-F♯-A♯) and the symmetrically related major third (E-G♯), both of which are held throughout the first phrase of the Episode. At the cadential point (m. 27) of this phrase, C is added to E-G♯, forming another augmented triad, E-G♯-C, above the primary one. Furthermore, the final bass note, F (m. 25), of strain 2 is held throughout the Episode as a pedal; at m. 28, the upbeat to the second phrase (Piú lento) adds a major third (A-C♯) above the F pedal, forming a third augmented triad (F-A-C♯) around the primary one (A♯-D-F♯). The new triad (F-A-C♯) is prominent in the structure of the second phrase, since a linear statement of the upper major third (A-C♯) also closes the Episode (m. 30), while the lower major third (F-A) of the same augmented triad is held as a pedal in all three measures. The latter (F-A-C♯), analogous to the symmetrical relationship between the primary triad (D-F♯-A♯) and strain 1, is basic to the symmetrical structure of the transposed tune in strain 2 (Ex. 64, whole notes). (In strain 2, mm. 18–25, the tune appears in F major-minor, tetrachords F-G-A-B♭ and C-D♭-E♭-F outlining a symmetrical scale.)

While modally ordered diatonic material and various symmetrical formations in the *Fourth String Quartet* progress from one to another primarily by means of intervallic expansions and contractions [16] (these special relations will be explored in subsequent chapters), a comparison of selected passages from the preliminary sketches and the final version of the work will illustrate, in terms of the compositional process, the transformation of diatonic material into symmetrical formations by a reordering of the original modal intervals. The sketch of Movement I at mm. 120–22 (i.e., within the

16 *Bartók Essays*, p. 381. The source is given in n. 9 of Chapter II.

modified recapitulation of the second-theme group), is based on a succession of various diatonic segments in vns, Ex. 65a. The first half of m. 121 yields the one complete and unambiguous diatonic mode of the excerpt (B major), simultaneously presented in two segments but nevertheless in its scalar order (B-C♯-D♯-E-F♯/G♯-A♯-B-C♯). In the final version (Ex. 65b), the pitch content of the latter is explicitly reordered as two linearly stated segments of the cycle of fifths in parallel major seconds (from m. 120 through m. 121, fifth eighth-note), with vnII containing one chromatic tone, B♯. Together, these perfect-fifth segments imply a symmetrical reordering of the original modal pitch-content as a seven-note cyclic segment, E-B-F♯-C♯-G♯-D♯-A♯. The final note, E♯, of this pattern in vnI (m. 121) cyclically extends this segment to eight notes, after which the pattern is broken. (The addition of E♯ suggests a shift to the pitch content of the B-Lydian mode; in the sketch, the adjacent segment A♭-E♭-B♭-F—in enharmonic spelling, G♯-D♯-A♯-E♯—supplies the E♯.)

At m. 135 of Movement II of the final version, the symmetrical vc figure (C-G-F♯-D♭) replaces a D♭-major scale in the preliminary sketch (Ex. 66). The final version, which does not reorder the entire D♭-major pitch-content, is based on three of the principal tones (D♭-F♯-C—in enharmonic spelling, D♭-G♭-C) of the D♭-major scale. A fourth nondiatonic tone (G) is added in the vc figure in the final version to symmetrize the modal segment, giving

65 *Fourth String Quartet*, Movement I, mm. 120–22, vn, comparison of
preliminary sketch with final version

(a) sketch (see Illustration 4)

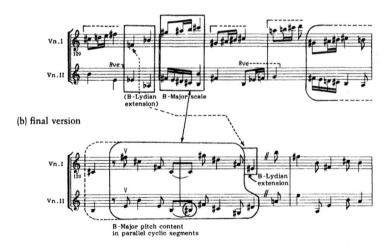

(b) final version

66   *Fourth String Quartet*, Movement II, comparison of preliminary sketch with the corresponding vc passage at m. 135

(a) preliminary sketch

(b) final version at mm. 134–35

us D♭-G♭-G-C.[17] Although the additional note, G, extends the D♭-major segment beyond the present diatonic spectrum of this mode, the comparison of the two versions nevertheless suggests Bartók's tendency toward symmetrical revision of traditional modal elements.

In Movement I of the *Third Piano Concerto*, the derivation of symmetrical pitch collections from the reordering of modal intervals is significant in terms of certain formal relationships. While the spun-out piano melody is based on shifting modes, the initial melodic segments of the piano (m. 2 through m. 5, opening) establish the priority of E-Mixolydian (Ex. 67). Pitch-class E is tonicized by its registral position in the melodic line (lowest and highest note), by the implied traditional root progression of V–I (B-E) in the timpani, and by the held boundary-interval (E-B) of the incomplete tonic triad in the clarinets. In the next thematic segment (m. 5 through m. 6, opening), the appearance of G♮ produces a bimodal melodic mixture of E-Mixolydian and E-Dorian.[18]

The entire bimodal pitch collection (through the local cadential point at m. 6) can also be understood as an eight-note symmetrical formation, D-E-F♯-G-G♯-A-B-C♯. This hypothesis is supported by the specific ordering of the modal material in the opening measures (1–5) of the orchestral accompaniment. The strings unfold a modal segment, E-F♯-A-B, that is symmetrically related to the eight-note pitch collection of the piano (D-E-F♯-G-G♯-A-B-C♯) (Ex. 68). The perfect fourth or fifth (E-B), of the timpani and clarinet

17 Ibid., p. 338. The original publication is given in n. 1 of Chapter I.
18 The accompaniment at this point (end of m. 5) is also in E-Dorian, except for the passing tone of A♯ between B and G♯. This implies a local octatonic alteration (E-F♯-G-A-A♯-()-C♯-()) of the E-Dorian mode (E-F♯-G-A-B-C♯-()).

67 *Third Piano Concerto*, Movement I, mm. 2–5

68 *Third Piano Concerto*, Movement I, opening strings

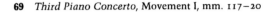

69   *Third Piano Concerto*, Movement I, mm. 117–20

parts, in addition to its tonality-defining role, appears as the boundary interval of the four-note symmetry E-F♯-A-B. A complete symmetrical reordering of the opening bimodal piano line (E-Mixolydian/Dorian) is established at the recapitulation (mm. 117ff.) (Ex. 69). The original four-note symmetry (E-F♯-A-B) of the orchestral accompaniment is replaced by the axial dyad, G-G♯ (enharmonic spelling of F×-G♯), in the trill figure of the violins. At the same time, segments of the modal thematic statement in the piano are contrapuntally aligned with their literal inversions, the first two piano chords giving us the original orchestral symmetry (E-F♯-A-B). The next piano chord, based on D-C♯, symmetrically expands this symmetry to D-E-F♯-( )-( )-A-B-C♯, outlining six of the eight notes of the original modal mixture in the initial four-note motive. The trill figure symmetrically supplies the remaining two (axial) pitches, G-G♯, to complete the eight-note symmetrical reordering (D-E-F♯-G-G♯-A-B-C♯) of the bimodal opening. Conversely, the lower strings (m. 119) reestablish E as the modal tonic by diatonically filling in the original timpani progression, B to E (V–I), with E now functioning as the tonal center of the E-Ionian mode.

CHAPTER IV

Basic Principles of Symmetrical Pitch Construction

The evolution of Bartók's musical language is represented in his set of six string quartets.[1] These works, composed over a period of thirty-one years, reveal a compositional trend. The first three (written in 1908, 1915–1917, and 1927) move from the lyrical, romantic style of the *First Quartet* to the intellectually abstract, expressionistic style of the *Third*; the last three quartets (written in 1928, 1934, and 1939) move in the opposite direction. The *Fourth Quartet*, which stands approximately at the midpoint of this quartet cycle, may be seen in many respects as the epitome of Bartók's compositional experimentation. An analysis of a piece in the traditional tonal system suggests general principles basic to all pieces written according to the rules of the tonal system. An analysis of the *Fourth Quartet* similarly suggests general principles that govern basic aspects of a larger body of "post-tonal" music. Thus, a general discussion of the principles of pitch relations underlying the *Fourth String Quartet* will serve as a basis for understanding the means by which tonality and progression are established in Bartók's music.[2]

In traditional tonal music, composers worked according to a system in which the octave was divided into unequal parts. The fundamental division

---

1 See George Perle, "The String Quartets of Béla Bartók," *Béla Bartók*, program notes for the recordings performed by the Tátrai String Quartet (New York: Dover, 1967), reprinted in *A Musical Offering: Essays in Honor of Martin Bernstein* (New York: Pendragon Press, 1977), p. 193.
2 The discussion in the present chapter is derived from Elliott Antokoletz, "Principles of Pitch Organization in Bartók's *Fourth String Quartet*" (Ph.D. dissertation, City University of New York, 1975), Chapter I.

70 System of interval cycles *

1/11	2/10	3/9	4/8	5/7	6/6	7/5	8/4	9/3	10/2	11/1	12/0	1/11
C				F♭		B♯				E	D	C
B				C♭		E♯				F	D	B
B♭				G♭		A♯				F♯	D	B♭
A				D♭		D♯				G	D	A
G♯				A♭		G♯				G♯	D	G♯
G				E♭		C♯				A	D	G
F♯	B♭ B			B♭		F♯			F♯ G	B♭	D	F♯
F	G♯ A			F		B			A♭ A	B	D	F
E	F♯ G	A♭ A B♭		C		E		A♭ A B♭	B♭ B	C	D	E
E♭	E F	F F♯ G	F♯ G G♯ A	G		A	B♭ B C C♯	F F♯ G	C C♯	C♯	D	E♭
D	D E♭	D E♭ E	D E♭ E F	D		D	D E♭ E F	D E♭ E	D E♭	D	D	D
C♯	C C♯	B C C♯	B♭ B C C♯	A	G♯ A B♭ B C C♯	G	F♯ G G♯ A	B C C♯	E F	E♭	D	C♯
C	B♭ B	A♭ A B♭	F♯ G G♯ A	E	D E♭ E F F♯ G	C	B♭ B C C♯	A♭ A B♭	F♯ G	E	D	C

* Due to lack of space, only the D cycle is included in the column of 12/0 cycles. If written out in unabbreviated form, this column would include all the 12/0 cycles, as follows: D-C♯-C-B-B♭-A-G♯-G-F♯-F-E-E♭-D. The specific permutation selected for the first cycle in each column is intended to correspond with certain derived tetrachordal segments of the cyclic system outlined in Example 189. The permutational ordering of each of the remaining cycles here is then systematically determined—i.e., the lowest notes of the cycles within each column form a series of ascending semitones.

was derived from the perfect fifth, which served as the basis of harmonic root function and as the primary structural interval of major and minor triads. In turn, the perfect fifth of the triad was unequally divided into major and minor thirds. In contrast, the pitch relations in Bartók's music are primarily based on the principle of *equal* subdivision of the octave into the complex of interval cycles. Each pair of complementary intervals—we will call this an *interval-class*—contains two intervallic differences that add up to an octave. In the pairs of complementary intervals other than that of the perfect fourth and perfect fifth, the smaller interval of each pair generates a cycle that subdivides one octave symmetrically. These other interval cycles include one cycle of minor seconds, two of major seconds, three of minor thirds, four of major thirds, and six of tritones (Ex. 70). The perfect fourth—or its harmonic inversion, the perfect fifth—is unique among the intervals: unlike the others, it generates a cycle that does not divide one octave symmetrically. Rather, the cycle of fourths must extend through many octaves before the initial pitch class returns. Thus, there is only one cycle of perfect fourths, or fifths.[3]

3 It will be unnecessary to refer to intervals according to their "perfect," "major," or "minor" qualities, since in the system of interval cycles the twelve tones are undifferentiated in terms of traditional tonal functions. Each degree of the chromatic scale will be assigned a corresponding number, from 0 to 11. We arbitrarily assign 0 (=12) to pitch-class C. Transposition numbers of pitch collections will also be designated by numbers from 0 to 11. We will assume a referential order in assigning a transposition number to a collection: the pitch-class number of the "first" note will designate that collection. If a referential collection is "based" on C, its

In Bartók's music, the interval cycles and derivative symmetrical segments have an important function in the large-scale structure. In order to demonstrate their functions and interrelations within the music, the properties of symmetrical pitch collections must first be defined. Any collection of two notes is symmetrical, since the two notes are equidistant from an imaginary axis. If we join a second dyad to the first, with the two notes of the second dyad equidistant from the same axis of symmetry, a four-note symmetry results (as in any of the tetrachords in Ex. 71). Such four-note symmetries are basic in the *Fourth Quartet*. In Example 71a, the axial intervals differ $(2 - 1 = 1; 3 - 0 = 3)$ but their sums are the same $(1 + 2 = 3; 0 + 3 = 3)$.[4] If a note from one dyad is combined with either note from the other dyad of the same sum, the remaining interval will be the same, as can be expressed in the equations $3 - 1 = 2 - 0$ and $3 - 2 = 1 - 0$. Each pair of intervals will be referred to as an *interval couple*.[5] Transposition changes the sum (i.e., the axis of symmetry) of a dyad, but not its interval class.

Example 71a is one of the three principal cells[6] of the *Fourth Quartet*. We will call this cell X.[7] The interval couples of X are demonstrated in Example 72. Cell X is a segment of the chromatic scale (interval-1 cycle). Of its three interval couples, the one expressed in the equation $3 - 2 = 1 - 0$ will be called *primary*, since it is based on the cyclic interval of X. The other interval couple that also has two equivalent intervals $(3 - 1 = 2 - 0)$ will be called *secondary*. The remaining interval couple, containing two non-

71   Four-note symmetries

(a)	(b)	(c)	or	(d)
0 1 2 3	10 0 2 4	8 1 2 7		2 7 8 1

transposition number is 0 $(=12)$. If the collection is transposed so that its "first" note becomes C♯, its transposition number becomes 1 $(=13)$. Intervals also imply their complements or harmonic inversions in the same interval-class and may be more specifically designated by double numbers: the perfect unison (or octave) will be interval 0/12; the minor second (or major seventh), interval 1/11; the major second (or minor seventh), interval 2/10; the minor third (or major sixth), interval 3/9; the major third (or minor sixth), interval 4/8; the perfect fourth (or perfect fifth), interval 5/7; and the tritone (which is equivalent in its harmonic inversion), interval 6/6.

4 Dyads separated by the tritone (e.g., Ex. 71c, C♯-D and G-G♯) have the same sum, $1 + 2 = 3$ and $7 + 8 = 15$—sums 3 and 15 are equivalent according to the present modulus of 12 (i.e., $15 - 12 = 3$)—since 6 is added to each note, and $2 \times 6 = 0$ (or 12). Therefore, any two dyads of the same sum can be shown to be symmetrically related around the same axis.

5 George Perle and Paul Lansky, "Twelve-Note Composition," *Grove's Dictionary of Music and Musicians*, ed. Stanley Sadie (6th ed., London: Macmillan, 1980), p. 292.

6 For a definition of *cell* see Chapter I, n. 27, above.

7 George Perle, in "Symmetrical Formations in the String Quartets of Béla Bartók," *Music Review* 16 (November, 1955), referred to this chromatic tetrachord as *set X*.

72 Primary, secondary, and tertiary interval couples of cell X

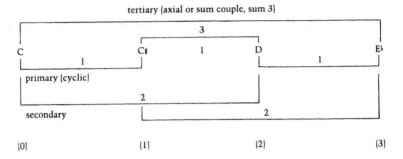

73 Primary, secondary, and tertiary interval couples of cell Y

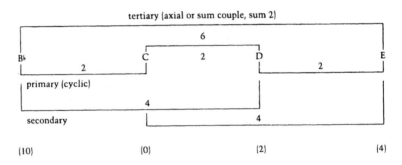

equivalent intervals $(2 - 1 = 1; 3 - 0 = 3)$, will be called *tertiary*; this is the sum couple,[8] since it is based on the two symmetrically related dyads of sum 3. Cell X is given at its basic transpositional level ("X-0") in Example 71a.

The three interval couples of another principal cell of the quartet—we will call this cell Y[9]—are shown in Example 73. Cell Y is a segment of the whole-tone scale (interval-2 cycle). Of its three interval couples, the one expressed in the equation $4 - 2 = 0 - 10$ (or $12 - 10$) is primary, since it is based on the cyclic interval of Y. The secondary interval couple is expressed in the equation $4 - 0 = 2 - 10$ (or $14 - 10$). The tertiary interval couple (the sum couple) consists, analogously to that of X, of two nonequivalent intervals that are symmetrically related $(10 + 4 = 0 + 2 = 2)$. The basic transpositional level of Y (Y-10) is shown in Example 71b.

---

8 *Sum couple* refers to two intervals that are symmetrically related, i.e., that have the same sum.

9 Perle, in "Symmetrical Formations," referred to this whole-tone tetrachord as *set Y*.

The third symmetrical cell (Z)[10] differs from X and Y in that the two intervals in *each* of its three interval couples are equivalent, and in that two of these interval couples are also sum couples (Ex. 74). Unlike X and Y, Z is not a segment of a uni-intervallic cycle. Its interval couple, expressed in the equation $7 - 1 = 8 - 2$, will be called *primary*, since it is based on two tritones, a property which enables Z to be permuted around either of two axes of symmetry, sum 3 or sum 9 (Ex. 74a, b). The other two interval couples of Z are the sum couples. The interval couple expressed in the equation $8 - 7 = 2 - 1$ has the sum of 3 $(8 + 7 = 2 + 1 = 3)$, which is symmetrically related

74   Primary, secondary, and tertiary interval couples of cell Z at sum 3 and sum 9

(a) Z-8 at sum 3

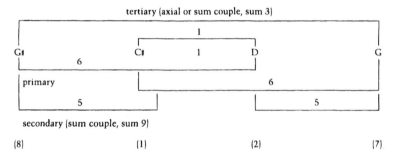

(b) Z-8 at sum 9

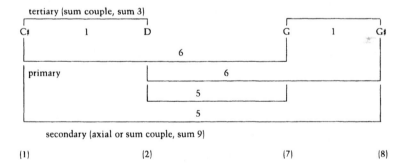

10 Leo Treitler first referred to this symmetrical tetrachord as *cell Z*, in "Harmonic Procedure in the *Fourth Quartet* of Béla Bartók," *Journal of Music Theory* 3/2 (November, 1959): 292–98, as a follow-up to Perle's designations of sets X and Y. (The Z nomenclature is not to be confused with that in the theoretical writings of Allen Forte.)

75   Permutations of cell Z-8/2 around either of two axes of symmetry

76   Permutations of cell Z-11/5 around either of two axes of symmetry

77   Alignment of two inversionally complementary semitonal cycles

dyads of	C	C♯	D	E♭	E	F	F♯	G	G♯	A	B♭	B	C
even-sum 0	C	B	B♭	A	G♯	G	F♯	F	E	E♭	D	C♯	C
pitch-class	0	1	2	3	4	5	6	7	8	9	10	11	0
number	0	11	10	9	8	7	6	5	4	3	2	1	0
interval	0	2	4	6	8	10	0	2	4	6	8	10	0

to the tertiary interval couple of X-0.[11] We will call this the *tertiary* interval couple. The interval couple that contains two interval-5 dyads ($7 - 2 = 1 - 8$, i.e., $7 - 2 = 13 - 8$) will be called *secondary*. Its sum is expressed in the equation $7 + 2 = 1 + 8 = 9$. We will assume that the basic transpositional level of cell Z is Z-8 (Ex. 71c), since this is the transposition number at its first appearance in the quartet (m. 22, va and vnI). At this occurrence, Z-8 is also a primary thematic element of the transition between first-theme and second-theme groups. If Z-8 (Ex. 75a) is transposed by the tritone to Z-2 (Ex. 75c), the axis of symmetry remains at sum 3 ($= 15$). If Z-8/2 is transposed by interval 3 to Z-11/5 (Ex. 76a, c), the interval couple that originally produces sum 3 in Z-8/2 now produces sum 9 in Z-11/5. Conversely, the interval couple that produces sum 9 in Z-8/2 (Ex. 75b, d) now produces sum 3 in Z-11/5 (Ex. 76b, d). The pivotal functions of both Z-8/2 and Z-11/5 are employed by Bartók as a means of exchanging one axis of symmetry for the other.

As was noted above, any symmetrical tetrachord can be analyzed into dyads that have the same sum. These sum dyads will form part of a series of symmetrically related dyads generated by aligning two inversionally complementary semitonal cycles (Ex. 77). The axis of symmetry is expressed by the sum of the two pitch-class numbers in any dyad. In this alignment of the

11 See Example 181 (left column).

cycles, each dyad has an even sum of 0 (= 12). Even sums of complementation produce even interval-classes; odd sums produce odd interval-classes. Each interval occurs at two pitch levels, separated by the tritone.

Each interval may be expressed numerically by subtracting the lower pitch-class number from the upper. In Example 77, the two complementary cycles intersect at the two 0/12 intervals—C-C and its tritone transposition F♯-F♯. These two points of intersection represent the dual axis of symmetry: they have the same sum (this is expressed in the equation 0 + 0 = 6 + 6 = 0). If these two cycles are realigned through the permutation of either cycle by one semitone relative to the other, the sum will become odd (Ex. 78). The axis of symmetry in this case is expressed by the sum of 1 (= 13). In the new alignment, the two complementary cycles intersect at the two 1/11 intervals, C-C♯ and its tritone transposition, F♯-G; the dual axis of symmetry is expressed in the equation 0 + 1 = 6 + 7 = 1.

If either cycle is permuted by an even number of semitones relative to the other, the same collection of interval classes will be generated at a new pitch level. Such a realignment of the cycles in Example 77 is shown in Example 79a. This realignment transposes the pair of cycles in Example 77 by a semitone, since the intersections now occur at C♯-C♯ and G-G; dyads of sum 0 change to dyads of sum 2. Through a number of such realignments, a

78 Realignment of two inversionally complementary semitonal cycles

dyads of	C♯	D	E♭	E	F	F♯	G	G♯	A	B♭	B	C	C♯
odd-sum 1:	C	B	B♭	A	G♯	G	F♯	F	E	E♭	D	C♯	C
pitch-class	1	2	3	4	5	6	7	8	9	10	11	0	1
number:	0	11	10	9	8	7	6	5	4	3	2	1	0
intervals:	1	3	5	7	9	11	1	3	5	7	9	11	1

79 Further Realignment of Two Inversionally Complementary
Semitonal Cycles

(a) Realignment of cycles in Ex. 77

dyads of	D	E♭	E	F	F♯	G	G♯	A	B♭	B	C	C♯	D
sum 2:	C	B	B♭	A	G♯	G	F♯	F	E	E♭	D	C♯	C
interval:	2	4	6	8	10	0	2	4	6	8	10	0	2

(b) Semitonal transposition of pair of cycles in Ex. 77

dyads of	C♯	D	E♭	E	F	F♯	G	G♯	A	B♭	B	C	C♯
sum 2:	C♯	C	B	B♭	A	G♯	G	F♯	F	E	E♭	D	C♯
interval:	0	2	4	6	8	10	0	2	4	6	8	10	0

80 Even array

81 Odd array

pair of inversionally complementary semitonal cycles that generate even interval-numbers will occur at six even sums, and a pair that generates odd interval-numbers will occur at six odd sums (illustrated in the two intervallic arrays, Exx. 80, 81).[12] Together, these arrays produce all intervals and sums. Each column, representing sums, consists of two inversionally com-

12 Perle and Lansky, "Twelve-Note Composition," p. 292.

plementary semitonal cycles, and each row, representing intervals, consists of two parallel semitonal cycles. The two dyads of a sum couple in a symmetrical tetrachord lie in the same column (e.g., X-0, C-C♯-D-E♭, may be partitioned into its symmetrically related dyads C♯-D and C-E♭ in the sum-3 column of the odd array at intervals 1/11 and 3/9). This symmetrical tetrachord may also be partitioned into two additional dyadic couples, each consisting of two identical intervals, i.e., intervals in the same row (e.g., X-0 may be partitioned into the C-D♭ and D-E♭ of its primary interval-couple, lying in row 1/11 of the odd array, or it may be partitioned into the C-D and C♯-D♯ of its secondary interval-couple, lying in row 2/10 of the even array). The sums of dyads C-D♭ and D-E♭ are expressed by the equations $0 + 1 = 1$ and $2 + 3 = 5$; the sums of C-D and D♭-E♭ are expressed by the equations $0 + 2 = 2$ and $1 + 3 = 4$. Thus, the four-note symmetry C-C♯-D-E♭ contains only one sum couple whose dyads C♯-D and C-E♭ have equivalent sums (i.e., are symmetrically related), expressed in the equations $1 + 2 = 3$ and $0 + 3 = 3$. The two sums in each of these three dyadic couples, whether equivalent or nonequivalent, complement each other to equal 6 ($1 + 5 = 2 + 4 = 3 + 3 = 6$). If two symmetrically related dyads (i.e., dyads in the same column, having the same sum) are separated by the tritone, the resultant four-note symmetry will have two sum couples each of whose dyads has equivalent sums. For example, Z-11/5, B-E-F-B♭, may be partitioned into the equivalent sum-dyads B-E and B♭-F (see Ex. 81, sum-3 column, intervals 5/7 and 7/5), expressed in the equations $11 + 4 = 3$ and $10 + 5 = 3$. This four-note symmetry may also be partitioned into the two equivalent sum-dyads B-B♭ and E-F, expressed in the equations $11 + 10 = 9$ and $4 + 5 = 9$. Equivalent sums in two of the three dyadic couples result from the double tritone.[13] (The tritone, represented by interval-number 6/6 in the even array, is the only interval that maintains the same pitch *and* interval content in its complementary inversion or at its own transposition. This principle will be referred to as *tritone equivalence*.) The development of symmetrical formations—significantly, of the basic cells—is largely based on such partitions into their sum or interval couples.

Interval 3 (the minor third), which divides the tritone symmetrically, is significant in the interrelationship of the cells: as is shown below in Example 181, the basic Z cell (Z-8/2) and its interval-3 transposition (Z-11/5) each has sums 3 and 9, which establish their relationship with each of the X transpositions of these sums. The axes of symmetry of sums 3 and 9 are separated by interval 3. The interval-3 relationship between Z-2/8 (D-G-G♯-C♯) and Z-11/5 (B-E-F-B♭) (Ex. 82), or any pair of symmetrically related Z cells (i.e., separated by interval 3), is also significant in the formation of a larger

13 See n. 4, above.

82 Octatonic scale formed by joining two Z cells separated by
interval 3/9

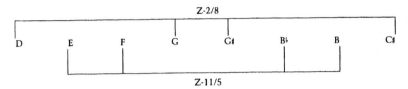

(symmetrical) octatonic scale.[14] Octatonic scales are extensively employed by Bartók throughout his works.

Interval 6 (the tritone) is also significant in the interrelationship of the cells: as is shown below in Example 137, the transpositional level of cell Z at its first explicit joining with cell Y in the *Fourth Quartet* is Z-1/7 (D♭-G♭-G-C). The two tritones of Z-1/7 (D♭-G and G♭-C), when filled in by whole tones, serve as the boundaries of two specific Y cells, Y-1 (D♭-E♭-F-G) and Y-6 (G♭-A♭-B♭-C) (Ex. 83a). These two Y cells (whole-tone tetrachords) can be systematically joined to form a larger (symmetrical) eight-note segment of the interval-5/7 cycle (Ex. 83b); the latter implies the presence of two diatonic sets.[15] The tritone boundaries of the original Y cells now form the boundaries of the two adjacent diatonic (interval-5/7) collections. Bartók often employs such eight-note interval-5/7 sets, frequently expressly partitioned into their adjacent seven-note diatonic components.

Thus, the tritones of cell Z can be employed as invariant structural intervals common to these two types of symmetrical eight-note sets, i.e., the octatonic scale and interval-5/7 collection based on two adjacent diatonic formations. Example 84 illustrates one instance of this relationship, where both sets are symmetrical extensions of Z-1/7. Because of the common tritones of Z, interactions and progressions are permitted among transpositions of one or the other of these sets, or between them.

14 The twelve tones can be partitioned into three mutually exclusive diminished-seventh chords, i.e., three cyclic-interval-3 tetrachords (see Ex. 70). If we pair any two of these three tetrachords, we get an eight-note scale based on regular alternations of whole tones and semitones; we will refer to this scale as *octatonic*. There are three possibilities for pairing the three interval-3 tetrachords, giving us the three octatonic scales—C-D-E♭-F-F♯-G♯-A-B, C♯-D♯-E-F♯-G-A-B♭-C, and D-E-F-G-G♯-B♭-B-C♯. In addition to pairing two interval-3 tetrachords, an octatonic set (e.g., D-E-F-G-G♯-B♭-B-C♯) can be formed by three other pairings of equivalent symmetrical subcollections: Z-2/8 (D-G-G♯-C♯) and its interval-3 transposition, Z-11/5 (B-E-F-B♭); the French-augmented-sixth chord, E-G♯-B♭-D, and its interval-3 transposition, G-B-C♯-F; and two minor tetrachords, D-E-F-G and G♯-B♭-B-C♯, separated by the tritone. We shall arbitrarily assume a referential position for each of the three octatonic scales, beginning with the whole tone. Any permutation of that scale that can begin with pitch-class C will be referred to as octatonic-0, that with pitch-class C♯ as octatonic-1, and that with pitch-class D as octatonic-2.

15 Any seven-note segment of the interval-5/7 cycle gives us the pitch content of a diatonic collection.

83   Tritones of Cell Z as Boundaries of Two Y Cells, and Systematic
Joining of Y-1 and Y-6 as Eight-Note Segment of Cycle of Fifths

(a) Cell Y/Z Construction

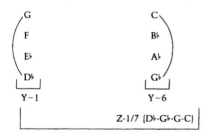

(b) Eight-Note Segment of Cycle of Fifths (Two Adjacent Diatonic Collections)
Interlocking Two Y Cells

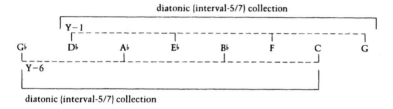

84   Cell Z and two symmetrical eight-note sets in *Fourth String Quartet*

(a) Movement I, mm. 40–43, vnI (in enharmonic spelling) *Diatonic*

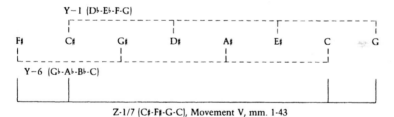

(b) Movement V, mm. 47–75, linear thematic material *Octatonic*

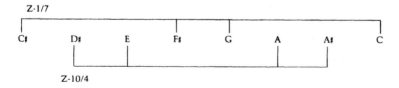

1. MS excerpt from draft of No. 1 (mm. 1–10) of *Eight Hungarian Folk Songs* (NYBA MS No. 17 Vo PS 1)

2. MS excerpt from draft of No. 4 (mm. 1–11) of *Eight Hungarian Folk Songs* (NYBA MS No. 17 Vo PS 1)

3. MS excerpt from draft of No. 5 (mm. 1–10) of *Eight Hungarian Folk Songs* (NYBA MS No. 17 Vo PS 1)

4. MS excerpt from draft of Mov. 1 (mm. 110–122, vns.) of *Fourth String Quartet* (NYBA MS No. 62 FSS 1)

5. MS excerpt from draft of Mov. 1 (No. 1, m. 6, through the measure before No. 3) of *Second String Quartet* (NYBA MS No. 42 FSS 1)

6. MS excerpt from draft of Mov. 1 (mm. 1–26, 49–52) of *Fourth String Quartet*
(NYBA MS No. 62 FSS 1)

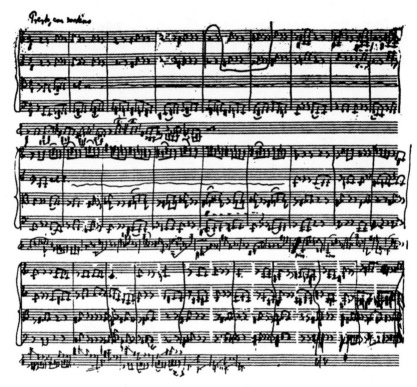

7. MS excerpt from draft of Mov. 2 (mm. 1–27) of *Fourth String Quartet* (NYBA MS No. 62 FSS 1)

8. MS excerpt from draft of Mov. 1 (fugue subject with inversion on page 1) of *Music for Strings, Percussion, and Celesta* (NYBA MS No. 74 FSS 1)

9. MS excerpt from draft of No. 2 (mm. 1–19) of *Eight Improvisations on Hungarian Peasant Songs*, Op. 20, for piano (NYBA MS No. 50 PS 1)

10.   MS excerpt from draft of Mov. 3 (mm. 16–34) of *Fourth String Quartet*
(NYBA MS No. 62 FSS 1)

11. MS excerpt from draft of Mov. 3 (mm. 22–56) of *Fourth String Quartet* (NYBA MS No. 62 FSS 1)

12. MS excerpt from draft of Mov. 3 (marginal sketch of theme from Mov. 4, m. 235f.) of *Music for Strings, Percussion, and Celesta* (NYBA MS No. 74 FSS 1)

13. MS excerpt from draft of Mov. 5 (mm. 121–148, 113–121) of *Fourth String Quartet* (NYBA MS No. 62 FSS 1)

14. MS excerpt from draft of Mov. 2 (mm. 19–41) of *Fourth String Quartet* (NYBA MS No. 62 FSS 1)

CHAPTER V

Construction, Development, and Interaction of Intervallic Cells

Even in some early works—significantly in the *Fourteen Bagatelles for Piano, Op. 6, First String Quartet,* and *Duke Bluebeard's Castle*—in which traditional triadic structures still contribute to the musical fabric, Bartók's new use of the diatonic scale led to a new conception of the chromatic scale.[1] Due to the free use of the modes, which led to a weakening of the hierarchical pitch relations inherent in the traditional dominant-tonic progressions, greater emphasis had to be placed on the *intervallic properties* of both the harmonic and melodic constructions as a means of establishing local and large-scale structural coherence. The new means of providing coherence in an idiom based on equalization of the semitones is primarily found in the intervallic pitch-cell.[2]

One of the most radical early departures from harmonic use of the triad occurs in *Bagatelle No. VIII.* The closing Ritenuto is melodically and harmonically permeated by all six transpositions of cell Z, which unfold above a G pedal (Ex. 85). This closing passage is a culminating point of various cell transformations throughout the piece. A modified recapitulation (più sostenuto) brings back the opening harmonic statements (forming a chromatic succession) of a nonsymmetrical three-note cell. The initial statement of the cell, G♯-B♯-C♯, returns at its original pitch-level (the grace-note G♯ moves on the downbeat to C-D♭, an enharmonic spelling of the original B♯-C♯). A significant transformation of the cell structure, which is based on the intervals of a minor second, major third, and perfect fourth (i.e., intervals 1,

---

1 See Chapter II, n. 1, above. The original publication is given in n. 8 of Chapter I.
2 See Chapter IV, n. 6, above.

85   *Bagatelle No. VIII*, closing

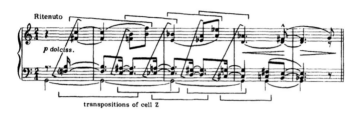

86   *Bagatelle No. VIII*, mm. 26–27

4, and 5), occurs in this section (mm. 24–27). In the first two phrases, the original major third is dropped from each harmonic statement of the cell, leaving only the parallel semitones. At mm. 26–27, not only does each of the cell statements now appear complete but a second major third is added. Each of the resulting four-note symmetrical chords joins the cell with its literal inversion (Ex. 86). (As one instance, the first chord of m. 26, B-G-C-Aᵇ, contains a prime form, G-B-C, and an inversion, G-Aᵇ-C.) Each four-note symmetry, which can also be understood as two semitones separated by a minor third (G-Aᵇ/B-C), anticipates cell Z (Ritenuto), which expands the minor third to a perfect fourth (e.g., F-F♯/B-C at m. 28). In addition, the tritones of cell Z are anticipated (mm. 25–27) by the cadential chords of these phrases. The two phrases at mm. 25 and 26 each end with an unresolved dominant-seventh chord (Eᵇ-G-()-Dᵇ and D-F♯-A-C), and the next two phrase segments (m. 27) similarly end with dominant-sevenths (B-D♯-F♯-A and F♯-A♯-C♯-E). Each of these four chords contains a whole-tone cell with one tritone (G-Dᵇ, F♯-C, D♯-A, and A♯-E). The successive pairs of tritones imply the presence of two Z cells (Dᵇ-F♯-G-C and E-A-A♯-D♯).

Significant transformations of the basic three-note cell begin with the second phrase (mm. 3–6) of the exposition. While the cell remains unchanged on the strong beats of mm. 3 and 4 (G♯-B♯-C♯, F♯-A♯-B, and E-G♯-A), its structure is partially altered in the other chords by the alignment of the original descending thirds against fifths instead of semitones as before. The cadential major-seventh chord, E-G♯-B-D♯ (m. 6), represents a significant transformation of the original cell, this four-note symmetry based on a joining of a prime form, B-D♯-E, with an inversion, D♯-E-G♯. The cell is also transformed in the upper line of the same phrase (Ex. 87, mm. 4–5). A gapped whole-tone segment A-B-( )-D♯, which retains the major third of the basic cell and expands the semitone to A-B, produces the new boundary A-D♯. This represents the first tritone occurrence in the piece. This melodic whole-tone cell is followed by a five-note diatonic segment in the bass line, E-F♯-G♯-A♯-B, the first four notes of which now give us a complete whole-tone tetrachord bounded by a second tritone, E-A♯. These two tritone boundaries, which encompass the linearly unfolding whole-tone segments A-B-( )-D♯ and E-F♯-G♯-A♯, together represent the first adumbration of the specific double-tritone combination of cell Z. In addition, the latter five-note cadential diatonic segment (m. 5) implies a partial Z cell, E-A♯-B-( ), in the principal modal tones.

A transitional passage (mm. 12–15) to the development section begins with the minor-third transposition (B-D♯-E) of the basic cell. Statements of the cell melodically overlap in two-note segments (Ex. 88): D♯-D-B♭ interlocked with its inversion, D-B♭-A, together produce the four-note symmetry D♯-D-B♭-A. (Such cell joining is significant in the recapitulation, mm. 26–27, where it precedes the expansion to the cell-Z constructions; see Ex. 86.) This symmetry implies the presence of two partial Z cells, D♯-D-A-( ) and D♯-B♭-A-( ); the former (in enharmonic spelling, A-E♭-D) explicitly appears as a melodic adjacency (mm. 14–15).

87 *Bagatelle No. VIII, mm. 4–6*

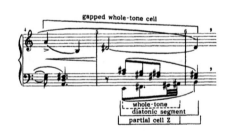

88 *Bagatelle No. VIII, mm. 13–15*

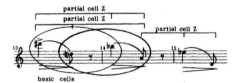

89   *Bagatelle No. VIII*, mm. 16–18

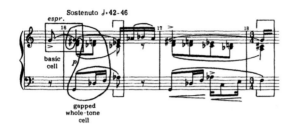

90   *Bagatelle No. VIII*, mm. 18, 21

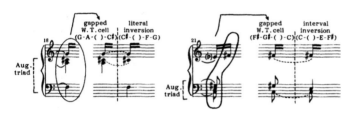

In the development section (mm. 16–23), intervallic transformations from the basic cell through the whole-tone cell to the properties of cell Z are unfolded in complex procedures. This section (Ex. 89) begins with the basic cell now at the tritone transposition, D-F♯-G, which moves at the second eighth-note of m. 16 to a passing statement of the gapped whole-tone cell D♭-( )-F-G. The following local cadential chord (middle of m. 16) contains an augmented (i.e., whole-tone) triad C♭-E♭-G in the right hand. The addition of A♭ in the left hand expands the latter to a four-note collection, which can be understood as a joining of the basic cell (E♭-G-A♭) with this whole-tone formation (C♭-E♭-G). At m. 18 the cadential chord, which ends the first half of the development section,[3] contains another augmented triad, F-A-C♯, in the quarter-notes. The addition of the sixteenth-note G expands the latter to a four-note collection that can be understood as a joining of two inversionally related gapped whole-tone cells, G-A-( )-C♯ and C♯-( )-F-G. (The descending phase of the following cadential flourish linearly establishes a transposition, F♭-( )-A♭-B♭, of the gapped whole-tone cell as part of a larger whole-tone scale, E-D-C-B♭-A♭-( )-F♭.) The cadential chord of the second half of the development section (Ex. 90, m. 21), analogous to that at m. 18,

---

3 The development section is divided into two analogous parts. The first (mm. 16–18) joins segments of the first two phrases of the piece, ending with a cadential flourish (m. 18); the second (mm. 19–23) represents an expansion and modification of the events of the first.

91 *Bagatelle No. VIII, mm. 21–23*

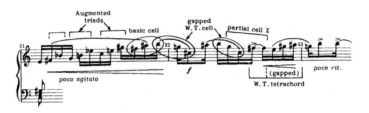

contains yet another augmented triad (C-E-G♯) in the left hand. The addition of F♯ in the right hand (following the sustained E♭ at mm. 20–21) expands the latter triad to a four-note collection, which, analogously to the chord at m. 18, can be understood as a joining of two inversionally related gapped whole-tone cells, F♯-G♯-( )-C and C-( )-E-F♯. However, the cadential four-note collection C-( )-E-F♯-G♯ (m. 21) is a literal inversion of that at the first cadence, F-G-A-( )-C♯ (m. 18). These inversionally related tetrachords, which respectively represent the two mutually exclusive whole-tone scales, each contain one tritone (G-C♯, C-F♯). Significantly, the two tritones together imply a background-level occurrence of cell Z (C♯-F♯-G-C), an anticipation of the final stage in the cellular transformation procedure. The cadential passage of the development (mm. 21–22) then joins, in interlocking succession, all the cell properties discussed thus far (Ex. 91). Measure 21 unfolds a series of augmented triads that culminates in a transposition of the basic cell (F♯-A♯-B). The latter intersects with gapped whole-tone cell G-( )-B-C♯, which is reiterated on the second quarter-note. The accented F♯ with the preceding G-C♯ forms a segment of cell Z, G-C♯-F♯-( ). (At the same time, F♯ completes the following gapped whole-tone cell to give us E-F♯-G♯-A♯. The latter with the cadential G-B forms the collection E-F♯-(G)-G♯-A♯-B, which is essentially identical to the diatonic segment that ended the second phrase of the piece, at mm. 5–6.) After a series of Z cells in the coda, the bagatelle ends with a return to the basic cell at the tritone transposition, D-F♯-G.

While these cell expansions and transformations are basic to the organic growth and structural coherence of the piece, a sense of tonality is produced by chordal structures other than those based on the cells. Certain local tonal areas suggest a larger tonal scheme reminiscent of the traditional sonata plan. The initial cell progression is interrupted at the cadential point (m. 2) of the first phrase by a C-minor triad. Then, at the main cadential point (mm. 9–10) of the closing idea, comes a shift to a dominant-pedal G, upon which are built major and then minor triads, the A and A♭ functioning as passing-tones. The development section opens (at mm. 16ff.) with an emphasis on the G-dominant in the bass and as a pedal in the right hand. The final chord of the development (m. 21) reestablishes the priority of C as the root of the augmented triad—perhaps an anticipation of the C triad (C-( )-G) at the cadence (m. 24) of the recapitulated first phrase. While these local traditional tonal assertions have little to do with the unfolding of the cells, they tend to establish a tonal framework for melodic and harmonic relations solely based on intervallic content. These seemingly contradictory principles in the formation of a single work are significantly integrated in the later works within a new set of unified relations.

The tritone, which serves as the primary determinant in the large-scale transpositions of the basic cell in *Bagatelle No. VIII* (i.e., the cell appears at the tritone transposition at the opening of the development, m. 16, and at the end of the work), is also basic in both the local and large-scale relations in *Bagatelle No. XIII.*[4] Although its triadic harmonic construction makes this piece appear traditional, in fact the relationship of these triads (which are separated exclusively by the tritone) has nothing to do with traditional tonal functions. An expressive melody is accompanied by only two chords— minor triads on E♭ and A—so that the progressions between these two chords are defined by their intervallic voice-leading properties. Thus, these two triads function more strongly as harmonic cells than as traditional chords.

These two triadic cells are systematically integrated with other cells that are linearly generated throughout the piece. Voice-leadings between the two alternating minor triads, E♭-G♭-B♭ and A-C-E, a tritone apart linearly outline three tritones, E♭-A, G♭-C, and B♭-E, of octatonic scale E♭-E-G♭-( )-A-B♭-C-( ). The latter appears complete in the final codetta (Ex. 92), where each triad is harmonically extended to a (symmetrical) minor-seventh chord (E♭-G♭-B♭-D♭ and A-C-E-G) by the addition of the fourth tritone, D♭-G.

92   *Bagatelle No. XIII*, mm. 23–26

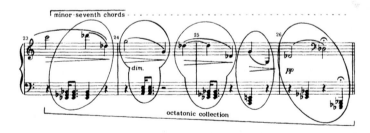

4 The form of this bagatelle is largely determined by the tritone. Two opening statements of an isorhythmic pattern (mm. 1–5 and 6–10, left hand) are exclusively based on an E♭-minor triad, except in the final measure (10) of the latter pattern, where this triad shifts to its tritone transposition. A new rhythmic pattern (to the codetta, mm. 15–16) is based on the latter chord (A-minor triad), the codetta then being based on both chords. The second section of the piece (mm. 17ff.) is based on regular alternations of these two chords, a tritone apart.

While these two minor-seventh chords appear here as two equivalent symmetrical partitions of the octatonic collection E♭-E-G♭-G-A-B♭-C-D♭, that collection also implies the presence of two Z cells, E♭-A-B♭-E and G♭-C-D♭-G. One of these (G♭-C-D♭-G) appeared at mm. 20–21 as a melodic detail near the climax of the piece (at the end of the agitato and crescendo) (Ex. 93). This local occurrence of cell Z, together with the two accompanying minor triads, gives us the first statement of the complete octatonic collection.

Cell Z also appears here as a culmination of successive cell transformations. The upper line of the opening phrase (Ex. 94, mm. 2–3) forms the major-seventh chord A-G♭-D-D♭ (in root position and enharmonic spelling, D-F♯-A-C♯), which returns, a half-step lower, near the end of the piece, at mm. 22–23. This formation can be understood as two inversionally related segments (G♭-D-D♭ and D-D♭-A), the same basic-cell structure as in *Bagatelle No. VIII.* The first segment, G♭-D-D♭, appears as a local melodic detail at mm. 5–6 of the second phrase, where it is interlocked with gapped whole-tone cell A♭-G♭-( )-D. The third phrase cadences at mm. 9–10 (Ex. 95) on a transposition of the basic cell, B♭-F♯-F. Interlockings then occur among the basic cell, gapped whole-tone cell, and cell Z in the remainder of the first large section. At mm. 13–14, tritone D-G♯, which encompasses the gapped whole-tone cell, D-( )-F♯-G♯, is also common to a partial statement of cell Z (D-G♯-G-( )); this unobtrusive statement is the first suggestion of cell Z in the work. In turn, partial cell Z is interlocked with a transposition of the basic cell G-G♯-C, the latter intersecting with yet another gapped whole-tone cell, C-( )-E-F♯. Tritone C-F♯ is joined at mm. 14–15 with another tritone, F-B, to give us the first complete melodic statement of cell Z (F♯-F-B-C) in the codetta of the first section. In the second large section (mm. 17ff.),

93 *Bagatelle No. XIII,* mm. 17–21

94 *Bagatelle No. XIII,* mm. 2–6

95 *Bagatelle No. XIII, mm.* 9–16

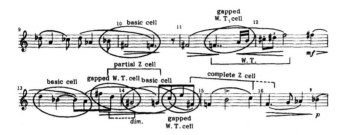

the melodic line unfolds pairs of semitones which form a series of interlocking four-note symmetries leading again to cell Z near the high point at mm.
20–21 (G♭-C♯-C-G) (see Ex. 93). Thus, the expansion and organic transformation of intervallic cells appear to be a fundamental means of progression
in works by Bartók.

With the disappearance, in the early part of the present century, of the
traditional triad as the basic harmonic premise, greater importance was
placed on the interval as a primary means of harmonic and melodic integration. The *First String Quartet* is historically transitional in its interaction of
triadic harmonies with fundamental melodic intervallic patterns. The thematically amorphous linear motions of the opening quasi-fugue movement,
which appear to determine the nontraditional chromatic progression of triads, contain the intervallic germ elements of the more clearly defined thematic constructions that emerge in the second and, especially, the third
movement. While this organic growth of themes from the initial appoggiatura patterns of the fugue subject may seem to have some relation to the
concept of motivic development found in traditional tonal music, the general dissociation of the basic intervallic constructions from any consistently
recognizable rhythmic patterns, harmonic bases, octave positions, or pitch-
class orderings suggests a cellular rather than motivic interpretation for
such emergent pitch formations. In the course of the quartet the initial appoggiatura elaborations of the underlying triadic harmonies are gradually removed from their traditional consonant-dissonant functions, so that subsequent intervallic manifestations derived from these appoggiatura motions
acquire a primal, perhaps even consonant, thematic and harmonic function.
The components of the opening thematic material are constantly modified throughout the work, so that they are only generally identifiable within
the contours of subsequent derivative thematic ideas. However, a closer
study of the intervallic content of the latter in their relationship with the
opening amorphous appoggiatura patterns suggests that specific cellular
properties are the primary integrative means in the organic growth process.

96 *First String Quartet*, Movement III, m. 5

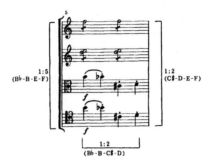

At the opening of Movement III, the va and vc present one of the most clearly identifiable themes of the work. This prominent unison statement serves as a focal point for the thematic morphogenesis of the preceding movements. A significant feature of this six-note melodic idea is the joining of two semitones that are separated (Ex. 96) by either a minor sixth (C♯-D/B♭-B) or a whole tone (B♭-B/C♯-D).[5] In the present context this linear thematic statement is harmonically dissociated from traditional triadic constructions, instead being harmonized by an ostinato figure, D-E-F. While pitch-class D of the latter duplicates a component of one of the thematic semitones, C♯-D, the two remaining ostinato tones, E-F, form a third semitone. The combination of three semitones implies a six-note segment of the octatonic scale (B♭-B-C♯-D-E-F). Within this pitch collection there are two ways of pairing the semitones: in an interval ratio of 1 : 2 (B♭-B/C♯-D or C♯-D/E-F), or 1 : 5 (B♭-B/E-F). At No. 1, mm. 1–2, the latter pairing emerges as the basis of a two-measure bridge, where it is explicitly ordered as two tritones, B♭-E and F-B. This symmetrical tetrachord is more systematically and extensively exploited (as cell Z) in the *Second, Fourth,* and *Fifth Quartet.*

These two four-note partitions (based on the interval-ratios 1 : 2 and 1 : 5) of the six-note octatonic segment are foreshadowed in the opening appoggiatura patterns of Movement I. Each of the imitative lines is permeated by a succession of semitones (Ex. 97). The vnI unfolds G-A♭, D♭-D, and E-F in the initial phrase of the subject (to m. 3, first eighth-note), which gives us another six-note segment of the octatonic collection that will appear in Movement III (see Ex. 96). The successive pairings (G-A♭/D♭-D and D♭-D/E-F) are exclusively based on the 1 : 5 and 1 : 2 ratios, respectively. In the second phrase of vnI (m. 3), the 1 : 2 pairing B♭-B/D♭-D is the transposition

5 We shall spell such cellular formations in their ascending pitch-class order, placing the smaller of the two intervallic gaps between the two semitonal components (e.g., B♭-B/C♯-D). This abstract designation is preferable, since we are presently dealing with intervallic content rather than with ordering.

that will appear as the basis of the opening linear thematic statement of Movement III. In the first phrase of vnII (mm. 1–2, seventh eighth-note), the pair of semitones, E♭-E and A-B♭, forms a 1:5 ratio which, together with the initial C, exclusively outlines a five-note octatonic segment.

These semitonal relations are subsequently transformed into other interval ratios. The first prominent transformation initiates the va melody at the opening of the middle section (No. 6, mm. 5–6); the two semitones D♯-E and G♯-A now form an interval ratio of 1:4. At the return of section A (No. 11f.), the priority of ratios 1:5 and 1:2 is reestablished in the opening linear thematic material and at the final enharmonically spelled semicadence in A minor, where the closing pair of semitones, A♭-A and C♭-C, suggest a diatonic setting for the basic ratio of 1:2. The latter moves attacca into the theme-1a motive of Movement II based on linearly stated semitones in parallel major thirds.

These opening semitonal combinations, which linearly suggest 1:1 ratios, initiate an interval-expansion process that culminates in prominent foreground statements of cell Z (1:5) in theme 1c (at No. 1, mm. 2ff., vnII and va). At m. 2, the priority of a 1:3 ratio is locally established in an isolated foreground statement of the theme-1a motive (A♯-B/C×-D♯). The thematic expansion of this motive near the end of the accelerando (mm. 11f.) is initiated by two parallel statements of the 1:4 ratio, A-A♯/C×-D♯ (vnI) and F-F♯/A♯-B (vnII), the vertical combinations of semitones giving us two successive 1:3 cells, A♯-B/C×-D♯ and F-F♯/A-A♯ (Ex. 98). A, 1:3 cell, C♯-

97 *First String Quartet*, Movement I, mm. 1–3

98 *First String Quartet*, Movement II, m. 11

99 *First String Quartet*, Movement II, No. 1, mm. 2–3

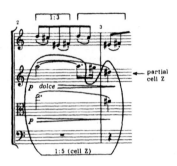

D/E♯-F♯, emerges at mm. 18 ff., vnI, as the basis of the theme-1b ostinato. At this point the latter is combined with an isolated foreground statement of the theme-1a motive in va and vc; the vertical combination of the three semitones A♯-B, C×-D♯, and E♯-F♯ implies the presence of interval-ratios 1:2 (C×-D♯/E♯-F♯), 1:3 (A♯-B/C×-D♯), and 1:4 (E♯-F♯/A♯-B). These are linearly and vertically expanded in theme 1c in vnII and va (No. 1, mm. 2ff.) to the basic 1:5 interval ratio (cell Z) (Ex. 99). While vnII plays a three-note segment of cell Z, A-G♯/D♯-( ), the prominently placed vertical interval-5 dyads E-A and A♯-D♯ give us a complete statement of the 1:5 ratio, or cell Z (A♯-D♯-E-A). This Z cell subsequently initiates the bridge section (No. 3, mm. 3ff.) as part of the linear thematic statement of vnII and va. At No. 5, near the end of the bridge, Z is intervallically contracted to ratio 1:4 (F♯-G/B-C), which also appears as an unobtrusive detail in the second theme (at No. 6, m. 4, with upbeat, in vnII and va).

These relationships of two semitones, which are extensively developed and transformed throughout the remainder of the work, serve as only one of the basic means of integration. Secondary cell formations that appear to grow out of the basic semitonal relations also serve significant functions in the organic growth of the work. As one instance, the second statement of the bridge passage in Movement III (No. 2) expands the original semitonal interval couple, B♭-B/E-F, of the 1:5 ratio at No. 1 to whole tones (A♭-B♭/C-D) to form a new interval ratio of 2:2 (Ex. 100). This expansion is anticipated in the initial six-note motive by the interval-2 dyad A-B. (Perhaps we may view the final tonic sonority of the work, A-B-E, as the ultimate expansion of the 1:5 ratio to 2:5. The latter is immediately preceded by a complete whole-tone scale, implying ratio 2:2, which can be seen as a local intervallic expansion of the semitonal figures at No. 39, mm. 5–9.) The expansion of the basic semitone to interval 2 is first manifested in Movement I (m. 4, vnI) in the third phrase of the fugue subject and again prominently at m. 12 of Movement II, where the pair of whole tones A♭-B♭/C-D expands the preced-

100   *First String Quartet*, Movement III, No. 2

ing linear 1 : 4 figures. At No. 14 of the development section, the eighth-note figures of vnI most significantly demonstrate the expansion of the semitones of the theme-1a motive to interval 2 (compare this figure at No. 14 with that at No. 1).

Like the *First Quartet, Bluebeard's Castle* (1911) is significantly based on the shifting relations of semitones, the various transformations of which appear to be associated with special dramatic situations. In connection with the emerging symbol of blood, combinations of semitones move from unobtrusive contexts (as part of larger thematic statements) to being the primary foreground event. The general tendency of the intervallic ratios between the semitones is to become increasingly dissonant (the most dissonant being the 1 : 1 ratio, based exclusively on semitones) in association with the main dramatic idea. The excerpt shown in Example 101—a prominent foreground statement of a 1 : 1 cell, G♯-A/A♯-B—occurs in the scene of the Torture Chamber (the first of the seven doors to be opened by Judith). The text at this point reveals that Judith has just noticed blood in Bluebeard's domain: "Deiner Feste Wände bluten!" ("Your castle walls are bleeding!").

This pair of semitones (G♯-A/A♯-B), the most dissonant relationship between two semitones, is divorced from any traditional modal construction. Prior to this point (see Ex. 101), combinations of semitones generally appeared as part of larger modal or polymodal thematic material. The opera opens with an introduction that unfolds a theme exclusively in F♯ pentatonic (F♯-A-B-C♯-E), a modal substructure totally devoid of semitones. Four of the notes (F♯-A-B-( )-E) are retained in the ensuing "menacing" motive (Ex. 102), which expands this pentatonic segment to an exotic non-diatonic mode, *F♯-G-A-B-C-( )-D♯-E*. (The expanded collection suggests a permutation of E harmonic-minor, E-F♯-G-A-B-C-D♯-E, which explicitly unfolds above the held F♯ tonic.) Three semitones (F♯-G, B-C, and D♯-E) are thereby introduced into the original pentatonic formation. In the second statement

101 *Bluebeard's Castle*, section b of Torture Chamber, No. 34f.

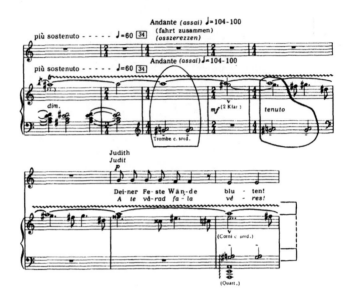

102 *Bluebeard's Castle*, m. 16 through No. 1

of the "menacing" motive (m. 18 through No. 1), the collection is further chromaticized by the addition of C♯—the one F♯-pentatonic note missing from the first statement—so we now get *F♯-G-A-B-C-C♯-D♯-E*. (The latter suggests a permutation of the "bimodal" combination of E harmonic-minor and E melodic-minor, E-F♯-G-A-B-C-C♯-D♯-E, unfolding above the held F♯.) Dissonance and tension are thereby introduced by a sudden incorporation of semitones into the opening pentatonic framework. In turn, in the final statements of the motive the supporting whole-tone bass motion becomes chromatic (No. 1, mm. 2ff.). In Bluebeard's first recitative (No. 2, m. 6, through No. 3, m. 6), an analogously progressive modal elaboration of another pentatonic scale (D-F-G-A-C) gradually introduces semitones, the basic means of producing dissonance and tension as Bluebeard and Judith enter the castle.

The opening instrumental punctuation at No. 2, mm. 6–7, lower strings, represents the first prominent statement of isolated semitones (D-D♯/F-F♯). Henceforth, in anticipation of blood, the primary transpositional level of two semitones at interval-ratio 1 : 1 (G♯-A/A♯-B) emerges with increasing prominence from the modal thematic material into a foreground event. At the return of the "menacing" motive (No. 4, mm. 5–6), both these semitones appear for the first time as basic local details in the larger thematic statement (Ex. 103), introducing Bluebeard's question: "Bleibst Du stehen? Willst nach Hause?" ("Are you anxious? Do you linger?"). At this point (No. 5, mm. 2–5, flutes and oboes), one of these semitones (G♯-A)

103 *Bluebeard's Castle*, No. 4, mm. 5ff.

104 *Bluebeard's Castle*, No. 11

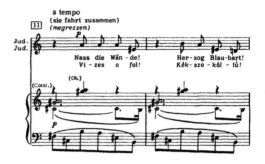

105 *Bluebeard's Castle*, No. 33f.

appears as the upper boundary of the successive eighth-note figures. At Judith's comment (No. 10, mm. 8–9), "Deine Feste ist so dunkel!" ("Your castle is so dark!"), the pitch content of the accompanying pentatonic collection (D♯-F♯-G♯-A♯-C♯) is disrupted by a single dissonant note in the voice (A), implying the presence of a partial statement of the basic 1:1 cell, G♯-A/A♯-(). At Judith's first allusion to blood (No. 11), "Nass die Wände!" ("Oozing walls!"), semitone G♯-A appears as a primary foreground event in the flutes, oboes, and horns (Ex. 104).

The components of this semitonal cell appear with increasing prominence in correspondence with the growing awareness of blood.[6] As the opening of the door (No. 30f.) produces a blood-red gap in the wall, the trilled semitone A♯-B appears as a dissonant element against the partially diatonic figurations. At No. 33 (Ex. 105), this semitone is briefly diatonicized as part of the scale figures, A♯-B-C♯-D♯-E and its inversion, B-A♯-G♯-F♯-E♯, the

6 For a systematic outline of these occurrences, see the essay by Sandor Veress, "Bluebeard's Castle," in *Béla Bartók: A Memorial Review* (New York: Boosey and Hawkes, 1950), pp. 45–49.

basic A♯-B forming an interval ratio of 1:4 with each of the other two diatonic semitones (A♯-B/D♯-E, and E♯-F♯/A♯-B). Then, at the main dramatic focal point of the symbol of blood (No. 34; see Ex. 101), A♯-B is dissociated from the latter diatonic context and joined with the other basic semitone, G♯-A, to form the dissonant 1:1 cell, G♯-A/A♯-B. Thus, *Bluebeard's Castle* significantly links an abstract intervallic cell with traditional modal formations, a relationship that contributes to the expression and integration of the drama.

The *Second String Quartet* marks a radical break from the harmonic progression in the *First Quartet*. In the earlier work (especially Movement I), contrapuntal alignment of the fluid chromatic lines harmonically results in a homogeneous succession of traditional triads. (The latter, however, are largely dissociated from the voice-leading properties of the major-minor scale system.) In the *Second Quartet*, contrapuntal alignment harmonically results in a heterogeneous succession of diverse chords that often are projections of the melodic intervals. Thus, a pitch formation that is melodically and harmonically undifferentiated can be analytically approached as a "collection" of pitches (i.e., an intervallic cell).

In the large-scale structure of the *Second Quartet*, cells function both as primary sources of melodic and harmonic integration and as a means of associating or transforming thematic statements. The modified return of the first-theme group (Movement I, recapitulation, No. 16, m. 8, to No. 18, m. 4) is linearly permeated by all six transpositions of cell Z (Ex. 106). The main thematic line in vnI (at No. 16, m. 9, beginning with D, through No. 17, m. 2, first eighth-note) is exclusively based on Z-2/8, D-G-G♯-C♯, while vc (No. 16, m. 8, to No. 17, m. 4, beat 2) unfolds Z-5/11, F-B♭-B-E, in counterpoint against it. At the same time, the inner voices unfold a syncopated ostinato first outlining Z-4/10, E-A-A♯-D♯ (No. 16, mm. 8–13), then Z-3/9, D♯-A♭-A-D (to No. 17, m. 4, beat 2). At No. 17, mm. 1–2, vnI linearly shifts from Z-2/8 to Z-1/7, D♭-G♭-A♭♭-C. The latter is then transformed (No. 17, mm. 4–8) into Z-4/10, E-A-B♭-E♭, which is exclusively established as the main foreground event at the cadence (No. 18, mm. 3–4). The remaining Z transposition, Z-0/6 (C-F-G♭-B), unfolds in the syncopated accompaniment (No. 17, m. 4, to No. 18, m. 2, vnII and va), becoming interlocked in the three lower instruments (No. 18, m. 2) with Z-1/7 (D♭-F♯-G-C).

The fusion of cells Z-0/6 and Z-1/7 a semitone apart is significant in the generation of a Z-variant, or secondary cell.[7] The first of each pair of chords (F♯-G-C) at No. 18f. forms an isolated three-note segment of Z, but the second chord (B-D♭-F) maintains only the tritone property of Z, expanding the

---

7 George Perle, "Symmetrical Formations in the String Quartets of Béla Bartók," *Music Review* 16 (November, 1955): 308–9, states that nonequivalent symmetries are employed as a means of differentiating the musical components.

107 *Second String Quartet,* Movement I

(a) Three interval couples of Z (vc)

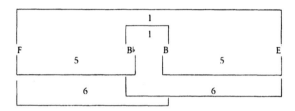

(b) Three interval couples of the Z-variant (vc, va, vnII)

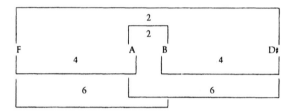

interval-1 property to interval 2 and contracting the interval-5 property to interval 4. At No. 18, m. 2, the addition of a held G in va and vc expands this nonsymmetrical variant, B-D♭-F, to a four-note symmetry, G-B-D♭-F. The latter joins two tritones, one from each of the two interlocking Z cells. This variant of cell Z is more prominently established as such at the opening of the recapitulation (No. 16, m. 8f.). Tritone F-B, which linearly forms part of Z-5/11 in vc, and tritone A-D♯, which linearly forms part of Z-4/10 in va and vn II, are vertically joined to form F-A-B-D♯ (see Ex. 106). The intervallic properties (i.e., interval couples) of cell Z and its variant are outlined in Example 107. Thus, the revised combination of the tritones of cell Z produces two new interval couples based on intervals 2 and 4, the tritones remaining common to both.

Both symmetries (cell Z and its variant) are foreshadowed as primary structures at the climax of the development section. Whereas Z unfolds as the basis of the linear contrapuntal motion in the recapitulation, it initiates the Sostenuto (No. 15) as the sole defining property of the harmonic structure (Ex. 108). The initial chord of the first phrase forms Z-1/7 (D♭-F♯-G-C), while that of the second phrase (No. 15, m. 2) forms Z-4/10 (E-A-A♯-D♯). The Z-variant is then established (No. 16, mm. 4–7) as the basic chordal structure at the end of the development section (Ex. 109). The transformation in this passage from Z to its variant is anticipated (No. 15) by the whole-tone neighbor motion from Z-1/7 (D♭-F♯-G-C) to Z-3/9 (E♭-G♯-A-D). Each

108 *Second String Quartet*, Movement I, No. 15, mm. 1–4

109 *Second String Quartet*, Movement I, No. 16, mm. 4–7

110 *Second String Quartet*, Movement I, No. 15

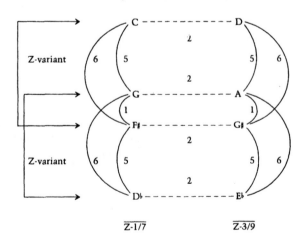

tritone of the initial transposition (Z-1/7) forms a Z-variant with the corresponding tritone of the upper neighbor, Z-3/9 (Ex. 110) (i.e., D♭-G moves to E♭-A to form E♭-G-A-D♭ and F♯-C moves to G♯-D to form G♯-C-D-F♯).[8] The second phrase duplicates the progression at the minor third.

Revised combinations of the two equivalent dyads common to each of the three interval couples of these basic symmetries (see Ex. 107a, b) serve as an important means of progression throughout the work. The climax of the development and the opening of the recapitulation, which are permeated by distinct, texturally differentiated statements of these cells, serve as focal points for the emergence of earlier unobtrusive cell statements set within larger thematic lines. Both cells (either partial or complete) are integrated as local details within the opening measures, together participating in a process of organic intervallic growth. The movement opens with a nonsymmetrical three-note cell, B♭-D-E♭, consisting of an interval-5 boundary filled in by intervals 4 and 1. This cell (a) is linearly projected into the thematic statement of vnI, A-D-C♯ (Ex. 111). The addition of G♯ transforms the latter into a four-note symmetry, G♯-A-C♯-D, by combining it with its inversion. At the same time, this produces a new intervallically expanded cell, D-C♯-G♯. In turn, the added G in vnI transforms the expanded cell (D-C♯-G♯) into a four-note symmetry, Z-8/2 (D-C♯-G♯-G), two of the interval couples (based on interval-1 and interval-5 dyads) of which are in common with the former. This cellular expansion is reflected in the chord progression of the first two measures. At the opening of m. 2, the initial form of cell a (B♭-D-E♭) is transformed into the first partial statement of the Z-variant, B♭-D-E, by the linear motion of E♭ to E. The result is an interlocking of cell a (B♭-D-E♭) with the partial Z-variant (B♭-D-E) and partial Z-4/10 (B♭-E♭-E). At the entry of E-A in vnI, the last cell (Z-4/10) is expanded to its four-note symmetrical form (B♭-E♭-E-A). Thus, cell a, which integrates certain intervallic properties of both cell Z and its variant, serves as a link between them.

111   *Second String Quartet,* Movement I, mm. 1–3

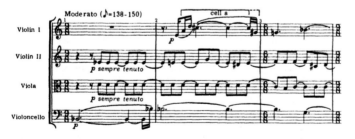

8 A similar progression occurs in the recapitulation (No. 17, m. 4, vnII and va), where a single tritone, linearly belonging to Z-3/9, moves by whole step to another, linearly belonging to Z-0/6; together these two tritones form a Z-variant.

112 *Second String Quartet,* Movement I

(a) m. 2, vnI   (b) No. 1, vc

113 *Second String Quartet,* Movement I

vc (mm. 3–6)

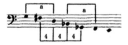

114 *Second String Quartet,* Movement I

m. 2, vn. I.   No. 1 (phrase 2), vc.   No. 3 (trans.), stretto No. 5 (theme 2), vns.

Intervals 4 and 5 of cell a (A-C♯-D) also serve as a link between the opening motive of theme 1 (m. 2, vnI) and the primary motive of theme 2 (No. 5, vns). The two disjunct interval-5 dyads, A-D and C♯-G♯, that linearly interlock cell a (A-D-C♯) with cell Z-8/2 (D-C♯-G♯-G) (Ex. 112a) are transformed at the next motivic statement (Ex. 112b) into two conjunct interval-4 dyads that interlock two statements of cell a. Furthermore, while the initial segment of the opening statement conjunctly joins two perfect fourths, E-A-D, around a local axis, A-A, the transformed motive joins two major thirds around the same local axis. Thus, the priority of interval 5 (a basic interval of cell Z) in the opening thematic statement is shifted to interval 4 (a basic interval of both the Z-variant and cell a) in the latter. This transformation is prepared by vc (mm. 3–6), which unfolds successive linear statements of cell a and its inversion (Ex. 113). The successive stages of transformation of the main motive, in which interval 4 of cell a emerges from its position as an unobtrusive detail to become the primary foreground element of theme 2, are outlined in Example 114.

A more direct link between the intervallic structure of cell a in theme 1 and that of theme 2 appears in an earlier sketch of the opening measures of the transition. The measure before No. 3 in the final version (Ex. 115a) replaces five measures of the original sketch (Ex. 115b). While the intervallic

structure of the theme-1 motive in the final version interlocks cell a (G-B-C)
with its literal inversion (F♯-G-B), the motive in the sketch linearly implies
the pitch content of minor-seventh chord C♯-E-G♯-B. However, in mm. 2–3
of the sketch, vc and va transform C♯-G♯ of this minor-seventh-chord outline into an inverted form of cell a (G♯-A-C♯), which, in turn, linearly intersects with the augmented triad A-C♯-E♯. The latter (A-C♯-E♯) is a local
adumbration of theme 2 at the proper pitch-level. This augmented triad is
then linearly overlapped by a prime form of cell a (C♯-E♯-F♯). These linearly
joined local statements of cell a and the augmented triad of theme 2 in this
transitional section support the hypothesis regarding the transformational
association between themes 1 and 2. The anticipation of theme 2 is also apparent in the contour of the two violins in this sketch. The movement closes
(No. 23, m. 2f.) with linear and vertical statements of this revised combination of the major thirds that form the second theme.

At the opening of the development (No. 10), the main motive appears as
a more isolated foreground event, now exclusively based on cell a (B♭-D-E♭)

115 *Second String Quartet,* Movement I (transition), comparison of final
version with original sketch

(a) one measure before No. 3 of the final version (va and vc)

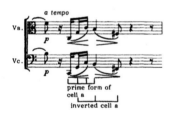

(b) five measures in place of the measure before No. 3, sketch (see Illustration 5)

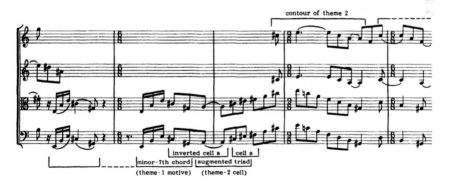

and cell Z (E♭-D-A-A♭). The remaining note, C, which expands the minor third of the original statement to a major third (A♭-C), produces an overlapping subordinate cell, A-A♭-C, that is a contraction of cell a. The next statement ends with F♯-F-A. The two together (F♯-F-A-A♭-C) form yet another interlocking relationship of major thirds. This three-note cell is extensively worked out in the second section (No. 12f.) of the development.[9] It also appears as a significant detail (No. 15, vnII, and No. 15, m. 4, vnI) at the climax of the development, where it cadentially punctuates the chords that are exclusively based on cell Z. The two cadential figures together (A-G♯-C-B-E♭) analogously form interlocking major thirds. As was shown in Example 109, vnI unfolds a chain of such interlocking major thirds. The specific combination of these major thirds, which results in secondary intervals of minor thirds and minor seconds, can also be seen as a revision of the major-third interval couple that forms each of the supporting Z-variant chords. Thus, such revisions of the interval couples that form symmetrical cells are essential in the organic development and transformation of the main themes and in the establishment of a new means of progression.

The basic cells play a more obvious role in defining the sections of Movement II.[10] The introduction distinctly isolates cells Z and a, which were ambiguously joined in the opening theme of Movement I (see Ex. 111). The cell Z-11/5 (B-E-F-B♭) is expressly partitioned into its two tritones (Ex. 116), the second (E-B♭) of which is filled in by cell a (F-A-B♭) and its inversion (E-F-A) to form a four-note symmetrical contraction of Z (E-F-A-B♭)—we shall call the latter symmetry cell a'. In the succession of tritones (mm. 5-7) that closes the introduction, three transpositions of Z are interlocked as primary cell statements, while two transpositions of cell a' (E-F-A-B♭ and

116 *Second String Quartet*, Movement II, mm. 1-7

9 See Halsey Stevens, *The Life and Music of Béla Bartók* (New York: Oxford University Press, 1954, rev. 1964), p. 179.
10 The movement appears to be a scherzo in rondo form: Introduction, A, B, A', B', A', Trio, B', A', Trio quote, A (= coda).

117 *Second String Quartet,* Movement II, mm. 5–7

118 *Second String Quartet,* Movement II, No. 10, mm. 1–4

A-B♭-D-E♭) are interlocked as secondary cell statements (Ex. 117). The main theme then begins with minor and major thirds unfolding above a constantly reiterated D; the three-note figure in turn forms a contraction of cell a.[11] At the local cadential points (No. 1, mm. 11–13, and No. 2, mm. 12–13, vnl), which punctuate the successive thematic statements, this contraction is transformed into the symmetrical formation F♯-E♯-D-C♯.

All three cells, two of which are contractions of basic cell Z, independently or jointly generate most of the remaining material. In the main motive of the first episode (No. 10), the relative priorities of Z and a' are reversed. The sixteenth-note figure based on a' now appears first, and the tail end of the motive then interlocks Z with a' (Ex. 118). The high point of the recapitulated episode reestablishes the priority of cell Z by systematically unfolding all six transpositions for the only time in the movement (Ex. 119).[12] Cell a' reappears as a secondary cell, also in all its transpositions in this passage.

The more relaxed thematic idea of the Trio (No. 27) is anticipated in the Tranquillo (No. 25, mm. 5–6), where segmental properties of all the cells are linearly joined.[13] The initial three notes imply Z-1/7, with an overlapping four-note segment outlining a complete form of the Z variant from Movement I (Ex. 120a). At the opening of the Trio (Ex. 120b), vnI revises the com-

11 This contraction prominently appeared in Movement I, at the opening of the development (mm. 70–72), as the tail end of the motive, then in the middle section (mm. 83ff.), and at the end of the development (see Ex. 109), where it was transformed in vnI into a symmetrical construction.

12 As shown by the parentheses in vnII of Example 119, the absence of note F in the final version, which leaves Z-11/5 incomplete, may be an error, since this note appears at this point in the earlier sketch.

13 Arnold Whittall states, in "Bartók's Second String Quartet," *Music Review* 32/3 (August, 1971): 268–69, that "the movement is a virtuoso display of dynamic, developmental conflict between [the cells] in which the most obvious moments of compromise are, appropriately, the most obvious moments of relaxation."

119 *Second String Quartet*, Movement II, No. 22f.

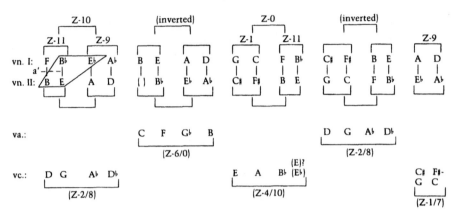

120 *Second String Quartet*, Movement II

(a) No. 25, mm. 5–6:   (b) No. 27, mm. 1–3:

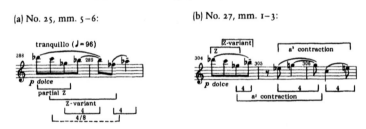

bination of major thirds (interval 4) so that E♭-G and C-E are linearly joined to form a cell-a' contraction, C-E♭-E-G. The final return of theme A (coda, No. 41, mm. 3f.) unfolds all the cellular properties observed thus far; the arch-form of this final section is largely established by interval expansions to and away from cell Z.

The slow finale opens with a motive that systematically joins basic cell Z with cell a and its contraction. The linearly stated tritones of Z-9/3 (A-D♯ and G♯-D) form the structural basis of the motive (Ex. 121). The local embellishments of the latter tritone in vnII produce foreground occurrences of the secondary cells: the cell-a contraction, F-G♯-A (m. 1), expands to cell a, B♭-D-D♯ (m. 2).[14] The latter represents a return to the pitch level of the opening chord (B♭-D-E♭) of Movement I. At the beginning of the second section (No.

---

14 For further manifestations of the cellular components in the finale, see ibid., pp. 209–10.

121 *Second String Quartet,* Movement III, mm. 1–2

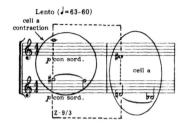

122 *Second String Quartet,* Movement III, No. 2, mm. 1–3, and No. 10, mm. 5–7, vnI

2, m. 2, vnI), cell Z returns to its original pitch-level (Ex. 122), which also appears as the final statement of the work (No. 10, mm. 5–7).

Although each of the *Eight Improvisations for Piano,* Op. 20 is a complete and individual musical entity, the pieces share a set of common cell properties. The closing passage (mm. 69ff.) of the *Eighth Improvisation* is a focal point for cellular development throughout the work. The folk tune, which linearly unfolds in octaves, is exclusively accompanied by five of the six transpositions of cell Z (see Ex. 249). Both linear and vertical combinations of these cell-Z chords imply the presence of secondary symmetrical cells, of which explicit foreground statements interact with cell Z in many of the preceding pieces.

The final chord of the last piece vertically joins Z-4/10 (E-A-B♭-E♭) with its interval-2 transposition, Z-6/0 (F♯-B-C-F) (Ex. 123). The corresponding upper 5/7 dyads (B♭-E♭ and C-F) of these two Z cells imply the presence of a pair of whole-tone dyads (E♭-F and B♭-C), both interval couples of which occur prominently in the *First Improvisation.* The accompaniment to strain 1 of the folk tune in the latter is exclusively based on whole-tone dyads E♭-F and B♭-C; the ornaments of the tune in strain 2 (m. 5) are initiated by the 5/7 dyads F-C and E♭-B♭. Furthermore, each statement of the C-Dorian tune

123 *Eighth Improvisation,* last chord

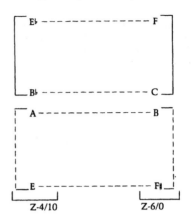

124 *First Improvisation,* mm. 9–10, beat 2

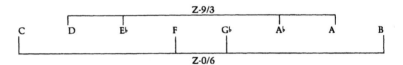

itself begins and ends with F-E♭ and B♭-C, the final cadence establishing the latter dyad.

The closing passage of the final piece also joins pairs of Z cells a minor third apart (the first two chords in each of mm. 70, 72, and 74). At the opening of strain 3 (m. 9) of the first piece, the lower 5/7 dyads (D-A and A♭-E♭) of the rolled chords—these are a continuation of the preceding ornaments—give us the first foreground occurrence of Z (A-D-E♭-A♭).[15] This cell, Z-9/3, is a symmetrical segment of octatonic collection C-D-E♭-F-G♭-A♭-A-B (mm. 9–10, beat 2, including the G♭ grace-note), the entire pitch content of which implies an interlocking of Z-9/3 (A-D-E♭-A♭) with its interval-3 transposition, Z-0/6 (C-F-G♭-B) (Ex. 124).

In the final passage of the last piece, one other type of combination occurs between a pair of Z cells. The succession of Z chords in the allegro (mm. 76-80) is based on alternations between Z-10/4 (A♯-D♯-E-A, or E-A-A♯-D♯) and its interval-1 transposition, Z-11/5 (B-E-F-B♭). The same relationship exists between Z-11/5 and Z-6/0 (m. 70, last two chords) and Z-2/8 and Z-1/7 (m. 72, last two chords), with the two Z chords in each pair

15 See Example 251 and the corresponding discussion in Chapter VII.

explicitly separated by interval 5/7. The combination of Z-2/8 and Z-7/1 (m. 72), for instance, implies the presence of a significant secondary symmetrical cell, D♭-D-G♭-G (Ex. 125). The latter—we shall call this cell a—opens the *Third Improvisation* as the harmonic basis of the first phrase (mm. 1–9) of the folk tune.[16] Each of these two 5/7 dyads (F♯-C♯ and G-D) of the first phrase (Ex. 126a) is cyclically extended in the second phrase (Ex. 126b) by a shift in the accompaniment to segments A♭-E♭-B♭ and A-E. At mm. 14–15,

125 *Eighth Improvisation*, m. 72, chords

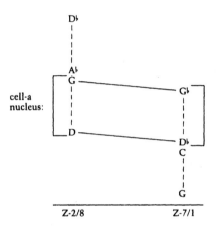

126 *Third Improvisation*, strain 1, mm. 1–15

(a) Phrase 1, mm. 1–9   (b) Phrase 2, mm. 14–15

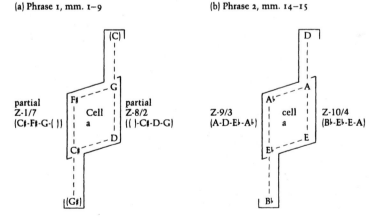

16 From the Kórógy collection.

127 *Third Improvisation*, mm. 42–45

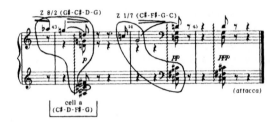

the alternation of these two segments under the cadential D of the tune extends the latter segment to D-A-E. This configuration (A♭-E♭-B♭ and D-A-E), which interlocks Z-10/4 (B♭-E♭-E-A) with its interval-1 transposition, Z-9/3 (A-D-E♭-A♭), contains a transposition of cell a (E♭-E-A♭-A) as its nucleus. The latter relationship supports the hypothesis that the initial statement of cell a (C♯-D-F♯-G) is a nucleus of an implied Z-2/8 and Z-1/7 combination (see Ex. 126a). This function is explicitly confirmed at the end of the coda (Ex. 127), where the original cell-a chord (C♯-D-F♯-G) is joined with two new notes, A♭ and C; while A♭ (in enharmonic spelling, G♯) completes Z-8/2 (G♯-C♯-D-G), C completes Z-1/7 (C♯-F♯-G-C) (see Ex. 126a). At the cadence of the first episode (m. 17), the Cell-Z combination of the second phrase (see Ex. 126b) is revised so that Z-10/4 (B♭E♭-E-A) is now joined with a partial linear statement of its interval-3 transposition, Z-1/7 (D♭-G♭-( )-C).

In the *Fourth Improvisation*, the opening phrase of strain 1[17] further establishes the relation between the Z-8/2 and Z-7/1 combination and its cell-a nucleus (C♯-D-F♯-G). The pitch content of the initial ostinato pattern contains all the pitch classes between F♯ and D (Ex. 128a). The rhythmic and registral partitioning of this chromatic continuum between the tune and accompaniment contributes to the definition of the basic cell properties. In m. 1, one semitone, C♯-D, of cell a vertically appears as the registral boundary, while the other, G-F♯, is prominently placed as the initial interval of the tune. The linear adjacency of three of these notes, G-F♯-D, in the tune also establishes the priority of cell a. At the same time, Z-2/8 functions as the basic structural property of the opening measure, since each of its 5/7 dyads, D-G and A♭-C♯, serves as a boundary for one of the two linear figures. At m. 2, however, the omission of one note (D) from the tune[18] produces a shift from the Z-2/8 structure to Z-1/7; that is, dyad F♯-G now serves as the lower boundary and C-C♯ as the upper boundary of the symmetrical chromatic figure. These cell properties of mm. 1 and 2 are summarized in Exam-

17 From Felsőiregh, Tolna (1907).
18 The original folk tune, from Felsőiregh, contains the D here.

128 *Fourth Improvisation, mm. 1–2*

(a)

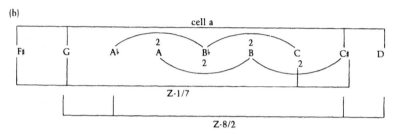

(b)

ple 128b. At the opening of the second phrase of this strain (m. 7), the initial motive is transposed by interval 5/7, so each linear figure is now bounded by the 5/7 dyads (G-C and Db-F#) of Z-1/7. The priority of Z-1/7 is established in the coda (m. 32, beat 2, through m. 37), where it emerges as the primary foreground event in the left hand.

These cell relationships in the third and fourth pieces are foreshadowed in the *Second Improvisation.* While neither Z nor a appears as a prominent foreground element, they are the basic midground- and background-level structures of the piece. Strain 1 of the folk tune[19] opens against two nonsymmetrical, chromatically expanding lower lines. The opening phrase-segment of the tune (mm. 2–5) is in C-Mixolydian, which contains one tritone, E-Bb. The accompaniment, which is based on a single semitone, B-C, supplies one new note, B. This Ionian seventh-degree B, which produces a modal conflict with the Mixolydian seventh-degree Bb, establishes a second tritone (B-F) within this bimodal complex. By reordering the bimodal pitch-content (C-Ionian and C-Mixolydian) into two adjacent seven-note segments of the cycle of fifths (Ex. 129a), we can conveniently demonstrate the structural role of the two tritones E-Bb and B-F. Together, these tritones imply the presence of Z-11/5 (B-E-F-Bb). The second half of the tune modulates (with the lowering of the third degree to Eb at m. 7) to C-Dorian, which contains one tritone, Eb-A. The two linearly implied tritones Bb-E and Eb-A form Z-10/4. These two Z cells (Z-11/5 and its interval-1 transposition, Z-10/4), which are basic to the polymodal structure of strain 1, explicitly appear as alternat-

19 From Hottó in the district of Zala.

129 *Second Improvisation*

(a) Strain 1, mm. 1–9

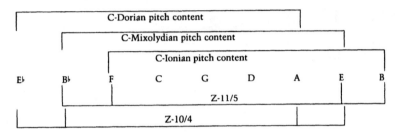

(b) Strain 2, mm. 14ff.

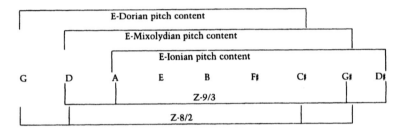

(c) Strain 3, mm. 30ff.

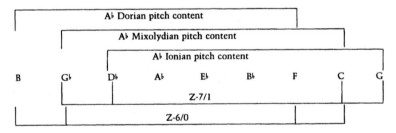

ing chords at the end of the final piece (mm. 76–80; see Ex. 249). The tritones implied in each of the next two polymodal strains (mm. 14–22 and 30–37) analogously establish background-level pairs of Z cells separated by interval 1. Strain 2 is based on Z-9/3 and Z-8/2 (Ex. 129b), and strain 3 is based on Z-7/1 and Z-6/0 (Ex. 129c). Thus, all six transpositions are systematically unfolded in descending order on the background level.

The first episode closes (mm. 12–13) with seven notes of an octatonic scale, B♯-D-D♯-E♯-F♯-( )-A-B, in which two implied Z cells (Z-0/6, B♯-E♯-

F♯-B, and partial Z-9/3, A-D-D♯-( )) are separated by interval 3. The missing note, G♯, from Z-9/3 is replaced by an A♯, thus implying the presence of cell a (A-A♯-D-D♯). The latter is a transposition of A♭-A-D♭-D (mm. 5–6), which appears as a local detail in the accompaniment of the opening strain. These unobtrusive occurrences of cell a, the first manifestations of this cell in the *Improvisations*, foreshadow the opening of the third piece, where cell a (C♯-D-F♯-G) emerges as an isolated foreground event.

Of all of Bartók's works, the *Fourth String Quartet* contains the most comprehensive and systematic interaction of symmetrical cells. The four-note symmetries C-C♯-D-E♭ and B♭-C-D-E are two of three basic cells (X, Y, and Z) in the quartet. Transpositions of cell X permeate the first-theme group (mm. 1–13) of Movement I. In this section, X progresses to Y at two points, first at mm. 5–6 (Ex. 130a) and again at mm. 10–11 (Ex. 130b). The third symmetrical cell (Z), G♯-C♯-D-G, first occurs at m. 22, va and vnI, where it is a primary pitch collection of the transition (Ex. 130c). (At this point cell Y also appears in vnII and vc.) This initial occurrence of cell Z is a focal point of a canon that began earlier in the transition (mm. 15ff., vns); the tritone boundaries (C♯-G and G♯-D) of these canonic lines are joined at m. 22 in va and vnI to give us cell Z.

The priority of these cell statements in the first-theme group and transition is significantly established by the principle of metric departure and return to the regular 4/4 barring. The opening two phrases (mm. 1–4) of the movement each begin at the barline. The third phrase gives us a stretto now beginning one eighth-note before the barline, culminating in a vertical alignment of the instruments in the first X-to-Y progression one eighth-note after the barline of m. 6. The fourth phrase is based on another stretto, again beginning before the barline. This stretto also culminates (mm. 10–11) in a vertical alignment of the instruments on the second X-to-Y progression (Ex. 131). The latter alignment is yet further removed from the barline. A final stretto, based on linear statements of cell X, begins in the middle of m. 11 and culminates at the final simultaneity in the middle of m. 13.

In the transition (mm. 14ff.), the lines together produce still more complex patterns, each implying an unequal-beat meter against the written barline. This combination of instruments produces a polymetric texture. The ostinato figure (C-D-E) of va (mm. 14–18) implies a regular 5/8 meter, while vc plays another ostinato figure in G♯ minor in varying meters (Ex. 132). The first vc statement implies 7/8, the second and third statements each 8/8, the abbreviated fourth statement 5/8, and the modified fifth statement 7/8. At the same time the violins play complex unequal-beat meters in canon (mm. 15–18). The subject and answer of this canon, which are bounded by the tritones of cell Z, have two metric parts, together implying 7+4/8. From mm. 18–21 all the patterns become yet more irregular. Then,

130 *Fourth String Quartet*, three symmetrical cells

(a) Initial X/Y progression (mm. 5–6) in the first-theme group

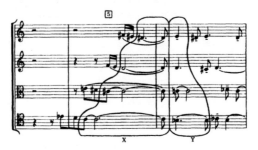

(b) X/Y progression (mm. 10–11) near the end of the first-theme group

(c) Initial occurrence of cell Z (m. 22, va and vnI) in the transitional group, stated simultaneously with Y (vnII and vc)

131 *Fourth String Quartet*, Movement I, mm. 1–13, shifts away from 4/4 barline in successive stretto and X-Y progressions

132 *Fourth String Quartet*, Movement I, transition, mm. 14ff., polymetric departure and return to regular barline at m. 22 (cells Y and Z)

at m. 22, we arrive at that significant point where vnI and va together give us the first foreground statement of cell Z, vnII and vc giving us cell Y (B♭-C-D-E) as a focal point of the earlier va ostinato (C-D-E) that was taken over by the cello.

At this prominent point (m. 22), some metric uniformity appears for the first time in this transition. The vnII gives us B♭ of cell Y at the barline; the C-D-E ostinato figure of cell Y in the cello also coincides with the downbeat, and the cell-Z statements in vnI and va respectively subdivide the measure into 2+3+3/8 and 3+3+2/8. At mm. 23–24, va establishes regular quarter-notes, while vnI plays a regular syncopation against them. Cell Z is even more prominently established as a focal point in an early sketch of these measures (Ex. 133, vnI and va). Most of the cadential points in the first-theme group (mm. 7, 10, and 13) and the prominent one in the transition (m. 26) conclude stretto passages by aligning the instruments vertically, but all these cadential chords occur on weak beats. Cell X again (Ex. 134) appears in stretto from the end of m. 26, as it did earlier (mm. 11–13). Each linear state-ment is now based on an arithmetic expansion of 4, 5, and 6 eighth-note units. The initial notes of the stretto together outline basic cell Y (B♭-C-D-E) at m. 26. Then, at the opening of theme II (m. 30), all the instruments are for the first time aligned on the downbeat. The vertical alignment gives us Y-8, A♭-B♭-C-D (the E♭ downbeat is an accented appoggiatura).

Intervals 3 and 6 are basic in the construction and interaction of cells X, Y, and Z. The boundary intervals of X (C-C♯-D-E♭) and Y (B♭-C-D-E) are, respectively, 3 and 6. In Movement I, at the conclusion of the first-theme group (m. 13), the B♭-E range of Y-10 (B♭-C-D-E) is chromatically filled through the conjunction of two transpositions of X (X-10 and X-1). The pro-cedure that leads to the filled-in tritone B♭-E (m. 13) occurs as follows. Mea-sures 11–12 are a stretto of the principal motive of the quartet, a linear state-ment of cell X. The stretto commences with X-0 (C-C♯-D-E♭) in vnI and va. The vnII and vc begin with an inversion of the motive that implies X-11 (B-C-D♭-( )) but shift the pitch level in the middle to A♯-B-C as a substitute for the "expected" literal completion (C-C♯-D), so we get X-10 (A♯-B-C-D♭) in-stead. The new note, A♯ (B♭), expands the total range of combined X-10 and X0 to B♭-E♭. In m. 12, vnII and vc repeat X-10 in the principal form of the

133   *Fourth String Quartet,* Movement I, mm. 22ff., early draft of vnI and
          va, which further elaborate cell Z (see Illustration 6)

134   *Fourth String Quartet,* Movement I ending of transition, m. 26, through opening of theme II, m. 30: arithmetic expansions leading to downbeat alignment of all voices

135   *Fourth String Quartet,* Movement I, mm. 11–13 (stretto of X statements)

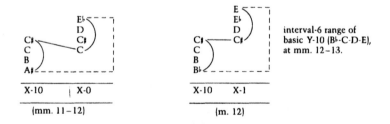

interval-6 range of basic Y-10 (B♭-C-D-E), at mm. 12–13.

X-10 ¦ X-0

(mm. 11–12)

X-10   X-1

(m. 12)

motive, with appropriate enharmonic spelling (B♭-B-C-D♭). The vnI and va transpose X-o (m. 11) to X-1, C♯-D-E♭-E (m. 12), the latter of which literally inverts the principal form based on X-10. The conjunct interval-3 ranges (B♭-C♯ and C♯-E) of X-10 and X-1 produce the interval-6 range (B♭-E) of Y-10 (Ex. 135).

This procedure, in which the interval-6 range of Y is produced through the conjunction of two transpositions of X, is anticipated throughout the first-theme group. The vnI and vnII transpose from X-3, D#-E-F-F# (m. 1 through the first eighth-note of m. 2) to X-0, C-C#-D-E♭ (m. 2, second and third eighth-notes) (Ex. 136). While C in vc and F# in vnI define the range of this phrase, the conjunction of the X-3 and X-0 ranges also produces the interval-6 range, C-F#. In the second phrase (mm. 3–4), X-0 is joined with its lower interval-3 transposition, X-9 (A-B♭-B-C). The latter opens the phrase in vnI and vnII (m. 3) and moves to vnII and va (m. 4) where it is joined with X-0 in vnI (mm. 3–4). The interval-3 ranges (C-E♭ and A-C) of X-0 and X-9 form the interval-6 range A-E♭. (The total range of the phrase, however, becomes C-E♭ in vnI and va, m. 4, third eighth-note, as va moves down by interval 9 from A to C. This A-C range of X-9 is a retrograde of the opening C-A in vc, m. 1, and C-A in vnI and vnII, m. 3.) In the third phrase (m. 5), interval 1 of X expands to interval 2 of Y. These expansions from interval 1 to interval 2 (mm. 5–6) and the shift in pitch level to B♭ in vc (m. 6) give us the interval-2 filling of B♭-E, which is Y-10, B♭-C-D-E (m. 6, second chord). The interval-6 range (C-F#) of combined X-3 and X-0 (m. 5) is also transposed by cyclic-interval 2 of Y to B♭-E of Y-10 (m. 6). The interval-6 range (B♭-E) of Y-10 at m. 7 is simultaneously subdivided into three interval-2s and two interval-3s: the four voices partition Y-10 into its cyclic-interval 2 and vc

136 *Fourth String Quartet,* Movement I, mm. 1–6

plays the principal motive spanning interval 3 (B♭-D♭). The interval-3 sub-division of tritone C-F♯ (m. 5) opened the phrase as X-3 was joined with X-0. Thus, while the semitones (intervals 1) of X are expanded to the whole tones (intervals 2) of Y, the boundary interval (3) of X is doubled to form the boundary interval (6) of Y. The semitones in the total pitch complex of the fourth phrase (mm. 8–10) expand to the whole tones of Y-10 in m. 10 as the voices become aligned. This expansion culminates in the final X-0 to Y-10 progressions at the end of m. 10 and the beginning of m. 11.

The interval-6 range of cell Y is basic in the construction of cell Z in the transition (mm. 14ff.). The primary interval of cell Z is 6. Basic cell Z-8/2 unambiguously appears for the first time in va and vnI at m. 22 of the transition,[20] where it coincides with Y-10 in vc and vnII. From the ending of the first-theme group (end of m. 12) to this point (m. 22), the interval-6 ranges (G♯-D and C♯-G) become the primary interval-couple of cell Z, analogous to the construction of interval 6 of Y from two conjunct transpositions of X. At the end of m. 12 and the beginning of m. 13, the B♭-E boundary is transposed by interval 2 to G♯-D of Y-8 and back to B♭-E in the final chromatic chord; Y-8 (A♭-B♭-C-D) initiates the imitative segments, which are based on the second half of the principal motive. Measures 15–18 of the transition are a canon between vnI and vnII, the statement in vnI encompassing tritone G♯-D. The specific tritone C♯-G is added in vnII in this canon to produce Z-8/2 (G♯-C♯-D-G), returning to the original axis of symmetry, C♯-D, of basic X-0 (at mm. 10–11). The first explicit connection between two transpositions of Y and a transposition of Z occurs (Ex. 137) at mm. 40–43 (vnI) of the second-theme group: the G♭-C range of Y-6 is joined with the D♭-G range of Y-1, these interval-6 ranges together outlining Z-1/7 (D♭-G♭-G-C).

The procedure that leads to the latter Y/Z construction in the second-theme group is analogous to the construction that led to Z-8/2 in the first-theme group and transition. The stretto (m. 12) between the principal motive based on X-10 and its literal inversion based on X-1, encompassing tritone B♭-E, is doubled in mm. 26–27. In the latter measures, the principal motive based on X-1 in vnII and its literal inversion based on X-10 in va are

137 *Fourth String Quartet*, Movement I, mm. 40–42

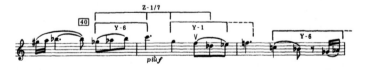

20 An incomplete form of Z-8/2 ((·)-D♭-D-G) appears at m. 2, fourth eighth-note, where it is introduced as the first nonsymmetrical formation of the movement. It is symmetrically completed at m. 22.

138 *Fourth String Quartet*, Movement I, mm. 38–42

doubled by their respective interval-2 transpositions, X-3 in vnI and X-8 in vc. Thus, the tritone range (Bb-E) in m. 12 becomes filled by whole tones in m. 26 as Y-10 initiates the latter stretto: vc and va play Bb-C in imitation of D-E in vnI and vnII (m. 26). Directly preceding the theme at m. 40, another stretto based on linear statements of X (m. 38, sixth eighth-note in vnI and vnII through the first half of m. 40) establishes A♯-E as its range. A linear statement of X-0 (B♯-C♯-D-D♯) in the middle of m. 38 through m. 39 (Ex. 138) initiates the stretto in vnI and vnII, imitated by X-10 (A♯-B-C-C♯) in vc. (This relationship of X-0 to X-10, which similarly initiated the stretto in m. 11, was followed by the transposition of X-0 to X-1 in m. 12.) From the end of m. 38 through the beginning of m. 40, vc presents these linear statements of X-10 and X-1, their conjunct interval-3 ranges outlining tritone Bb-E. The vnI imitates these conjunct vc statements of X with X-4, E-F-F♯-G (m. 39, fourth eighth-note) and X-7, G-G♯-A-Bb, the interval-3 ranges of the latter two transpositions of X also outlining tritone E-Bb. The tritone E-Bb is transposed by interval 2 to Y-6 (boundary Gb-C) in vnI at the end of m. 40 through m. 41. Cell Y-6, in turn, is joined with Y-1 (Db-Eb-F-G) in the same voice to outline Z-1/7 (Db-Gb-G-C). (This procedure is analogous to the construction in which Y-10 was transposed by its cyclic-interval 2 to Y-8 in mm. 12–13 of the first-theme group, the tritone range of the latter transposition of Y then being joined with C♯-G to produce basic cell Z-8/2 in the transition.) Tritone E-B♭ is explicitly confirmed as the range of Y-4 (E-F♯-G♯-B♭), which occurs in m. 40ff. as linear cadential points in the four voices.

The X-Y-Z progressions (Ex. 139) that begin the development section (mm. 49–52) are analogous to the progressions from X-0 to Y-10 in mm. 10–11 of the first-theme group and Y-10 to Z-8/2 in mm. 14–23 of the transition. The significance of the relationship between these two sets of X-Y-Z progressions can be seen in the correspondence with tonal relations of the

139 *Fourth String Quartet,* Movement I, X-Y-Z progressions in exposition, mm. 10–23, and development, mm. 49ff.

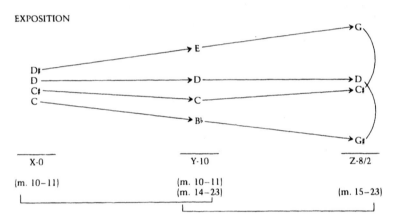

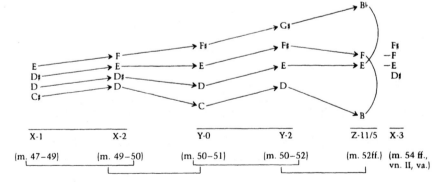

traditional sonata plan. In traditional schemes, the common principle of modulation entails tonal motion by the components of the tonic triad. That is, if we move from the tonic area of the first-theme group to the dominant area of the second-theme group and development section, the motion has its reference in the root and fifth degrees of the tonic triad. The same principle is demonstrated in minor keys where the tonality shifts by way of the root to the third degree of the tonic minor-triad. Analogously, in the present work, tonal motion from the exposition to the opening of the development occurs through the cyclic intervals of the basic chords (i.e., cells). Cell X-1 (C#-D-E♭-E), which is prominent in the cello part of the second theme (mm. 41–43) and at the end of the exposition (mm. 47–49), is a semitone above the basic X-0 (C-C#-D-E♭) of the opening. Cell X-1 is then transposed by its cyclic-interval 1 to X-2 (D-E♭-E-F) in mm. 49–50. The latter expands to Y-0 (C-D-E-F#) on the second quarter-note of m. 50; this Y transposition is a whole-tone above the basic Y-10 (B♭-C-D-E) of the exposition. Cell Y-0 is then transposed by its own cyclic-interval 2 to Y-2 (D-E-F#-G#) at the end of m. 50 through m. 51. Measure 52 ends the progression, as Y-2 expands to Z-11/5 (B-E-F-A#). Cell Z-11/5 (m. 52) is an interval-3 transposition of the original Z-8/2 (m. 22), the intervallic relationship that permits two Z cells to be permuted around the same two axes of symmetry (in this case, sums 3 and 9).[21] In m. 53, Z-11/5 is joined with X-3, which is a cyclic-interval 1 transposition of the preceding X-2 statement (mm. 49–50). At mm. 54–60 (va and vnII), X-3 becomes the nucleus of the passage. The recapitulation (m. 92) is ushered in by the reverse procedure, in which X-3 (m. 82) moves down by its cyclic-interval 1 through X-2 and X-1 to X-0.

The X-Y-Z progressions are basic in the final section of the coda (mm. 152–60). In mm. 152–56, the sforzando chords are Y-8 collections (A♭-B♭-C-D). Each of these cell-Y statements is preceded by a grace-note chord based on X-9 (A-B♭-B-C), giving us X-9 to Y-8 progressions. This progression of X to Y is significant in that it is the last of three in the movement and forms a long-range inversional relationship with the first, X-0 to Y-10 (see Ex. 130a, b).[22] The priority of X-9 to Y-8 as a focal point in the coda is established by the principle of metric departure and return to the barline. An arithmetically expanding stretto occurs at mm. 149–51, which culminates in an alignment of all the instruments at the downbeat of m. 152 (i.e., the initial statement of X-9 to Y-8) (Ex. 140); this arithmetic progression is analogous to that which introduced the second-theme group beginning with the same transposition of Y (see Ex. 134). At this point the X-9 to Y-8 progression also initiates a decreasing arithmetic progression of X-Y statements

---

21 These symmetrical relations based on axes (i.e., sums of complementation) will be discussed in Chapter VI.
22 The function of this large-scale inversional relationship will be discussed in Chapter VI.

140 *Fourth String Quartet*, Movement I, mm. 150ff.

141   *Fourth String Quartet*, Movement I, mm. 157–60; the three odd-
numbered Z cells marked by accents and sforzandi

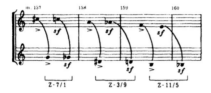

that form a pattern of 1 × 3, 2 × 2, and 3 × 1 (mm. 152–56), thus moving
away from the barline again. Precisely at the end of the latter pattern, vnI
and va initiate a sequence of intervallically expanded linear statements of
the X motive, canonically imitated by vnII and vc at the tritone. The tritone
range (A♭-D) of Y-8 (mm. 152–56) is transposed by the cyclic-interval 2 of Y
to F♯-C, which initiates the canon on the last eighth-note of m. 156 and second eighth-note of m. 157 (vnII and vc). Tritone F♯-C also occurs at the end
of m. 157 (now marked "sforzando"), juxtaposed in this measure with the
accented tritone C♯-G. These two tritones (C♯-F♯ and C♯-G) together form
Z-7/1 (G-C-C♯-F♯), which completes the progression (mm. 156–57) from
X-9 through Y-8 to Z-7/1. This transposition of Z initiates a sequence of
, Z cells each of whose tritones is specifically marked by the pairs of accents
and sforzandi throughout the canon. Each Z cell shifts to the next one by
interval 4 (Ex. 141): cell Z-7/1 (G-C-C♯-G♭) in m. 157 is transposed by interval 4 to Z-3/9 (D♯-A♭-A-D) at m. 158 through the first eighth-note of m.
159, which, in turn, is transposed by interval 4 to Z-11/5 (B-E-F-B♭) at mm.
159–60 to conclude the sequence.

The last transposition of cell Z (Z-11/5) of this sequence, which is one of
the two primary Z cells (Z-8/2 and Z-11/5) of this movement (see Ex. 139), is
also the basis of mm. 1–4 of Movement II. The tritones of Z-11/5 outline the
main chromatic theme (Ex. 142a): E and A♯ encompass the chromatic ascent, and B and E♯ encompass the chromatic descent. At the end of Movement II (mm. 243–46, va), Z-8/2 and Z-11/5 are joined to produce the octatonic scale D-E-F-G-G♯-A♯-B-C♯ (Ex. 142b). This interval-3 relationship
between the two Z cells also occurs in Movement V. Z-1/7 (D♭-F♯-G-C) is
the basis of mm. 1–43, appearing prominently as the opening chord and in
the vc ostinato (mm. 12ff.). The main theme of this movement (mm. 15–18,
vns) and its accompaniment include Z-1/7 as part of an incomplete octatonic collection (C-C♯-D♯-( )-F♯-G). (This theme is derived from the canon
between vnI and vnII in the transition of Movement I, mm. 15ff., which led
to Z-8/2 in m. 22 of that movement.) Cell Z-1/7 (mm. 1–43) is transposed by
interval 3 in vnI and vnII (m. 45) to Z-4/10 (E-A-B♭-E♭); the latter is the basis

142 *Fourth String Quartet,* Movement II

(a) mm. 1–4, theme

(b) mm. 243–46, va

of the thematic material in the violins (mm. 63–74). In this section, which is initiated by Z-4/10 (m. 45), the main partial-octatonic theme is completed in the linear thematic material of mm. 47–74 (first the violins, then with va added). Thus, Z-1/7 and its interval-3 transposition, Z-4/10, are combined to form the complete octatonic collection (C♯-D♯-E-F♯-G-A-A♯-B♯) in Movement V, analogous to the combination of Z-8/2 and Z-11/5 in the octatonic scale at the end of Movement II (see Ex. 142b).

At the end of Movement I, the canonic lines based on the intervallically expanded X motives and the sequential pattern of Z cells outlined in Example 141 are interrupted by a shift in pitch level (m. 160, second and sixth sixteenth-notes) to tritone D-A♭ in place of an "expected" C♯-G. Thus, the tritone (A♭-D) that occurred as the range of Y-8 in mm. 152–56 also ends the canon. In the sixteenth-note figures in m. 160, this concluding tritone is joined with tritone D♯-A to produce Z-9/3 (A-D-D♯-A♭). The latter transposition of Z establishes the harmonic area of the opening of Movement III (mm. 1–6), where the tritones A-D♯ and D-G♯ are the ranges of Y-9 (A-B-C♯-D♯) and Y-2 (D-E-F♯-G♯) (Ex. 143). (Notes D♯ and D are played by vc at m. 6.) This construction that opens the central movement contains a symmetrical balance of the three basic cells—X-1 (C♯-D-D♯-E) forms the nucleus, while Y-9 and Y-2 are bounded by the tritones that form Z-9/3 (A-D-D♯-G♯). Cell Z-9/3 is anticipated near the end of the development section in Movement II (mm. 161–64), where tritone A-D♯ is joined with tritone G♯-D in each of the four voices of the stretto (Ex. 144). However, each tritone of Z-9/3 in this passage of Movement II is subdivided into two interval-3s (D♯-F♯-A and G♯-B-D) instead of the subdivisions that later appear in the opening of Movement III into the three interval-2s of Y-9 (A-B-C♯-D♯) and Y-2 (D-E-F♯-G♯). (These interval-3 subdivisions are reminiscent of the construction of the cell-Y tritone boundary from two conjunct cell-X boundaries; see Ex. 135.)

143 *Fourth String Quartet, Movement III, mm.* 1–6

144 *Fourth String Quartet, Movement II, mm.* 161–64

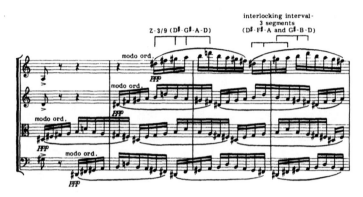

The importance of one of these tritones (A-D♯) of Z was established in the opening of the development section of Movement II by the use of Y-3 as a held chord (mm. 79–94) in the violins. Cell Y-3 occurs here as part of a large interval-expansion procedure (mm. 76–136). In mm. 78–94, sixteenth-note figures based on interval 2 appear in sequence in the violins. (These may be associated with similar interval-2 figures in Movement I—vc in m. 40 and all the instruments in mm. 45–46 and 127–35—that outlined the second-ary interval couple of X.) Each of the interval-2 figures in mm. 79–94 of Movement II is filled in by a pedal tone, and the sequence of these pedal tones (E♭-F-G-A) distinguishes Y-3 from the entire chromatic complex (Ex. 145). While the interval-6 range (E♭-A) of Y-3 in the violins is partitioned into the three cyclic-interval 2s (mm. 79–94), va and vc in mm. 76–83 and 93–99 simultaneously partition X-10 (B♭-B-C-D♭) into its tertiary interval-couple (intervals 1 and 3) in the ostinato patterns. (Y is also rhythmically distinguished from the two-against-three X ostinato of vc and va. The held notes of cell Y in the violins form a decreasing arithmetic progression in which the successive distances from one long-note articulation to the next outline a pattern of 4, 4, 3, and 2 eighth-note durations.) At mm. 76ff., cell X-10 is joined with X-0 (m. 95, in the glissandi of vnI and vnII). This X-10/X-0 combination, which had preceded the construction of the tritone range (B♭-E) of Y-10 in m. 11 of Movement I (see Ex. 135), again precedes the con-

145   *Fourth String Quartet*, Movement II, mm. 76–90

struction of this tritone in mm. 95–97 of Movement II (Ex. 146): the X-10/ X-0 combination in m. 95 changes to X-10/X-1 in mm. 96–97 at the shift from X-0 to X-1 in the glissandi. The resultant tritone range (Bb-E) based on these conjunct interval-3 ranges of X-10 and X-1 (Bb-Db and C#-E) is transposed down by interval 2 in m. 102 to the tritone range (Ab-D) of Y-8. (The latter is part of the X-9 to Y-8 progression from m. 100 to the first eighth-note of m. 102. An expansion from interval 1 to interval 2 can also be seen in the partitioning of X-9 in this progression into its secondary interval couple, A-B and Bb-C, in mm. 100–101.)

At mm. 113–36, the imitation between vnII and va (vc, at mm. 129ff.) generates sequences of tritones, each tritone of which is subdivided into two interval-3s. (These ostinati based on two conjunct interval-3s may be seen as

a doubling of the interval-3 range of the vc ostinato in mm. 76–83 and
93–99, which outlined X-10.) Each ostinato encompassing a tritone in mm.
113–36 is transposed several times. At each shift of the ostinato, the two
linearly adjacent tritones together outline a transposition of cell Z (Ex. 147).
Of the four transpositions of Z in this passage, the tritones of Z-9/3 (E♭-A
and A♭-D) are pervasive (mm. 115–28, va, and mm. 127–36, vnII). Throughout the passage (mm. 79–136) these two tritones have been variously subdivided into cyclic-intervals 2 and 3. In mm. 161–64, these tritones of Z-9/3
are linearly interlocked in each of the four voices of the stretto (see Ex. 144).
Thus, the symmetrical construction of the three basic cells from one another appears to be a consistent underlying principle in cellular development and interaction throughout the first three movements.

In *Music for Strings, Percussion, and Celesta*, the intervallic properties
of cells X, Y, and Z are basic structural links between chromatic and diatonic

146   *Fourth String Quartet*, Movement II, mm. 95–97

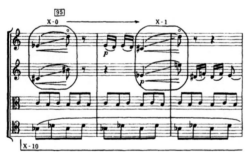

147   *Fourth String Quartet*, Movement II, mm. 113–36

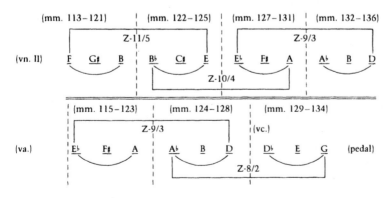

material. Transpositions of these cells emerge from their positions in Movement I as unobtrusive details within larger thematic statements to being primary foreground events in the two central movements. In Movement IV, certain cell properties return to their original unobtrusive positions or are dissolved altogether.

Movement III opens with a primary foreground statement of cell Z-6/0 (F♯-B-C-F), a partial statement (F♯-( )-C-F) of which closes the movement. Movement IV opens with an A-Lydian theme, the pitch content (A-E-B-F♯-C♯-G♯-D♯) of which contains one tritone, A-D♯. At m. 19, in violins 1/2, the first new melodic note of the movement (D) extends the A-Lydian content to an eight-note segment of the cycle of fifths, D-A-E-B-F♯-C♯-G♯-D♯. This extended pitch-collection includes a second tritone (D-G♯), which with the first (A-D♯) implies the presence of a symmetrically placed statement of Z-9/3 (Ex. 148).

Therefore, in the opening of Movement IV, Z-9/3 (A-D-D♯-G♯), which is the symmetrical complement of Z-6/0 (F♯-B-C-F) of Movement III (i.e., they have the same two axes of symmetry), appears as a background event in the diatonic context. At mm. 45–51 of Movement I, which is a bridge leading to the high point of the middle section on E♭ (m. 56), the cellos and basses establish the main foreground statements of cell Z in the movement. These sequentially ascending figures unfold five of the six transpositions of cell Z (Ex. 149). Above this series of Z cells (mm. 45–51), the upper strings present repetitious thematic segments, which imply the properties of the missing transposition, Z-10/4 (B♭-E♭-E-A): the repeated initial phrase of the fugue subject in violins 1/2 begins with E♭-E, which, with the two notes (B♭-A) of violins 3/4 (m. 45), produces the latter transposition of Z. Leading into this passage, violins 3/4 and violas 1/2 (upbeat to m. 42 through m. 43) anticipate the series of Z cells with Z-8/2 and Z-10/4, the first foreground statements in the work.

This passage near the high point of Movement I, which represents the first explicit appearance of cell Z in the work, serves as a focal point for the series of thematic statements that unfold throughout the fugue exposition. The first statement of the fugue subject (mm. 1–5, beat 1) is based on four phrases that together produce all the chromatic tones between A and E. Two

148 *Music for Strings, Percussion, and Celesta*, Movement IV,
opening theme

A-Lydian pitch content extended

| D | A | E | B | F♯ | C♯ | G♯ | D♯ |

(symmetrical placement of the tritones of Z-9/3 (A-D-D♯-G♯))

149   *Music for Strings, Percussion, and Celesta,* Movement I

tritones (A-E♭ and B♭-E), which imply the presence of Z-10/4 (B♭-E♭-E-A), are symmetrically hidden within this chromatic continuum (Ex. 150a; see also Ex. 158). These two tritones, while remaining on the background level of the theme, also appear as important thematic structural elements. The first and second phrases unfold the chromatic tones between A and E♭; the third and fourth phrases unfold the chromatic tones between E and A (Ex. 150b). The penultimate note, B♭ (m. 4), is interrupted, before its resolution to A, by the next subject entry on E; this event produces a focus on the second tritone (B♭-E) contained within the fugue subject. One may observe the same structural position of cell Z in the chromatic theme of Movement II of the *Fourth String Quartet,* where the chromatic line first ascends from E to A♯ and then descends from B to E♯ to outline Z-11/5, B-E-E♯-A♯ (see Ex. 142a).

Cell Z, which is implied by the two tritones contained within the fugue

150 Z-Cell Structure of Opening Chromatic Fugue Subject in *Music for Strings, Percussion, and Celesta*, Movement I, mm. 1–5

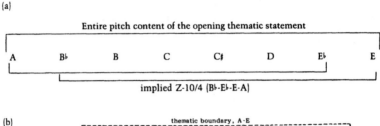

(a)

Entire pitch content of the opening thematic statement

| A | B♭ | B | C | C♯ | D | E♭ | E |

implied Z-10/4 (B♭-E♭-E-A)

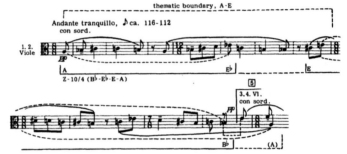

(b)

151 *Music for Strings, Percussion, and Celesta*, Movement I

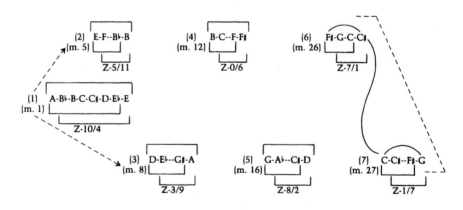

subject, is transposed with each subsequent thematic statement. The first section of the movement (to m. 31) unfolds seven complete statements of the subject (Ex. 151). Together, these imply the presence of all six transpositions of cell Z, the sixth and seventh statements (mm. 26–31) of which converge on the same transposition, Z-1/7 and Z-7/1 (C♯-F♯-G-C). The latter is the symmetrical complement of the initial transposition, Z-10/4 (i.e., they

152 *Music for Strings, Percussion, and Celesta,* Movement I, mm. 26–27

can be permuted around the same two axes of symmetry).[23] The priority of cell Z as a basic structural element of the theme is further established by this convergence on Z-1/7. These two concluding fugue statements represent the first appearance of the subject in stretto. While the two linear statements simultaneously contain the same two tritones (F#-C and G-C#) of Z-1/7, their combined perfect-fifth ranges (F#-C# and C-G) also establish the structural priority of this cell. Furthermore (Example 152), this close stretto permits the components of Z-1/7 to come into closer proximity as a more foreground event in the first two notes of each statement. The entire series of implied Z cells in the succession of thematic statements appears in the middle of the movement (see Ex. 149) as a foreground realization for the first time. At the high point (m. 56), the first chord establishes the priority of Z-10/4, the basic cell of the movement, by presenting a partial statement of it (Bb-Eb-E-( )) in triple forte.

In the first thematic statement, the semitones that fill in the tritone range (A-Eb) of the second and fourth phrases are expanded (at m. 5) in the opening segment of the countersubject to the whole tones of another basic cell, Y-9 (A-B-C#-D#). The following chromatic segment, a linear statement of a third cell, X-11 (B-C-C#-D), complements cell Y by filling in its upper whole tones (Ex. 153a). This explicit Y-9/X-11 progression retrospectively suggests that these two cells are hidden within the chromatic second and fourth phrases of the opening thematic statement (Ex. 153b). At m. 6 of the countersubject, X-11 (B-C-C#-D) moves to a linear statement of X-1 (C#-D-

23 As shown by the brackets in Example 151, the chromatic filling of the perfect fifth, which defines the pitch content of each statement, is symmetrically encompassed by the two tritones of cell Z. Each transposition of Z explicitly appears in its permuted position within the perfect-fifth boundary; e.g., Z-10/4 (Bb-Eb-E-A) appears as A-Bb-Eb-E in the initial statement.

153 *Music for Strings, Percussion, and Celesta*, Movement I

(a) countersubject (mm. 5ff.)

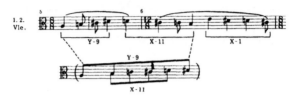

(b)

D♯-E), the latter progression (X-11/X-1) retrospectively suggesting the presence of these two X cells in the chromatic third phrase of the opening thematic statement (see Ex. 153b). At the first appearance of the celesta, in the coda (mm. 78ff.), X-1 emerges as a primary foreground event. Thus, the properties of cells X and Y, in addition to cell Z, appear to be basic structural elements of the fugue subject and countersubject.

In Movement II, primary foreground statements of cell Z are placed at prominent structural points of the traditional sonata plan.[24] At mm. 40–57 of the first-theme group, partial (three-note) statements of all six transpositions of Z prominently emerge in imitation. Then the inverted stretto (Ex. 154, mm. 57–66) of the two antiphonal string sections brings the first-theme group to a close with the first complete statements of cell Z in the movement. The passage (mm. 40–66) begins and ends with partial statements of Z-1/7 (F♯-C♯-B♯-( ), at mm. 40–42, vnI, and its retrograde inversion, ( )-G-F♯-C♯, at mm. 64–66, upper strings), one of the two symmetrically related Z cells (Z-10/4 and Z-1/7) that were basic to Movement I (see Ex. 151). Toward the latter part of the second-theme group (mm. 114–24, upper strings), all six transpositions of Z are again unfolded, now exclusively

24 According to Bartók, *Béla Bartók Essays*, ed. Benjamin Suchoff (New York: St. Martin's Press, 1976), p. 416, this plan follows the traditional scheme in both sectional divisions and tonal outline. A more detailed outline is as follows: theme 1 in C (to m. 67); theme 2 in G (mm. 68–154); closing theme in G (mm. 155–85); development—part 1 (mm. 185–242), part 2 (mm. 242–310), part 3, fugato (mm. 310–71); free recapitulation—theme 1a (mm. 372–412), theme 2a (mm. 412–79), closing theme (mm. 479–90); coda (mm. 490–520). The original publication is "Aufbau der Musik für Saiteninstrumenten" ("Structure of Music for String Instruments"), preface to the score (Vienna: Universal Edition, 1937), ii–iii (in German, English, and French). This also appeared in reprint (New York: Boosey and Hawkes, 1939), iii (in English only).

as partial (three-note) statements (Ex. 155). This time, Z-10/4 (B♭-E♭-E-A) both initiates and ends the series (mm. 114–15, upper strings, ( )-E♭-A-E, and m. 124, B♭ tremolo with the first sixteenth-note chord, E-( )-A-E♭). The priority of Z-10/4 in this series is further established by its alternations with the other five Z transpositions. In turn, the closing section of the exposition begins (mm. 155ff., piano) with a complete single statement of Z-7/1 (G-C-

154 *Music for Strings, Percussion, and Celesta*, Movement II, mm. 56–66

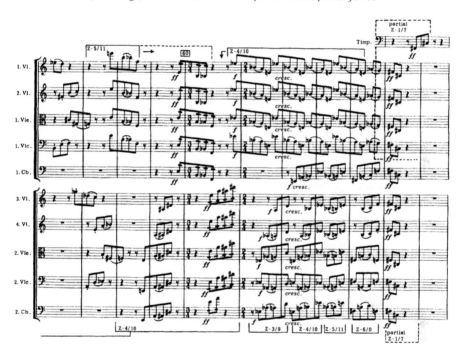

155 *Music for Strings, Percussion, and Celesta*, Movement II,
mm. 114–124

C#-F#), a partial statement ((|)-F#-G-C) of which will later close the movement (mm. 517ff., timpani and piano).

These foreground occurrences of cell Z—especially Z-7/1 (G-C-C#-F#)—at prominent structural points of the movement are foreshadowed by the main theme. By comparing the final modified statements of the main thematic segment (mm. 489–94, at the beginning of the coda) with its original form (mm. 5–8), the thematic function of Z-7/1 becomes apparent. The opening statement is initiated (Ex. 156a) by a nonsymmetrical three-note cell, A-C-D♭, a retrograde inversion of the initial three notes (A-B♭-C#) of the fugue subject of Movement I. The initial minor third (A-C) is expanded at the opening of the coda (Ex. 156b) to a perfect fourth (G-C), giving us three notes (G-C-D♭-(|)) of Z-7/1. (This expansion is suggested in the opening statement, at mm. 7–8 by the timpani and lower strings, where the cadential punctuation on G-C overlaps with D♭-C of the melodic line.) At the next statement in the coda (mm. 491–93), the lower strings invert the theme, so that its initial three notes, C-G-F#, form an inversional complement of the prime form (G-C-D♭), which together imply the presence of complete Z-7/1 (G-C-D♭-F#).

In addition to the initial three-note cell (A-C-D♭), the theme contains another cell that was foreshadowed in the fugue movement. The ascending five-note segment, C-D-E-F-F#, is a modified version of the initial countersubject segment, A-B-C#-D#-D (Movement I, m. 5), in which the upper whole-tone of Y-9 (A-B-C#-D#) is chromatically filled in by the following note, D. At the high point of Movement I (mm. 55–56, upper strings), the same countersubject segment reverses the order of the last two notes to produce A-B-C#-D-E♭, thereby anticipating its transposition (C-D-E-F-F#) in the theme of Movement II. Furthermore, while Y-9 (A-B-C#-D#) of Move-

156 *Music for Strings, Percussion, and Celesta*, Movement II

(a) Opening thematic statement (mm. 5–8)

partial Z-7/1

(b) Final thematic statements (mm. 489ff., coda)

complete Z-7/1 (G-C-D♭-F#)

interval expansion

157 *Music for Strings, Percussion, and Celesta,* Movement II, mm.
421–24, piano

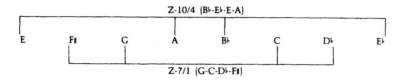

158 *Music for Strings, Percussion, and Celesta,* Movement III, mm. 20ff.

ment I encompasses one of the tritones (A-E♭) of Z-10/4 (B♭-E♭-E-A) (Exx.
150b, 153), implied Y-0 (C-D-E-F♯) in the theme of Movement II now encompasses one of the tritones (C-F♯) of the symmetrically complementary
Z-7/1 (G-C-D♭-F♯). The symmetrical relationship between Z-10/4 and
Z-7/1 occurs as a prominent foreground event for the first (mm.
421–23, piano) near the beginning of the recapitulated second-theme group
in the only octatonic scale of the work (E-F♯-G-A-B♭-C-D♭-E♭) (Ex. 157).
Thus, basic cells Y and Z serve as significant structural elements within the
thematic material of Movement II[25] as well as within that of Movement I.

The first X/Y/Z foreground progression occurs in Movement III (Section
II, mm. 20–31). This contributes to the general sense of intervallic expansion that occurs on the background level of the work (i.e., chromatic to
diatonic themes). At m. 20, immediately following the first phrase of the
original chromatic-fugue subject, the trill figures of vnIII open with X-7 (G-
A♭-A-B♭).[26] Then vnIV enter with X-3 (D♯-E-F-G♭). The essential tones (D♯-
F-G-A) of these combined trill figures outline a whole-tone tetrachord, Y-3,
and the inessential tones (E-G♭-A♭-B♭) form a secondary whole-tone tetrachord, Y-4 (Ex. 158). The tritone boundaries (D♯-A and E-B♭) of these two Y

---

25 While the complete forms of cells Y and Z appear in the theme as background events (Z
emerges as a complete cell on the foreground level only at mm. 57ff.), other subordinate intervallic structures do appear within the theme and introductory pizzicato phrase as local cellular
components. These are confirmed as cells by their subsequent development within the first-
theme group. A detailed account of these other thematic components is given by Robert Smith
in "Béla Bartók's *Music for Strings, Percussion, and Celesta*," *Music Review* 20/3, 4 (August–November, 1959): 268–71.
26 Cell X-7 (G-A♭-A-B♭) is symmetrically related to the opening Z-6/0 statement (mm.
1–5) in its sum-5 permutation, F-F♯-B-C.

159   *Music for Strings, Percussion, and Celesta,* Movement III,
mm. 31–33

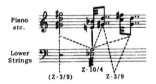

cells imply the presence of Z-10/4 (B♭-D♯-E-A).[27] Above these sustained trill patterns, the glissandi of vnII and the piano chords (mm. 22–27) unfold repetitions of a third chromatic tetrachord, X-11 (B-C-C♯-D). At mm. 28–30, the latter is chromatically extended through pitch-class G. The successive downbeats in these glissandi outline a new whole-tone tetrachord, Y-0 (C-D-E-F♯), giving us a third tritone boundary (C-F♯). (The latter, C-F♯, and the boundary of the essential notes of the trills, D♯-A, are the two basic tritones of the work, as was discussed earlier.) Then, at the cadential measures of this passage (mm. 31–33), the three cell-Y boundaries (D♯-A, E-B♭, and C-F♯) that have unfolded in the ostinato patterns emerge as foreground events. The tritone E♭-A (from Y-3) is held as a tremolo in the lower strings, above which the tritone E-B♭ (from Y-4) appears as thirty-second notes (Ex. 159). Together, these two tritones form Z-10/4 (B♭-E♭-E-A), which also encompassed the preceding trill figures (see Ex. 158). While the third tritone, C-F♯ (from Y-0), also appears as a thirty-second note, one new tritone (G♯-D) is prominently added. The latter (G♯-D), together with the held E♭-A, forms a second Z cell, Z-3/9 (E♭-A♭-A-D). This transposition of cell Z, which is the most prominent in these cadential measures, maintains the axis (sum 5) of the preceding passage, the latter having been centralized around the X-7 nucleus (see Ex. 215). Furthermore, both Z cells (Z-10/4 and Z-3/9), which have emerged into the foreground level at this focal point (mm. 31–33), are joined (m. 40, middle of next section) in the harp glissandi. These partial cell-Z statements (A♭-D-E♭/E♭-F♭-B♭) establish the priority of the basic axis of symmetry (sum 6) of the work (see Ex. 217). Thus, this X/Y/Z progression in Section II of Movement III serves as a focal point for the larger intervallic expansion of the work.

   Bartók referred to this work as an example of "extension in range" of a theme, in which the opening chromatic fugue subject is expanded into diatonic themes in later movements (the reverse, which occurs near the end of

27 This chromatic continuum, which fills in the perfect fifth from D♯ to B♭, is the tritone transposition of the chromatic content of the fugue subject that opens Movement I (see Ex. 150a). Perhaps the reference to the first phrase of the subject (Movement III, mm. 18–19) immediately preceding these trill figures serves to support this long-range connection, in which the tritones of Z-10/4 form the common boundary.

the work, is called *chromatic compression*). Through this procedure, he stated, "we will get variety on the one hand, but the unity will remain un-destroyed because of the hidden relation between the two forms."[28] Thus far, the expansion from the chromatic fugue subject of Movement I to the A-Lydian theme of Movement IV has been foreshadowed, or suggested, by sys-tematic intervallic expansions as is seen in the X/Y/Z relations in the in-tervening movements. The long-range thematic transformation results in expansion of the semitones within the boundary of a perfect fifth (A-Bb-B-C-C#-D-Eb-E) to the diatonic whole- and half-steps of the Lydian scale within the boundary of an octave (A-B-C#-D#-E-F#-G#-A). Furthermore, of the two tritones, A-Eb and E-Bb, contained within the fugue subject, only A-D# (en-harmonic spelling of A-Eb) is retained in the A-Lydian theme. These the-matic connections were established at the outset of the work (m. 5, va), where the countersubject begins with the lower A-Lydian tetrachord, or Y-9 (A-B-C#-D#), bounded by tritone A-D#.

In the reverse procedure, chromatic compression, the final section of Movement IV presents a return to the chromatic structure of the fugue sub-ject. At the Molto moderato (mm. 203ff., or letter F), we get a modified dia-tonic statement of the fugue subject. By association with the Lydian theme that opens this movement, we may take the liberty in this special case of referring to the mode of this statement as "C-Lydian" with flatted seventh (C-D-E-F#-G-A-Bb-C). However, the pedal-tone doubling of the sixth and seventh degrees (A and Bb) tends to weaken the C priority of this hybrid mode and, more significantly, suggests the initial half-step of the chromatic fugue subject at its original pitch level on A. Furthermore, while the pure Lydian mode contains only one tritone, this "altered" modal version con-tains two tritones, C-F# and Bb-E, thereby bringing us closer to the original fugue subject, which also contains two tritones, A-Eb and Bb-E. The former pair (separated by a whole-tone) is chromatically compressed in the latter (separated by a semitone). The second tritone (Bb-E) is common to both and will serve as one of the links between the diatonic and chromatic forms of the subject in the following passage (mm. 209–22).

A nonliteral inversion of the theme (Ex. 160a) is now presented in coun-terpoint against the reiterated hybrid "C-Lydian" version of the fugue sub-ject that began several measures earlier. (The primary form occurs, mm. 209ff., upper three strings of both string groups, in parallel motion at three pitch-levels, C, Eb, and Ab, giving us a series of first-inversion triads.) Through a succession of chromatic fillings within the inverted counter-idea, the intervallic structure of the hybrid C-Lydian theme is gradually com-pressed into chromatic phrases associated with the original fugue subject (mm. 214ff.). In m. 210, the first note in the inverted theme outside of the

28 *Bartók Essays*, p. 381. The source is given in n. 9 of Chapter II.

160 *Music for Strings, Percussion, and Celesta,* Movement IV

(a) Inverted theme in pno and vcl (mm. 209ff.)

(b) Stretto (mm. 215–22)

hybrid C-Lydian modal content (C-D-E-F♯-G-A-B♭-C) is F, which forms part of a five-note segment, C-D-E-F-G♭. The latter reminds us of segment C-D-E-F-F♯ of the main theme at the opening of Movement II (upper strings), and, further back (high point of Movement I, mm. 55–56), at its original transpositional level, A-B-C♯-D-E♭; this appeared as the first five notes, A-B-C♯-D♯-D, of the countersubject (m. 5, violas; see Ex. 153), which was understood as a partial diatonic expansion of the fugue subject.

While the reiterated primary form of the hybrid C-Lydian theme in the present passage of Movement IV spans an octave (C-C), the boundary of the inverted form, through m. 211, third eighth-note, spans a fifth (C-G). The next, more chromatic segment presents another new note in this inversion (E♭), so now only one chromatic tone (D♭) is missing between C and G. This chromatic filling of the lower modal pentachord (C-D-E-F♯-G) is completed at m. 213, the thematic inversion thus far giving us A-B♭/C-D♭-D-E♭-E-F-G♭-G. The filled C-G is a minor-third transposition of the original content of the fugue subject (A-B♭-B-C-C♯-D-E♭-E). At the cadence (mm. 214–15), we get a new (contracted) boundary, tritone A-E♭, the original one that defined the first two phrases of the fugue subject: A-E♭ is entirely chromatically filled at this point. The absence of one note (A♭) in the inverted thematic statement contributes to the distinction between the chromatically filled fifth (C-G) and the chromatically filled tritone (A-E♭). Thus, the transformational procedure that brings us back to the compressed pitch content to reestablish the basic fugue subject is analogous to those Y/X relations of the original countersubject in Movement I (see Ex. 153) where A-B-C♯-D♯ was filled, or chromatically elaborated, by successive semitonal additions (D-C♯-C-B and E-D♯-D-C♯) to form A-( )-B-C-C♯-D-D♯-E.

The next passage, based on modified chromatic segments of the fugue subject, represents a return from the whole-tone separation of tritones (a property of the hybrid C-Lydian form of the fugue subject, i.e., C-F♯/B♭-E) to the chromatically compressed relation of tritones (a property of the original chromatic subject, i.e., A-E♭/B♭-E). The reestablishment of the compressed relation begins in the stretti, at mm. 215–22 (Ex. 160b). These measures are based on a succession of chromatic phrase segments that are close in contour to those of the original fugue subject. In the first two phrases of the three respective stretto groups (vnI/vnII, vcI/vcII, and vnIV/vaII), three tritones unfold as boundary intervals (C-F♯, B♭-E, G♯-D) separated by whole-tones. The first two are those of the hybrid C-Lydian mode. In the last two phrases of the stretto (mm. 217–19), the remaining three tritones (A-E♭, B-F, C♯-G) unfold in the same whole-tone relationship. The first tritone (A-E♭) is basic to the structure of the original chromatic fugue subject. However, in the linear motion of the string groups at mm. 218–22, pairs of tritones now unfold in a chromatically compressed relationship. The upper violins, bounded by A-E♭, move to B♭-E of a new stretto, while the lower violins and violas, bounded by C♯-G, move to C-F♯ of the new stretto. Significantly, these two implied Z cells, Z-10/4 (B♭-E♭-E-A) and Z-1/7 (C♯-F♯-G-C), are precisely those that initiated and ended, respectively, the series of fugue-subject statements in Movement I (see Ex. 151). While C-F♯ of the latter is one of the basic tritones of the hybrid C-Lydian mode, A-E♭ of the former is one of the basic tritones of the chromatic subject, B♭-E being in both. Thus, the entire passage (mm. 209–22) represents a return to the chromatic structure of the fugue by means of both the Y/X (diatonic/chromatic) intervallic relations and the chromatic compression of the double-tritone property of the hybrid C-Lydian theme to the original Z-cell structure of the opening statement of the fugue subject.

CHAPTER VI

Tonal Centricity Based on Axes of Symmetry

Symmetrical pitch collections, which tend to negate those properties of traditional major and minor scales that establish a sense of tonality, have a fundamental function in many of Bartók's works in establishing a new sense of pitch-class priority. The concept of a *tonal center* in Bartók's music has two general meanings. One is the establishment of a given pitch-class as the primary tone of a traditional mode; here the term *center* is a misnomer. The other meaning is the establishment of a given sonic area by symmetrical organization of a conglomerate of pitches around an axis of symmetry. Such symmetrical configurations or progressions may be based on recurrent and, therefore, clearly identifiable symmetrical cells. In such symmetrical relations, the term *tonal center* has a literal designation. Both the traditional and nontraditional concepts are relevant to Bartók's music. These two seemingly unrelated means of establishing a sense of pitch-class priority are often integrated by means of special interactions and transformations.

Local occurrences of symmetrical formations are prominent in most of Bartók's *Fourteen Bagatelles for Piano*, Op. 6, but the pitch organization in the *Bagatelle No. III* foreshadows the new concept of symmetrical organization. An exotic melody (characterized by the augmented second and tritone)[1] unfolds in the left hand, while the right accompanies with a rotating five-note chromatic figure, G-B-Bb-A-Ab (Ex. 161a). The relationship of this

[1] The augmented second is a feature of certain oriental melodies; see *Béla Bartók Essays*, ed. Benjamin Suchoff (New York: St. Martin's Press, 1976), p. 363. The source is given in n. 9 of Chapter II.

161 *Bagatelle No. III*

(a) mm. 3–6

(b) mm. 11–19

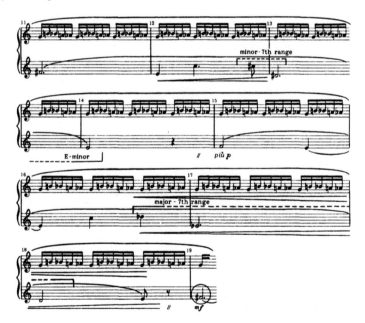

"C-major"[2] tune to the rotating figure suggests a new concept of defining musical space. The boundary interval of this figure (G-B) is symmetrically filled in by the intervening chromatic tones.[3] The four-measure tune that unfolds against it is temporally bounded by a tritone (F#-C), the notes of which are brought into melodic proximity at mm. 6–7 by the phrasal repetition. While the remaining melody notes, E-D#-B, do not support the symmetry of the rotating figure, the tritone boundary of the melody (F#-C) is a symmetrical chromatic expansion of it (*F#-G-A♭-A-B♭-B-C*).

The next two melodic phrases (mm. 11–18) before the modified recapitulation chromatically fill in the complementary space between F# and C to give us all twelve tones. The following phrase (mm. 11–14), which cadences in E minor, has an expanded range of a minor seventh (C#-D#), giving us a new note, C# (Ex. 161b). In the final phrase of the middle section (mm. 15–18) a high point is reached by a further extension of the range to a major seventh (D♭-D) and the inclusion of the remaining tones (F and D) of the chromatic continuum. The one note missing from the latter phrase is F#, and this gap is filled (m. 19) by the first note of the recapitulated tune. Thus, while this piece has an Oriental, folklike modal character, it is based on a tendency toward symmetrical pitch organization in which the material revolves around a nucleus (or axis).

At this point we may briefly observe that symmetrically filled-in rotating figures that serve a nuclear function within the larger context appear in other works of Bartók. One prominent later example that comes to mind is the trio section in the *Scherzo* of the *Fifth String Quartet* (Ex. 162). The opening rotating figure of vnI (and subsequently the other instruments) is registrally encompassed by the two semitones (F-G♭ and B-C) of a Z cell

162 *Fifth String Quartet, Scherzo,* trio section

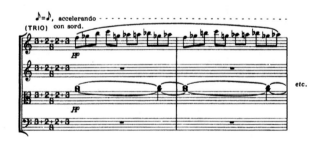

2 *Béla Bartók Letters,* ed. János Demény, trans. Péter Balabán and István Farkas, rev. Elizabeth West and Colin Mason (London: Faber and Faber; Budapest: Corvina Press, 1971), p. 98.

3 This device of immediately filling in a given interval is found in most of Bartók's chromatic works—e.g., the fugue subject of *Music for Strings, Percussion, and Celesta* and the viola theme of the *Sixth String Quartet.*

163 *Bagatelle No. II*, mm. 3–4

164 Axis of symmetry A-A or E♭-E♭

(G♭-B-C-F). The perfect-fourth gap (G♭-B) is linearly filled in by an X-cell (G-A♭-A-B♭) to form the larger rotating symmetrical collection. While the other voices are not symmetrically related to this figure (analogous to the tune and ostinato in *Bagatelle No. III*), they move, in the first eleven measures, exclusively within its registral confines.

Bagatelle No. II is almost exclusively based on a large-scale symmetrical organization around a single axis. The opening eighth-note pattern establishes the priority of a major second (A♭-B♭), which is symmetrical around an implied axis A-A. This serves as a nucleus for symmetrical expansion in the left hand (mm. 3–4) (Ex. 163). The melodically unfolding pairs of tones, B-G, C-G♭, D♭-F, D-F♭, and E♭-(E♭), form, with A♭-B♭, a series of symmetrically related intervals that are generated by aligning two inversionally complementary semitonal cycles intersecting at A-A and its tritone E♭-E♭ (Ex. 164). The middle section opens at m. 7 with the symmetrical whole-tone collection F-G-A-B-D♭, which locally reaffirms the A-A axis.

At the second metric change to 3/2 (m. 17), the repeated major second returns at the tritone transposition, D-E. The implied axis is E♭-E♭, the dual intersection of the original axis (see Ex. 164). The original symmetrical expansion (see mm. 3–4) is now switched to the right hand, expressly around the same axis (E♭-E♭). A significant change occurs in the last two measures (22–23) of this recapitulated phrase. Whereas the analogous point of the exposition (mm. 5–6) departed from the axis (A-A) in the left hand, mm. 22–23 now maintain the axis in the right-hand chromatic figure, B♭-B♭♭-A♭ (Ex. 165). The final return of the first phrase (mm. 23ff.) is based on the original symmetrical expansion around the major-second A♭-B♭ (or implied axis A-A). Thus, in the outer sections of this piece, a new concept of tonal cen-

165 *Bagatelle No. II*, mm. 22–23

tricity is established by means of a single axis of symmetry (A-A or E♭-E♭).[4] The developmental middle section (mm. 7–17, beat 2), which departs from the basic axis after the first four notes of m. 7, consists of a series of diverse symmetrical segments many of which are derived from the interval cycles (e.g., linearly unfolding augmented triads, whole-tone tetrachords, and chromatic segments). The rounded form of the piece is supported by the return to the original axis of symmetry.

The *First String Quartet* illustrates both traditional and progressive tendencies in its melodic and harmonic constructions and in the means by which tonal areas are established. Bartók usually considered certain works of his to be in a particular key, his decision in many cases being based only on the assertion of a given tonality at prominent structural points. In this way accordingly the *First Quartet* may be assigned the tonality of A. While this work has been more specifically considered to be in the minor mode of this tonality, the ambiguity produced by a general hovering between major and minor or nontraditional configurations that are built on pitch-class A weakens the argument for such modal specificity. Furthermore, the constantly shifting tonalities in the first part of the work only gradually focus on the primary tonal region of A, which by the end of the work is unambiguously established.[5] Nevertheless, a sense of tonal priority is apparent within every textural fiber and at every cadential turn in this quartet and, indeed, in all of Bartók's compositions.

The means by which Bartók achieves a sense of tonal integration in a context of emergent tonality must be viewed as part of an historical transition between two chromatic tonal systems. The chromatic (but still somewhat functional) voice-leading properties found in late-nineteenth-century Romantic music are mingled with more radical chromatic configurations

4 Bartók's designation (in a letter, *Bartók Letters*, p. 98) of D♭ major as the basic tonality of the piece can only be due to the local occurrence of pitch-class D♭ and its dominant (A♭) in the final chord.

5 This procedure is appropriately described as *emergent tonality* by David Gow, in his article "Tonality and Structure in Bartók's First Two String Quartets," *Music Review* 34 (August–November, 1973): 259.

that defy analysis based on traditional hierarchical tonal functions. For example, traditional chord progressions based on dominant-tonic relations are juxtaposed with progressions of alternating major and minor triads, the latter combination of which forms a symmetrical pitch collection. Such interrelationships of traditional (functional) and nontraditional (symmetrical) constructions and progressions on the middle and background levels of the quartet contribute to the establishment of the primary tonality of A.

Much of the finale sounds in A, a phenomenon largely determined by the assertion, at the main points of the sonata-rondo form,[6] of certain properties we tend to associate with the traditional tonal system. Each of the three large sections (exposition, development, and recapitulation) is initiated by an ostinato eighth-note pattern on the dominant degree (E) of the key. In each case, these dominant assertions lead to a cadential focal point on the A tonic: at m. 14 of the exposition, the first cadence is based on a progression of V7/vi-V7-I; at No. 14, m. 4, of the development, the first cadence establishes the tonic major-seventh chord, followed at the Meno vivo by a statement of the main theme in A minor; and, at No. 30, mm. 4–6, of the recapitulation, the E ostinato is absorbed into the tonic chord. Furthermore, the closing measures of the movement (beginning at the Molto agitato) linearly and vertically establish a pentatonically derived trichord (A-B-E, or A-E-B) built on the tonic degree.

The asserted tonality of A, which contributes to the formal definition of the finale, also serves as a tonal nucleus for the background-level unfolding of symmetrically related keys throughout the work.[7] The quasi-fugue of Movement I opens with a i6-V6 triadic progression in F minor (Ex. 166), the tonality of which is immediately obscured in the following chromatic succession of triads. At the first cadential point (m. 7), the original suggestion of F minor is replaced by an implied V2–I6 progression in A major-minor. The priority of this major-third tonal polarization between F and A is further established (at No. 1) at the second pair of entries in F minor, bringing the two keys into temporal proximity. Henceforth, A and its lower major third (F) emerge with increasing prominence throughout section A of the ABA′ form. For the next seven measures (No. 1f.), the chords do not remain long enough to establish an unambiguous tonal region. At No. 1, m. 5, F minor is asserted only briefly, by a rhythmic convergence of the voices and the first crescendo molto. At the peak of the second crescendo (No. 2, m. 3), we get the first held

6 The form of the finale is as follows: exposition (m. 1 through No. 14)—theme 1a (m. 1 through No. 1), theme 1b (No. 1, m. 3, through No. 8), theme 1c (Nos. 8–11), theme 2 (No. 11 through No. 11, m. 12), return of theme 1c (No. 12 through No. 13, m. 9); development (Nos. 14–27)—fugato (No. 17f.), transition to recapitulation (No. 27 through No. 27, m. 14); recapitulation (No. 28f.)—theme 1a (No. 28 through No. 30, m. 6), theme 1b (No. 30, m. 7, through No. 34, m. 4), theme 2 (No. 34, m. 5, through No. 35, m. 4), return of theme 1c (No. 35, m. 5); coda (No. 37f.).

7 This tonal scheme is discussed by Gow, "Tonality and Structure."

chord on A major-minor. At the next plateau (No. 4, m. 3), which is produced by increased rhythmic agitation and the first fortissimo of the piece, F minor is clearly asserted by prominent alternations of the tonic and dominant triads (Ex. 167). The main climax of section A (No. 6) then establishes A major-minor as the primary foreground event.

At the opening of section B (No. 6, m. 5), occurs a significant event that will play a fundamental role in the large-scale relation of the basic tonalities. Against the held C-G of vc, which suggests that we have arrived at either the dominant of F or the relative of A, the viola introduces a rhapsodic

166 *First String Quartet*, Movement I, mm. 1–8

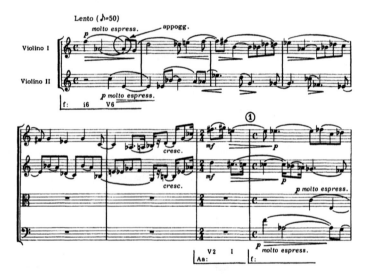

167 *First String Quartet*, Movement I, No. 4, mm. 2–3

168 *First String Quartet,* Movement I, opening of section B

theme in C♯ minor (Ex. 168). While the latter is somewhat obscured by its polytonal relation with C, it offers the first suggestion of the symmetrical polarization with F around the A nucleus (i.e., F-A-C♯).

We may perhaps view the C-C♯ polytonal relation that opens the B section as an expansion of the two third-degrees (i.e., the axis C-C♯) of the A major-minor symmetry at the climax of the preceding section. This projection of the A major-minor axis is significant in that it permits a link to be established between the traditional relative key area (C) and the upper major-third (C♯) of the symmetrical scheme of tonal regions. It may be observed that this relationship is a culmination of a series of major-minor chords that occur at the ending of section A. The focal point on A major-minor at No. 6 is approached (Ex. 169) by a sequence of three phrases (No. 4, m. 4, to No. 6), in which the fortissimo in each phrase locally establishes the priority of a major-minor symmetry (E♭-G♭-G-B♭, F♯-A-A♯-C♯, and A-C-C♯-E). At the opening of section B (No. 6, m. 5), following modified reiterations of these chords, the combination of C-G in vc with the E-D♯ of the C♯-minor va theme harmonically establishes a C major-minor symmetry (in enharmonic spelling, C-E♭-E-G). The latter completes the sequence of major-minor chords, the root progression of which outlines a series of minor thirds (E♭-F♯-A-C), forming a background-level linear symmetry as well. In the first half of section B (to No. 8, m. 3), the bass progression, C-F♯, brings two of these roots into temporal proximity; this tritone suggests a symmetrical balance around the basic A nucleus. Thus, while the triadic harmonies and modal melodic lines are reminiscent of the traditional tonal system, the local major-minor juxtapositions and the background-level root relations tend toward symmetrical divisions of the chromatic continuum.

Thus far, A and its lower major third, F, have emerged in the large-scale progression of tonalities as primary focal points in section A, while the upper major third (C♯) has only been touched on in the opening polytonal context of section B. The tonal areas of both A and C♯ appear with increasing prominence throughout the remainder of the work. The cadential segment of Movement I closes on a minor third, A♭-C♭, which, in enharmonic spelling (G♯-B) suggests the third and fifth degrees of the dominant triad (E-G♯-B)

169 *First String Quartet,* Movement I, No. 4, m. 4, to No. 6

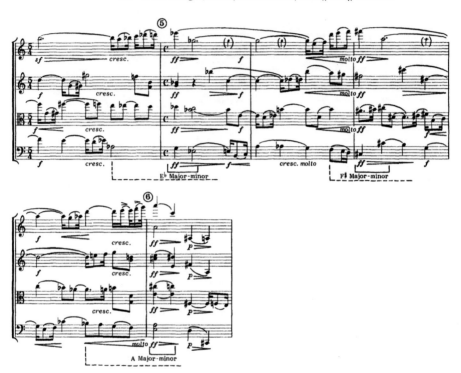

of A minor. This implied dominant then moves *attacca* to the tonic chord of A major to begin Movement II. The first-theme group cadences (one measure before No. 3) on an F-major triad, immediately followed by a linearly outlined A-major triad. The roots of these two basic tonal areas are then vertically joined with C♯ in the opening chord of the bridge section (in enharmonic spelling, C♯-F-A). Within the bridge section (at No. 5, mm. 3–4), we find local occurrences of the same symmetrical configuration. Then, at the opening of the second-theme group (No. 6, mm. 1–2), the melodic line in the inner voices first establishes A major (in enharmonic spelling), followed by a shift to an enharmonically spelled C♯ minor (Ex. 170). The latter tonality is subsequently supported (No. 6, m. 9, to No. 7, m. 3) by a D♭-major-minor harmonic framework. While the ending of the exposition (No. 11, mm. 6–15) suggests arrival at the dominant areas (C and E) of F and A, respectively, the first cadential point (at No. 12, m. 11) establishes V-I in F, and C is expanded at No. 14f. The recapitulation of the first-theme group importantly focuses (No. 26, mm. 3–4) on the upper major-third tonality (C♯ minor) at the first prominent cadential point. The tonalities of A major and C♯ minor are then asserted at, respectively, No. 28f. and the Poco sostenuto (Ex. 171), and local reiterations of the three tonalities (C♯-F-A) prominently appear in the appoggiatura motions in the violins at No. 28 and again at No. 31f. The movement closes in A major-minor (No. 32, mm. 3ff.) with a cadence in the unexpected key of B major.

In the *Introduzione* to the finale, assertions of C♯ now appear at cadential focal points (e.g., mm. 4, 8, 13) and throughout the vc solo at the Meno vivo. In the finale, C♯ emerges within the opening phrase as an expanded tonal area in juxtaposition to the A tonality of the va/vc theme and main cadence at m. 14 (Ex. 172). Following the continually shifting tonalities of themes 1a and 1b, the cadential point of the latter (one measure before No. 8) clearly establishes C♯ minor before moving into theme 1c. Though the new subtheme harmonically begins in F♯ minor, the tune in vnI linearly unfolds in the C♯-Dorian mode against the chromatic lines of the accompaniment. At the first cadential point (No. 14, mm. 4–5) in the development section, the E-dominant ostinato moves to the tonic A-major-seventh chord, which can be interpreted as a vertical joining of A-major and C♯-minor triads.

170   *First String Quartet*, Movement II, theme 2 at No. 6f.

171 *First String Quartet*, Movement II, No. 28f.

172 *First String Quartet*, Movement III, mm. 1–14

173 *First String Quartet,* Movement III, 1 m. preceding No. 17 through
No. 17, mm. 1–3

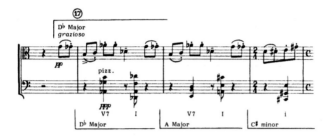

These two keys alternate throughout the first half of this section. At the
Meno vivo, the main theme, which first appears in A minor, introduces a
fugue (two measures before No. 17) based on a rhythmically diminished version of the latter theme. The entry of the subject in va is in D♭ major (in
enharmonic spelling, C♯ major), the supporting harmonies alternating V-I
progressions in D♭ and A (Ex. 173). (At No. 18, mm. 6–7, we get the explicit
C♯ spelling in alternation with the A-major triad.) The tonality of C♯ is
most significantly asserted at the opening of the recapitulation (No. 28, mm.
1–7), where it replaces the original tonality of A as the basis of theme 1a (Ex.
174). The tonality then abruptly shifts from C♯ minor to C major, a relationship that reminds us of section B in Movement I, where the two tonalities
were stated simultaneously. The A-minor tonality is reestablished (No. 30,
mm. 4–6) at the cadence of theme 1a. At No. 38f. of the coda, A is forcefully
asserted on the downbeats of each thematic statement, followed at the
Più vivo by the final alternations of C-minor and C♯-minor segments, before moving to the tonic sonority, A-E-B. The latter pervades the ending of
the movement. Thus, while major-minor, perfect-fifth, and other types of
symmetrical chords are meaningful only as local foreground sonorities, the
primary emergent tonalities of F, A, and C♯ form the basis of the background-level scheme of symmetrically organized tonalities. The priority of
pitch-class A is thereby established both as the root of traditional and nontraditional constructions and as the nucleus of this large-scale tonal scheme.

As early as the *Second String Quartet* (1915–1917), cell Z played a significant role in establishing axes of symmetry on the background level of
the work.[8] In the opening of Movement I, the linear thematic statement in

---

8 According to George Perle, "Symmetrical Formations in the String Quartets of Béla Bartók," *Music Review* 16 (November, 1955): 306–7, symmetrical formations on the local level of
each movement do not revolve, as they do in the *Fourth* and *Fifth Quartets*, around stable axes
that function as tonal centers, but are freely employed around constantly shifting axes of symmetry. On the local level, a sense of tonality is established by assertion of certain elements of
the traditional modes.

174 *First String Quartet*, Movement III, Recapitulation at No. 28f.

vnI (mm. 2–3) contains a sum-9 permutation (D-C♯-G♯-G) of Z-8/2 (Ex. 175a). While this transposition of Z appears only as an unobtrusive local configuration within the larger melodic line, it emerges at the opening of the recapitulation (No. 16, m. 9, beginning on D in vnI, through No. 17) as the sole generator of the linear statement in the same instrument. The latter expressly unfolds cell Z around both axes of sums 9 and 3. This transposition, Z-8/2, is also the final transposition of cell Z in the movement, appearing in its original sum-9 permutation within the final two statements of the main motive in vnI (No. 21, mm. 5–6 and No. 22, m. 2) and finally in its sum-3 permutation in the anacrusic chord (No. 22, m. 4) to the Poco più mosso. At the opening of Movement II (mm. 1–6, beat 1), all the voices now present Z-11/5 (B-E-F-B♭) as a more prominent foreground event (Ex. 175b), the latter transposition of Z being symmetrically related to Z-8/2 at sum 9 or 3.[9] Significantly, the initial statements of these two Z cells (Z-8/2, opening of Movement I, and Z-11/5, opening of Movement II) are explicitly presented around the same axis of symmetry (sum 9), Z-8/2 in permutation D-C♯-G♯-G, and Z-11/5 in permutation B-E-F-B♭ (Ex. 175c). In Movement III, the first

9 In ibid. Perle does not discuss sums of complementation, a principle that is essential in understanding the special symmetrical properties of pairs of related Z cells.

occurrence of Z (No. 2, m. 2, vnI, immediately following the *Lento* introduction) is Z-8/2 in its permutation, also explicitly of sum 9. This axis is now supported by a held sum-9 dyad, C-A (No. 1, m. 13, to No. 2, m. 3, va and vc). The movement closes with the same permutation of Z-8/2 (sum 9) in vnI, again accompanied in va and vc by the same sum-9 dyad (C-A). This dyad then occurs alone in the last two measures.

While the establishment of a single primary axis (i.e., sum 9) is exclusively a background event, the symmetrical polarity of Z-8/2 and Z-11/5 (both of sum 9) in the tripartite arch-form of the quartet is locally reflected in the recapitulation of Movement I. Cell Z-2/8 (D-G-G♯-C♯) emerges as a primary foreground event in the return of the main theme in vnI (Ex.. 176a: No. 16, m. 9, to No. 17, m. 2, first eighth-note). At the same time, vc linearly unfolds a statement of Z-5/11 (F-B♭-B-E), completed by No. 17, m. 2, beat 1. These two basic transpositions of Z are separated by interval 3 in their referential positions (D-G-G♯-C♯ and F-B♭-B-E). An ostinato in the inner voices

175 *Second String Quartet*

(a) Movement I, mm. 2–3, vnI

(b) Movement II, mm. 1–6

(c) Sum-9 permutations of Z-8/2 and Z-11/5

176 *Second String Quartet*

(a) Recapitulation in Movement I

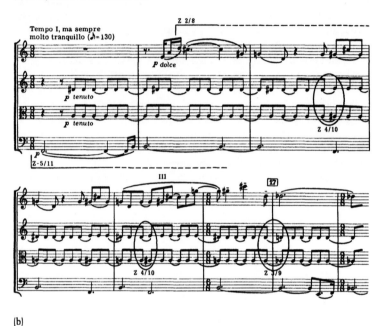

(b)

is initiated by tritone A-D♯. At No. 16, mm. 10, 11, and 12, the latter moves to an upper-neighbor tritone, A♯-E, the tritones thus forming Z-4/10 (E-A-A♯-D♯). At No. 17, the initial tritone (A-D♯) then moves to a lower-neighbor tritone, A♭-D, forming Z-3/9 (D♯-A♭-A-D). The gap between Z-2/8 and Z-5/11 is thereby symmetrically filled in (Ex. 176b). This conglomerate of four Z cells can be shown to be symmetrical around either of two axes of symmetry, sum 6 (A-A or D♯-D♯) or sum 0 (C-C or F♯-F♯). If we choose the former (sum 6), we see that the only two notes (C and F♯) missing from the excerpt implicitly encompass either of the axial dyads, A-A or D♯-D♯. (The exclusion of tritone C-F♯ contributes to the symmetrical definition of the entire pitch collection.) If we choose sum 0, the converse occurs: the explicitly stated tritone, A-D♯ (inner voices), encompasses the implied axial dyads C-C and F♯-F♯. Thus, this large symmetry, in which basic cells Z-2/8 and Z-5/11 (both of sums 9 and 3) together symmetrically encompass the axes of either sum 6 or sum 0, contributes to the establishment of certain basic tonal areas (A, E♭, C, and F♯) in the quartet.[10]

The main thematic line in vnI (No. 17, mm. 2–4, third note) dissolves this large symmetry by shifting to a new Z transposition, Z-1/7 (in enharmonic spelling, D♭-G♭-G-C) (Ex. 177). The latter overlaps with Z-5/11 (vc) and one of the tritones (A♭-D) of Z-3/9 (va and vnII), which continue from the preceding measures. In va and vnII (No. 17, m. 4, beat 3), a new tritone, G♭-C, initiates the remaining Z cell, Z-0/6 (C-F-G♭-B), which forms the pitch content of the inner voices for the next seven measures. As Z-1/7 (vnI) is thematically transformed (at No. 17, mm. 8f.) into Z-4/10 (E-A-B♭-E♭), the two new Z transpositions (Z-1/7, D♭-F♯-G-C, and Z-0/6, C-F-F♯-B) of this passage converge (No. 18, m. 2) in the three lower voices to form the exclusive pitch-content of the accompaniment. These two new Z-transpositions (Z-1/7 and Z-0/6) interlock at a common tritone, C-F♯, which was precisely the axial structure (i.e., around axis A-A) missing from the large symmetry in the opening section of the recapitulation (see Ex. 176b).

The last seven measures of the movement establish the priority of A through a combination of nonsymmetrical modal material and two symmetrical constructions (Ex. 178). Against the eighth-note melody in A minor, a (symmetrical) augmented triad, F-A-C♯, unfolds linearly and vertically. This formation, which is derived from theme 2, can be permuted

---

10 The basic tonality of the quartet may be considered to be A, since the complex of pitch relations moves toward that goal in the final measures of the work. Within the first movement, this tendency of growth into the key of A is already apparent, first at the return of theme 2 (m. 141), then at the closing section (mm. 156f.), which begins and ends in A major-minor. The secondary tonal areas, i.e., the tritone (E♭) and minor thirds (C and F♯) of A, are also established at primary structural points of the sonata form. The transition (mm. 20ff.) to theme 2 suggests C minor, touching upon A major-minor at m. 28. Theme 2 (m. 32) then establishes F♯ minor, which is anticipated by two measures of its enharmonically spelled major-minor dominant. The closing theme (mm. 63–69) reestablishes F♯ as the tonic of the Dorian mode, following a lengthy transition initiated (m. 38, beat 3) by A major-minor. The opening of the development (m. 70) suggests E♭.

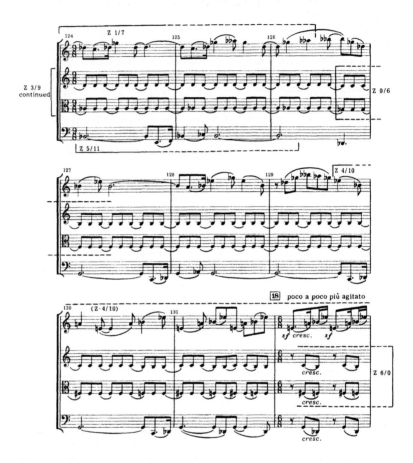

around axis A-A. The latter is introduced (No. 23, mm. 1 and 3) by a symmetrical chord, Bb-C♯-F-G♯, which is also symmetrical around the A-A (or Eb-Eb) axis.

Tonal priority in the *Sixth Improvisation for Piano*, Op. 20, is established by a combination of traditional modal properties in a symmetrical scheme of keys. The principal key of the piece is primarily determined by three statements of an Eb-pentatonic folk tune.[11] The pitch content of the latter (Eb-Gb-Ab-Bb-Db) is anticipated in the introduction (mm. 1–5, left

---

11 This folk tune from the district of Csík-Gyimes is the basis of the formal outline, as follows: introduction (mm. 1–5); strain 1 of the tune (mm. 6–11, right hand); strain 2 (mm. 12–19, left hand); strain 3 (mm. 20–26, left hand); and coda (mm. 27–32).

hand), where it forms the basis of a highly modified statement of the original folk tune. This five-note pitch collection (black keys) is complemented in the right hand by the remaining seven pitch-classes (white keys), the two together giving us all twelve tones.[12] Within each of these five- and seven-note partitions, certain traditional diatonic properties tend to establish a sense of tonal priority. The harmonic basis of the right hand is triadic, the opening two-and-a-half measures exclusively alternating the dominant (in enharmonic spelling, ( )-B-D) and tonic chords in C major (Ex. 179). While the pentatonic collection of the left hand is somewhat tonally ambiguous in these introductory measures, the continuation of the latter in strain 1 (mm. 6ff., right hand) establishes the priority of E♭. Against this statement of the tune, the left hand (mm. 6–7) implies tonic-dominant alternations in G♭-minor. (The tonic chord, in enharmonic spelling, G♭-B♭♭-D♭, which is

178 *Second String Quartet*, Movement I, No. 23, mm. 1–7

12 At m. 5, only one "odd" pitch class (C♯) appears in the diatonic (white-key) spectrum of the right hand. The significance of this note is referred to in n. 13, below. The use of the white-note diatonic and the black-note pentatonic collections to derive all twelve notes is basic in Berg's *Lulu*, as discussed by Douglas Jarman, in "Dr. Schön's Five-Strophe Aria: Some Notes on Tonality and Pitch Association in Berg's *Lulu*," *Perspectives of New Music* 8/2 (Spring-Summer, 1970).

179 *Sixth Improvisation*, mm. 1–6

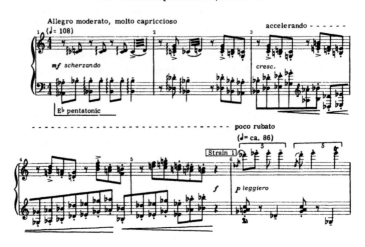

180 *Sixth Improvisation*, mm. 15–19

formed by both hands, contains one dissonant tone, C.)[13] Thus far, the two keys (C major and G♭ minor) that appear in polytonal conflict with the basic mode of E♭-pentatonic form a symmetrical scheme of minor-third tonalities around it. The remaining succession of chords in the left hand of strain 1 reestablishes the C-major pitch content (m. 8, with upbeat, and m. 10), both measures ending on the dominant-seventh chord of the latter key, before moving to the main cadential point (m. 11) in E♭ major.

In strain 2 (mm. 12–19), the successive tonalities of the accompaniment, in conjunction with the E♭ tonality of the tune, form a revised symmetrical scheme of tonal roots, so that the primary E♭ axis is shifted to the secondary

---

13 At the crossover point of the two hands (mm. 5–6), the single dissonant (or "odd") note, C, in the G♭-minor tonic chord of the left hand may perhaps be considered part of an interchange with the single "odd" note, C♯ (m. 5), in the C-major tonality of the right hand. Such interchanges between components of different or opposing sets of pitches are common in Bartók's works—for example, in Movement III of the *Fourth String Quartet* (see Ex. 337).

one of C. The first three measures (12–14) of the accompaniment are in C, with the exception of the chromatically embellishing triplet figures. At mm. 15–16, a chromatically embellished C major-minor triad moves (mm. 17–18) to an A major-minor modal mixture (Ex. 180). Tonic A of the accompaniment and tonic E♭ of the tune, which are equidistant from pitch-class C, converge at the cadence (m. 19) on an unharmonized statement of the latter axis.

These two symmetrical schemes of tonal roots, first C-E♭-G♭ (strain 1) and then A-C-E♭ (strain 2), outline four equidistant tonalities (A-C-E♭-G♭) that rotate around the primary (E♭) and secondary (C) tonics. These two axes (E♭ and C), which represent the two opposing diatonic spectra of the introduction, are exclusively polarized in strain 3 and the coda as the roots of the E♭-pentatonic and C-major-minor modal pitch collections. Thus, tonal priority in this *Improvisation* is established by an interlocking of principles from two different systems, modal and symmetrical.

The large-scale arch form of the *Fourth String Quartet*[14] serves as a framework within which Bartók organizes diversified pitch-formations into a highly systematic network of symmetrical relations. Of the three basic cells (X, Y, and Z), symmetrical relationships may be shown only between X and Z (Ex. 181), since the sum of complementation (as represented by the axis of symmetry) for each of their transpositions is odd. In correspondence with X-0 (C-C♯-D-E♭) of sum 3 and X-3 (D♯-E-F-F♯) of sum 9, Z-8/2 and

181 *Fourth String Quartet*, symmetrical relations between basic X and Z transpositions of Movement I

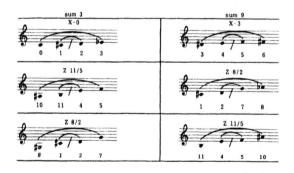

14 The five movements are symmetrically related, with the first and second mirroring the fifth and fourth, respectively, in tempi and thematic material. The central movement, in a slow parlando-rubato style, is enveloped by two scherzo movements. All five movements are in ternary (A-B-A′) forms with codas, the first movement more specifically outlining a sonata-allegro plan: exposition (mm. 1–49), first-theme group (mm. 1–13), transition (mm. 14–29), second-theme group (mm. 30–43), closing (mm. 44–49); development (mm. 49–92); recapitulation (mm. 93–134), first-theme group (mm. 93–104), transition (mm. 104–119), second-theme group (mm. 119–126), closing (mm. 126–134), coda (mm. 134–161).

Z-11/5 occur most importantly at sums 3 and 9. However, while X-0 and X-3 are each based on a single axis of symmetry (one of sum 3, the other of sum 9), each of these two Z cells simultaneously contains both axes of sums 3 and 9; that is, both these transpositions of Z can be permuted around either axis of symmetry.

In the first phrase (mm. 1–2) of the first-theme group, vnI and vnII transpose from X-3, D♯-E-F-F♯ (m. 1 through the first eighth-note of m. 2) to X-0, C-D♭-D-E♭ (m. 2, second and third eighth-notes). The axis of symmetry of X-3 is sum 9, and the same sum is expressed in the C-A of vc, while the axis of symmetry of X-0 is sum 3, and that sum is expressed in the A-F♯ of vc (Ex. 182). (In the recapitulation, m. 93, these two sum dyads, C-A and A-F♯, explicitly appear in vc as double stops.) In the second phrase (mm. 3–4), X-0 is joined with its lower interval-3 transposition, X-9 (A-B♭-B-C). The latter opens the phrase in vnI and vnII (m. 3), again at sum 9,[15] and moves by way of a lower-neighbor (X-8, A♭-A-B♭-B) to its cadential statement in vnII and va (m. 4). At this point it is joined with X-0 in vnI (mm. 3–4) for a simultaneous

182 *Fourth String Quartet*, Movement I, mm. 1–6

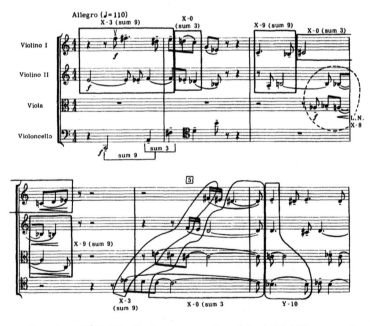

[15] Since X-9 (A-B♭-B-C) is the tritone transposition of X-3 (D♯-E-F-F♯), at m. 1, it will have the same axis of sum 9. This is demonstrated in Example 81, in the sum-9 column at rows 1/11 and 3/9 (X-3) and rows 9/3 and 11/1 (X-9) of the odd array.

statement of sums 9 and 3. At m. 4, the sum-9 range (A-C) of va is a retrograde of the opening C-A in vc (m. 1) and C-A in vnI and vnII (m. 3). In the third phrase (m. 5), X-3 (E♭-E-F-F♯) of sum 9 is reestablished at the opening of a stretto, moving down again to X-0 (C-C♯-D-D♯) of sum 3. The latter transposition (X-0) is then established as the basic pitch-level of X as it expands for the first time to basic Y-10 (B♭-C-D-E) on the second chord of m. 6. In the fourth phrase (mm. 8–10), the sum-9 to sum-3 progression occurs once more as X-3 (m. 8, second chord of the stretto) moves to X-0 (m. 10) at the cadential alignment of the voices. At this point (mm. 10–11), we get the second X-0 to Y-10 progression. Thus, sums 9 and 3 are locally established as the basic axes of symmetry of the first-theme group.

Measures 15–18 of the transition contain a canon between vnI and vnII, the statement in vnI encompassing tritone G♯-D. A specific tritone, C♯-G, is added in vnII in this canon to imply the presence of Z-8/2 (G♯-C♯-D-G), returning to the original sum 3 of X-0 (C-C♯-D-E♭) (Ex. 183). At m. 22 of the transition, Z-8/2 emerges as a local foreground event for the first time in va and vnI, vertically stated as G♯-C♯-D-G and linearly in vnI as D-G-A♭-D♭; both permutations are based on the sum-3 axis.

The X-Y-Z progressions at the beginning of the development section (mm. 49–52) are analogous to the progressions from X-0 to Y-10 in mm. 1–11 of the first-theme group and Y-10 to Z-8/2 in mm. 14–23 of the transition (see Ex. 139). At the end of the new progression (m. 52), Y-2 (D-E-F♯-G♯) expands to Z-11/5 (B-E-F-A♯). The latter, which explicitly establishes the axis of sum 9, is an interval-3 transposition of the original Z-8/2 (G♯-C♯-D-G), which explicitly established sum 3 at m. 22. At mm. 53–60, sum 9 is confirmed as the primary axis of symmetry (Ex. 184), as X-3 (D♯-E-E♯-F♯) appears as the basis of an ostinato in vnII and va (mm. 54–58); vnI and vc form a stretto around the X-3 ostinato. (These two imitative voices are based on motivic segments that primarily encompass linear interval-3s, i.e., B♭-G and D-B. Since the stretto specifically begins at interval 4/8, B♭-D, in m. 54, dyads D-G and B-B♭, each of which has a sum of 9, can occur vertically.) In m. 53, Z-11/5 (B-E-F-A♯) is joined with X-3 (D♯-E-F-F♯), the latter becoming the nucleus of the passage from m. 54 to m. 60. (Thus far, the symmetrical relationships between cells X and Z shown in Ex. 181, sum-3 and sum-9 columns, have formed the basis of a large-scale tonal motion from the exposition to the development of the sonata plan. This motion, from sum 3 to sum 9, is a background-level unfolding of the local alternations between these two axes that permeated the opening of the exposition.) In the remainder of this passage (to m. 60), all the sum-9 transpositions of cells X and Z are firmly established. On the first beat of m. 55, X-9, the tetrachord A-B♭-B-C (vc and vnI), is joined with X-3 and Z-11/5. In mm. 56–58, B-B♭ of Z-11/5 in the inverted stretto between vc and vnI symmetrically contracts around D-G in these two voices to form a sum-9 permutation of Z-8/2 (C♯-D-G-A♭) in

183 *Fourth String Quartet*, Movement I, mm. 14–22 of transition

m. 57, the fifth through seventh eighth-note. In m. 58, the G-A♭ in vnI is aligned with D-C♯ in vc, forming a Z-8/2 ostinato (specifically at sum 9) around the X-3 nucleus in vnII and va. Thus, both transpositions of X (X-3 and X-9) and Z (Z-8/2 and Z-11/5) of sum 9 are joined in this passage (mm. 53–60).

The final symmetrical contraction around the X-3 (sum 9) nucleus (at m. 58) is made more prominent by the metric departure and return to the barline at this point. In the stretto (mm. 54–58), the linear statements in vnI and vc at first adhere to the barline, though implying local metric displacements in the slurred eighth-notes (m. 54). At the end of m. 56 through m. 57

they change to implied overlapping 3/8 meters. The vnII and va, which are based on the X-3 ostinato, imply alternating metric groups of 3/4 and 3/8. At the beginning of m. 57, an "expected" 3/8 group does not occur. This pattern, which begins on the second eighth-note of m. 54, correspondingly ends with an eighth-note chord at the end of m. 57, permitting all the voices to be vertically aligned on the downbeat of m. 58, marked by a sforzando. At this point the final contraction to Z-8/2 (around the sum-9 nucleus) occurs.

At the end of the development section (mm. 85–92), X is transposed by its cyclic-interval 1 from X-3 of sum 9 (m. 85) through X-2 and X-1 to X-0 of sum 3 (m. 92) at the beginning of the recapitulation. This shift from sum 9 to sum 3 is a reverse of the original large-scale progression from basic X-0 (sum 3) in the exposition to X-3 (sum 9) in the opening of the development. In these final measures (85–92) of the development, the transposing state-

184   *Fourth String Quartet*, mm. 53–60 of development

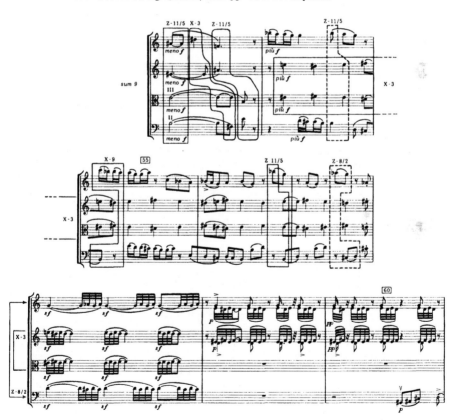

ments of the X motive are separated by a prominently placed arithmetic progression in the thirty-second notes. These thirty-second notes occur twice in groups of three (mm. 82–84), three times in groups of two (mm. 85–87), and seven instead of an "expected" six occurrences of a single group (mm. 88–92), the final "odd" one cadencing on the downbeat of m. 92 in anticipation of the final X statement, which ushers in the recapitulation (Ex. 185). In the corresponding movement (V) of the symmetrical arch form, the middle section (mm. 151–237) analogously moves by way of descending X transpositions from sum 9 to sum 3. This section ends with the interval-3 boundary (C-E♭) of X-0 (sum 3) in all the voices. At mm. 162–64, vc plays X-3 (sum 9)—the first linear statement of the X motive in this section. A stretto in mm. 182–95 is initiated by the latter transposition (X-3) in vc and vnI. In m. 185, vnI and vc then play X-2, returning at mm. 187–89 in all the instruments of the stretto. This is followed by X-1 in all the instruments from m. 190 to m. 192. The vnI and vnII shift to X-5 (F-F♯-G-A♭) in mm. 193–95, while X-1 (C♯-D-E♭-E) stays in vc and va. This X-1/X-5 combination (C♯-D-E♭-E/F-F♯-G-A♭) is a return to the original E-F axis of sum 9 of the stretto. From m. 221 to m. 237, X-2 is the basis of a motivic ostinato in va and vc, while the cadential interval-3 boundary (C-E♭) of implied X-0 (m. 237) is prepared in vnI and vnII (mm. 227–37). Cell X-0 is explicitly anticipated in vnII at mm. 218–19.

In the coda of Movement I (mm. 134–45), sum 9 is again established explicitly around the axis of symmetry, E-F. Principal and inverted linear statements of the expanded X motive (marked "forte") are aligned in vnI and vc around axis of symmetry E-F in vnII and va. These linear statements of the X motive in vnI and vc are initiated (fourth eighth-note of m. 134) by G-D (sum 9), which expands to B-B♭ of Z-11/5 (m. 135, first eighth-note). The latter dyad then contracts around D-G in the successive statements of the X motive (mm. 136–41). In turn, D-G symmetrically contracts to F-E (mm. 142–45) (Ex. 186).

Cell Z-11/5 (B-E-F-B♭), which prominently opens the coda (m. 135), is a focal point for a series of intervallic expansions that lead to this sum-9 symmetry. At mm. 126–34 (Più mosso), the closing of the recapitulation unfolds in stretto. Each linear statement of the rhythmically expanded X motive in this stretto is initiated by a sforzando. The range of the opening statement of the motive in each voice (the end of m. 126 through the beginning of m. 128), which begins on C, is expanded to interval 5 (C-G). (In the closing of the exposition, mm. 44ff., each linear statement of the motive encompassed interval 4.) In mm. 128–29, beginning with the sforzando on D, the range of each linear statement expands to interval 6 (G♯-D). In mm. 130–31, beginning with the sforzando on F, the interval-6 range of each linear statement shifts to F-B, which also appears in inversion in vc. (These two interval-6 ranges, G♯-D and F-B, outline the interval-3 collection G♯-B-D-F.) The range F-B in mm. 130ff. is not chromatically filled as was G♯-D in mm. 128–29

185 *Fourth String Quartet*, Ending of development section (mm. 82–92);
arithmetic progression in thirty-second-note groups (2×3, 3×2, 7×1,
instead of "expected" 6×1), ending at bar line to usher in Recapitulation

186 *Fourth String Quartet*, Movement I, mm. 135–45 (contraction
around axis E-F of sum 9)

but, rather, encompasses the symmetrical formation F-F♯-G♯-A♯-B in the three upper instruments and its inversion, F-E-D-C-B, in vc. Then, at the sforzando in mm. 131–32, the three upper instruments move up, and vc down, from F-B to G♯-D. At m. 134, the fourth eighth-note, G♯, becomes G in vc, and D is retained in vnI, resulting in an expansion from interval 6 (G♯-D) to interval 7 (G-D). At this point, the appearance of E in va produces an expanded interval 9 above G, while the appearance of F in vnII produces interval 9 below D. The new axis of symmetry is E-F (sum 9). In vnI and vc, G-D expands to B-B♭ (m. 135, first eighth-note). Thus, the specific tritone F-B (closing, mm. 130–31) recurs in vnII and vc (m. 135, first eighth-note), where it is joined with tritone E-B♭ in va and vnI to produce Z-11/5 (at sum 9).

In the final section of the coda (mm. 152–60) an X-Y-Z progression again asserts the priority of sum 9. The sforzando chords (mm. 152–56) are based on the progression X-9 (A-B♭-B-C) to Y-8 (A♭-B♭-C-D), this transposition of X having an axis of sum 9 (see Ex. 140). Cell Y-8 then leads (at m. 157) to a canon at the tritone (Ex. 141), in which the series of sforzandi and accents defines a background-level unfolding of the three odd-numbered Z cells (Z-7/1, Z-3/9, and Z-11/5). The last one (Z-11/5), at mm. 159–60, is a return to sums 9 and 3. (Sum 9 initiated the coda at mm. 134ff. and the X-9/Y-8 progression in mm. 152–56.)

This X-Y-Z progression is significant in establishing the priority of basic sums 9 and 3, and the progression X-9 to Y-8 also plays a fundamental role in establishing pitch-class C as the basic tonal frame of the quartet. Symmetrical relationships cannot be shown between cells X and Y, since these two cells do not have a common axis of symmetry (the sum of complementation for any transposition of X is odd, whereas for any transposition of Y it is even). However, since the nonsymmetrical expansion from X-9 (sum 9) to Y-8 (sum 10) is a mirror of the original nonsymmetrical expansion from X-0 (sum 3) to Y-10 (sum 2), a long-range symmetry is produced (Ex. 187). The axis of symmetry of the two inversionally related progressions is C, which is the only pitch class common to all four tetrachords. This procedure contributes to the establishment of C as the basic tonality.

The dual establishment of pitch-class C as a tonal priority—on the one hand, as a traditional root of the quasi-Phrygian segment at the final cadence of Movement I (and Movement V), and on the other, as an axis of symmetry (see Ex. 187)—is common in many of Bartók's works. In terms of the axial function of C-C (sum 0), we find a significant relationship with the basic odd axes of sums 3 and 9. While X-0 and X-9 (Ex. 187) are of sums 3 and 9, respectively, the combination of the two X transpositions forms a larger symmetry of sum 0 intersecting at C-C. The same relations are found in the combination of the two basic Z cells (Z-2/8 and Z-11/5) of these odd sums, 3 and 9. This combination forms the larger octatonic scale D-E-F-G-G♯-A♯-B-C♯,

187 *Fourth String Quartet*, Movement I, basic X-0/Y-10 progression (mm.
10–11) mirrored by X-9/Y-8 (mm. 152–56)

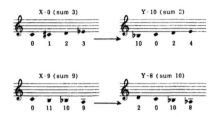

which expressly occurs in Movement II at mm. 243–46, va. The latter can be
permuted around any of four axes—two odd (sums 3 and 9) and two even
(sums 0 and 6). The sum-0 intervals, B-C♯ and F-G, in this scale are implicitly based on the sum-0 axial dyads C-C and F♯-F♯, respectively. These
axial relations are more extensively developed in *Music for Strings, Percussion, and Celesta* (see Ex. 220, and corresponding discussion). The interrelations of these four odd and even sums are suggested in the opening phrases
of Movement I of the quartet. At mm. 1–2, X-3 (E♭-E-F-F♯) and X-0 (C-C♯-
D-E♭) of sums 9 and 3 in the violins intersect at E♭-E♭, while the opening
linear segment of the sum-9 and sum-3 dyads in vc (C-A-F♯) has an intersection of A-A. At m. 4, the new combination of X-0 (C-C♯-D-E♭) with X-9 (A-
B♭-B-C) of the same two odd sums forms a new intersection at C-C (see Ex.
182). Furthermore, the first two notes of the movement (E and C) traditionally suggest C major. Thus, a link between the somewhat traditional
tonal frame of C of the quartet and the primary odd axes of sums 9 and 3 is
suggested in the interrelations of the basic symmetrical cells.

The symmetrical relations between cells Z-8/2 and Z-11/5, both of
sums 3 and 9, also play an important role in Movement II. While Z-8/2 was
the first to appear in the work (m. 22), specifically at sum 3, Z-11/5 initiates
Movement II (mm. 1–4) also specifically permuted around sum 3. The tritones (E-A♯ and B-E♯) of Z-11/5 outline the ascending and descending
phases of the chromatic theme (see Ex. 142), so the two tritones together (E-
E♯-A♯-B) have a sum-3 axis of G-G♯. At the same time, the initial two notes
(E-F), which are prominently reiterated in the first two measures of the accompaniment, ambiguously suggest the other axis (of sum 9). The presence
of the sum-9 dyad, E-F, is even more prominent in the original sketch of this
opening thematic statement, as a comparison of the early draft with the final version demonstrates (Ex. 188a, b). At the end of this movement (mm.
243–46, va), Z-8/2 and Z-11/5 are symmetrically joined to produce octatonic scale D-E-F-G-G♯-A♯-B-C♯, explicitly permuted around sum 3 (see Ex.
142b).

188 *Fourth String Quartet*, Movement II, mm. 5–10 (comparison of early draft with final version)

(a) Early draft (see Illustration 7)

(b) Final version

Whereas the odd sums of 9 and 3 are established as the primary axes of symmetry in the outer movements,[16] a new set of symmetrical relations is established at the center of the arch form (Movement III). In order to understand the significance of these centrally located axes in terms of their relationship to the original axes, certain larger generative implications of the basic cells must first be demonstrated. An X/Y-generated system of symmetries can be produced by selecting a four-note segment from each of the interval cycles: from the chromatic complex (interval-1/11 cycle), one can select the tetrachord C-C♯-D-E♭ (cell X-0) to generate the other tetrachords in the system by means of an interval-expansion process. The intervals in these other tetrachords consecutively expand (Ex. 189) through each of the cyclic intervals from 2/10 (cell Y-10) to 12/0 before a cyclic return to 1/11 (cell X-0). While each tetrachord is part of a particular cycle, four complete cycles occur (see Ex. 189, horizontal rows), initiated by each of the tones of X-0 (tetrachord C-C♯-D-E♭) in the interval 1/11 column. The uppermost row extends from E♭ through the octave by a succession of ascending 1/11

16 As discussed above, these axes are reestablished in Movement V (mm. 162–237 of the middle section) by the progression of X motives from X-3 (sum 9) to X-0 (sum 3) and by Z-11/5 of sum 3 (or 9) (mm. 384–85 of the recapitulated coda from Movement I; see Ex. 141).

intervals, i.e., an interval-1/11 cycle. The row from D to D is an interval-0/12 cycle, from C# to C# a descending interval-1/11 cycle, and from C to C a descending interval-2/10 cycle. This entire system is itself one large cycle, since the initial tetrachordal collection (X-o) returns at interval 1/11. Significantly, certain elements have a central position in the system: D-D at 12/o, and D-G# at 6/6, each represents a dual axis of symmetry; that is, the intervallic properties of the preceding tetrachordal structures recur in their retrograde order after this point.

Analogous to their positions in this system, pitch-class D and tritone D-G# have central positions in the arch-form of the quartet. The basic tonality of Movement III is D and, with G#, D appears as the axis of symmetry in the middle of this movement.[17] In mm. 47–52, the ostinati in vnI and vc together form a segment of the interval-5/7 cycle (Gb-Db-Ab-Eb-Bb) (Ex. 190). The axis of symmetry is Ab-Ab (in enharmonic spelling, G#-G#) of even-sum 4. At the end of m. 52, this collection shifts in the same voices to another symmetrical collection, F-G-D-A-B. The expressed axis of symmetry of the latter is D-D (also sum 4). In va at mm. 48–49, the collection B-C-D-E-F has D-D as the axis of symmetry. In vnII and va at mm. 51–55, C-E, which implies the same axis (D-D), emerges as the basis of the entire symmetrical passage, as follows. The va and vnII at mm. 50–51 are based on a segment of the interval-5/7 cycle, F-C-G-D-A-E-B (sum 4), which explicitly appears as the diatonic collection C-D-E-F-G-A-B. At the end of m. 51, these two instruments cadence on C-E, which then appears as the explicit axial interval through m. 55. Segments C-E (va and vnII) and F-G-D-A-B (vc and vnI, end of mm. 52ff.) have the common axis of symmetry D-D. Thus, the axis of symmetry (D-D) of the va statement in mm. 48–49 emerges in mm. 50–55 as the axis of symmetry of the entire pitch-collection. The axis (Ab-Ab) of the

189 *Fourth String Quartet*, X-o/Y-10-generated tetrachordal system derived from the complex of interval cycles

	1/11	2/10	3/9	4/8	5/7	6/6	7/5	8/4	9/3	10/2	11/1	12/0	1/11
1/11:	Eb	E	F	F#	G	G#	A	Bb	B	C	C#	D	Eb
0/12:	D	D	D	D	D	D	D	D	D	D	D	D	D
1/11:	C#	C	B	Bb	A	G#	G	F#	F	E	Eb	D	C#
2/10:	C	Bb	Ab	F#	E	D	C	Bb	Ab	F#	E	D	C

X-0   Y-10   Y-0   X-1   (X-0)

17 This movement is in three parts: A (mm. 1–34), codetta (mm. 34–41); middle section (mm. 42–55); A' or free recapitulation (mm. 55–63), codetta (mm. 64–71). According to Bartók, *Bartók Essays*, pp. 412–13, the first codetta and middle section together (mm. 34–55) comprise the second part of this movement.

190 *Fourth String Quartet*, Movement III, mm. 47–55

ostinati in vnI and vc (mm. 47–52) becomes subordinate at the end of m. 52, as the ostinati shift to the D-D axis. This hierarchical relationship between A♭ and D is echoed in m. 71: G♯ in vnII is released, while vnI alone retains D: this corresponds to the hierarchical relation within the X/Y-generated system (see Ex. 189).

The held tritone G♯-D at m. 71 serves as a focal point for a background-level unfolding of this tritone in the codetta (Ex. 191; mm. 64–71). The three lower instruments return to the held chord, A-B-C♯-E-F♯-G♯, that opened the movement. This hexachord is based on two equivalent whole-tone trichords, A-B-C♯ and E-F♯-G♯. The joining of a third trichord, B♭-C-D (vnI), with the pedal trichords (A-B-C♯ and E-F♯-G♯) produces a new symmetrical collection F♯-G♯-A-B♭-B-C-C♯-D-E, now of sum 10, to which tritone G♯-D (which combines the original sum-4 dual axes, D-D and G♯-G♯, as a sum-10 dyad) is symmetrically related. Movement IV then opens with an ostinato pattern based on a sum-10 chord, D-E♭-G-A♭, which is bounded by tritone D-A♭. Furthermore, at the entry of va (m. 6), the first six notes (A♭-B♭-C-D-E♭-F-( )-( )) symmetrically expand the ostinato chord to a seven-note segment of the cycle of fifths (A♭-E♭-B♭-F-C-G-D). This segment is the tritone transposition of the seven-note chord D-A-E-B-F♯-C♯-G♯ at mm. 70–71 of Movement III (Ex. 192), which led to the held tritone G♯-D. These two seven-note symmetries (A♭-E♭-B♭-F-C-G-D/D-A-E-B-F♯-C♯-G♯) together form a permutation of the entire 5/7 cycle that is symmetrically related to the basic 5/7 collection (F-C-G-D-A-E-B) established at sum 4 (axis D-D) at the center of Movement III (mm. 50–51, va and vnII). Thus, the dual axis (D-D and D-G♯) of the X/Y-generated system is established, as both foreground and background events, as the axis of the large-scale arch-form of the quartet.

The successive stages of the X/Y-generated system, although depicted in Example 189 as one large progression, do not all occur as progressions in the quartet. Rather, each stage occurs prominently at a significant structural point. Furthermore, certain stages have functions in the quartet that are analogous to those they have in the system. The dual axis of symmetry in the middle of Movement III, for example, is formed by D-D and D-G♯. Certain stages, however, do progress directly in the quartet from one to another, e.g., tetrachords in the system at intervals 1/11 and 2/10 (X-0 to Y-10), at intervals 5/7 and 4/8 [18] and at intervals 11/1 and 12/0 (X-1, C♯-D-E♭-E, to the D-D axis). This last progression is basic to the background-level unfolding of axes in Movement III. Measures 1–13 of Movement III are partitioned into a solo line in vc and a pedal chord in the other three instruments. The pedal chord unfolds two whole-tone trichords, G♯-F♯-E and C♯-B-A, separated by interval 3 (C♯-E). Through the addition of the axial dyad D-D♯ in vc

---

18 The significance of this progression will be discussed in Chapter VIII, where both the 5/7 (or 7/5) tetrachords play a prominent role in the generation of the interval cycles.

191 *Fourth String Quartet*, Movement III, mm. 64–71

192 *Fourth String Quartet*, end of Movement III (mm. 70–71) and
beginning of Movement IV (m. 1 through m. 7, first eighth-note)

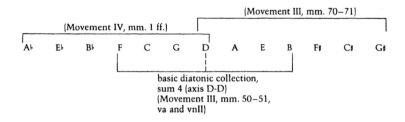

basic diatonic collection,
sum 4 (axis D-D)
(Movement III, mm. 50–51,
va and vnII)

193 *Fourth String Quartet*, Movement III, mm. 1–6

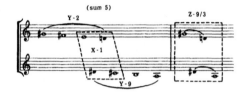

at m. 6, the C♯-E gap of the large hexachordal symmetry (G♯-F♯-E-( )-( )-C♯-
B-A) is symmetrically filled. The axial dyad D-D♯ also expands the two
whole-tone trichords to Y-2 (D-E-F♯-G♯) and Y-9 (A-B-C♯-D♯). This collection symmetrically joins the basic cells (X-1, Y-2 and Y-9, and Z-9/3) around
the sum-5 axis (Ex. 193). (While D-D♯ is established as the axis in these
measures, the rhapsodic vc line at mm. 6–9, tends to emphasize pitch-class
D through the greater duration of the latter. This foreshadows the local shift
in vc at mm. 10–11 to the diatonic collection F-C-G-D-A-E-B with an axis of
symmetry D-D, and the prominent establishment in the middle section of
this axis.) Cell Y-2 (m. 6) is ultimately transposed at the codetta of this section (mm. 34–39, the four lowest tones of the pedal chord) by interval 4 to
Y-10, while Y-9 (m. 6) is analogously transposed (mm. 34–39, the two highest pedal tones and vnI) by interval 4 to Y-1. The transposed collection
(Y-10/Y-1) in mm. 34–39 is based on the same axis of symmetry (sum 5) as
the initial Y-2/Y-9 collection (Ex. 194). These two passages—one of which
initiates the first section, the other of which closes it—thus intersect at
their common tones C♯-D-D♯-E. The latter (X-1) is the last stage of the X/Y-
generated system before the convergence at interval 12/0 on D-D. At mm.
50–55, the middle section of the movement establishes the D-D axis of
symmetry.

Cell Z-9/3 (A-D-D♯-G♯), which is implied in the boundary tritones of

194 *Fourth String Quartet*, Movement III, establishment of sum 5 at the opening (mm. 1–6) and closing (mm. 34–39) of section A

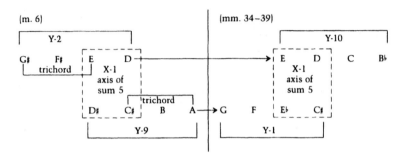

Y-2 (D-G♯) and Y-9 (A-D♯) at m. 6, plays a fundamental role in establishing certain symmetrical relations in the A section analogous to the relations in Movement I between sums 3 and 9. Cell Z-9/3 is explicitly stated at sum 5 (at m. 6), the same sum being reestablished in the codetta (at mm. 34–39). In a transitional passage (mm. 22–29) between these two points, a new pedal chord contains five notes of one whole-tone scale (G♯-B♭-C-D-E) and an "odd" note (F) in va, while vc unfolds the other whole-tone scale (G-A-B-C♯-D♯-F) and an "odd" note (F♯) at m. 23. Although these two odd notes (F-F♯) are interchanged between vc (m. 23) and the lower va pedal, they are in their registral positions with regard to their respective cycles. Dyad F-F♯ (sum 11) is the other axis of symmetry of the opening Z-9/3 (in the sum-11 position, D-D♯-G♯-A). This passage also maintains maximal relationship with the opening and closing passages of section A, by presenting D and D♯ as its lowest and highest tones, respectively. Thus, the opening section of Movement III establishes the two axes (sums 5 and 11) of Z-9/3 analogously to the establishment in Movement I of the two axes (sums 3 and 9) of either Z-8/2 or Z-11/5.

In the *Fifth String Quartet*, as in the *Fourth*, the principle of symmetry is basic to both the large-scale formal design [19] and the underlying pitch relations. Pitch-class B♭, which is asserted as a primary tonal event at the opening of the work, is explicitly established as an axis (mm. 216–18) at the final cadence of Movement I (Ex. 195a). The inversionally symmetrical motion of the paired instruments (first in stretto, then in homophony) that produces this axis is demonstrated (Ex. 195b) by aligning two inversionally com-

19 See Chapter VI, n. 14. The central movement of the *Fifth String Quartet*, however, is a scherzo rather than a slow movement, and this is enveloped by two slow movements rather than scherzi.

plementary semitonal cycles that intersect at B♭-B♭ and its tritone, E-E. Whereas both cadential phrases are initiated by axial dyad E-E, the final cadential point converges on the B♭-B♭.[20]

Pitch-classes B♭ and E, which are prominently placed within the opening canonic subject, are brought into temporal proximity (m. 5) at the entry of the canonic answer. The vertical foreground occurrence of this tritone forms part of a local four-note symmetry, B♭-E♭-E-A (Z-10/4) (Ex. 196), the properties of which are basic to the linear thematic structure. While Z-10/4 is based on an axis of either odd-sum 7 (B♭-E♭-E-A) or odd-sum 1 (E♭-E-A-B♭), a long-range mirroring of this initial statement of Z ultimately contributes to the establishment of the main axis of even-sum 8 (B♭-B♭). The vio-

195   *Fifth String Quartet*, Movement I

(a) Movement I, mm. 216–18

(b)

dyads of even-sum 8:	E	E♭	D	D♭	C	C♭	B♭
	E	F	G♭	G	A♭	A	B♭

in pitch-class numbers:	4	3	2	1	0	11	10
	4	5	6	7	8	9	10

20 The tonal priority of axial pitch classes B♭ and E is also established at primary structural points within the first and last movements. In Movement I, the initial B♭ theme is transposed to E (m. 59) at the opening of the development section, and back to B♭ (m. 159) at its inverted restatement in the recapitulation. In Movement V, the opening theme (m. 14) of the exposition now conversely establishes the priority of pitch-class E. At mm. 367ff., middle section, the fugato entries are alternately initiated by E and B♭, with the latter order of these two pitch-classes thematically reestablished (mm. 546ff.) at the opening of the recapitulation.

196 *Fifth String Quartet*, Movement I, mm. 4–6

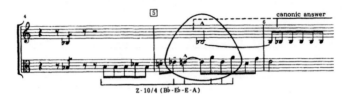

197 *Fifth String Quartet*, Movement V

(a) Movement V, last three measures

(b)

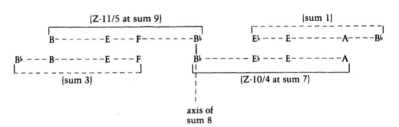

lins in the last three measures of Movement V (Ex. 197a) play an eight-note symmetry outlined by Z-11/5 (B-E-F-B♭) of sum 9. The inversional relationship between this and the initial statement (Z-10/4) is demonstrated in Example 197b. At the final cadence, the inversional motion of va and vc against the violins establishes the priority of the B♭-B♭ axis as a primary foreground event. In Movement I, at mm. 167ff. of the recapitulation, the inverted return of the canonic subject implies a partial statement of the same inverted transposition, Z-11/5 (( )-E-F-B♭), so basic sum 8 is also suggested through the long-range inversion of Z-10/4 by Z-11/5 in the symmetrical formal design of this movement.[21]

The two pairs of odd axes (sums 1 and 7 and sums 9 and 3), which together symmetrically encompass basic sum 8 (see Ex. 197b), significantly contribute to the articulation of the symmetrical formal divisions of Movement V.[22] Let us first observe the inversional pitch-relations between the thematic statements in the symmetrical formal design of the exposition. Theme 1 (mm. 14ff.) outlines the basic tritone, Bb-E, the inverted return of this theme (at mm. 113ff.) establishing a new tritone, B-F; the two tritones together form a background-level occurrence of Z-11/5 (B-E-F-Bb) of either sum 9 or sum 3 (see Ex. 197b). Analogously, theme 2 (mm. 55ff.) linearly establishes tritone Gb-C, the inverted return of this theme (mm. 75ff.) outlining tritone G-Db; the two tritones together form a background-level occurrence of Z-1/7 (Db-Gb-G-C), which has the same two sums (7 or 1) as Z-10/4 (see Ex. 197b). Furthermore, at mm. 18ff., the va/vc accompaniment to the opening statement of theme 1 forms a six-note symmetry, F-G-A-Bb-C-D, of sum 7; the accompaniment to the inverted closing statement of this theme forms a six-note symmetry, F-Gb-A-C-D#-E, of sum 9; together these accompanying figures support the long-range symmetrical motion around the basic axis of sum 8. As is shown in Example 198, the sum-7 symmetry, F-G-A-Bb-C-D, in the accompaniment to the first statement of theme 1 replaces a Bb-Lydian segment, Bb-C-D-E-F, in the preliminary sketch, the latter segment being modally completed by the figure F-G-A-Bb in the violins. The change from segment Bb-C-D-E-F in the sketch to the symmetrical segment F-G-A-Bb-C-D in the final version is a significant illustration of how Bartók absorbed properties of the folk modes into a set of abstract pitch relations. The sketch further reveals that the basic tritone Bb-E, components of which form the primary dual axis of sum 8, Bb-Bb and E-E, of the work, was originally conceived (in the sketch of the present passage) exclusively in terms of the diatonic source, Bb-Lydian mode.

The two cadential passages (at mm. 184–200) preceding the trio section serve as focal points for these inversional relations. The passage at mm. 184–88 mechanically unfolds a symmetrical progression generated from the axial dyad G-Ab of sum 3, and the codetta (mm. 188–200) unfolds a similar

21 In Movement I, the principal subject, bridge, and subordinate subject not only return in reversed order in the recapitulation, but the totality of pitch relations of each is inverted (see George Perle, "The String Quartets of Béla Bartók," in *A Musical Offering: Essays in Honor of Martin Bernstein* (New York: Pendragon Press, 1977), p. 6.
22 Movement V is a sonata-rondo with a suggestion of a double trio, as follows: introduction (mm. 1–14); exposition—theme 1 (mm. 14–54), theme 2 (mm. 55–75), inverted repeat of theme 2 (mm. 75–92), transition back to theme 1, introduction to theme 1 (mm. 109–12), inverted repeat of theme 1 (mm. 113–49), transition initiated by the return of the introduction (mm. 150–88), codetta (mm. 188–200); trio (mm. 201–356); introduction as transition (mm. 455–77); trio quote (mm. 480–527); introduction (mm. 527–45); recapitulation—theme 1 (m. 546), theme 2 (m. 624), codetta (m. 673), "Allegretto con indifferenza" (m. 699), theme 2 (m. 721), codetta (m. 763); coda (m. 781).

198 *Fifth String Quartet*, Movement V, comparison of sketch with final version at mm. 13ff.

(a) Sketch

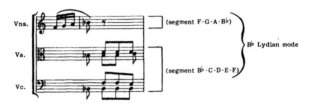

(b) Final version

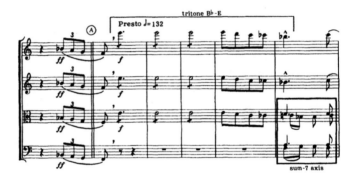

symmetrical progression at a new pitch-level generated from the axial dyad C-D♭ of sum 1 (Ex. 199); these sums, 3 and 1 (= 13), analogous to sums 9 and 7, also symmetrically encompass basic sum 8. The latter progression (codetta) then culminates at mm. 196–200 on isolated statements of both its axial (sum-1) dyads, F♯-G and C-C♯, which together form a prominent foreground statement of Z-1/7 (C♯-F♯-G-C). The trio then joins Z-1/7 (of sums 1 and 7) and Z-8/2 (of sums 9 and 3) in a stretto based on a new thematic idea. The initial notes of the eighth-note figures (Ex. 200) outline Z-1/7 (in enharmonic spelling, C♯-F♯-G-C). Certain axial properties of these two Z cells that open the trio also appear at the end of the trio (mm. 337ff.) as the basis of an inversionally complementary linear motion (Ex. 201a). At mm. 337–45, these lines intersect at the sum-9 dyads, A♯-B and E-F (downbeats) implying the presence of Z-11/5. At m. 345, last eighth-note, through m. 349, this symmetrical progression is revised: the inversionally complementary lines now intersect at the sum-1 dyad, F♯-G. The latter dyad is the axis of Z-1/7, which closes the trio (mm. 351–56) at sum 1 or sum 7 (Ex. 201b).

These interactions, which are significant in balancing the local sym-

199 *Fifth String Quartet*, Movement V, mm. 184–200

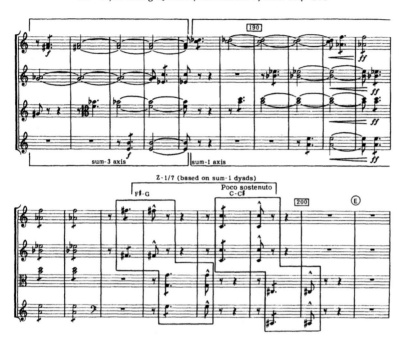

200 *Fifth String Quartet*, Movement V, mm. 202–6

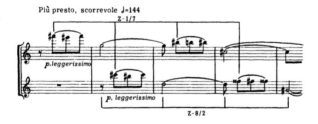

metrical areas (odd axes) on either side of the primary sum-8 axis, B♭-B♭ or E-E, are also basic to the symmetrical formal design of the movement. The central fugato section (mm. 368ff.) explicitly reestablishes the priority of primary pitch-classes B♭ and E in the successive thematic entries and in the accompanying ostinato patterns. The trio (mm. 480ff.) and exposition (mm. 546ff.) return in reversed order, the brief trio quote being reintroduced (mm. 477–80) by the odd axes (Ex. 202). At the end of the recapitulation of theme

201 *Fifth String Quartet*, Movement V

(a) mm. 337–48

(b) mm. 351–56

202 *Fifth String Quartet*, Movement V, mm. 477–80

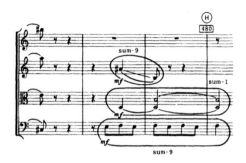

2 (mm. 673–98), the entire cadential passage is now strictly symmetrical around the axial dyads A-B♭ (explicitly stated as the outer elements of the initial chord) and E♭-E (implied at the center). (These two sum-7 dyads are the dual axis of Z-10/4, B♭-E♭-E-A, which appeared at m. 5 near the opening of Movement I.) A curious childlike tune marked "Allegretto, con indifferenza," appears as a grotesque contrast; this diatonic variant of the more chromatic second subject unfolds in A major over tonic and dominant ostinato chords. While these chords in A major are mechanically reiterated, the tune shifts to B♭ major, the two keys together transforming the sum-7 axial dyad (A-B♭) of the preceding symmetrical passage into traditional tonal centers.[23] This diatonic tune—in A major, then B♭ major (Ex. 203a)—is foreshadowed in Movement I, mm. 45ff., by the contour of the chromatic third theme, against which A and B♭ are held as pedals (Ex. 203b).

The recapitulation closes (prestissimo, mm. 763–80) with contrary linear motions derived from the main thematic material of the movement. While these scales are neither linearly symmetrical nor form a larger symmetry through their simultaneous statements in contrary motion, certain symmetrical background-level properties of these scales reestablish pitch-classes A-B♭ as an axis of symmetry. Each of the two linearly joined diatonic tetrachords that form each scalar statement is bounded by a perfect fourth, these two perfect fourths a tritone apart together outlining a Z cell (Ex. 204). The inverted contrapuntal alignments of these cell-Z structures, together with the successive pairs of long notes, establish a series of symmetrically related (sum-7) dyads that intersect at the dual axis, A-B♭ or E♭-E. At m. 788, the held G♯ moves up to A, but the lower held note, B, does not make the corresponding move down to B♭. Therefore, A departs from its position in

---

23 See Perle, "String Quartets," pp. 6–7. Also, some of the following concepts and procedures are discussed by Perle, "Symmetrical Formations."

(a) Movement V, mm. 699ff. ("Allegretto con indifferenza")

(b) Movement I, mm. 44ff. (Theme 3)

204 *Fifth String Quartet*, Movement V, mm. 763–80

the axis, A-B♭, and, in association with B, becomes part of a new symmetrical structure (with an axis B♭-B♭, or E-E) that is explicitly established at the
beginning of the Stretto (mm. 781ff.).

Throughout the coda (Stretto, mm. 781ff.), B♭-B♭ and E-E remain the
primary dual axis, established almost exclusively by literal inversional relationships of segments derived from the introduction and main theme. While
the simultaneously stated introductory statements (vnI and vc) are each linearly nonsymmetrical, together they form a larger symmetry converging on
the axis B♭-B♭. The vnII and va enter with a chromatic figure initiated by the

205 *Fifth String Quartet*, Movement V, mm. 781–91

other axial dyad, E-E. At mm. 783–91 (see Ex. 205), the embellishing inversional motion around the E pedal immediately establishes E-E as an axis. At the same time (mm. 783–91), the outer instruments expand the initial diatonic figure by prefixing it with the E-E axis. This explicitly establishes both axial dyads as the first and last notes of each figure, and symmetrizes the linear aspect of these diatonic segments as well.

At mm. 794ff., an E pedal appears in vc as a substitute for the mirror image of the upper voice, thereby dissolving the preceding symmetrical relations. After two nonsymmetrically extended statements of the figure in vnI (mm. 795–99), which fill in the octave from E to E, linear symmetry returns through the substitution of the final E by E♭ (Ex. 206). This alteration momentarily restores the former sum-7 axis (based on dyads A-B♭ and E♭-E), the entire linear symmetry outlining the original Z-4/10, E-A-B♭-E♭ (see Ex. 196).

At mm. 804ff., the E♭ is joined with B to form one of two alternating major thirds (B-E♭ and F-A) that rotate around an implied B♭-B♭ (or E-E) axis. At the same time, the violins unfold a symmetrical linear figure in imitation at the tritone, the axis of each (A and E♭) of which explicitly occurs as a local

206 *Fifth String Quartet*, Movement V, mm. 795–804

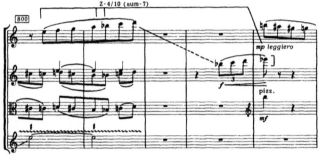

cadential resolution. These secondary axis tones, A and E♭, relate to the earlier prestissimo passage (see Ex. 204), where each formed part of the dual
sum-7 axial dyads A-B♭ and E♭-E. In the present passage (mm. 804–10), they
are analogously associated with the single axial dyads, B♭-B♭ and E-E, of the
accompanying thirds (Ex. 207). However, the contextual separation of the
two tones (A from B♭ and E♭ from E) in this passage ultimately serves as
preparation for the final transformation to the primary sum-8 axis (B♭-B♭
and E-E). While va and vc (mm. 810–20) hold the secondary axial dyad, D♯-
E, as a focal point for this stretto, the violins continue their preceding linear
figure, but at a new pitch level. At mm. 815–24, this figure is symmetrically
stabilized around the implied B♭-B♭ axis, the held D♯-E in the lower instruments being replaced (mm. 821–23) by the inverted figure around the B♭-B♭
axis. At m. 825, the cadential point closes the passage on D-F♯ in the upper
strings, implying the primary axis (B♭-B♭ or E-E) of sum 8, against D-F in the
vc, based on the conflicting secondary axis (E♭-E or A-B♭) of sum 7 (see last
paragraph of Preface, above, regarding a discrepancy in this measure between
different published versions of the score). The cadential passage then symmetrically converges on the primary axis (see Ex. 197). The overall sym-

207 *Fifth String Quartet*, Movement V, mm. 804–10

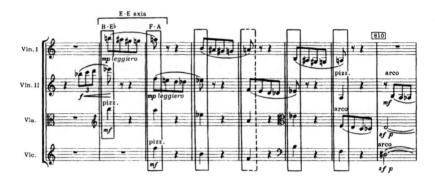

208 *Fifth String Quartet*

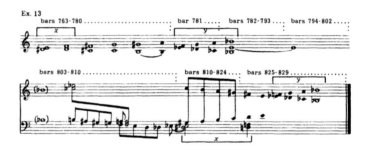

metrical organization of the last sixty-six measures of the movement is outlined in Example 208.[24]

In *Music for Strings, Percussion, and Celesta*, tonal priority is established according to two contrasting principles. The chromatic sections are
primarily organized around axes of symmetry, while the modal diatonic
ones are based on traditional key-centers. However, significant interrelations occur between these seemingly irreconcilable methods of establishing
tonal centers.[25]

Movement IV is primarily set within the diatonic framework of the A-
Lydian mode, the tonic priority of A being established at the opening of the

24 My thanks are due to George Perle for permission to reproduce example 13 from his
"Symmetrical Formations."

25 Furthermore, these two methods correspond to long-range transformations from chromatic to diatonic themes. See *Béla Bartók Essays*, ed. Benjamin Suchoff (New York: St. Martin's Press, 1976), p. 381, and the corresponding discussion regarding the principles of *diatonic
expansion* and *chromatic compression*. The source is given in Chapter II, n. 9.

movement by the repeated strumming of the tonic triad as well as by the two opening A-Lydian thematic statements. The pitch content of this mode also appears earlier in the work as the basis of a set of nontraditional tonal relations. The A-Lydian mode contains one tritone (A-D♯), which can be shown to be the boundary of the symmetrically reordered A-Lydian pitch content (A-E-B-F♯-C♯-G♯-D♯). This pitch collection, which appears in its Lydian scale order in Movement IV, unfolds on the background level of the opening fugue movement explicitly in the perfect-fifth ordering given above. The first statement of the chromatic fugue subject, in violas 1/2, begins and ends on A. Violins 3/4 answer this opening statement a fifth higher (on E). In turn, celli 1/2 answer on D, a fifth below the original statement. Through the end of the first section (to m. 31), the subsequent entries continue this unfolding of inversionally related fifths, ending on F♯ and C of the last two overlapping statements (Ex. 209a). The middle section of the movement (from the end of m. 33)[26] continues the succession of fifths, but with octave displacements (Ex. 209b). At the high point of the movement (m. 56), marked "*FFF*," the two inversionally related cycles converge at E♭ (tritone distance from A) in unisons and octaves. The dyads A-A and E♭-E♭ represent the dual axis (sum 6) of the alignment of the cyclic segments that have unfolded in the movement thus far. Thus, the ascending cycle (A-E-B-F♯-C♯-G♯-E♭) of the inversional pair of cycles unfolds the A-Lydian pitch-content in its perfect-fifth ordering. (Ex. 212).

209 *Music for Strings, Percussion, and Celesta*, Movement I

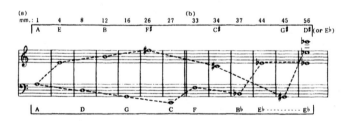

210 *Music for Strings, Percussion, and Celesta*

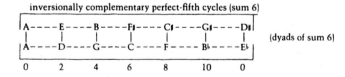

---

26 The middle section is defined as such by the fragmentation of the subject now in stretto, the removal of mutes, and first entry of a percussion instrument.

211 *Music for Strings, Percussion, and Celesta,* Movement I

The remainder of the middle section through the recapitulation (to m. 77) represents the return phase of these unfolding cycles. The high point on the held E♭ (m. 56) is extended by fifths at the next held notes, B♭ and F, the initial segment of the retransition (upbeat to m. 65) in turn extending the last to C. This section then closes with stretto entries on C and F♯, the entry pitches that closed the first section (see Ex. 209a). The recapitulation (end of m. 68 through m. 77), which now presents inverted statements of the fugue subject in close stretto, continues the cycles in the successive entry pitches (Ex. 211). The opening of the coda (mm. 77ff.) is a focal point for the reconvergence of both cycles on A-A. Then, both the prime and inverted forms of the subject are symmetrically aligned throughout this final section, the tritone range (A-E♭) of the final alignment (mm. 86–88) explicitly defining the dual axis as a primary foreground event. The held notes, D-E♭-E, which define the pitch content of the string accompaniment (to m. 81), are also symmetrical at sum 6, around the E♭-E♭ axis. Thus, the basic modal properties of the A-Lydian theme of Movement IV are foreshadowed in the symmetrical relations of the opening chromatic-fugue movement.

Another property of the diatonic theme of Movement IV is foreshadowed in the coda of the fugue movement. In Movement IV, the exclusively A-Lydian pitch-content of the first two linear thematic statements (mm. 5–13) is altered in the melodic variant of the theme. At m. 19, in the middle of this stretto, three new notes (D, A♯, and Fx) appear in the local cadential figure of violins 1/2. These notes are the first disruptive melodic elements outside the A-Lydian pitch-content. The note D first expands the latter (A-E-B-F♯-C♯-G♯-D♯) to an eight-note segment of the cycle of fifths; the next two notes (A♯ and Fx) further symmetrically expand this to nine and then ten notes. The first new note (D) linearly implies the presence of a second modal tritone (D-G♯). With the first (A-D♯), this second tritone implies the linear presence of cell Z-9/3 on the background level of the theme (Ex. 212). A special property of cell Z is that its two tritones allow it to be permuted around either of two axes of symmetry; in this case, the axis is explicitly sum 5 (A-D-D♯-G♯) or implicitly sum 11 (D-D♯-G♯-A). In the coda of Movement I

212 *Music for Strings, Percussion, and Celesta,* Movement IV

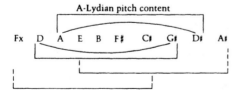

symmetrical expansion
around an axis of sum 5
(implied Z-9/3, A-D-D♯-G♯)
in the first two tritones, A-
D♯ and D-G♯)

213 *Music for Strings, Percussion, and Celesta*, Movement I, Coda

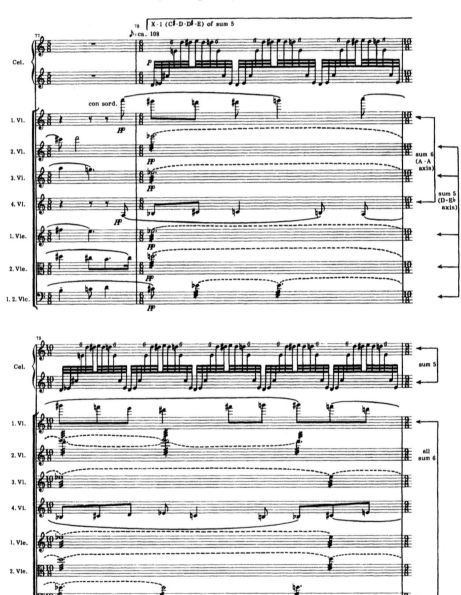

(mm. 78ff.), the first appearance of the celesta produces a sum-5 conflict with the sum-6 axis of the strings. The celesta simultaneously unfolds an ostinato pattern exclusively based on a chromatic tetrachord, cell X-1 (C♯-D-D♯-E), of sum 5.[27] The initial held D-E♭ of the strings (m. 78) is a pitch-class duplication of the X-1 axis (Ex. 213). However, the addition, at m. 79, of the third held note, E, extends the first two (D-E♭) to D-E♭-E. This produces a pivotal relationship between the sum-5 axis of the celesta and the sum-6 axis of the string group.

This conflict between sum 6 (axis A-A or E♭-E♭) and sum 5 (axis D-E♭ or G♯-A) is developed in Movement III. The movement closes with a progression from a partial statement of Z-6/0 (F♯-( )-C-F),[28] which is based on an implied axis of either sum 11 or sum 5, to the remaining tritone, C-F♯, of sum 6. Section I of the movement opens (mm. 1–5) with a complete statement of this Z cell (F♯-B-C-F). One of its tritones (B-F) is dropped after m. 5, leaving the sum-6 tritone (C-F♯) to be held as a pedal (Ex. 214). Then the rhapsodic viola theme, which unfolds above the held C-F♯, cadences at m. 9 on D-E. The dyads D-E and C-F♯ form the whole-tone tetrachord C-D-E-F♯, which represents a cadential convergence at sum 6.

Sections II (mm. 20f.) and III (mm. 35f.) of the movement, which round out the first phase of the arch-form,[29] further establish these interactions between sums 5 and 6. In section II, a new theme (mm. 23f., celesta) is introduced and accompanied by a combination of distinct ostinato patterns that unfold various transpositions of cell X. Violins 3 (in divisi) initiate the section with trill figures based on X-7 (G-A♭-A-B♭), at sum 5. The other cell-X ostinato patterns symmetrically unfold around the X-7 (sum-5) nucleus (Ex. 215): violins 4 (in divisi) enter in stretto with trills based on X-3 (D♯-E-F-G♭), a major third below X-7; the pitch content of the remaining patterns (glissandi in violin 2, chords in the piano, and tremolos in viola 1 and cello 1), through the opening of m. 28, is exclusively based on X-11 (B-C-C♯-D), a major third above the X-7 nucleus. (This large sum-5 symmetry is then dissolved in the cadential measures, 28–31, by the chromatic shifting away from the upper X-11 component.) At the same time, the celesta theme un-

27 This celesta statement of X-1 appears to be derived from one of the symmetrical segments (at m. 6) of the countersubject.

28 Cell Z-6/0 is the symmetrical complement of Z-9/3 and can be permuted around sum 5 (B-C-F-F♯) to form a symmetrical relationship with both Z-9/3 (A-D-D♯-G♯) and X-1 (C♯-D-D♯-E) of the same axis.

29 The arch form of Movement III can be outlined as follows:
(Bartók's lettering: ( )   A   B   C   D   E)
                            I   II   III   IV   V   VI
                            A   B   C   D   CB   A
The various factors that contribute to the formation of the arch (metronomic relationships, dynamics, orchestration, etc.) are given a detailed account by Judith Shepherd Maxwell in "An Investigation of Axis-Based Symmetrical Structures in Two Compositions of Béla Bartók" (D.M.Ed. thesis, University of Oklahoma, 1975), pp. 88–89, 101–3, 110–12.

214 *Music for Strings, Percussion, and Celesta,* Movement III, opening

folds all the chromatic tones (excluding E♭) between the initial E (m. 23) and the final D (m. 31), thus establishing the pitch content of the melodic line at sum 6 against the sum-5 accompaniment.

Section III is introduced (mm. 33–34) by a statement of the second phrase of the original fugue subject. The registral boundary of this statement is the tritone A-E♭, the two notes of which have represented the dual axis

215 *Music for Strings, Percussion, and Celesta*, Movement III,
mm. 20–28

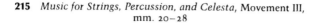

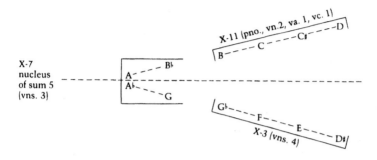

(A-A and E♭-E♭) of sum 6.[30] At the same time, tritone A-E♭ appears as part of a larger held chord, E♭-A-G♯-D (lower strings, piano, and celesta), that forms cell Z-3/9 (E♭-G♯-A-D) at sum 5. Throughout Section III (mm. 35–43), which is near the center of the arch-form, these two axes (sums 6 and 5) now appear in their most prominent and extensive development since the coda of Movement I. The E♭ is held throughout the entire section (in contrabass 2, the left hand of the piano, together or alternately in the two harps, and in the timpani). The dyad E♭-E♭ (or A-A) is immediately established as an axis at sum 6 (at m. 35) by the symmetrical harp figure (E♭-F♭-G♭-A♭-B♭-C-D-E♭) and the piano glissando from F♭ to D (Ex. 216). At the same time, the celesta plays two alternating pentatonic scales, E-G-A-B-D and E♭-G♭-A♭-B♭-D♭. These symmetrical scales (one with an axis of A-A, the other an axis of A♭-A♭) together produce a larger symmetry with an axis of A♭-A, or sum 5. Both sums (6 and 5) are supported by the opening piano figure (m. 35). The sum-6 dyad, F♭-D, which encompasses the glissando, is immediately joined by dyad D♭-E♭, and together they form a larger symmetry, cell X-1 (D♭-D-E♭-F♭). This produces a shift to sum 5 in the latter tetrachord (see Ex. 216).

At the beginning of the crescendo (m. 38), the harps begin to build symmetrically around the E♭-E♭ axis of sum 6. At this point, two new notes, A♭ and B♭, are added to the E♭ glissandi to form two alternating fourth dyads, E♭-A♭ and B♭-E♭, which together form a larger sum-6 symmetry (A♭-E♭/E♭-B♭). At m. 40, these harp glissandi add two new notes, D and F♭. (The latter two notes also form the sum-6 boundary of the piano glissando.) These alternating three-note groups imply partial Z-3/9 (E♭-A♭-( )-D) and Z-10/4 (B♭-E♭-F♭-( )), which together symmetrically intersect at the common tone, E♭ (i.e., axis E♭-E♭ of sum 6) (Ex. 217). The common missing note is the

<hr>

30 The significance of its position here as the boundary of the linear chromatic fugue segment (A-B♭-B-C-C♯-D-E♭), where the two notes together define an axis of sum 0 (C-C), will be discussed below in relation to Section IV and the final movement.

216 *Music for Strings, Percussion, and Celesta,* Movement III

Griffbezeichnung / indique la manière de toucher

other sum-6 axial dyad, A-A. (In the introductory passage to this section, at mm. 31–33, both these Z cells, E♭-A♭-A-D and B♭-E♭-E-A, appear complete, the common tritone A-E♭ being held in the tremolo and serving as the boundary of the fugue subject.)

At mm. 36–43, the tremolos of the two string groups form a large-scale symmetrical balance with the figures of the other instruments, the combination of which establishes the priority of the sum-6 axis on the background level of this section. At m. 36, the two string groups begin to unfold separate patterns of cell-X transpositions. The tremolo figures of the upper string group unfold a series of ascending X transpositions that begins with X-11 (C♭-C-D♭-D), at mm. 36–37, and ends, at mm. 41–43, with X-4 (E-F-F♯-G) in violins 1 and 3. This series of X cells (from mm. 36–43, upper strings), which produces all the semitones between the lowest note (C♭) of initial X-11 and the highest note (G) of cadential X-4, compositely forms a larger chromatic symmetry (C♭-C-D♭-D-E♭-E-E♯-F♯-G) around the basic axis (E♭-E♭) of sum 6 (Ex. 218). At the same time, the tremolos of the lower string group (above the held E♭ of contrabass 2) exclusively unfold ostinato repetitions of X-8 (A♭-B♭-B♭-C♭), which has an axis of symmetry of sum 7. The latter symmetrically balances sum 5 (celesta and piano) around the central sum-6 axis. Thus, on the highest architectonic level of Section III, the combination of texturally distinct symmetrical patterns (i.e., sum 5 in the celesta and piano; sum 6 in the timpani, harps, upper string group, and contrabass 2; and sum 7 in the remaining lower-string ostinato) compositely establishes the priority of the basic axis of symmetry (sum 6).

The symmetrical function of the two tritone components, A and E♭, as the dual axis of sum 6 (A-A or E♭-E♭) is transformed at the opening of Sec-

217 *Music for Strings, Percussion, and Celesta,* Movement III, mm. 40ff.

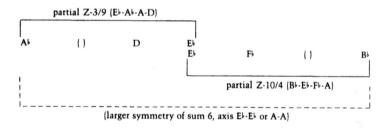

218 *Music for Strings, Percussion, and Celesta,* Movement III, mm. 36–43

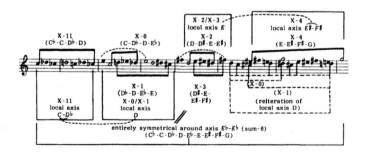

tion IV (mm. 45f.). At this point, which initiates the return phase of the arch-form of the movement,[31] these two pitch classes are absorbed into a new symmetrical context, where they now explicitly form a sum-o tritone (A-E♭) around a dual axis of either C-C or F♯-F♯.[32] From m. 46 through m. 54, the pitch content of the linear thematic material forms a five-note symmetrical segment, A-B♭-C-D-E♭, in which tritone A-E♭ is the boundary and C-C the axis. The held accompanying chord (mm. 45–54), which comprises all the remaining tones of the passage, outlines two diminished triads (F-A♭-B/C♯-E-G) (Ex. 219). Together, the latter form a six-note symmetrical segment also around the sum-o axis (C-C or F♯-F♯). This symmetrical reinterpretation, in which the two components of tritone A-E♭ are transformed from their positions in Section III as the sum-6 dual axis (A-A and E♭-E♭) to being a local tritone detail of a larger sum-o symmetry, foreshadows the diatonic role of this basic tritone in Movement IV (i.e., as the boundary interval of the symmetrical A-Lydian pitch content, A-E-B-F♯-C♯-G♯-D♯).

These two axes of even sums 6 and o, foreshadowed in Section II by specific transpositions of cell Y (at mm. 20ff., the essential notes of the violin trills outline Y-3, D♯-F-G-A, of sum o, while the successive downbeats of the violin glissandi outline Y-o, C-D-E-F♯, of sum 6), are further established in Section V, which follows the two middle sections of the movement. However, these basic even axes now appear in conjunction with new secondary odd axes. Whereas the movement opens and closes with Z-6/o at sum 11 (F♯-B-C-F) or sum 5 (B-C-F-F♯), Section V opens (m. 63) with a tremolo figure in the piano (then harps) exclusively based on the new odd axis B♭-C♭ of sum 9. Against this axis (mm. 63ff.), a theme unfolds in the strings in six canonic statements, the successive entry pitches outlining the three tritones D♭-G, A♭-D, and C♭-F. The first two are the tritones of Z-8/2 (A♭-D♭-D-G), while the third (C♭-F) forms part of Z-5/11 (F-B♭-C♭-F♭), the latter Z cell appearing complete at the end of the canon (mm. 73–74, strings). (Above this canon, the celesta arpeggiation begins, at m. 65, and ends, at mm. 72–73, with complete statements of Z-5/11.)[33] These six canonic entries and Z-5/11, which supplies the additional tritone B♭-E,[34] together form an octatonic

31 The juxtaposition of prime and retrograde statements of the theme, which leads to the dynamic climax at m. 54, contributes to the central position of this section in the symmetrical arch-form of the movement (see also n. 29, above).

32 As can be seen in Example 210, this is the converse of that relationship where tritone C-F♯ appeared as a sum-6 dyad around the dual axis of symmetry, A-A or E♭-E♭ (see also n. 30, above).

33 While the axial dyad B♭-C♭ of Z-5/11 is maintained in the celesta arpeggiation throughout, the other axial dyad, F♭-F, of this Z cell is chromatically altered, beginning with E♭ and D at m. 65. These and the subsequent chromatic alterations in the celesta are simply doublings of the tremolo figures in vnIII that unfold all the chromatic tones between D and A♭ (mm. 65–70). The latter (D-A♭) is one of the tritones of the presently unfolding canon outlining Z-8/2.

34 The canon is also introduced by the third phrase of the fugue subject, which is encompassed precisely by this tritone (B♭-E) that is missing from the octatonic-collection unfolding in the canonic entries.

219 *Music for Strings, Percussion, and Celesta,* Movement III,
mm. 44–47

*) kleineres instrument mit höherem Ton / instrument plus petit au son plus clair

220 *Music for Strings, Percussion, and Celesta,* Movement III, mm. 63ff.

(a)

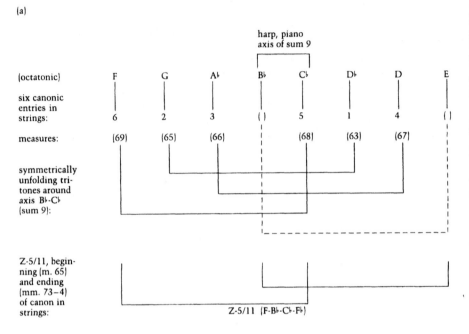

(b) Octatonic scale

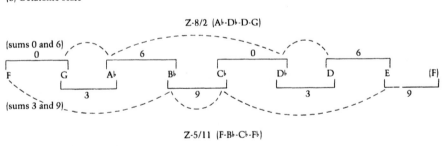

collection (Ex. 220a), the four tritones of which symmetrically unfold around the Bb-Cb axis (sum 9) of the harps and piano. This collection, on the one hand, is based on alternating dyads of odd sums 9 and 3 (i.e., the sums of Z-8/2 and Z-5/11), and on the other, on alternating dyads of even sums 6 and 0, which are the essential ones of the movement (Ex. 220b). Thus, while this canonic section produces a shift from the initial odd axes of the movement (sums 11 and 5) to sums 9 and 3, the basic axes of even sums 6 and 0 are maintained. (Section VI ends, at mm. 81–83, with a partial return to the opening Z-6/0, F♯-(·)-C-F, of sums 11 and 5, which then moves to the cadence on C-F♯ of basic sum 6.)

The significance of the main symmetrical scheme (see Ex. 220b), which is based on the axial relations of the primary even sums of the work (6 and 0) and the secondary odd sums (9 and 3), is supported by an earlier idea of Bartók regarding the fugue subject of Movement I. In the final version of the work, the only simultaneous statement of the fugue subject (on A) against its literal inversion (also on A) occurs in the coda of Movement I (mm. 77ff., vnI and vnIV). This inversional symmetry contributes to the establishment of sum 6 (A-A or E♭-E♭) as the primary axis of symmetry (Ex. 221a). However, on the first page of the early manuscript draft, Bartók presented a sketch of the fugue subject (on A) against its inversion (on C), suggesting the importance of one of the secondary odd axes (sum 9) (Ex. 221b). Thus, Bartók's sketch, which suggests sum 9 as a potentially basic axis of symmetry, supports the hypothesis that Bartók was interested in systematically generating the other axial possibilities inherent in the relationship of the primary even axes A-A (or E♭-E♭) and C-C (or F♯-F♯) of sums 6 and 0; that is, at the midpoint between any pairing of these sum-6 and sum-0 dyads (as one instance, between A-A and C-C, in which we find either the sum-9 dyad B♭-B or E-F), we have an odd axis of either sum 9 or sum 3.

221   *Music for Strings, Percussion, and Celesta*

(a) Movement I, coda, mm. 77ff., vnI and vnIV: axis of sum 6 (A-A or E♭-E♭)

(b) Sketch of fugue subject and its inversion (on C); first page of manuscript draft: axis of sum 9 (B♭-B or E-F) (see Illustration 8)

222 *Mikrokosmos,* No. 131, mm. 1–4

223 *Mikrokosmos,* No. 131, mm. 9–12

Strict inversional symmetry was demonstrated as early as 1908 in *Bagatelle No. II,* and similar procedures systematically occur in various pieces from the *Mikrokosmos* (1926–1939). These progressive pieces for piano were composed during Bartók's mature period, in which we find the most intensive and comprehensive exploitation of symmetrical pitch relations. *No. 131* ("Fourths") is entirely built on symmetrical chords, the opening measures of which establish the priority of sum 4 based on the axis of symmetry, D-D. A local disruption of sum 4 is produced (on the last chord of m. 3) by a sum-5 chord, A-D-E♭-A♭, which immediately returns to the original D-D axis at the first cadence (Ex. 222). Phrase b (mm. 9–12) introduces a new disruption (a sum-3 chord, G-C-E♭-A♭), which is locally juxtaposed with a symmetrical chord (G-C-F-B♭) of the earlier sum-5 disruptive axis (Ex. 223). This combination of sums 3 and 5 forms a larger symmetrical balance around the basic sum-4 axis. The latter is explicitly represented by the initial chord (F♯-B-F-B♭) of this phrase. The remaining two measures (11 and 12) of this phrase are now exclusively based on sum 3; thus, this prominent disruption of phrase b complements that (sum-5) of phrase a to establish exclusively the large-scale priority of sum 4 in section A (mm. 1–16). In section B (mm. 16ff.), the opening simultaneities (based on the original chord, B♭-E♭-D♭-G♭) and the complementary neighbor motions maintain the sum-4 axis. In the recapitulation (mm. 26ff.), an intervallic mutation occurs (m. 28) in the inverted statement of phrase b, so that the final chord of the measure (C♭-F♭-C-F) replaces the earlier sums 5 and 3 combination (m. 9) with basic sum 4 (Ex. 224). Thus, the formal scheme of symmetries is analogous to that of *Bagatelle No. II.*

In *No. 133* ("Syncopation"), two opposing concepts of tonal priority are established simultaneously by the juxtaposition of triadic and symmetrical constructions. The first phrase opens (mm. 1–2) with reiterations of a G-major triad against an unfolding symmetrical chromatic tetrachord, E♭-E-F-F♯ (Ex. 225). While the tonal priority of G is supported by the final statements of the dominant and tonic degrees (D and G) of this key, the opening juxtaposition tends to weaken the sense of G as the primary tonic sonority. Furthermore, the prominent addition of a held B♭ at the first cadential point transforms the traditional G-major construction into a major-minor symmetry (G-B♭-B-D), so that the latter now forms a symmetrical relation with E♭-E-F-F♯ around the same axis (either E-F or B♭-B) of sum 9 (Ex. 226). The closing dominant and tonic reiterations (D and G) of the traditional key of G

224 *Mikrokosmos*, No. 131, m. 28

225 *Mikrokosmos*, No. 133, mm. 1–3

226 *Mikrokosmos*, No. 133, mm. 1–3, analysis

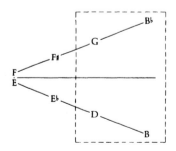

major also imply the sum-9 axis. Thus, both traditional and nontraditional pitch-constructions are ultimately absorbed into a scheme of symmetrical relations.

   The *Sixth Quartet* (1939) to some extent represents a return to the lyrical, Romantic style of the *First*. While the *Sixth Quartet* is less ambiguous than the *First* in its use of traditional harmonic functions, the fusion of such conservative elements as triadic constructions with the progressive concepts of symmetrical tonal relations reveals a mastery beyond that of the earlier work. Like the *First Quartet*, the *Sixth* is based on a large-scale symmetrical scheme of keys, the tonal priority of D in the latter work being established by an interlocking of traditional with progressive principles.[35] The opening segment of the Mesto theme (Ex. 227) contains, in microcosm, those tonal priorities that are telescoped into the large-scale tonal scheme of the four movements. The thematic segment temporally spans the tritone G♯-D, the significance of which is fully realized in the cadential extension of this segment in the concluding measures of the work. The thematic structure of Example 227 is outlined by the four tones of an interval-3/9 cycle, G♯-B-F-D, a symmetrical scheme from which the keys (D-B-F-D) of the four movements appear to be derived. (In the thematic material of the middle section, Rubato, of Movement II, G♯ occurs as a prominent pitch-class.) The priority of the D tonality is therefore established both as the axis of the symmetrical tonal scheme and as the root of the cadential triadic harmonies of the outer movements. Another set of symmetrical tonal relations is established by the cycle of transpositions of the Mesto theme by perfect fifths throughout the work: the first Mesto statement is initiated by G♯, the second by E♭, the third by B♭. In the opening of the finale, the theme appears in canon between vnI and vc, these two statements initiated, respectively, by C and F♯. This tritone is symmetrically related to the transpositional scheme of the preceding Mesto statements (giving us the overall symmetrical outline of G♯-C-E♭-F♯-B♭). Thus, in the *Sixth Quartet* Bartók returns to an interlocking of the triadic and symmetrical principles that had characterized the design of the *First Quartet*.

227   *Sixth String Quartet*, Movement I, opening segment of Mesto theme
in va

---

35 See Perle, "String Quartets," p. 8.

228 *Third Piano Concerto,* Movement I, mm. 4–6

In Movement I of the *Third Piano Concerto,* too, tonal centricity is established by an interlocking of principles from the two different tonal systems. While tonality is significantly determined by the use of the diatonic folk modes, tonal priority is also established by means of axes of symmetry. The movement outlines traditional key relationships that contribute to the establishment of a sonata plan. The primary key is E-Mixolydian, established by the piano in theme 1a and by the prominence of the E-major triad and final flute segment in the closing section. However, the melodic mixture of E-Mixolydian with E-Dorian produces major and minor thirds (G and G♯) (Ex. 228), which function both diatonically and as an axis of symmetry. This axial dyad (G-G♯), which is implied in the accompanying orchestral symmetry, E-F♯-( )-( )-A-B, expressly appears in the symmetrically related pitch-content (D-E-F♯-G-G♯-A-B-C♯) of the bimodal piano theme (mm. 2–6, beat 1).

In the remaining theme groups of the exposition and in the development section, axial pitches G and G♯ are expanded into separate keys in the larger traditional sonata scheme.[36] Axial pitch G is established as the initial tonality of theme 2 (m. 54) by the assertion of both the G-major and G-minor triads (Ex. 229). The latter mixture forms a four-note symmetry, G-B♭-B-D, that both establishes the tonal priority of the mediant, G, and produces a change from the original axis (G-G♯) of sum 3 to a new axis (B♭-B) of sum 9.

Whereas the former axis of symmetry resulted from the major–minor-third mixture of two diatonic modes, the latter axis (B♭-B) results from the G-major–minor mixture (G-B♭-B-D) that initiates the larger octatonic collection (m. 54), G-A♭-B♭-B-C♯-D-E-F (see Ex. 229). (The last note, F, is supplied by the trill on one "odd" note, E♭.) The alternating sum-3 and sum-9 dyads (G-A♭, B♭-B, C♯-D, E-F) that generate this octatonic scale (Ex. 230) reflect the long-range axial shift from sum 3 (G-G♯, or C♯-D) to sum 9 (B♭-B, or E-F). (The significance of these axes a minor-third apart was demonstrated in Ex. 181 in connection with the *Fourth String Quartet.*) The closing theme (mm. 68–74) reaffirms both the secondary key area of G, in the prominent statements of the G-major–minor chord (mm. 71–74), and the resulting B♭-B axis of sum 9.

36 Local traditional triadic progressions, such as the implied V-I root progression of E-Mixolydian/Dorian at mm. 1ff., timpani, and the explicit V-I progression initiating the relative major, G-Lydian, at mm. 18–19 (orchestral statement of theme 1a'), play a decisive role in establishing these traditional tonal areas.

229 *Third Piano Concerto*, Movement I, m. 54

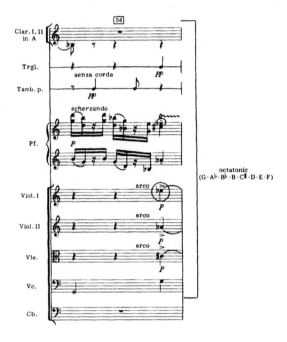

230 *Third Piano Concerto*, Movement I

The development section (mm. 75–112) begins a half-step higher, in A♭ major, which is prepared for (at mm. 73–74) by its dominant-seventh chord in the theme-1a segment. The A♭ root represents a tonal shift from the first component (G) to the second (G♯) of the original sum-3 axis (G-G♯). The entire development section then prolongs the key of A♭ by progressing from A♭ major through an ascending whole-tone sequence of major keys to G♯ major (m. 110, full orchestra, marked *fortissimo*). At the end of the retransition, based on a descending series of half-step trills, the G♯ tonality of the development returns (at mm. 117ff.) to its foreground position as one of the components of the original axis of symmetry, G-G♯. This contraction of the G and G♯ tonalities to their original axial positions in the trill figure, at mm. 117ff., ushers in the recapitulation (see Ex. 69). At this point, the opening motivic segment of theme 1a (m. 118), by being contrapuntally aligned with its literal inversion, forms three sum-3 dyads (E-B, F♯-A, and D-C♯) around the G-G♯ axial trill-figure. At the same time, the E-major–minor tonic chord, which was only implied in the original E-Mixolydian/Dorian mixture, is now explicitly established by its prominent placement in the first five measures (mm. 118–22) of the recapitulation. After some tonal digression, the closing theme (beginning at m. 175) reestablishes the E-major–minor tonic chord. The minor-third degree (G) is then dropped in the remainder of the movement (mm. 180ff.), implying a return to the opening E-Mixolydian mode. However, the final four measures add two notes (A♯ and F) to the exclusively Mixolydian pitch content (mm. 184–87), giving us seven notes (E-F-( )-G♯-A♯-B-C♯-D) of the octatonic scale that initiated theme 2 (m. 54). Thus, the movement ends with a foreground reflection (in this octatonic scale) of the axial dyads that alternate basic sums 3 and 9.

CHAPTER VII

Interaction of Diatonic, Octatonic, and Whole-Tone Formations

In even their earliest studies of Hungarian peasant music, Bartók and Kodály were aware that the traditional major and minor scales were generally absent from the authentic folk melodies. Instead, they had found a prevalence of the Greek or medieval church modes as well as some that were entirely unknown in modal art music.[1] The latter, unlike the church modes, are nondiatonic. One instance (G-A-Bb-C-Db-Eb-F)[2] is given in Example 231, where certain overlapping segments of the mode (Bb-C-Db-Eb-F and G-A-Bb-C-Db-Eb) are isolated by brackets. These segments are often extended by Bartók in his own compositions in order to derive larger divergent pitch collections; among these, the most significant are complete diatonic and octatonic scales.[3] While the diatonic extensions themselves appear as one or another of the church modes in the authentic folk melodies, the octatonic extensions represent abstract transformations of the original nondiatonic folk sources. In addition, in certain instances in Bartók's music, whole-tone scales may be understood as abstract extensions of one or another of the folk modes. All these extensions, whether or not they can be found among the authentic peasant melodies (the completed octatonic and whole-tone scales cannot), are exploited both melodically and harmonically by Bartók as pitch sets, that is, as divorced from traditional tonal functions. The diatonic and

1 *Béla Bartók Essays*, ed. Benjamin Suchoff (New York: St. Martin's Press, 1976), p. 363. The source is given in n. 9 of Chapter II.
2 As is pointed out by Suchoff, ibid., n. 1, Bartók transposed the *tonus finalis* of this as well as almost all of his folk-music transcriptions to G, after the system of Finnish ethnologist Ilmari Krohn.
3 See the definition of *octatonic* in Chapter IV, n. 14.

231 Non-diatonic mode found in Hungarian peasant music, with divergent overlapping modal segments

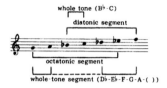

232 Diatonic and octatonic extensions of the nondiatonic folk mode in Example 231

(a) octatonic extension

(b) diatonic extensions (B♭-Aeolian mode)

(B♭-Dorian mode)

233 Diatonic modes of Example 232b represented as adjacent seven-note segments along the cycle of fifths

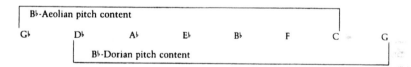

octatonic extensions of the nondiatonic folk mode given in Example 231 are illustrated in Example 232. While segment G-A-B♭-C-D♭-E♭ can be extended to a complete octatonic scale (G-A-B♭-C-D♭-E♭-F♭-G♭), segment B♭-C-D♭-E♭-F can be extended to either of two complete diatonic scales (B♭-Aeolian, B♭-C-D♭-E♭-F-G♭-A♭, or B♭-Dorian, B♭-C-D♭-E♭-F-G-A♭). Since these diatonic scales (as is the case with any of the modes) will appear in various permutations in Bartók's music, making a primary ordering ambiguous or undetermined, we shall conveniently represent the pitch content of these two diatonic collections as seven-note segments of the cycle of fifths (Ex. 233). While the interactions of diatonic, octatonic, and whole-tone sets are basic in many of Bartók's works, the derivation of these three sets from such nondiatonic folk modes as are given in Example 231 is most directly exploited in the *Cantata Profana* (1930) (discussed below).

In works as early as the *Fourteen Bagatelles for Piano*, Op. 6, diatonic and octatonic scales primarily function as pitch sets, which are fundamental in the generation of both melodic and harmonic material. In *Bagatelle No. XI*, diatonic-octatonic interactions are based on the development of segments common to the two sets. Near the end of the first large section (Ex. 234), the statement of the complete octatonic scale D♯-E♯-F♯-G♯-A-B-C-D (mm. 27–28, right hand) against the white-key diatonic collection F-C-G-D-A-E-B (mm. 26–29, left hand) serves as a basic frame of reference for octatonic-diatonic interactions throughout the piece. The fourth chords, which are intervallically reordered segments of the partial diatonic modes that unfold in the linear voice-leading,[4] mark a radical departure from the triad, the traditional harmonic structure.

The opening period is initiated by two antecedent-phrase segments (Ex. 235: mm. 1–4), of which the upper line outlines a five-note segment D-C-B-A-A♭ of the basic octatonic scale (see Ex. 234). The first four notes of this octatonic segment are harmonized by a succession of fourth chords (as occurs later at mm. 27–28 with the complete octatonic scale), these fourth chords together unfolding an eight-note segment of the cycle of fifths (B♭-F-C-G-D-A-E-B). The latter implies the presence of two adjacent seven-note

234   *Bagatelle No. XI*, mm. 26–29

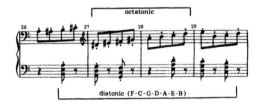

235   *Bagatelle No. XI*, mm. 1–4

4 These incomplete linear modal statements are foreshadowed at mm. 7–8 and 16–17 by complete white-key diatonic scales.

236 *Bagatelle No. XI, mm.* 5–9

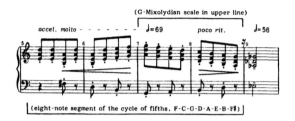

(diatonic) segments along the cycle of fifths (Bᵇ-F-C-G-D-A-E and F-C-G-D-A-E-B). (At the melodic addition of Aᵇ in mm. 2 and 4, which unambiguously establishes the upper melodic line as octatonic, the supporting minor-seventh chord Aᵇ-Cᵇ-Eᵇ-Gᵇ extends the entire eight-note interval-5/7 collection to eleven notes, Bᵇ-F-C-G-D-A-E-Cᵇ-Gᵇ-(-)Aᵇ-Eᵇ.) The upper melodic line of the consequent phrase (mm. 5–8) is now based on a complete G-Mixolydian (diatonic) scale (Ex. 236). While the G-Mixolydian pitch content implies the presence of a seven-note segment of the cycle of fifths (F-C-G-D-A-E-B), the melodic addition of Gᵇ at m. 9 extends the latter to eight notes (F-C-G-D-A-E-B-Gᵇ), that is, two adjacent seven-note (diatonic) collections along the cycle of fifths, F-C-G-D-A-E-B and C-G-D-A-E-B-Gᵇ. The harmonization (at mm. 5–8) by fourth chords is exclusively derived from these eight notes. (At the melodic addition of Gᵇ at m. 9, the new supporting fourth chord again extends the entire eight-note interval-5/7 collection to eleven notes.)

Diatonic considerations dictate that certain intervallic mutations within some of the perfect-fourth chords must occur in these harmonic progressions. These intervallic mutations include three-note simultaneities in the right hand, each segment of which joins a perfect fourth and a tritone (specific instances include C-F-B at mm. 1, 3, and 8; Bᵇ-E-A at mm. 1 and 3; and F-B-E at mm. 6 and 7). While the perfect-fourth chords are exclusively diatonic, the mutated type can be found in both diatonic and octatonic sets. This three-note structure prominently emerges at mm. 30–33 as a melodic cell in a series of linear overlappings.[5] At the Vivo, which immediately precedes the recapitulation (m. 61), overlapping transpositions and inversions of the cell appear as the basis of the melodic line, forming the four-note symmetry F-Bᵇ-B-E (i.e., cell Z-5/11) (Ex. 237). This four-note figure represents a transformation of the original three-note modal segment into a larger

---

5 According to Bartók, *Bartók Essays*, pp. 336–38, "Rumanian and Slovak songs show a highly interesting treatment of the tritone . . . in a Lydian mode. . . . These forms brought about the free use of the augmented fourth." (The original publication is given in n. 1 of Chapter I.) Bartók derived the present three-note cell from the principal tones of certain diatonic modes (see Ex. 236), in certain chords of the diatonic harmonization.

237 *Bagatelle No. XI, mm. 55–60*

symmetry, a transformation having little to do with the original diatonic material.[6]

The significance of the inversional symmetry in this context lies in its role as a link between the opening eight-note segments of the cycle of fifths (mm. 1, 3, 5–8) and the complete octatonic scale (mm. 27–28). An eight-note interval-5/7 segment, Bb-F-C-G-D-A-E-B (at m. 1), implies two adjacent seven-note diatonic collections along the 5/7 cycle (Ex. 238), the boundaries of which are the tritones Bb-E and F-B, precisely the two that form the cadential four-note symmetry F-Bb-B-E, or Z-5/11 (at mm. 55–60), leading into the recapitulation. (These two tritones originally appeared as unobtrusive details in the third and fourth chords of m. 1.) Furthermore (Ex. 239a), the eight-note 5/7 collection F-C-G-D-A-E-B-F♯ (mm. 5–8) similarly has two tritone boundaries, F-B and C-F♯, which form one (F♯-B-C-F) of two equivalent symmetrical partitions (Z cells) of the octatonic scale at mm. 27–28 (Ex. 239b). Thus, Bartók employs diatonicism in a nontraditional role here, in that certain of its symmetrical properties generate much of the basic harmonic material (perfect-fourth chords) while other diatonic derivations (the cell based on the perfect fourth and tritone) generate both new harmonic and melodic constructions (F-Bb-B-E, at mm. 55–60, and the octatonic scale).

In *Bagatelle No. XIV* the melodic and harmonic details are primarily based on interactions of diatonic and whole-tone formations. The melodic line (mm. 9–43) unfolds a series of held notes, C♯-F♯-B-E-A, outlining a perfect-fifth ordering of a pentatonic scale. The chordal accompaniment below the held axis note (B) of this pentatonic outline forms (through m. 26), together with the B, a five-note segment (G-A-B-C♯-Eb) of a whole-tone scale (Ex. 240). The held note (B) simultaneously appears as a common axis (or focal point) for both the melodic pentatonic outline and the chordal whole-tone collection. Furthermore, the specific symmetrical ordering (C♯-F♯-B-E-A and G-A-B-C♯-Eb) of both five-note groups is supported by the symmetrical placement of their common whole-tone segment, A-B-C♯.

The whole-tone collection, which remains incomplete (G-A-B-C♯-Eb-( )) through m. 26, is explicitly partitioned into two tritones, C♯-G and A-Eb,

6 See ibid., p. 338. The original publication is given in ibid.

238   *Bagatelle No. XI*, m. 1 or 3

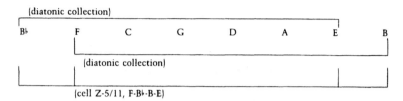

239   *Bagatelle No. XI*

(a) mm. 5–8

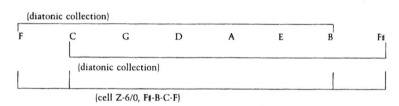

(b) mm. 27–28

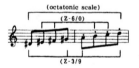

240   *Bagatelle No. XIV*, mm. 18–26

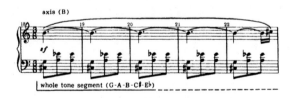

and the axis-note, B. At the ritard. molto (m. 27), one new note, E♯, is melodically added to complete the whole-tone scale and the third tritone, B-E♯. This tritone, which is melodically filled in by whole tones, anticipates a shift to the following diatonic passage (m. 28, last note, through m. 36). This passage, in C major, contains one tritone, F-B, an enharmonic spelling of the tritone (B-E♯) that temporally and registrally encompassed the entire melodic line of the preceding whole-tone passage (mm. 18–27). Furthermore, tritone F-B, as in the whole-tone passage, prominently encompasses the diatonic melody—F initiates it (m. 28, last eighth-note) and B (m. 36) is the highest and last of the diatonic pitch-classes to emerge (Ex. 241). Tritone F-B is also the boundary of an implied whole-tone tetrachord (F-G-A-B), that is, it can be formed by the only tones common to both these whole-tone and diatonic passages. At mm. 37ff., an incomplete segment (F-G-A-B-C♯-( )) of the whole-tone collection returns, this time presenting pitch-class F at the outset. Therefore the implied whole-tone tetrachord F-G-A-B remains the invariant subcollection between the larger alternating whole-tone and diatonic collections.

Such interactions of diatonic and whole-tone formations are established at the outset of the piece, where the D-major (tonic) triad appears in alternation with a whole-tone chord, F♯-G♯-B♭. At mm. 9–12, the addition of the first held note, C♯, extends the tonic triad to a major-seventh chord, D-F♯-A-C♯, and the whole-tone chord to an incomplete pentatonic formation, F♯-G♯-B♭-C♯-( ) (Ex. 242). The only apparent connection between these two alternating diatonic formations is the common perfect-fifth, C♯-F♯, melodically unfolding as the first two held notes. Thus, important invariants, or

241   *Bagatelle No. XIV*, mm. 28–36

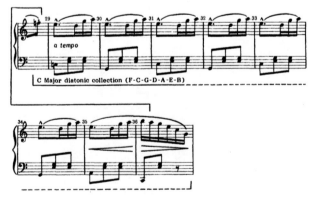

242   *Bagatelle No. XIV, mm. 9–12*

243   *Bagatelle No. VI, mm. 20–25*

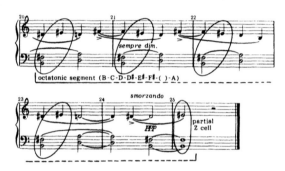

common segments, serve as links between these two different types of pitch collections.

In *Bagatelle No. VI*, basic pitch cells serve as links between larger octatonic and whole-tone collections. The final chord (B-E♯-F♯) is a subcollection of a larger octatonic segment (B-C-D-D♯-E♯-F♯-( )-A), the exclusive pitch-content of the last six measures, mm. 20–25 of the recapitulation (Ex. 243). In this passage, segment B-E♯-F♯ anticipates the cadential chord as a local detail on the second beat of each measure. This three-note segment, which similarly occurs in the opening phrases (mm. 2–4), represents an incomplete statement of cell Z. The complete four-note form (B-C-E♯-F♯) of the latter is symmetrically mapped into a larger segment of the octatonic scale (*B-C*-D-D♯-*E♯-F♯*), which includes the entire pitch-class content of the first phrase (excluding the initial A♯). The perfect-fifth boundary (B-F♯) of this octatonic segment, and of the present permutation of cell Z, is the only harmonic structure in the opening phrase.

The implied presence of this Z cell is also suggested in the opening, where its two tritones (F♯-C and B-E♯) are melodically contained within two gapped whole-tone cells, F♯-( )-A♯-C and B-( )-D♯-E♯, as the implied interval-class boundaries (Ex. 244). The last two measures (14 and 15) of the middle section anticipate the recapitulation with two expanded whole-tone segments, D-E-F♯-G♯-B♭-( ) (right hand) and D♯-F-G-A-B-( ) (both hands, beginning with m. 15, beat 2). The left-hand chromatic segment, D-C♯-C-B, may be understood as an interchange between C♯ and C, which complete the two whole-tone cycles (Ex. 245). Thus, the intervallic properties of cell Z link the larger octatonic and whole-tone collections.

In *Bagatelle No. IX*, a set of variations in unison, ambiguous melodic segments serve as links among whole-tone, diatonic, and octatonic formations. The second (repeated) phrase cadences, at m. 4, with a gapped whole-tone segment, E♭-( )-G-A (Ex. 246). At the opening of m. 5 this cadential for-

244 *Bagatelle No. VI, mm. 1–4*

245 *Bagatelle No. VI, mm. 14–15*

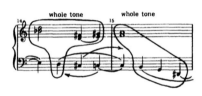

246 *Bagatelle No. IX, mm. 1–5*

247 *Bagatelle No. IX, mm. 11–14*

248   *Bagatelle No. IX*, mm. 17–19

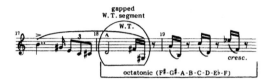

mation is extended by whole tones to A-( )-C♯-E♭-E♯-G. At the end of this section (m. 11, beat 2, through m. 12, beats 1–2), the latter, in turn, appears as a complete whole-tone scale, A-B-C♯-E♭-E♯-G. At the main thematic cadence (m. 12), a segment (A-B-C♯) from this whole-tone scale is reinterpreted, with the addition of the note D, as a diatonic segment, A-B-C♯-D (Ex. 247).

In the first variation (Tempo I), the second phrase (mm. 17–18) cadences on a transposition (D-( )-F♯-G♯) of the original gapped whole-tone segment, this time representing the other whole-tone scale. Whereas the first occurrence (m. 4) was expanded by whole tones in the following measure, the present occurrence is expanded by a complete octatonic scale, D-( )-F♯-G♯-A-B-C-D-E♭-F (mm. 18–19) (Ex. 248). Thus, the latter whole-tone segment (D-( )-F♯-G♯) serves as an invariant segment between whole-tone and octatonic scales. Such links appear to be a primary means of melodic progression throughout this as well as other bagatelles.

In the last of the *Eight Improvisations on Hungarian Peasant Songs*, Op. 20, for piano, interactions among four statements of a diatonic folk tune[7] and octatonic collections are primarily established by the intervallic properties of cell Z. Toward the end of strain 3 (end of m. 63), cell-Z formations emerge from their positions as incomplete details in larger pitch collections to being primary foreground events. Episode 3 (mm. 65–68) is partitioned into two transpositions of this cell, Z-10/4 (A♯-D♯-E-A) and Z-8/2 (G♯-C♯-D-G). In the remainder of the piece (mm. 69ff.), the final statement of the tune (strain 4) is exclusively accompanied by Z chords, three new transpositions, Z-7/1 (G-C-D♭-G♭), Z-11/5 (B-E-F-B♭), and Z-6/0 (F♯-B-C-F), being mixed with the former two. Thus, from the ending of strain 3 (mm. 63ff.), we get all but one (Z-9/3, A-D-E♭-A♭) of the six transpositions of cell Z.

The specific juxtapositions of these cell-Z statements in this final section (mm. 70ff.) produce both complete and incomplete octatonic collections (Ex. 249). The first pairing (m. 70, Z-8/2 and Z-11/5) produces the oc-

7 This tune, which was collected at Diósad in the district of Szilágy in 1914, is the basis of the following formal outline: strain 1 (mm. 5–12); episode 1 (mm. 13–27); strain 2 (mm. 28–38); episode 2 (mm. 38–52); strain 3 (mm. 53–64); episode 3 (mm. 65–68); strain 4 (mm. 69–82).

249 *Eighth Improvisation*, Op. 20, mm. 69ff.

tatonic collection G♯-B♭-B-C♯-D-E-F-G, the last Z chord of the measure
(Z-6/0) implying a shift to a new, partial octatonic formation, F♯-( )-( )-B-
C-( )-( )-F. The initial pairing (Z-8/2 and Z-11/5) returns at the second phrase
segment of the tune (m. 72), and the third chord of the measure (Z-7/1) is
paired at m. 74 with Z-4/10 to produce the final octatonic collection, E-G♭-
G-A-B♭-C-D♭-E♭. The remaining chords of the piece then juxtapose these Z
cells as incomplete octatonic segments.

These accompanying octatonic (Z-cell) chords, which at first appear to
be unrelated to the underlying diatonic folk-tune statement (strain 4), actually form a basic structural relationship with it. Strain 4 begins in the C-
Dorian mode (C-D-E♭-F-G-A-B♭-C), but at m. 74 a lowering of the sixth de-

gree, A, to A♭ produces a modal shift to C-Aeolian (C-D-E♭-F-G-A♭-B♭-C). The C-Dorian mode contains one tritone, E♭-A; C-Aeolian contains D-A♭. These two modal variants can be understood as two adjacent seven-note segments of the cycle of fifths (A♭-E♭-B♭-F-C-G-D and E♭-B♭-F-C-G-D-A), each explicitly bounded by its modal tritone (Ex. 250). These two tritones, A♭-D and E♭-A, together supply the one Z cell, Z-3/9 (E♭-A♭-A-D), or partial octatonic collection, that is missing from the accompanying chords.

This complementary relationship between the diatonic bimodal folk tune and the octatonic accompaniment is melodically implied in the structure of the strain-4 statement of the tune. While the bimodal melody, from m. 69 through m. 80, beat 2, is exclusively based on the pitch content outlined in Example 250 (see also Ex. 249), a codetta (m. 80, beat 3) is initiated by a new, chromatically altered note, G♭. This melodically produces a partial statement of Z-6/0 (G♭-( )-C-F) with the preceding two notes. The latter Z cell and its octatonic complement, Z-3/9 (E♭-A♭-A-D), which is implied by the tritones of the bimodal theme (see Ex. 250), together form seven notes of the octatonic collection, G♭-A♭-A-( )-C-D-E♭-F, that remained incomplete in the accompaniment. Thus, the tritone properties of cell Z link the bimodal folk tune with the octatonic chords.

This complementary diatonic-octatonic interaction is also a culmination of a long-range relationship in the piece. The introductory measures are based on a tetrachord, C-E♭-A♭-D, that implies the presence of a partial statement of Z-3/9 (E♭-A♭-( )-D).[8] This transposition of Z is precisely the one missing from the final Z chords of the piece and is supplied by the tritones (E♭-A and A♭-D) of the final C-Dorian/C-Aeolian statement of the tune. One chromatic alteration, from A♭ to A, (at m. 6, accompaniment), completes Z-3/9 (E♭-A♭-A-D) (Ex. 251); A and A♭ also represent the chromatic

250 *Eighth Improvisation*, Op. 20, mm. 69ff., theme, C-Aeolian and C-Dorian as overlapping segments of the cycle of fifths

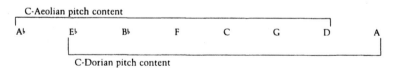

C-Aeolian pitch content

| A♭ | E♭ | B♭ | F | C | G | D | A |

C-Dorian pitch content

251 *Eighth Improvisation*, Op. 20, m. 6, Z-3/9 (E♭-A♭-A-D)

8 The significance of the remaining note, C, will be discussed below.

252   *Eighth Improvisation, Op. 20, opening*

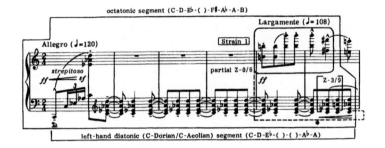

253   *Eighth Improvisation, Op. 20, opening, shared tritone boundary of C-Aeolian and B-Dorian pitch content*

difference between the final C-Dorian and C-Aeolian mixture in strain 4 (see Ex. 250). Furthermore, both these diatonic modes are foreshadowed in the pitch content (C-D-E♭-( )-( )-A♭-A-( )) of the opening chordal accompaniment (mm. 1–6). At the same time, the latter collection ambiguously implies an octatonic segment, and this is confirmed by the entry (mm. 5–6) of the first two pitch-classes, B and F♯, of the theme (Ex. 252). While all four notes of Z-3/9 (E♭-A♭-A-D) are present, these two notes, B-F♯, and the remaining held note, C, together form a partial occurrence of Z-0/6 (C-( )-F♯-B). The thematic entry, therefore, expands the ambiguous bimodal-octatonic accompaniment to a seven-note octatonic segment, C-D-E♭-( )-F♯-A♭-A-B.

The initial B-F♯ of the theme, an octatonic extension of the accompaniment (i.e., one of the perfect fourths, or fifths, of Z-0/6, C-( )-F♯-B), simultaneously functions as the basic fifth of the B-Dorian melody (mm. 5–12). Although this mode represents a shift from the introductory C-Aeolian tonality, it contains the same tritone (D-G♯, or D-A♭) as the latter (Ex. 253). (By reordering the pitch content of both modes as seven-note segments of the cycle of fifths, we see that one is the tritone transposition of the other, their tritone boundary being the only element in common.) The tritone D-A♭, because it is also found in the opening Z-3/9 (E♭-A♭-A-D), serves as a link between the B-Dorian folk tune and the ambiguous C-Aeolian or octatonic accompaniment.

Not only do the two tritones of Z-3/9, E♭-A and A♭-D, serve as the octatonic link with the C-Aeolian/C-Dorian combination of the chords, mm. 1–6 (see Ex. 250), but tritone A♭-D also functions as a link with a similar bimodal combination in the melodic line, from the opening of the theme (m. 5) through the first local cadential point of Episode 1 (m. 17, beat 1). The B-Dorian mode of the theme is altered at m. 17 of the episode by a lowering of the sixth degree (G♯) to G, which produces a modulation to B-Aeolian. The B-Dorian mode (B-C♯-D-E-F♯-G♯-A-B) contains the tritone D-G♯, the latter (B-C♯-D-E-F♯-G-A-B), C♯-G. The pitch content of these two modal variants (B-Dorian and B-Aeolian) can be understood as two adjacent seven-note segments of the cycle of fifths, each bounded by its modal tritone (Ex. 254). These two tritones, D-G♯ and G-C♯, form a new Z cell, Z-8/2 (G♯-C♯-D-G), implying a shift to a new octatonic collection, G♯-( )-( )-C♯-D-( )-( )-G. The latter is then established, at mm. 17–18, by a linear joining of D-G from Z-8/2 with its complete complement, Z-11/5 (B-E-F-B♭) to give us six notes (D-E-F-G-( )-B♭-B-( )) of this octatonic collection. Then, at m. 19, articulations 1–4, this is expanded to seven notes, D-E-F-G-A♭-( )-B-D♭.

The accompanying chords (mm. 7–16), which unfold consecutive complete and partial octatonic collections (Ex. 255), produce maximal diver-

254 *Eighth Improvisation, Op. 20, mm. 5–17, theme, B-Dorian and B-Aeolian as overlapping segments of the cycle of fifths*

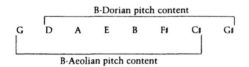

255 *Eighth Improvisation, Op. 20, mm. 7–17*

256   *Eighth Improvisation*

(a) mm. 28–29

basic octatonic collection
(C-D-Eb-F-Gb-Ab-A-B)

(b) mm. 38–40

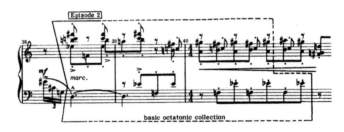

gence from the bimodal linear thematic material. However, at the first variation of the folk tune (strain 2, m. 28), the ambiguous diatonic-octatonic
tetrachord (D-C-B-A) of the melodic line, together with the accompaniment
(mm. 28–29, third eighth-note), return to a complete statement of the original octatonic collection (C-D-Eb-F-Gb-Ab-A-B) (Ex. 256a). After a dissolution of this union between melody and accompaniment, Episode 2 (mm.
38–40) more extensively reestablishes this basic octatonic collection (Ex.
256b).

Strain 3 (mm. 53–64), the second variation of the folk tune, is a focal
point in the development of diatonic and octatonic interactions. A tritone
relationship similar to that (see Ex. 253) which links the C-Aeolian and B-
Dorian modes on midground and background levels of the piece is established in strain 3 as a primary foreground event. This strain is unique among
the four in that it simultaneously presents two diatonic lines in canon at the
tritone. The upper line is in the E-Dorian mode; the lower line mixes Bb-
Dorian with Bb-Aeolian. The pitch content of the E-Dorian and Bb-Dorian,
which are tritone transpositions of one another, have only one element (tritone G-C#) in common (Ex. 257). At m. 58, the chromatic lowering of the
Bb-Dorian sixth degree (G) to Gb produces a modulation to Bb-Aeolian, permitting the only other melodic implication of a modal tritone (Gb-C) in the

passage. These two tritones imply the presence of Z-1/7 (D♭-G♭-G-C), which then explicitly emerges (end of m. 62 through beginning of m. 63) as a local harmonic intersection of the canonic lines. The specific contrapuntal alignment immediately preceding this point also permits an harmonic occurrence of Z-10/4 (B♭-E♭-E-A); these two complementary Z cells (Z-1/7 and Z-10/4 form an octatonic intersection (D♭-E♭-E-F♯-G-A-B♭-C) between the modal canonic lines (Ex. 258). At m. 63, beat 2, through m. 64, the two melodic (diatonic) fourths, B♭-E♭ and E-A, are then vertically aligned to form Z-10/4 as the exclusive harmonic basis for the ending of the canon. The initial alignment of the canonic statements (mm. 53–56) also permits an intersection between two melodic (diatonic) fourths, F-B♭ and B-E, to produce Z-5/11 (F-B♭-B-E) harmonically (Ex. 259). The remaining notes, A♭-C♯-D-G (through m. 56, A♭ of the lower line), form its complement (Z-8/2) to give us this initial octatonic intersection between the canonic lines. The next episode (mm. 65–68) is exclusively based on Z-8/2 from the initial octatonic collection and Z-10/4 from the final one of the canon. Thus, while the canon of strain 3 is a focal point of the large-scale diatonic-octatonic relations, it also foreshadows, with Episode 3, the two complete octatonic collections of the final section (see Ex. 249).

257 Modes of *Eighth Improvisation*, strain 3

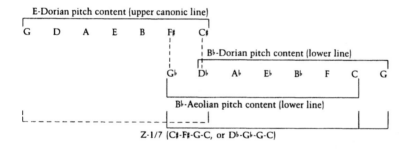

258 Complementary Z Cells Forming Octatonic Intersection in *Eighth Improvisation*, Op. 20, mm. 61–64

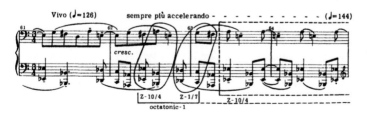

259 Complementary Z Cells Forming Octatonic Intersection in *Eighth Improvisation*, Op. 20. mm. 53–56

These diatonic-octatonic interactions are suggested in the *First Improvisation*, which is based on three statements of a Hungarian folk tune in C-Dorian. The combined pitch-content of the first statement and its accompaniment (mm. 1–4) remains exclusively within the C-Dorian mode. From m. 9 through m. 10, beat 2, the initial C-Dorian tetrachord, C-D-Eb-F, of the third melodic statement and the accompaniment (through the grace-note, Gb) exclusively produce the only complete octatonic collection (C-D-Eb-F-Gb-Ab-A-B) of the movement (Ex. 260).[9] Tetrachord C-D-Eb-F, therefore, serves as the link between the C-Dorian melodic line (C-D-Eb-F-G-A-Bb-C) and this octatonic collection (C-D-Eb-F-Gb-Ab-A-B). At m. 10, beats 3–6 (see Ex. 260), the tune unfolds the diatonic notes G-A-Bb, giving us a partial statement of the remaining upper C-Dorian tetrachord, G-A-Bb-C. The latter is complemented by the accompanying segment, Gb-Db-Bb, to form a new, partial octatonic collection, Db-()-()-Gb-G-A-Bb-(). Therefore, while the lower diatonic tetrachord, C-D-Eb-F, appeared as the invariant element between the C-Dorian mode and complete octatonic-0 (Ex. 261a), the upper diatonic tetrachord (G-A-Bb-()) appears as the invariant element between the C-Dorian mode and partial octatonic-1 (Ex. 261b).

The second statement of the tune (mm. 5–8) serves as a transition between the exclusively diatonic first section (mm. 1–4) and the exclusively octatonic opening of the third (mm. 9–10). The grace-note, Gb, at m. 10, which functions as an elision between the octatonic-0 and octatonic-1 collections (see Ex. 260), appears at the opening of the second statement (m. 5) as the first disruptive element outside the C-Dorian mode. Both the tune and the accompaniment, from m. 5 through m. 6, beat 2, are entirely within the spectrum of C-Dorian, except for one chromatic note, Gb (Ex. 262). The presence of Gb transforms the diatonic properties of this accompanying segment into a partial octatonic-1 collection, ()-Eb-()-Gb-G-A-Bb-C, thereby producing a diatonic-octatonic conflict between the C-Dorian tetrachord, C-

260 *First Improvisation*, Op. 20, mm. 9f.

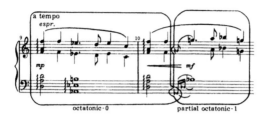

261 Invariant Tetrachords (or Tetrachordal Segments) between Diatonic
and Octatonic Collections in *First Improvisation*, Op. 20

(a) m. 9f.

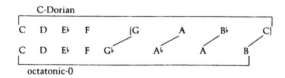

(b) m. 10, beats 3–6

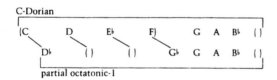

262 Octatonic Interpenetration of C-Dorian in *First Improvisation*,
Op. 20, mm. 5–8

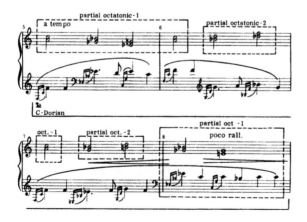

D-E♭-F, and the accompaniment. In the remainder of the second statement (see Ex. 262), the alternations between segments of the octatonic-1 and octatonic-2 collections in the accompaniment continue such conflicts with the tune. The ending of this statement (m. 8) is a return to a revised segment (E♭-G♭-G-B♭) of the initial octatonic-1 collection. This time, however, the accompanying and melodic segments, rather than conflicting with each other, map into a larger octatonic-1 segment, ( )-E♭-E-G♭-G-( )-B♭-C. This segment then moves, at the opening of the third statement (mm. 9ff.), to the complete octatonic-0 collection.

In the *Second Improvisation*, diatonic and octatonic collections appear in alternating folk-tune and episodic passages. The four identical strains of the tune are transposed by major thirds (in C, E, A♭, and C). The first linear thematic statement (mm. 1–9) begins in C-Mixolydian and modulates, at m. 7, to C-Dorian (Ex. 263a). This bimodal combination contains two tritones (E-B♭ and A-E♭), implying a midground-level presence of Z-10/4 (B♭-E♭-E-A). Each successive transposition of the theme, which similarly moves from a Mixolydian to a Dorian mode, presents two new tritones: strain 2 (mm. 14–22), in E-Mixolydian/Dorian, implies the presence of Z-2/8 (D-G-

263   *Second Improvisation*, Op. 20

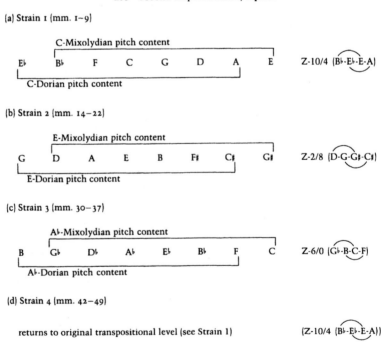

(a) Strain 1 (mm. 1–9)

C-Mixolydian pitch content

| E♭ | B♭ | F | C | G | D | A | E | Z-10/4 (B♭-E♭-E-A) |

C-Dorian pitch content

(b) Strain 2 (mm. 14–22)

E-Mixolydian pitch content

| G | D | A | E | B | F♯ | C♯ | G♯ | Z-2/8 (D-G-G♯-C♯) |

E-Dorian pitch content

(c) Strain 3 (mm. 30–37)

A♭-Mixolydian pitch content

| B | G♭ | D♭ | A♭ | E♭ | B♭ | F | C | Z-6/0 (G♭-B-C-F) |

A♭-Dorian pitch content

(d) Strain 4 (mm. 42–49)

returns to original transpositional level (see Strain 1)   (Z-10/4 (B♭-E♭-E-A))

264   Bimodal Combinations in *Second Improvisation*, Op. 20

(a) Strain 1 (mm. 1–5)

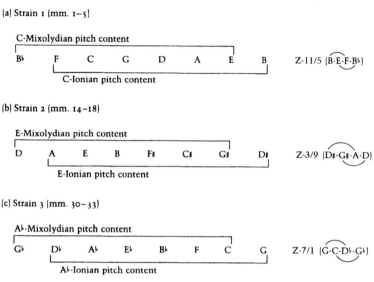

On the contrapuntal level, the first half of each thematic statement (through the first local cadential point), with the accompanying semitone, produces a second bimodal mixture. Semitone B-C (mm. 1–5) adds a raised seventh degree (B) to strain 1 to produce a bimodal combination of C-Mixolydian/Ionian (Ex. 264a). The two tritones (B-F and E-B♭) contained within imply a midground-level presence of Z-11/5 (B-E-F-B♭). Each successive combination of theme and semitone, which similarly produces a Mixolydian/Ionian mixture, contains a new tritone pairing: strain 2 (mm. 14–18), in E-Mixolydian/Ionian, implies the presence of Z-3/9 (D♯-G♯-A-D) (Ex. 264b); and strain 3 (mm. 30–33), in A♭-Mixolydian/Ionian, implies the presence of Z-7/1 (G-C-D♭-G♭) (Ex. 264c). (The recapitulation, at strain 4, eliminates the original semitone, B-C, from the accompaniment.) These pairs of modal tritones together imply a background-level unfolding of all three odd-numbered Z cells (Z-11/5, Z-3/9, and Z-7/1).

G♯-C♯) (Ex. 263b); strain 3 (mm. 30–37), in A♭-Mixolydian/Dorian, implies the presence of Z-6/0 (G♭-B-C-F) (Ex. 263c); and strain 4 (mm. 42–49) returns to the original transpositional level (Ex. 263d). Within the succession of thematic statements, therefore, the pairs of modal tritones together imply a background-level unfolding of all three even-numbered Z cells (Z-10/4, Z-2/8, and Z-6/0). The latter may be considered a background-level adumbration of the same three Z cells (see Ex. 249, mm. 81–82 of *Improvisation No. VIII*) that emerge as the final primary foreground events of the work.

In the original sketch of the first thematic statement, the left hand at m. 4 contains a minor-third dyad, B♭-D♭, instead of the semitone B-C of the final version. This dyad (B♭-D♭) of the early version (Ex. 265a) forms part of a local symmetrical chromatic progression (mm. 3–4) from B-C to B♭-D♭, whereas the final version (Ex. 265b) retains B-C in both measures, perhaps so that the exclusive bimodal pitch collection (C-Mixolydian/C-Ionian) of the first phrase (mm. 1–5, first eighth) is not disrupted.

The pitch content of Episode 1 (mm. 10–13), with the exception of one chromatic note, A♯, is exclusively based on seven notes of octatonic-0, B♯-D-D♯-E♯-F♯-( )-A-B (Ex. 266). One of the two Z cells (Z-3/9, D♯-( )-A-D) that form this collection remains incomplete. At the opening of strain 2 (see Ex. 264b), the bimodal tritones (D♯-A and G♯-D) imply the complete form of the latter. Episode 3 (Ex. 266b: m. 37 through the opening of strain 4, m. 42, beat 1), with the exception again of the chromatic note, A♯, represents a return to seven notes of octatonic-0 (C-D-( )-F-F♯-G♯-A-B). (This time, however, G♯ is supplied and D♯ is missing.) The end of the middle episode (m. 25, beat 2) through the opening of strain 3 (m. 30, beat 1) (Ex. 266c) is based exclusively on a segment of octatonic-2, D-( )-( )-G-A♭-B♭-B-( ). In the following linear thematic statement of strain 3 (see Ex. 266c), partial Z-8/2 (D-G-A♭-( )) from the latter octatonic collection is completed by its inversion, G-A♭-D♭, at m. 30. Thus, the tritone properties of cell Z, which serve as significant structural elements on the midground level of the bimodal folk-tune statements, function as links between the latter and the octatonic episodes.

In the *Seventh Improvisation*, diatonic and octatonic collections again have elements in common. The prevailing tonality of the opening statement

265   *Second Improvisation*, Op. 20, first thematic statement, comparison of original sketch with final version

(a) Preliminary sketch, mm. 3–5 (see Illustration 9)

(b) Final version, mm. 1–5

266 *Second Improvisation,* Op. 20

(a) Episode 1 (mm. 10–13)

(b) Episode 3 (mm. 37–42)

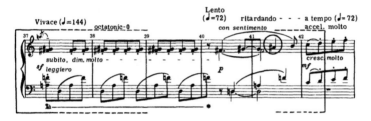

(c) Episode 2 (mm. 25–30)

of the folk tune (mm. 1–11) is C;[10] the first two phrases suggest C-Aeolian, the last two C-Phrygian. The local cadential points of the tune are punctuated by symmetrical chords, each of which produces a modal conflict with the linear diatonic material. The first vertical construction, C-E♭-A♭-B (or A♭-major–minor chord, A♭-B-C-E♭), introduces one new note, B (Ex. 267), which is a chromatic alteration of the Aeolian seventh degree, B♭ (m. 4); this produces a bimodal conflict in the first two phrases between the modes of C-Aeolian (C-D-E♭-F-G-A♭-B♭-C) and C-harmonic-minor (C-D-E♭-F-G-A♭-B-

---

10 While the opening melodic segment (mm. 1–3) is tonally ambiguous, the original folk tune, from Lengyelfalva in the district of Udvarhely (originally transcribed in the key of G, as are Bartók's other folk-tune transcriptions), is initiated by an ornament that supplies the tonic.

267 *Seventh Improvisation*, Op. 20, strain 1, mm. 1–11

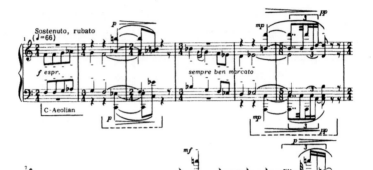

C). At mm. 5–6, a second vertical construction, A-B-C-D (A-minor tetra-chord), introduces two new notes, A and B, which are chromatic alterations of the Aeolian sixth and seventh degrees, A♭ and B♭; this produces another bimodal conflict with the tune by suggesting C melodic-minor (C-D-E♭-F-G-*A*-*B*-C). The final vertical construction of strain 1, F♯-A-D-F (or D-major–minor chord, D-F-F♯-A), which punctuates the ending of the tune (mm. 10 and 11), introduces two new notes, F♯ and A, against the linearly unfolding C-Phrygian scale, C-D♭-E♭-F-G-A♭-B♭-C. Whereas the first two chords (C-E♭-A♭-B and A-B-C-D) remain within the limits of certain tradi-tional modal scales built on C, the last one (D-major–minor) produces a nontraditional modal conflict with the tune by preparing for the octatonic scale (C-D-E♭-F-F♯-G♯-A-B)[11] that opens Episode 1 (mm. 12–13, beat 2) (Ex. 268).

The pitch relations that establish the D-major–minor chord as a pivot between the C-polymodal context of strain 1 and octatonic-0 of the Episode are as follows: the first symmetrical chord, C-E♭-A♭-B, which is ambigu-ously common to both the C-harmonic–minor and octatonic-0 scales, sym-metrically expands in contrary minor tenths to the next chord, A-C-B-D; the latter, which is ambiguously common to both the C-melodic-minor and

11 The priority of C in this nontraditional, symmetrical collection is established by the C pedal from the final note of the tune (mm. 11–12).

octatonic-o scales, expands in contrary minor tenths to the final symmetry, F♯-A-D-F. This cadential statement of the D-major–minor chord completes the octatonic collection that has been ambiguously unfolding in the first two (C-modal) chords (Ex. 269). At m. 13 (beats 1–2) of the Episode, the two major-minor chords of strain 1 (C-E♭-A♭-B and F♯-A-D-F) then appear in symmetrical proximity to give us the octatonic collection as an isolated foreground event.

A direct link between the linearly stated folk-tune and the octatonic-o collection is established at each of the local cadential points of the melodic statement. The held cadential diatonic tones of the tune (F, at mm. 2–3, E♭,

268 *Seventh Improvisation*, Op. 20, Episode 1, mm. 12–13

269 *Seventh Improvisation*, Op. 20, strain 1, three chords

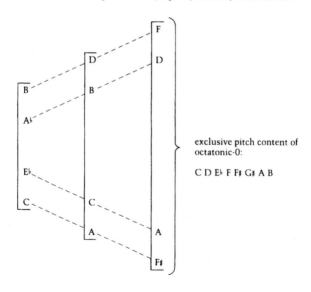

at mm. 5–6, and C, at mm. 10 and 11) are each harmonically given an octatonic interpretation by the accompanying chord, so that F becomes part of
octatonic segment C-E♭-*F*-A♭-B, E♭ part of A-C-*E♭*-B-D, and C part of F♯-
A-*C*-D-F. Furthermore, these three prominent cadential tones, which together represent a segment of the lower tetrachord built on C, are the only
elements common to all four C modes of strain 1 (Aeolian, harmonic-minor,
melodic-minor, and Phrygian) and octatonic-0. This pitch-class invariance
contributes to the establishment of C as the principal tonality of the piece.
(The cadential chord of strain 1, F♯-A-*C*-D-F, also serves as a focal point for
embellishing motions in Episode 1, the opening of strain 2, and the last
three measures of the coda.)

The second strain of the tune (mm. 16–21, left hand, then right) is transposed to the bimodal key of G-Aeolian–Phrygian, the previously held cadential C of strain 1 and the episode becoming the initial note of the new melodic statement. The first three diatonic notes of this strain, C-D-E♭ (m. 16),
are harmonically interpreted by the accompanying chords as part of a complete statement of octatonic-0 (Ex. 270). Furthermore, the new pitch level of
the tune (on G) permits yet another diatonic-octatonic link. The pitch content of the G-Aeolian-Phrygian melodic line can be conveniently ordered as
two adjacent seven-note segments of the cycle of fifths (Ex. 271), each encompassed by the two implied modal tritones, E♭-A and A♭-D. Together,
the latter form one (Z-3/9, E♭-A♭-A-D) of two equivalent symmetrical seg-

270   *Seventh Improvisation*, Op. 20, strain 2, m. 16

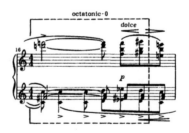

271   *Seventh Improvisation*, Op. 20, strain 2, mm. 16–21

G-Aeolian pitch content							
A♭	E♭	B♭	F	C	G	D	A

G-Phrygian pitch content

Z-3/9 (E♭-A♭-A-D)

272 *Fourth String Quartet*, Movement I, mm. 40–43, vnI

(a) Two whole-tone (or diatonic) tetrachords, Y-6 and Y-1

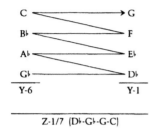

Y-6   Y-1

Z-1/7 (D♭-G♭-G-C)

(b) Eight-note segment of the interval-5/7 cycle

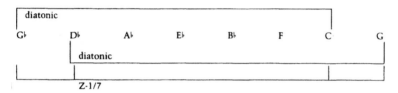

ments of octatonic-0. This implicit cell-Z connection between the bimodal and octatonic structures anticipates a more foreground expression of this relationship at the opening of the *Eighth Improvisation* (see Ex. 251). Thus, various symmetrical partitions of the octatonic scale serve as invariant or common links between the octatonic scale and the bimodal diatonic properties of the folk tune.

In the *Fourth String Quartet*, the tritones of cell Z are fundamental in linking whole-tone, diatonic, and octatonic collections. At mm. 40–42 of Movement I, the linear thematic statement in vnI (Ex. 272a) outlines two transpositions of cell Y (Y-6/Y-1), the tritone ranges (G♭-C and D♭-G) of which produce Z-1/7 (D♭-G♭-G-C). The two whole-tone Y tetrachords can be reordered to form the pitch content of an eight-note interval-5/7 segment (Ex. 272b), the latter of which implies the presence of two adjacent seven-note diatonic collections (G♭-D♭-A♭-E♭-B♭-F-C and D♭-A♭-E♭-B♭-F-C-G) along the cycle of fifths. The two tritones of cell Z (D♭-G and G♭-C) also encompass these interval-5/7 (i.e., diatonic) formations. At m. 41 of this linear thematic statement (Ex. 273), a gapped segment D♭-( )-F-G, whose tritone range is subdivided into intervals 2 and 4, is filled in by E♭ on the final eighth-note of the measure to complete this whole-tone tetrachord. At m. 42, an interval-5/7 transposition (G♭-( )-B♭-C) of this gapped segment is anal-

273   *Fourth String Quartet*, Movement I, mm. 41–42, vnI

274   *Fourth String Quartet*, Movement II, mm. 243–46, va and vc

275   *Fourth String Quartet*, Movement I, mm. 16–18, vns

ogously filled by A♭. At the opening of the quartet (third quarter-note of m. 1), an equivalent gapped cell (C-( )-E-F♯) is stated vertically. In vnI at mm. 1–2, the linear descent from F♯ to C fills in this C-( )-E-F♯ cell by whole-tones. Thus, the linear statement in vnI at mm. 40–42 and the opening phrase (mm. 1–2) *symmetrically* fill in the tritone of gapped cell Y or the double tritones of cell Z as whole-tone (or diatonic) segments.

   Near the end of Movement II, va and vc at mm. 243–46 present a complete octatonic scale, D-E-F-G-G♯-A♯-B-C♯ (Ex. 274). This scale, which joins four tritones, can be symmetrically partitioned into two Z cells, Z-2/8 (D-G-G♯-C♯) and Z-11/5 (B-E-F-A♯). This octatonic statement, which (analogous to the eight-note interval-5/7 segment) is bounded by the tritones of cell Z, retrospectively serves as a frame of reference for incomplete octatonic collections that unfold throughout Movement I. The vnII and vnI at mm. 15ff. play canonic statements that encompass the two tritones (C♯-G and G♯-D) of Z-8/2. The canonic subject in vnII contains (end of mm. 16–17) a linear statement of a gapped segment, C♯-D♯-( )-G, and the canonic answer in vnI (end of mm. 17–18) its interval-5/7 transposition, G♯-A♯-( )-D (Ex. 275). These segments are intervallically equivalent to the opening C-( )-E-F♯ cell and the two gapped Y cells, D♭-( )-F-G and G♭-( )-B♭-C, in Ex. 273.) At this point, however, each of these two gapped segments is filled in by interval 5/7, giving us the nonsymmetrical tetrachords C♯-D♯-(F♯)-G in vnII and

G♯-A♯-(C♯)-D in vnI. Thus, in contrast to the linear thematic statement in vnI at mm. 40–42, the canonic statements in vnII and vnI at mm. 15ff. *non-symmetrically* fill in the tritone of gapped cell Y or the double tritones of cell Z as partial octatonic segments.

Throughout the first three movements, diatonic and octatonic collections and their ambiguous derivative segments (discussed above) are unfolded generally independently of one another, whereas in the last two movements they are joined in special ways to form hybrid diatonic-octatonic sets. In the coda of Movement I, which begins at the end of m. 134, tetrachord D-E-F-G (fourth eighth-note of m. 134)—one of two equivalent partitions of the basic octatonic scale (D-E-F-G/G♯-A♯-B-C♯)—symmetrically expands to Z-11/5 (first eighth-note of m. 135)—one of two other equivalent partitions (Z-11/5 and Z-8/2) of the same octatonic scale (see Ex. 274). The axis of symmetry (sum 9) is the principal one of the movement. In the development section, the sforzandi and accents at mm. 58ff. mark this tetrachord (D-E-F-G). In vc and va at mm. 60ff., the linear statement from the canon (at mm. 16ff., vnI), which is based on tetrachord G♯-A♯-C♯-D, is now joined with tetrachord D-E-F-G, which initiates each thirty-second-note figure in vnI and vnII. These two tetrachords together imply the basic octatonic collection, D-E-F-G-G♯-A♯-( )-C♯ (Ex. 276). At the change of ostinato in vnI and vnII at mm. 63ff., D-E-F-G is transposed by interval 5/7 to G-A-A♯-C, which initiates each of these new thirty-second-note figures. This tetrachord (G-A-A♯-C) is juxtaposed with C♯-D♯-F♯-G in the linear statements of va and vc. These two tetrachords imply another octatonic collection, G-A-A♯-C-C♯-D♯-( )-F♯. The linear statements in vnI and vc at mm. 65–67 are expansions of the preceding linear statements (mm. 60–64), and these expanded statements imply a third octatonic collection, C-D-D♯-E♯-F♯-G♯-( )-B. In va and vnII (mm. 65–68), the prominent pedal-tone A completes the last octatonic collection, giving us C-D-D♯-E♯-F♯-G♯-A-B. Thus, all three octatonic collections are presented in the development section.

Measures 30–31 and 33 of Movement II present the first complete statement of a diatonic collection, F-G-A-B-C-D-E. (Although its seven tones are simultaneously stated in m. 31, they are registrally arranged in their diatonic-scale order, as shown below in Ex. 354.) In the pedal tones at mm. 113–36 in the middle section of the movement, a six-note segment, B-E-A-D-G-C, of this basic diatonic collection is explicitly reordered as a partition of the interval-5/7 cycle (Ex. 277). It is of interest to note that the octatonic-segment Z-1/7, D♭-F♯-G-C, in vc at m. 135 is a replacement of the diatonic scale of D♭ major in an early draft. Segment D♭-G♭-C of Z-1/7 is common to the latter.

In the last two measures of this movement, the glissandi unfold the basic diatonic scale (F-G-A-B-( )-D-E) against the interval-5/7 pizzicato chords based on the complete diatonic collection, G-D-A-E-B-F♯-C♯. Thus, we get

276   *Fourth String Quartet*, Movement I, mm. 60–68

277 *Fourth String Quartet*, Movement II, mm. 113–36

277 continued

two diatonic collections, one in its diatonic-scale order, the other as a seven-note segment of the 5/7 cycle. The basic collection (F-C-G-D-A-E-B) is explicitly presented in both orderings in various passages of the movement.

In Movement III, the basic diatonic collection appears in both orderings (i.e., as a C-major scale at mm. 50–51, as a series of 5/7 dyads at cadential points in vc in the free recapitulation—A-E at m. 57, G-D at m. 59, and F-C at mm. 62–63, and as both diatonic and 5/7 segments at mm. 10–11 and 17–19 in vc), but it is significant that eight-note 5/7 collections (i.e., two adjacent seven-note diatonic collections in perfect-fifth ordering) are developed throughout. The final chord at mm. 70–71 is a seven-note diatonic collection, D-A-E-B-F♯-C♯-G♯. At mm. 56–57 of the free recapitulation, the first phrase of vnI implies the diatonic collection A-E-B-F♯-C♯-G♯-D♯, which at m. 58 is cyclically expanded by the addition of D to eight notes, D-A-E-B-F♯-C♯-G♯-D♯. Thus, the latter, which joins two seven-note diatonic collections (A-E-B-F♯-C♯-G♯-D♯ and D-A-E-B-F♯-C♯-G♯), is confirmed as such by the first phrase of vnI (mm. 56–57) and the final chord at mm. 70–71. This eight-note 5/7 collection, which is established at mm. 1–6 of the movement, also opens the codetta at mm. 64ff. Analogous to the Y/Z construction in Example 272, this collection (D-A-E-B-F♯-C♯-G♯-D♯) is bounded by the double tritones (D-G♯ and A-D♯) of Z-9/3 (A-D-D♯-G♯).

The chord that is held from the end of m. 13 through m. 20 is based on two gapped Y cells, G-A-( )-C♯ and D-E-( )-G♯, the tritone ranges of which outline Z-8/2 (G♯-C♯-D-G) (whereas vnI at mm. 40–42 of Movement I filled in such gapped Y cells with whole tones, the present two gapped Y cells remain unfilled). At mm. 42ff., the pedal chord implies the presence of two other gapped Y cells, D-E-( )-G♯ and F-( )-A-B (Ex. 278). The tritone boundaries D-G♯ and F-B form an interval-3 cycle, G♯-B-D-F, which occurs at intervals 3/9 and 9/3 of the X/Y-generated system (see Ex. 189). This structure occurs on either side of the dual axes D-D and D-G♯ within the form of this movement also. At mm. 50–51, the gapped Y-5 cell (F-( )-A-B) is expanded in

va and vnII to the basic diatonic collection, F-C-G-D-A-E-B, while in the
final chord at mm. 70–71 the gapped Y-2 cell (D-E-(·)-G♯) is expanded to
the diatonic collection D-A-E-B-F♯-C♯-G♯. Thus, the ambiguously gapped
whole-tone cells are expressly realized as diatonic collections in Movement
III.

Dual realizations of whole-tone segments as either larger whole-tone or
diatonic formations are also manifested in Movement III. The whole-tone
passage of vc at mm. 22–28 (with one odd-note F♯ at m. 23) prominently
contains local occurrences of gapped Y cells, which are immediately filled
by whole tones. At mm. 29–30, complete Y cells are now absorbed into
larger diatonic segments that move to a complete diatonic collection at mm.
31ff. A comparison of the vc line of the final version (Ex. 279) with preliminary sketches (Ex. 280) reveals that Bartók tended toward mutual exclusive-
ness between whole-tone and diatonic collections in his first thoughts and

278 *Fourth String Quartet*, Movement III, mm. 42–46

279 *Fourth String Quartet*, Movement III, mm. 22–33, vc

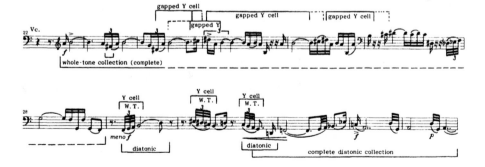

280 *Fourth String Quartet*, sketches of Example 279 (see Illustrations 10 and 11)

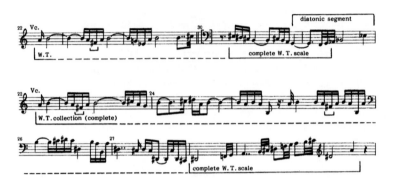

281 *Fourth String Quartet*, Movement IV, mm. 6–13, va

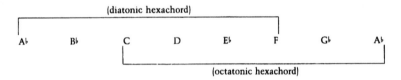

toward smoother connections and greater interactions between them in his final decisions.

In Movement IV diatonic and octatonic collections are joined to form hybrid sets. At mm. 6–13, the theme in the viola joins a diatonic hexachord (A♭-B♭-C-D-E♭-F) with an overlapping octatonic hexachord (C-D-E♭-F-G♭-A♭) (Ex. 281). At mm. 1ff., the accompaniment presents the tetrachord D-E♭-G-A♭, the G of which completes the diatonic collection in the linear thematic statement of the viola. Thus, from m. 1 through the first eighth-note of m. 7 (which includes the diatonic hexachord of the viola), the entire content is based on the diatonic formation A♭-B♭-C-D-E♭-F-G. As was shown in Example 192, this formation, A♭-E♭-B♭-F-C-G-D, is the tritone transposition of the diatonic chord, D-A-E-B-F♯-C♯-G♯, that ended Movement III. The symmetrical relation of these two diatonic collections to the basic one, F-C-G-D-A-E-B, establishes the structural priority of the interval-3/9 collection, A♭-B-D-F, of the X/Y-generated system.

In the recapitulation (mm. 88ff.), the theme, which appears in stretto between vnI and vc, becomes increasingly fragmented. At the end of m. 94, vnI and then vc play a segment based on the first six notes of the theme (Ex. 282). This ascending diatonic segment (A♭-B♭-C-D-E♭-F) is followed by another (G♭-A♭-B♭-C♭-D♭), which, in turn, is followed by a descending octatonic segment (D-C♯-B-A♯-G♯). In the remainder of the movement, the thematic material is based either on complete diatonic formations or on octatonic segments. At mm. 102–4, va and vnII present a complete diatonic collection, D♭-C-B♭-A♭-G♭-F-E♭. At m. 105, a shift to D♮ alters this collection, producing an overlapping octatonic segment (D-E♭-F-G♭-A♭) (Ex. 283). At mm. 106–11, the stretto in all the instruments is again based exclusively on the complete diatonic collection D♭-C-B♭-A♭-G♭-F-E♭. At m. 112, another shift, this time to A♮ in vc and vnI, again produces an octatonic segment (e.g., vc at mm. 112–13 plays E♭-F-G♭-A♭-A). At mm. 112–16, vc and va play a sequence of chords each of which is a gapped whole-tone Y cell. In mm. 112–18, one of these cells, G♭-( )-B♭-C (m. 118), is filled by whole tones, giving us Y-6 (G♭-A♭-B♭-C). The ambiguous chord E-( )-A♭-B♭, which appears at the Sostenuto (m. 119), also appears in m. 120, vnI, in a sequence that forms an incomplete octatonic collection (A♯-G♯-G-F-E-D-D♭-( )) (Ex. 284). The vnII imitates this at interval 5/7, giving us another incomplete octatonic collection, D♯-C♯-C-B♭-A-G-G♭-( ). At mm. 122–23, these linear statements in both vnI and vnII become chromatic. (While va at mm. 120–21 is initiated by a gapped Y cell, C-D-( )-G♭, which is intervallically equivalent to those that begin the octatonic statements in vnI and vnII, the intervallic content in each of its successive three-note groups is altered.) At the same time, vc unfolds a diatonic collection E♭-B♭-F-C-G-D-A.

The nonsymmetrical theme at mm. 15–18 (vnI and vnII) of Movement V consists exclusively of tones from the octatonic scale. The accompaniment, which is based on Z-1/7 (D♭-F♯-G-C), adds C to the thematic pitch-content, giving us an expanded octatonic segment, C-C♯-D♯-( )-F♯-G. In vnI and vnII at mm. 47ff., this octatonic segment is further expanded to six notes, C♯-

282 *Fourth String Quartet*, Movement IV, mm. 94–97, vnI and vc

283 *Fourth String Quartet*, Movement IV, mm. 103–5

284   *Fourth String Quartet,* Movement IV, mm. 119–end

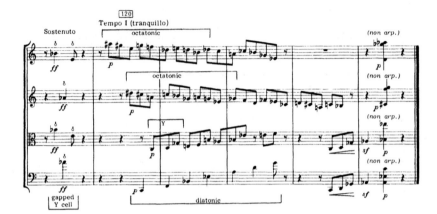

D♯-( )-F♯-G-A-( )-B♯. Preceding this statement, vnI and vnII at m. 45 are based on Z-10/4 (B♭-D♯-E-A), which contains the tritone (B♭-E) missing from the linearly stated octatonic segment. The pitch collection in vnI and vnII at mm. 44–75 and va at mm. 57–75 then unfolds the complete octatonic collection, C♯-D♯-E-F♯-G-A-B♭-B♯. At the same time (mm. 44ff.), the accompaniment in vc and va is based on the diatonic hexachord F-C-G-D-A-E. At mm. 68–70, vc adds B and then F♯, which complete the basic diatonic collection, F-C-G-D-A-E-B (mm. 44–68) and an adjacent one, C-G-D-A-E-B-F♯ (mm. 58–71). Thus, the entire passage (mm. 44–71) is exclusively partitioned between the linear thematic material based on the octatonic collection (C♯-D♯-E-F♯-G-A-B♭-B♯) and the ostinato accompaniment based on an eight-note segment of the 5/7 cycle (F-C-G-D-A-E-B-F♯). The two collections are symmetrically encompassed by the properties of cell Z (Ex. 285).

Measure 151 begins the middle section of the movement with the ostinato 5/7-tetrachords C-G-D-A and E-A-D-G in vc and vnII. This partial diatonic collection (C-G-D-A-E) accompanies the secondary theme of the movement (mm. 156ff., vnI and va). Whereas the main theme (mm. 15–18) of the movement is an octatonic segment, each statement of this secondary theme contains a complete diatonic scale (e.g., D♭-E♭-F-G♭-A♭-B♭-C-C♯, the last eighth-note of vnI at m. 156 through the first sixteenth-note of m. 162). Example 286 illustrates the succession of these diatonic collections (in interval-5/7 cyclic ordering) in the thematic statements at mm. 156–79.

Throughout the remainder of the movement, octatonic segments are juxtaposed or joined with diatonic segments to form hybrid sets. At the end of m. 272 through m. 274 an octatonic hexachord, C♯-D♯-( )-F♯-G-A-( )-C,

285   *Fourth String Quartet*, Movement V, mm. 44–71

(a) Linear thematic material based on the octatonic scale

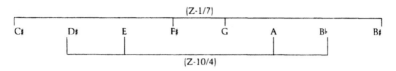

(b) Ostinato accompaniment based on two adjacent 5/7 (diatonic) sets

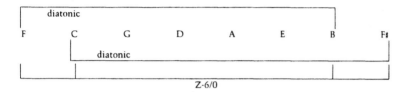

286   *Fourth String Quartet*, Movement V, mm. 156–79

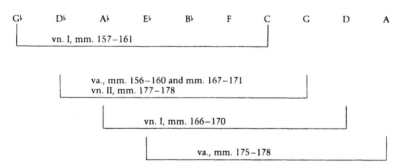

that outlines the initial Z cell (Z-1/7) of this movement (see Ex. 285a, above) is joined with a hexachordal segment C-D-E-F-G-A of the basic diatonic collection at mm. 274–77 (Ex. 287). At mm. 281–84 the chords, which are based on the interval-5/7 pentachord C-G-D-A-E of the basic diatonic collection, alternate with a unison C♯. Such juxtapositions of octatonic with diatonic material continue through m. 299.

At mm. 300–6, the octatonic theme of mm. 15–18 is transformed into diatonic material. Each of the instruments in this inverted canon outlines a diatonic hexachord: vnI consists of D♭-E♭-F-G♭-A♭-B♭; va, A♭-B♭-C-D♭-E♭-F; vnII, E♭-F-G-A♭-B♭-C; and vc, B♭-C-D-E♭-F-G. These hexachords outline a succession of interval-5/7 transpositions (Ex. 288). At mm. 320–40, linear statements of the octatonic theme alternate with chords based on the

287   *Fourth String Quartet,* Movement V, mm. 272–79

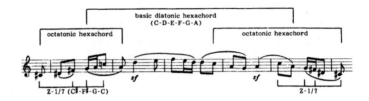

288   *Fourth String Quartet,* Movement V, mm. 300–306

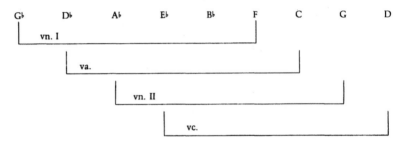

289   *Fourth String Quartet,* Movement V, mm. 365–69

diatonic hexachord F-C-G-D-A-E. This hexachord, an interval-5/7 expansion of the pentachord (C-G-D-A-E) in the chordal passages at mm. 281ff. and 296ff., ends the recapitulation (mm. 333–40) in the chords marked "col legno." At mm. 357–69 of the coda, C-G-D-A-E is unfolded for the last time as a series of 5/7 pedals (E-A, D-G, C), against which the linear thematic statements (mm. 365ff.) appear in stretto (Ex. 289). Each statement is initiated by one of two of the incomplete octatonic tetrachords (C♯-D♯-( )-F♯-G and G-A-( )-C-D♭). (At mm. 369ff., this pattern changes, for the statements now begin with chromatic segments.) The incomplete octatonic segment that initiates each of the first two statements is joined with an incomplete diatonic segment. In vnI and va, the combined octatonic-diatonic collection C♯-D♯-F♯-G-A-B-C, ending with the pedal-note C, is outlined by the initial Z cell (Z-1/7, C♯-F♯-G-C) of the movement. In vnII and vc, the combined collection G-A-C-D♭-E♭-F-G♭, ending with the pedal-note G♭, is also outlined by this Z cell. Thus, the tritones of cell Z serve as a link between octatonic and diatonic segments that are joined to form such hybrid sets.

In Bartók's *Cantata Profana*, development and transformation of both diatonic and nondiatonic folk modes appear to correspond with dramatic symbolization in the text. The legend concerns a father who had nine sons, who learned no trade, for he taught them only how to hunt in the mountains. One day, the nine sons, pursuing the tracks of a great stag, lost their way and were themselves transformed into stags. The father pleaded with them to come home, but the largest stag, the eldest son, answered that they would not go with him. This legend may be applied to Bartók's deep commitment to the principles of independence and freedom—the *Cantata* had originally been planned as part of a trilogy that would express the idea of brotherhood among three neighboring nations, Rumania, Slovakia, and Hungary.[12]

The authentic Rumanian folk-song texts that form the basis of the *Cantata Profana* are supported by these diatonic and nondiatonic folk modes, which are transformed into several other diatonic modes, as well as octatonic and whole-tone collections, in support of the main idea of the story. A transposition (D-E-F-G-A♭-B♭-C) of the nondiatonic folk mode given in Example 231, above, is established as a fundamental scale structure in the strings at the outset of the work (Ex. 290).[13] The excerpt shown in Example 291[14]—a transformation of the original mode—occurs as a local collection near the ending of the first large section.[15] The text at this point reveals that

12 The history of the text of the *Cantata Profana* goes back to April 1914, during a folk-song expedition in Transylvania, where Bartók recorded two versions of a Rumanian *colindă* text, that is, a Christmas song with many verses. From 1924 through 1926, while writing his book on Rumanian Christmas songs, he outlined a new version of the ballad in Rumanian by combining and rewriting the two original folk ballads. See László Somfai, *Cantata Profana*, preface to the score (Vienna: Universal Edition, 1934; New York: Boosey and Hawkes, 1955).

13 Benjamin Suchoff, Head of the New York Bartók Archive, has kindly pointed out to me that this "nondiatonic folk mode" is Pattern 10 of Table 2 of Béla Bartók, *Rumanian Folk Music*, Vol. IV, ed. Benjamin Suchoff, trans. E. C. Teodorescu et al. (The Hague: Martinus Nijhoff, 1975), p. 19, the scale family to which belongs *colinde* melody nos. 12i and 12bb, the only two versions of the epic *text* on which the *Cantata* is based.

14 I am also grateful to Dr. Suchoff for informing me that this thematic idea is a transformation of Melody No. 46 from Bartók-Kodály, *Erdélyi Magyarság. Népdalok* (see Bibliography in *RFM* IV, ibid., p. 44), a Székely tune from Bukovina collected by Kodály and used in his *Spinning Room* and also in No. 5 of his *Hungarian Folk Songs for Voice and Piano*.

15 Bartók divided the *Cantata Profana* into three main sections: (1) the sons are changed into stags; (2) the father meets his sons; and (3) the chorus recapitulates the tale. The formal

290   *Cantata Profana*, mm. 1–5

291   *Cantata Profana*, Ancora più lento, mm. 178–79

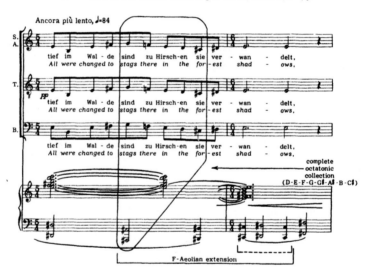

the nine sons, after a long period of hunting and wandering, are transformed into stags: "sind zu Hirschen sie verwandelt" ("all were changed to stags"). At this point in the dramatic action, the basic mode is extended in the combined descending choral segment (G-F-E-D-C♯) and accompanying chord

outlines of these sections are as follows: (I) introduction (mm. 1–26), A (mm. 27–58), B (mm. 59–63), A' (mm. 164–98); (II) introduction (mm. 1–8), A (mm. 9–37), transition (mm. 38–41), B (mm. 42–95), transition (mm. 96–102), A' (mm. 103–60), transition (mm. 160–66), B' (mm. 167–87), C (mm. 188–215); (III) A (mm. 1–34), B (mm. 35–64), A' (mm. 65–79), coda (mm. 79–93). The three large sections are without break.

(A♯-E-F-G♯-B-D) to the complete octatonic collection D-E-F-G-G♯-A♯-B-C♯. At the same time, the linear segment in the double basses and celli, A♯-B♯-C♯-D♯ (in enharmonic spelling, B♭-C-D♭-E♭), adds two new notes (D♭ and E♭) to the original mode, thus also implying the presence in this excerpt of the Aeolian extension F-G-A♭-B♭-C-D♭-E♭. The pitch content at this focal point in the tale (a transposition of the relationships given in Exx. 231–33) is analyzed in Example 292. While the remaining diatonic extension (F-Dorian pitch-content) cannot be meaningfully demonstrated in this complex, it prominently occurs in vnI in the preceding contrapuntal passage (m. 173, beat 2, through m. 175). In anticipation of the transformation into stags, "irrten wegverloren" ("nor knew where they wandered"), the F-Dorian pitch-content, F-G-A♭-B♭-C-D-E♭ (implied in the original nondiatonic folk mode), explicitly occurs here as a C-Aeolian permutation (C-D-E♭-F-G-A♭-B♭) (Ex. 293). The latter appears as part of the larger vnI line, which is exclu-

292   *Cantata Profana,* m. 178, beat 3, through m. 179, beat 4

(a) Basic nondiatonic folk mode

D	E	F	G	G♯	A♯	B♯

(basic mode)

(b) Octatonic extension

(octatonic collection)

D	E	F	G	G♯	A♯	B	C♯

(basic modal segment)   (extension)

(c) Aeolian extension

F-Aeolian

D	E	F	G	G♯	A♯	B♯	C♯	D♯

(basic mode)

293   *Cantata Profana,* mm. 171–75, strings

Un poco più lento, ♩=100
sul tasto
div.

Vln. 1.   transposed non-diatonic folk mode
permutation of F-Dorian content as a C-Aeolian scale
(diatonically extended mode)

sively based on a transposition of the original mode (A-B-C-D-E♭-F-G) and this diatonic extension, giving us A-B-C-D-E♭-F-G-A♭-B♭ (Ex. 294). The remaining violin lines, in parallel motion with vnI, unfold other transpositions of the basic mode and their corresponding diatonic extensions. The remaining contrapuntal lines of the strings and choral parts mix octatonic and diatonic segments. Thus, at this significant point in the tale, where the sons are transformed, the basic nondiatonic folk mode that opens the work is transformed into complete diatonic and octatonic sets.

Another significant extension of the original nondiatonic folk mode occurs at the textual cadence of this first large section (Ex. 295: mm. 188–89). The pitch collection at this point includes the basic mode, D-E-E♯-(-)-G♯-A♯-C (in enharmonic spelling, D-E-F-(-)-A♭-B♭-C); the two remaining notes, B and C♯, serve to imply the presence of the octatonic extension, D-E-E♯-(-)-G♯-A♯-B-C♯. Significantly, the violins and harps unfold E-D-C-A♯ from the

294 *Cantata Profana,* vnI at mm. 171–75

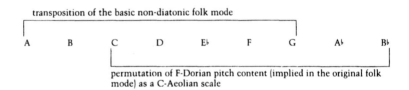

transposition of the basic non-diatonic folk mode

| A | B | C | D | E♭ | F | G | A♭ | B♭ |

permutation of F-Dorian pitch content (implied in the original folk mode) as a C-Aeolian scale

295 *Cantata Profana,* mm. 188–89

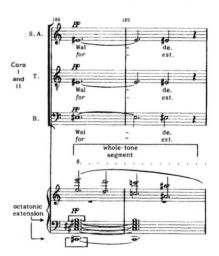

296 *Cantata Profana*, mm. 186–87

pitch content of the basic folk mode, thereby bringing four of the five notes (E-D-C-A♯-G♯) of the main whole-tone segment into linear proximity. This is immediately preceded in vnI by a complete statement of the complementary whole-tone scale, beginning with pitch-class A (m. 186, beat 3). This whole-tone scale (Ex. 296) is an extension of a permuted statement of the transposed folk mode, F♯-G♯-A-B-C♯-D♯-F (in original modal order, D♯-F-F♯-G♯-A-B-C♯). At this point, these statements of the two whole-tone scales, which are indeterminate in terms of a tonal priority, appropriately support the textual reference to the *roving* of the enchanted stags through the forest. In the orchestral postlude of this section (mm. 188–98), the harps, with some doubling by the winds and strings, then alternately unfold four-note segments from both whole-tone scales; this generates the complete whole-tone scales. (The one note, B, that is missing from one of the whole-tone cycles in these alternations is held as a pedal tone in vnI.) Against the final whole-tone segment (C-B♭-A♭-G♭) in the harps and lower strings (m. 196 through beat 3 of m. 198), the pitch content of the winds exclusively unfolds the complete octatonic extension (D-E-F-G-A♭-B♭-B-C♯) of the original folk mode (D-E-F-G-A♭-B♭-C) (Ex. 297). Thus, all three possibilities—diatonic, octatonic, and whole-tone—for extending the basic

297 *Cantata Profana*, mm. 196–98

nondiatonic folk mode, as was shown in Example 231, are realized in this work in correspondence with the main dramatic points of the text.

A final transformation of the folk mode occurs in the closing section of Part III, beginning with the tenor solo at m. 72. The text at this point, which represents the final allusion to the physical transformation of the sons, in a more general sense suggests their ultimate freedom: "Und ihr Mund wird nie mehr volle Becher leeren, Trinket nur aus klarem Quell" ("Now their mouths no longer drink from crystal glasses, only from cooling mountain springs"). In correspondence with the meaning of the text, a new nondiatonic folk mode D-E-F♯-G♯-A-B-C replaces the original folk mode (D-E-F-G-A♭-B♭-C) on the same tonic, D.[16] This new mode appears first in the solo tenor line and then as the basis for the closing string stretto that unfolds against the final choral statements (Ex. 298). While this new mode at first appears to be an extensive intervallic revision of the original folk mode on a common tonic, it is actually a literal intervallic inversion (D-C-B-A-G♯-F♯-E-D) of the latter (Ex. 299a). This inversion retains the original intervallic structure of the basic folk mode while permitting a sense of modal transformation to occur. At the same time, the inversion can be understood as a systematic rotation of the original mode transposed to the tonic (Ex. 299b); that is, if we begin the original scale at B♭, we get the rotation B♭-C-D-E-F-G-A♭-B♭, which, when transposed to the tonic (D), gives us the final (inverted) scale D-E-F♯-G♯-A-B-C-D. The rotation (B♭-C-D-E-F-G-A♭-B♭) is already suggested at m. 4 in the harmonic structure (Ex. 299c). The basic folk mode

298   *Cantata Profana,* mm. 72–87, tenor solo and string stretto

16 Dr. Suchoff has further informed me that this "new nondiatonic mode" (Ex. 298) is Pattern 15 of Table 2 of *RFM*, Vol. IV, ibid., p. 20, the scale family to which belongs *colindă* melody No. 121 (a melodic variant of the basic melody type to which belongs Nos. 12i and 12bb, mentioned in n. 13, above). According to Bartók's footnote, the latent harmony of Ex. 290 is the half-cadence F-A♭-C resolving to the major triad C-E-G as a semi-cadence close of the melody; therefore, it is the so-called Yugoslav cadence that infiltrated Rumanian Transylvania. Thus, Suchoff has suggested that this "new nondiatonic mode" (D-E-F♯-G♯-A-B-C), which is linked to the basic "nondiatonic folk mode" (D-E-F-G-A♭-B♭-C) as its inversion, must be termed the "new nondiatonic *folk* mode." Bartók refers to the Patterns as "scale families" with chromatic alteration of the less important degrees (see *RFM*, Vol. IV, ibid., p. 18). These folk-source connections reveal the importance Bartók gave to the *colinde,* which served as "motto" material for the *Cantata.*

299 *Cantata Profana,* two intervallically equivalent transformations of
the basic nondiatonic folk mode

(a) Basic folk mode and its inversion at the original pitch-level

(b) Basic folk mode and its rotation at B♭

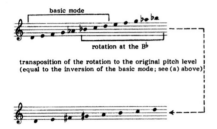

(c) mm. 1–5, strings, harmonically suggesting the B♭ rotation at m. 4

300 New Nondiatonic Folk Mode from *Cantata Profana* as Basis of
Octatonic and Diatonic Expansions in Other Works

(a) *Fourth Quartet*, Movement IV, va at mm. 6ff. and va/vnII at mm. 103–5

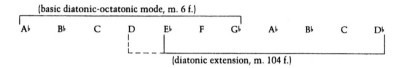

(b) *Concerto for Orchestra*, Movement V, mm. 486ff. and mm. 570–72

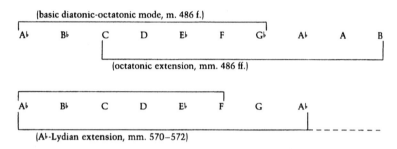

can, therefore, be transformed in two, intervallically equivalent ways. Thus, the physical transformation of the sons is symbolized musically by a complex set of abstract transformations of the nondiatonic folk mode that opened the *Cantata*.

The transformed mode (D-E-F♯-G♯-A-B-C), which is inversionally related to the folk-modal source in the *Cantata Profana*, is significantly employed in other works of Bartók as the basis of octatonic and diatonic extensions. Instances from the *Fourth String Quartet* and the *Concerto for Orchestra* are illustrated in Example 300. Diatonic and octatonic interactions stemming from a specific inverted transposition (A♭-B♭-C-D-E♭-F-G♭) of the folk mode are discussed in depth in this chapter in connection with the latter two works (see Exx. 281 and 282, concerning Movement IV of the *Fourth Quartet*, and Exx. 322 and 323, concerning Movement V of the *Concerto for Orchestra*). Example 300a illustrates the diatonic extension of the inverted mode; Example 300b illustrates both octatonic and diatonic extensions.

Diatonic, octatonic, and whole-tone sets are less extensively (and somewhat more ambiguously) integrated in the *Music for Strings, Percussion, and Celesta* than in many other works of Bartók, but prominent examples of these overlapping sets are occasionally apparent in the scale passages of certain movements. In Movement II (mm. 412–15), for example, vaII adds a new countermelody at the beginning of the recapitulated second theme, which elides a seven-note ascending octatonic segment with a complete descending whole-tone scale (Ex. 301). At mm. 421–25, the octatonic segment is completed by the first scale in the piano, the second scale then being based on overlapping octatonic and whole-tone segments (Ex. 302). This combination produces an unobtrusive interlocking diatonic segment as well (Bb-C-Db-Eb-F). In most of the other scale passages in the work, either such overlapping sets are obscured by constantly shifting modal patterns or the scales are exclusively diatonic. A significant example of the latter emerges as the basis of the main theme of the last movement (Ex. 303). The A-Lydian mode is unambiguously established at the outset of the movement, but Bartók's earlier sketches of this theme in Bulgarian rhythm reveal that he had experimented with the possibility of joining diatonic, octatonic, and whole-tone properties similar to the excerpts shown in Examples 301 and 302.

301 *Music for Strings, Percussion, and Celesta*, Movement II, mm. 412–15 (recapitulation of theme 2), new countermelody in vaII

302 *Music for Strings, Percussion, and Celesta*, Movement II, mm. 421–25, piano

303 *Music for Strings, Percussion, and Celesta*, main theme (A-Lydian) of Movement IV

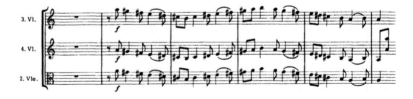

304 *Music for Strings, Percussion, and Celesta,* crossed-out sketches of the finale theme (m. 235f.), appearing in Movement III about ten bars after No. 55 (see Illustration 12)

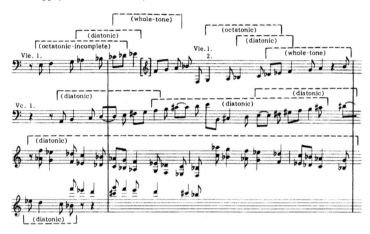

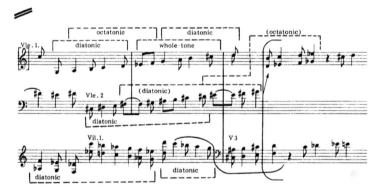

These thoughts seem to have preoccupied Bartók during his preliminary working-out of Movement III (Ex. 304), where crossed-out sketches of the finale theme occur ten bars after No. 55.[17]

In certain pieces from the *Mikrokosmos,* the transformation of diatonic folk-modal material into abstract symmetrical pitch-sets (most significantly, the octatonic scale) is produced by means of polymodal coordination. *No.*

---

17 I have used dotted brackets to designate these overlapping set segments.

305 *Mikrokosmos*, No. 101, mm. 1–5

306 *Mikrokosmos*, No. 101, mm. 26–34

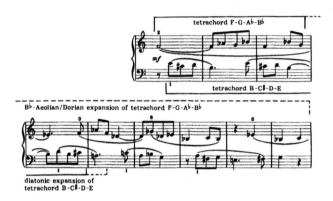

101 ("Diminished Fifth"),[18] for instance, opens with the simultaneous statement of two minor tetrachords (E♭-F-G♭-A♭ and A-B-C-D) a tritone apart, a combination of which produces a complete octatonic collection (Ex. 305). After a series of thematic transpositions that unfolds all three octatonic collections, the passage at mm. 26–34 (immediately preceding the final thematic return at the original pitch level) confirms the diatonic interpretation of the linear tetrachordal segments. In this statement, tetrachord F-G-A♭-B♭ (mm. 26–28, right hand) is bimodally expanded in the same line to a complete B♭-Aeolian-Dorian pitch collection, B♭-C-D♭-E♭-F-G♭-G-A♭-B♭ (to m. 34), while tetrachord B-C♯-D-E in the left hand is expanded to a larger diatonic segment on A (A-B-C♯-D-E) (Ex. 306).

In *No. 109* ("From the Island of Bali"), unlike *No. 101*, the linear partitioning of the octatonic set into two nontraditional symmetrical tetrachords (i.e., Z cells) unambiguously establishes the priority of the octatonic scale (Ex. 307). In *No. 150* ("Third Dance in Bulgarian Rhythm"), however, we find

18 See Kenneth Louis Gaburo, "Studies in Pitch Symmetry in Twentieth-Century Music," (Ph.D. diss., University of Illinois, 1962), Chapter II, for a discussion of the "Bartók Tetrachord" in this work.

more complex and ambiguous interactions between polymodal and octatonic sets than in *No. 101*. In the opening thematic statement (Ex. 308:
mm. 1–4), the tonal priority of E is established by the prominence of the
E-major triad. While the A♯ belongs to an implied E-Lydian segment in the
left hand (E-(   )-G♯-A♯), tetrachord B-C♯-D-E of the right hand implies an E-
Mixolydian expansion of the basic E-major triad, E-(   )-G♯-(   )-B-C♯-D-E. The
modified thematic return at mm. 23–26 (Ex. 309) expands the original E-
Mixolydian–Lydian pitch content (E-(   )-G♯-A♯-B-C♯-D-E) to a complete octatonic scale, E-F-G-G♯-A♯-B-C♯-D, by the addition of two nondiatonic
tones, F and G. The final return of the main theme (at mm. 79ff.), which is
transposed to another complete octatonic collection, A-B♭-C-C♯-D♯-E-F♯-
G, contains a new diatonic tetrachord, E-F♯-G-A, in the right hand. This diatonic shift is foreshadowed first (at mm. 5–22) in the E-Dorian pitch-content
(E-F♯-G-A-B-C♯-D-E) of the subordinate theme and again (mm. 58–78) in

307 *Mikrokosmos*, No. 109, mm. 1–4

308 *Mikrokosmos*, No. 150, mm. 1–4

309 *Mikrokosmos*, No. 150, mm. 23–26

the polymodal context of E-Aeolian–Mixolydian in the final occurrence of the latter theme. Thus, the opening ambiguous combination of polymodal and octatonic segments is transformed (through expansion) into separate and complete diatonic and octatonic collections. (Similar relations are basic to the organic growth of the thematic and harmonic material in Movement I of Bartók's *Piano Sonata*, written in 1926.)

In the *Concerto for Orchestra*, diatonic, octatonic, and whole-tone formations are either independently developed or elided to form hybrid pitch-collections at prominent structural points. The significance of these developments is that the diatonic as well as octatonic and whole-tone formations, whether employed as the basis of traditional folk-like themes or as abstract scale patterns, primarily function as pitch sets, i.e., they are usually divorced from their traditional major-minor harmonic roles. The first theme of Movement I (m. 76), which is based on two contrasting motives, begins these developments. Motive a (F-G-A♭-B♭-B) is a five-note segment of an octatonic scale, while motive b (C-F-E♭-A♭) is an ambiguous four-note segment of either an octatonic or diatonic scale (Ex. 310). At mm. 86–91, the pitch content of motive b is expanded in both the motivic and chordal material to a complete diatonic collection, the cadence establishing the priority of the F-Phrygian permutation (F-G♭-A♭-B♭-C-D♭-E♭). At m. 79 the inverted form of motive a (B♭-A♭-G♭-F-E) links these octatonic and diatonic formations. Through the lowering of G from the octatonic form of motive a to G♭ in the partially diatonicized inverted form, an F-Phrygian segment (B♭-A♭-G♭-F) is produced in the first four notes. Thus, the two basic motives generate two contrasting types of sets, the first an octatonic segment on F (F-G-A♭-B♭-B), the second a complete diatonic (Phrygian) collection on the same tonic (F-G♭-A♭-B♭-C-D♭-E♭).

The ending of the first-theme group (mm. 131–44) serves as a focal point for these developments; motive a is expanded into a larger octatonic, motive b into a larger diatonic, collection. A transposition of motive a (A♯-B♯-C♯-D♯-E) (Ex. 311: mm. 131–32) is accompanied by linear statements of Z-10/4 (B♭-E♭-F♭-A) and Z-7/1 (G-C-D♭-G♭), which together form the first complete octatonic collection in the movement, B♭-C-D♭-E♭-F♭-G♭-G-A (in enharmonic spelling, A♯-B♯-C♯-D♯-E-F♯-G-A). The latter is an expansion of the motive-a statement in the upper winds (A♯-B♯-C♯-D♯-E). At mm. 134–44, a transitional trombone theme transforms motive b into a six-note C♯-Aeolian or Dorian segment (C♯-D♯-E-F♯-G♯-(-)-B), which has a tetrachordal segment (C♯-D♯-E-F♯) in common with the latter octatonic scale.

The most significant expansions of motives a and b occur in the development (mm. 231ff.). At mm. 246–48, a motive-a stretto in the strings culminates in expanded octatonic formations: While the violins (at mm. 247–48) end one of the stretto lines with a six-note octatonic segment (C♯-D♯-E-F♯-

310 *Concerto for Orchestra*, Movement I, mm. 76–91

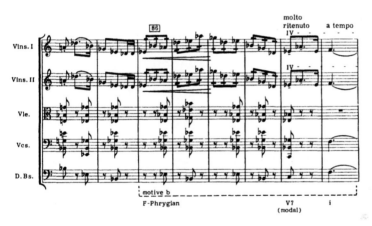

G-A), the lower strings (at mm. 246–47) end the other stretto line with a complete statement of the "primary" octatonic scale, B-C♯-D-E-E♯-F×-G♯-A♯-B (in enharmonic spelling, B-C♯-D-E-F-G-A♭-B♭-B), i.e., containing motive a at its original pitch-level (F-G-A♭-B♭-B). At mm. 248ff. (Ex. 312), a motive-b stretto now produces, through sequential expansions, octatonic associations of motive b with motive a. The first six measures of this stretto expand the pitch content of motive b to six notes, A-D-C-F-E♭-A♭, that are a segment of the third octatonic scale (A-( )-C-D-E♭-F-( )-A♭). At mm. 258ff., the tail end of this stretto expands the pitch content of motive b to a complete octatonic collection, G-C-B♭-E♭-D♭-G♭-E-A (in octatonic-scale ordering, G-A-B♭-C-D♭-E♭-E-G♭).

311 *Concerto for Orchestra*, Movement I, mm. 131–32

Motive a reappears at m. 18 of Movement II (in the closing phrase of section a),[19] where it is simultaneously stated as octatonic segment C♯-D♯-E-F♯-G (bassoon I) and diatonic segment E-F♯-G♯-A♯-B (bassoon II). The octatonic form is linearly encompassed by two diminished-seventh chords (A-F♯-D♯-B♯ and G-E-C♯-A♯), which together outline a complete octatonic collection (A♯-B♯-C♯-D♯-E-F♯-G-A), that is, an octatonic expansion of the intervening a-motive (C♯-D♯-E-F♯-G) (Ex. 313). At the same time, the diatonic form of motive a (bassoon II) is linearly encompassed by two (diatonic) dominant-seventh chords (C♯-A♯-F×-D♯ and B-G♯-E♯-C♯) that are contrapuntally aligned with the diminished-seventh chords of bassoon I (see dotted brackets in Ex. 313) to form two octatonic segments. These octatonic-diatonic interactions are a focal point for the opening bassoon phrase, which contains linearly overlapping ambiguous segments from these two sets.

19 The first large section (mm. 9–122), following a brief introduction, outlines a chain of five smaller sections (a, b, c, d, e), each based on a different pair of wind solos. A varied da capo (mm. 165ff.) follows a central trio section.

312   *Concerto for Orchestra*, Movement I, mm. 248ff.

313   *Concerto for Orchestra*, Movement II, mm. 17–19

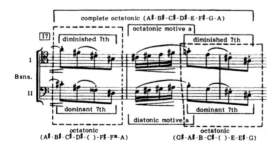

314 *Concerto for Orchestra*, Movement II, mm. 25–28

At the opening of section b (mm. 25–26), a new thematic idea in the paired oboes is based on the transposed octatonic pitch-content of motive a (F♯-G♯-A-B-C). At the same time (Ex. 314), each of these parallel melodic lines (from m. 25 through m. 27, first note) separately unfolds a diatonic segment, D♯-E-F♯-G♯-A (oboe II) and F♯-G-A-B-C (oboe I). From m. 27 through m. 28, first note, two statements of motive a are played in parallel minor thirds, so that these linear octatonic segments together produce a larger seven-note octatonic formation (D♯-E-F♯-G-A-B♭-C-( )). After some linear mixing of these sets, the opening of the concluding passage (mm. 32–34) is initiated by octatonic segment A-( )-C-C♯-D♯-E-F♯-G in the combined oboes. At the same time, oboe I linearly unfolds the complete diatonic mode of G major, while oboe II (mm. 35ff.) unfolds first G-Mixolydian, then G major.

At the opening of section d (mm. 60–62), all three octatonic collections are simultaneously represented in a new theme (in parallel fifths) and the accompanying chords. The flI (mm. 60–61) unfolds a segment (A♯-B♯-C♯-( )-E) from one of the octatonic scales, flII a segment (D♯-E♯-F♯-( )-A) from another, while the pitch content of the accompaniment (mm. 60–62) unfolds a segment (G♯-A♯-B-C♯-D) from the third. At m. 62, the flutes separately unfold two complete octatonic scales (A♯-B♯-C♯-D♯-E-F♯-G-A and E♯-F×-G♯-A♯-B-C♯-D-E), giving us the first occurrences in this movement of complete octatonic collections explicitly in scalar order. The remainder of section d (to m. 82) is then permeated by both partial and complete diatonic scales.

At the cadential point of section d (mm. 82–83), the final scales in the flutes form linear interlockings of diatonic and octatonic formations (a significant foreshadowing of Movements IV and V, where linear overlappings of these sets serve as the basic means for generating the thematic material.) The scale in flI interlocks the complete G-major and G-Mixolydian modes and a transposition of the octatonic a-motive (D-E-F-G-G♯); analogous relations form the scale in flIII.

In Movement IV, diatonic and octatonic segments are linearly interlocked to form the basic properties of the main thematic material. At mm. 4–12 (oboe), the initial statement of theme A outlines an incomplete dia-

315   *Concerto for Orchestra*, Movement II, mm. 60–62

316   *Concerto for Orchestra*, Movement II, mm. 82–83

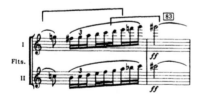

tonic scale (B-C♯-( )-E-F♯-( )-A♯-B), which suggests B major (i.e., at m. 15, the major-third degree, D♯, is supplied by an inverted bassoon countermelody, which unfolds against the first part of the repeated theme-A statement, mm. 12–17). At m. 18, the repeated theme-A statement introduces the minor-third degree (D) of the key, the octatonic role of which becomes more evident at the next thematic return (mm. 32ff., oboe and flute); in the latter passage, pitch-class D appears in the flute as part of linear octatonic segment

317   *Concerto for Orchestra*, Movement IV, mm. 32–40, flute and oboe

G♯-A♯-B-C♯-D, now in counterpoint against the main diatonic one (E-F♯-A♯-B) (Ex. 317). Together, these two lines form a larger diatonic-octatonic overlap, E-F♯-G♯-A♯-B-C♯-D. (At mm. 38–40, a chromatic shift in the flute produces a new octatonic segment, C♯-( )-E-F♯-G-( )-A♯, which together with the final oboe segment, B-C♯-E-F♯-A♯, implies another larger diatonic-octatonic overlap, B-C♯-( )-E-F♯-G-( )-A♯.)

At mm. 42–50, va, this diatonic-octatonic overlap is manifested in the transposed scalar structure of theme B (Ex. 318a).[20] At mm. 42–45, the C melodic-minor pitch-content (G-A-B-C-D-E♭-F) that opens the first phrase suggests an overlapping of the diatonic and octatonic segments G-A-B-C-D and A-B-C-D-E♭-F (Ex. 318b). At mm. 46–47, the B♭ melodic-minor pitch-content (F-G-A-B♭-C-D♭-E♭) that opens the second phrase similarly suggests an overlapping of the diatonic and octatonic segments F-G-A-B♭-C and G-A-B♭-C-D♭-E♭.[21] At mm. 45–46, the linear cadential overlapping of segments from these two melodic-minor modes outlines a hybrid collection, F-G-A-B♭-B-C, which may perhaps be considered a subtle manifestation of the transformed motive-a statement that initiated the return of theme 1 at mm. 488–89 of Movement I. The latter form of motive a implies a partial diatonic alteration, through the raising of one note, A♭ to A, of the original octatonic structure of the motive, F-G-A♭-B♭-B.

In the return phase of the large-scale arch-form of the movement, themes B (m. 119) and A (m. 134) appear in reversed order. The six-note octatonic segments, A-B-C-D-E♭-F and G-A-B♭-C-D♭-E♭, in theme B represent

20 Traditional harmonic relations contribute to the establishment of tonal areas within this theme. At mm. 42–43, a V7-i progression in C melodic-minor supports the linear unfolding of this key. At the cadence of the first phrase (mm. 45–46), a V7-I progression in F-Mixolydian similarly supports a linearly stated segment of the latter key. The cadential tonic chord, on F, is then established as a dominant-seventh anacrusis to B♭ melodic-minor, which initiates the second phrase. This phrase (mm. 46–50) then moves by way of transitory tonal areas (G♯ and A) to the final cadence on the dominant of the initial key (C). The tonic chord of the latter is reestablished at the opening of the repeated thematic statement.

21 At mm. 108ff. of the Interroto section, an inverted statement (in the strings) of a theme quoted from the *Seventh Symphony* of Shostakovich is a transposed diatonic extension (in A-Mixolydian) of the partial diatonic scales (either G-A-B-C-D or F-G-A-B♭-C) from theme B. This related thematic parody contributes to the establishment of the diatonic properties contained in theme B.

318 *Concerto for Orchestra*, Movement IV, mm. 42ff.

(a) Movement IV, mm. 42–50, theme B

(b) mm. 42–45, va

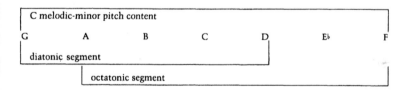

mm. 46–47, va.

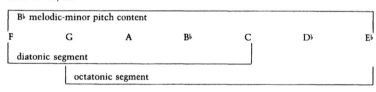

two of the octatonic scales, and the clarinet (mm. 130–35) in the bridge passage between the two themes exclusively outlines an expanded seven-note segment (D-E-F-G-A♭-B♭-B-( )) of the remaining octatonic scale. At the modified recapitulation of theme A (mm. 135–39), the English horn and clarinet together expand the original pitch-content to E-F♯-G♯-A♯-B-C♯-D-E, giving us expanded overlapping diatonic and octatonic segments (Ex. 319). A segment of the flute line then unfolds a seven-note octatonic formation, A-( )-G♭-F-E♭-D-C-B (Ex. 320). At this point, the accompaniment (mm. 140–42), which is based on this octatonic collection (with the exception of one note,

319   *Concerto for Orchestra,* Movement IV, mm. 135ff.

320   *Concerto for Orchestra,* Movement IV, mm. 140–42

321 *Concerto for Orchestra*, Movement V, mm. 594–98

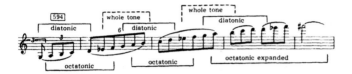

G, in va), supplies the one note (A♭) that is missing from the octatonic flute segment. Thus, this passage unfolds the first complete octatonic collection in the movement. At mm. 144ff., resumption of this theme-A subsection re-establishes the partial B-major scale (B-( )-D♯-E-F♯-( )-A♯-B) with which the movement opened, this time linearly including the major-third degree (D♯).

The linear diatonic-octatonic elisions that were established as the basis of the main thematic constructions in Movement IV are expressly developed as hybrid scale-patterns in various sections throughout Movement V. At mm. 573–99, the large fanfare section [22] preceding the coda serves as a focal point for these developments. At the end of this section (Ex. 321: mm. 594–98), the diatonic-octatonic scale (G-A-B-C-D-E♭-F) that initiated theme B of Movement IV (see Ex. 318) is presented at its original pitch-level. This scalar statement unfolds through three octaves, the final octave punctuated (m. 598) by a new note, F♯. This chromatic alteration of the scale expands the original six-note octatonic segment of theme B from Movement IV to seven notes, A-B-C-D-E♭-F-F♯-( ), while the scalar permutation in the piccolo (m. 602, coda) expands the original five-note diatonic segment to six notes, F♯-G-A-B-C-D-( ). Furthermore, as a result of the scalar extension through three octaves, a whole-tone formation, E♭-F-G-A-B-( ), is produced.

At mm. 482–558 the fanfare section, which forms a long crescendo to the closing theme, unfolds all three types of pitch sets (diatonic, octatonic, and whole-tone) in their complete forms. At the opening of this section (Ex. 322: mm. 482ff., più presto), the violas and celli initiate a stretto, each of the entry statements of which is based on a diatonic-octatonic elision (A♭-B♭-C-D-E♭-F-G♭).[23] At m. 484, a transposed diatonic-octatonic elision in va (D-E-F♯-G♯-A-B-C), based on D-Lydian (D-E-F♯-G♯-A-B) and octatonic (F♯-G♯-A-B-C) segments, is unfolded in parallel motion against the original elision (A♭-B♭-C-D-E♭-F-G♭). The two simultaneously stated Lydian tetrachords (A♭-B♭-C-D and D-E-F♯-G♯) form a complete whole-tone scale. At the third stretto entry (m. 486), the violins expand the octatonic segment to its complete form (C-D-E♭-F-F♯-G♯-A-B), in parallel motion with transposed state-

22 The fanfare theme, which serves as an introduction to the movement, also intermittently appears between or within the sections of the sonata plan.

23 The five-note octatonic segment C-D-E♭-F-G♭ appears to be a manifestation of motive a (F-G-A♭-B♭-B) from Movement I.

322   *Concerto for Orchestra*, Movement V, mm. 482–93

*as near the bridge as possible

ments. At m. 489, the bassoon enters with the fanfare theme, the pitch content of which forms an incomplete octatonic scale, D-C-( )-( )-A♭-G♭-( )-E♭-D;[24] the missing notes are supplied by the complete octatonic statements in the accompanying violins. Of the three types of overlapping sets, two, octatonic and whole-tone, are expanded to their complete forms in this stretto.

24 This statement of the fanfare theme is an octatonic variant of the original diatonic (F-Lydian) form in the introduction (mm. 1–2).

The subsequent scale passages in this large fanfare section undergo a series of intervallic transformations that lead, at the end of the crescendo (mm. 558–59, beginning of the closing-theme group), to a prominently placed Dᵇ-major scale. At mm. 498–514, a transitional scalar form expands the former octatonic interval-ratio of 2 : 1 (i.e., consecutive whole and half-steps) to 3 : 1 (consecutive minor thirds and half-steps). At the same time, the two interlocking augmented triads contained within each of these scale statements (e.g., vc at m. 498, Gᵇ-Bᵇ-D and A-Dᵇ-F) anticipate the two mutually exclusive whole-tone scales at mm. 533ff. At mm. 539–42, segments of the latter are then mixed, giving the first complete diatonic scale (A-Lydian) of the section. Whole-tone and interval-ratio-3 : 1 scales return, in reversed order, at mm. 543 and 556, respectively, prior to the establishment of Dᵇ major in the closing-theme group (m. 558).

While certain scale passages in the closing-theme group are based on elided diatonic, octatonic, and whole-tone segments (e.g., mm. 560–61), the context is now predominantly diatonic; that is, of the three sets, only diatonic scales appear in their complete forms, and these prominently initiate and close the section. The closing theme, presented by trpt and trbI (mm. 556–72), is exclusively based on a pentatonic pitch collection, C-Eᵇ-F-Aᵇ-Bᵇ.[25] The opening scale passage (mm. 558–59) establishes this thematic pitch-content as part of Dᵇ major; then the cadential scale passage (mm. 570–72) and final chord (m. 572) reinterpret it as part of the Aᵇ-Lydian mode (or F-Dorian permutation of the latter) (Ex. 323). These modal permutations of the pitch content link the closing theme and the return of the fanfare theme (mm. 573–75, flute and strings) in the same diatonic spectrum. This statement of the fanfare theme is the first recurrence of its diatonic form since the exposition (mm. 148ff.), where it was the basis of a fugato preceding the second-theme group.

The cadential passage (mm. 621–65) of the "alternative ending" connects the introductory diatonic fanfare with the octatonic a-motive (F-G-Aᵇ-Bᵇ-B) of Movement I. At the recapitulation of Movement I (m. 488), motive a was altered to form a partially diatonicized segment (F-G-A-Bᵇ-B). The bimodal significance of the latter (as a combination of F-Lydian and F-Mixolydian tetrachords, F-G-A-B and F-G-A-Bᵇ) can now be assumed in retrospect of the final ascending scales of Movement V. The woodwinds and strings unfold the complete F-Lydian pitch-content of the introductory fanfare theme (F-E-( )-C-B-( )-G-F), while the horns are based on the F-Mixolydian pitch-content (F-G-A-Bᵇ-C-D-Eᵇ) from the cadential phrase of the introduction (mm. 3–4). Their combined lower tetrachords imply the presence of the diatonicized variant of motive a (F-G-A-Bᵇ-B). This association of

---

25 The initial phrase of this theme (mm. 556–63) may be considered a transformation of motive b from Movement I (see mm. 77–78), since it is based on the original pitch content of the latter (C-Eᵇ-F-Aᵇ).

323 *Concerto for Orchestra*, Movement V, mm. 570–75

324 *Concerto for Orchestra*, Movement V, mm. 1–9

the diatonic fanfare with motive a is further established in the opening measures of this movement. The ascending F-Mixolydian scale (mm. 3–4) is transformed at the opening of the first-theme group (m. 8) into an ascending octatonic segment (C♯-D♯-E-F♯-G), a transposed extension of the octatonic a-motive (Ex. 324).

The unfolding of theme 1 is based on increasingly ambiguous diatonic-octatonic elisions. At the first cadential point in this section (m. 35, beat 2, through m. 43), these sets become more contrapuntally distinct. The upper first violins (in divisi) now expand the original six-note octatonic segment to seven notes, C♯-D♯-E-F♯-G-A-B♭-( ), while the remaining string parts (from m. 36, beat 2, through m. 43, beat 1) exclusively produce the complete A-Mixolydian mode (Ex. 325). The repeated A-major triad of the accompaniment is common to the octatonic (C♯-D♯-E-F♯-G-A-B♭-( )) and diatonic (A-B-C♯-D-E-F♯-G-A) sets. Toward the ending of the first-theme group (m. 88 through the beginning of m. 95), the unison strings present a new, complete octatonic collection, D-E-F-G-A♭-B♭-C♭-C♯, against the exclusive G♯-major pitch content in the woodwinds and brass (with some enharmonically spelled fragments). Thus, Movement V extensively develops the diatonic and octatonic figurations and themes that were juxtaposed or elided in the preceding movements.

325   *Concerto for Orchestra*, Movement V, mm. 35–43

In Movement I of the *Third Piano Concerto*, long-range relationships are established between the opening diatonic theme (1a) and an octatonic scale. The movement opens in the mode of E-Mixolydian (mm. 1–5, cadential point) and shifts at the next melodic segment to a mixture of E-Dorian and E-Mixolydian (see Chapter III, n. 18). Near the ending of the movement (mm. 184–86), the flute plays a segment (E-( )-G♯-( )-B-C♯-D-E) from the opening E-Mixolydian mode. However, in the last two measures of the movement (186–87), the piano adds a new note, F, to the tonic triad (E-G♯-B), while in the preceding measure (184), vnI adds an A♯ to the same triad (Ex. 326). The incomplete E-Mixolydian segment of the flute and the two new notes (F and A♯) exclusively form a seven-note segment of an octatonic scale, E-F-( )-G♯-A♯-B-C♯-D, in the final four measures. (The latter is a focal point of the closing theme, mm. 175ff., in which various octatonic segments emerge, mm. 180–83, strings, from the initial chromatic context. Measure 182 foreshadows the primary octatonic statement of the last four measures.) Thus, the thematic segment in the flute, which is common to the octatonic and E-Mixolydian scales, establishes this long-range connection.

A similar connection between the opening diatonic theme (1a) and the final octatonic collection occurs (mm. 18ff.) at the opening of the orchestral exposition (theme 1a'). The tonal priority of G is established by the V-I pro-

gression in the first two chords, the pitch collection in the orchestra (mm.
18–20, beat 2) outlining the G-Lydian mode, G-A-B-C♯-D-E-F♯. Although
this represents a modal change from the opening E-Mixolydian/E-Dorian
mixture, the pitch content of the present G-Lydian statement (G-A-B-C♯-D-
E-F♯) is the same as that of E-Dorian (E-F♯-G-A-B-C♯-D) from the opening
bimodal theme. The G-Lydian statement (mm. 20 to m. 21, beat 1) overlaps
a six-note segment of the same octatonic scale (( )-( )-B-C♯-D-E-F-G) that ends
the movement, extended (at m. 22) by the cello A♭ to A♭-( )-B-C♯-D-E-F-G
(Ex. 327). (One odd note, cello thirty-second-note A, functions as an insig-
nificant passing-tone.) The notes common to this diatonic/octatonic elision
are B-C♯-D-E-G. The latter segment and the one near the end of the movement (B-C♯-D-E-G♯), at mm. 185–86, flute, have the same pitch-content except for their respective notes G and G♯, the chromatic difference between
the opening E-Mixolydian and E-Dorian modes (i.e., the axis of their symmetrical ordering).

A significant formal relationship is implied between theme 1a and
theme 2 (m. 54, or m. 162 of the recapitulation), the former in E-Mixo-
lydian/Dorian and the latter initiated by the basic octatonic collection. The
opening of theme 2 (m. 54) represents the first complete octatonic statement, G-A♭-B♭-B-C♯-D-E-F (see Ex. 230). (A trill on the one odd note, E♭,

326   *Third Piano Concerto*, Movement I, mm. 184–87

327   *Third Piano Concerto*, Movement I, mm. 20–22

supplies the missing note, F.) Of the three possible octatonic scales, only the basic one selected by Bartók for this movement can be permuted (to D-E-F-G-G♯-A♯-B-C♯) to produce a symmetrical relationship with the E-Mixolydian/Dorian collection (D-E-F♯-G-G♯-A-B-C♯). This relationship contributes to the establishment of the main axis of symmetry (G-G♯) of the movement (see Exs. 67–69).

CHAPTER VIII

Generation of the Interval Cycles

The functions and interrelations of symmetrical cells are basic in the generation of the interval cycles in many of Bartók's works. The total complex of cycles (see Ex. 70) consists of one cycle of minor seconds, two of whole tones, three of minor thirds, four of major thirds, only one of perfect fourths, and six of tritones. In *Bagatelle No. X* for piano, any of the three interval couples of cell Z (see Ex. 74)[1] may serve as the basis for cyclic interval expansion. Cell Z (G-C-D♭-G♭) appears as a primary thematic construction at mm. 17–18 (Ex. 328). The cell is partitioned between the two hands into two perfect fourths (or fifths), G-C and D♭-G♭. While one of the fifths (G-C) is sustained in the left hand (mm. 15–19), the right hand unfolds a complete melodic statement of the cell, ordered both as fourths (G♭-D♭/C-G) and tritones (D♭-G/C-F♯). At the return of the theme (mm. 54–55), the left hand presents the complete cell as a pair of semitones (C-D♭/F♯-G), while the right hand melodically outlines an incomplete statement (D♭-G-C-( )), suggesting the modal (Lydian) source of cell Z.[2]

One perfect fifth of Z, G-C, appears in the bass (m. 19), and the right hand outlines F♯-C♯-G♯-( )-A♯, a cyclic expansion of the other perfect fifth (F♯-C♯). This incomplete cyclic segment defines both whole-tone (F♯-G♯-A♯) and perfect-fifth (F♯-C♯-G♯) properties. At m. 20, while the right hand has G-C, the left (A♭-E♭, or its enharmonic equivalent, G♯-D♯) completes the preceding perfect-fifth segment to give us the "black key" pentatonic

---

1 This symmetrical tetrachord can be analyzed into three different interval couples: (1) a pair of perfect fourths a tritone apart; (2) a pair of tritones a perfect fourth or minor second apart; and (3) a pair of minor seconds a tritone apart.

2 See Chapter VII, n. 5, above. The original publication is given in n. 1 of Chapter I.

328 *Bagatelle No. X, mm. 17–18*

329 *Bagatelle No. X, mm. 19–20*

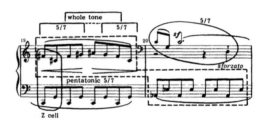

330 *Bagatelle No. X, mm. 54–56*

collection, F♯-C♯-G♯-D♯-A♯ (Ex. 329). At the same time, C-G of the right hand is cyclically expanded to C-G-D of the "white keys." Thus, cell Z is the basis for cyclic interval expansion resulting in two simultaneously stated pentatonic (or diatonic) areas.

At m. 56, following the thematic return, the left hand expands tritone F♯-C of cell Z by whole tones (E-F♯-( )-B♭-C) by joining it with a new tritone, E-B♭. This new tritone is immediately filled in by whole tones (end of m. 56) to form E-G♭-A♭-B♭ (Ex. 330). Therefore, the entire bass line of m. 56 cyclically expands tritone F♯-C to the five-note whole-tone segment E-G♭-A♭-B♭-C. At m. 61, the right hand expands D♭ of cell Z by whole tones to D♭-E♭-F-G, which represents the other whole-tone cycle. Thus, the tritones of cell Z are the basis for cyclic expansion to the larger symmetrical whole-tone segments.

The theme (mm. 15ff.) is introduced by a succession of phrases that prepare us for the cell-Z thematic structure. Each of the opening chords in the right hand (A-C-G♭ and B♭-D♭-E) contains a tritone. The first bass note, F, with the tritone G♭-C implies the presence of a partial Z cell (C-F-G♭-( )), and the next bass note, D♭, again with G♭-C, implies the presence of another partial Z cell (D♭-G♭-( )-C). When the tritone B♭-E of the next chord expands to B♭-F, the bass adds E to imply yet another partial Z cell (F-B♭-( )-E). This pattern is consistent in the ensuing progression. Furthermore (Ex. 331), partial Z cells occur as local melodic details in this passage (e.g., B♭-B-F at m. 4, bass), with complete forms (Z-0/6 and Z-1/7) elided at mm. 6−7, left hand. While modal (Lydian) segments are implied in these partial Z-cell occurrences, the two tritones of Z, when filled in by whole tones (G♭-A♭-B♭-C and D♭-E♭-F-G), represent segments of the two mutually exclusive whole-tone cycles. The grace-note anacrusis to m. 15 outlines the whole-tone segment G♭-A♭-B♭-C, the boundary (G♭-C) of which forms one of the two tritones of the following cell-Z theme (Ex. 332). Such mutual representations of the two whole-tone collections appear in the preceding chordal alternations and combinations, beginning in the second phrase (mm. 5ff., first in the right hand and then in both hands) (Ex. 333). Thus, this bagatelle is based on interactions between modal and cyclic segments with the properties of cell Z serving as a link between them.

In the *Fourth String Quartet*, the whole-tone filling of the two tritones of cell Z serves as the primary source for generation of both complementary whole-tone cycles. The tritones of cell Z are produced when the ranges of two specific transpositions of cell Y are joined (Ex. 334). While one whole-tone–filled tritone (cell Y) is a segment of one of the whole-tone cycles, two whole-tone–filled tritones that specifically outline cell Z are respective segments of the two mutually exclusive whole-tone cycles.

Let us observe how such Y/Z constructions contribute to the simul-

331 *Bagatelle No. X*, mm. 4, 6−7

332 *Bagatelle No. X*, mm. 14ff.

333 *Bagatelle No. X*, mm. 5–15

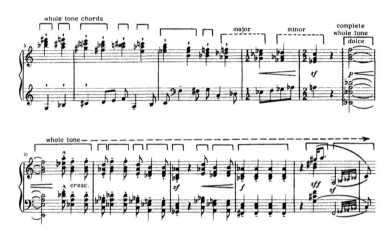

334 *Fourth String Quartet*, prominent examples of cell Y/Z constructions

(a) Movement I, mm. 40–43, vnI

(b) Movement III, mm. 1–6

taneous unfolding of both whole-tone cycles, first in Movement III. Measures 1–13 are partitioned into a solo line in vc and a pedal chord in the other three instruments. This pedal chord unfolds trichords G♯-F♯-E and C♯-B-A, which together form a diatonic hexachord. Through the addition of D and D♯ in vc at m. 6, these two trichords are expanded to whole-tone tetrachords D-E-F♯-G♯ (Y-2) and A-B-C♯-D♯ (Y-9) (see Ex. 334b). In the final section of this movement (mm. 64–71), trichords E-F♯-G♯ and A-B-C♯ are again presented as a pedal chord. The vc (m. 64) leads into these trichords with a triplet figure containing D and D♯ (the C♯ becomes a pedal tone), implying the presence of Y-2 and Y-9 (Ex. 335). (The return to the initial Y-2 and Y-9 cells at m. 64 is anticipated in the pitch content in the first two phrases of vnI at the free recapitulation, mm. 56–59.)

In the pedal chord of mm. 1–13, the two whole-tone trichords G♯-F♯-E and C♯-B-A are separated by interval 3 (C♯-E), which is chromatically filled by the axial dyad D-D♯ (vc entrance at m. 6). The primary whole-tone tetrachord, Y-2 (m. 6)—*primary* since it belongs to the whole-tone cycle that contains the basic cell-Y transposition (Y-10) of the quartet and the other even transpositions of Y—is ultimately transposed by interval 4 to another primary tetrachord, Y-10, at the end of the first section (mm. 34–39, four lowest tones of the pedal chord), while the secondary whole-tone tetrachord, Y-9 (m. 6), is analogously transposed by interval 4 to another secondary tetrachord, Y-1, in mm. 34–39 (two highest tones of the pedal chord and vnI) (Ex. 336). The transposed collection (Y-10/Y-1) in mm. 34–39 maintains

335   *Fourth String Quartet*, Movement III, m. 64

336   *Fourth String Quartet*, Movement III, generation of the two whole-tone cycles by interval-4 transpositions of Y-2 and Y-9 (m. 6) to Y-10 and Y-1 (mm. 34–39)

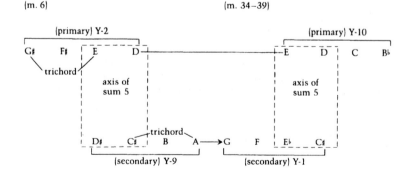

337   *Fourth String Quartet*, Movement III, mm. 22–29

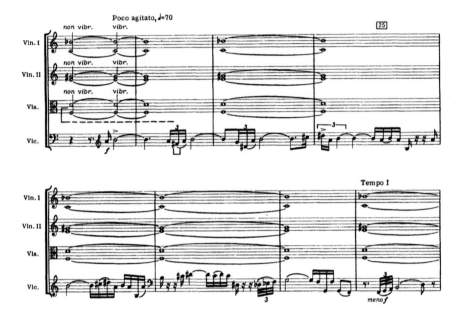

the same axis of symmetry (sum 5) as the initial Y-2/Y-9 collection (see Ex.
336), and these two passages intersect at the common tones C♯-D-D♯-E
(X-1). At the same time, they contain the respective tetrachordal segments
(D-E-F♯-G♯ and B♭-C-D-E) of the primary cycle and the respective tetrachordal segments (A-B-C♯-D♯ and C♯-E♭-F-G) of the secondary cycle. The
transposition from Y-2 to Y-10 adds B♭-C to complete the primary whole-
tone hexachord, B♭-C/D-E-F♯-G♯, while the transposition from Y-9 to Y-1
adds dyad F-G to complete the secondary whole-tone hexachord, A-B-C♯-
D♯/F-G.

In this procedure mm. 22–29 are transitional. The pedal chord contains
five notes (G♯-B♭-C-D-E) of the primary whole-tone cycle and vc contains
five notes (G-A-B-C♯-D♯) of the secondary whole-tone cycle (completed by
F-G at mm. 28–29) (Ex. 337). The two odd notes (F and F♯) of the respective
cycles are interchanged between the lower va pedal (F) and vc (F♯) at m. 23.
Although these two tones are interchanged, they are in their registral positions with regard to their respective cycles. The trend toward the two mutually exclusive cycles begins in m. 14. Analogously to the pedal chord in mm.
1–13, which is based on the two whole-tone trichords E-F♯-G♯ and A-B-C♯,
the pedal chord in mm. 14–20 implies equal segments from both whole-
tone cycles. This pedal chord presents G-A-C♯ (va and vnI) and D-E-G♯ (va
and vnII), implying the presence of two transpositions of Y (Y-7 and Y-2)

whose tritones (G-C# and D-G#) outline Z-8/2 (G#-C#-D-G). In vc, the secondary whole-tone cycle is represented by prominently placed whole-tone dyads (G-F in mm. 14–16, A-B in mm. 22–26, C#-D# in mm. 26–27, and F-G in mm. 28–29), each of which appears as a thread within each successive phrase. In m. 21, the primary whole-tone cycle emerges as the basis of the partition G/G#-B♭-C-D-E in the pedal chord. The odd-note G in va at m. 21 shifts by interval 2 to the odd pedal-note F in va at m. 22. The addition of dyads A-B and C#-D# in vc, mm. 22ff., to F-G of these pedals generates the secondary whole-tone cycle.

At mm. 64–71 (codetta), a primary whole-tone trichord, B♭-C-D, unfolds in the thirty-second-notes of vnI (Ex. 338). This trichord, with the up-

338 *Fourth String Quartet*, Movement III, mm. 64–71

per pedal-note G♯ in vnII, produces a new transposition of Y (Y-8, G♯-B♭-C-D). (This Y cell follows Y-2 and Y-9 at m. 64; cf. Ex. 335.) The resultant tritone (G♯-D), which opened this concluding passage (m. 64) as the range of Y-2 (D-E-F♯-G♯), appears as the range of Y-8 (G♯-B♭-C-D). This extension of Y-2 by Y-8 completes the primary whole-tone cycle in the passage, while the secondary whole-tone cycle (represented by Y-9, A-B-C♯-D♯, at m. 64, and the pedal trichord A-B-C♯) remains incomplete. The primary whole-tone cycle in this passage (D-E-F♯-G♯-B♭-C-D) has G♯-D as a fundamental structure: G♯-G♯ (sum 4) is the axis of symmetry of this permutation of the cycle and D-D (sum 4) is its boundary interval (see Ex. 189, the dual axis at intervals 6/6 and 12/0, the axis also of this central movement).

At the center of the arch-form of the quartet (mm. 51–55), C-E in vnII and va is a focal point, representing both the axis of symmetry (sum 4) and the primary whole-tone collection. At mm. 42–46, the pitch content of the pedal chord in vc, va, and vnI implies the presence of two incomplete transpositions of Y, Y-2 (D-E-( )-G♯), and Y-5 (F-( )-A-B). This is analogous to the pitch content in the pedal chord at mm. 14–20, which was based on incomplete Y-7 (G-A-( )-C♯) and Y-2 (D-E-( )-G♯). In both passages the primary and secondary whole-tone cycles are equally represented in each pair of incomplete Y segments. The implied Y-2/Y-5 combination in the pedal chord at mm. 42–46 is directly preceded (mm. 34–39) by the combination of two complete Y cells (Y-10/Y-1), which also represent both whole-tone cycles (see Ex. 336). From the end of m. 44 through the beginning of m. 46, vnII plays Y-4 (F♭-G♭-A♭-B♭), a cyclic extension of pedal tones D-E-( )-G♯ (Y-2) (Ex. 339). In mm. 47–49, vnII joins linear statements of X-9 (A-B♭-B-C) and X-0 (C-D♭-D-E♭), which intersect at C-C. Each of these transpositions of X is partitioned into its whole-tone interval couple: X-9 is ordered into A-B/B♭-C and X-0 into C-D/D♭-E♭. Together B♭-C of the former and C-D of the latter outline a primary whole-tone trichordal axis (B♭-C-D) of this linear statement. This is juxtaposed in mm. 48–49 with the symmetrical va figure B-C-D-E-F, which contains the axial trichord C-D-E. Thus, in the middle section of Movement III (mm. 42–55), the primary whole-tone cycle unfolds from pentachord D-F♭-G♭-A♭-B♭ (Y-2 segment in the pedal chord and Y-4 in vnII) through B♭-C-D in vnII at mm. 47–49 to C-D-E in va at mm. 48–49. In vnII and va at mm. 51–55, the interval-4 range (C-E) of the last collection concludes the section.

At mm. 14ff. of Movement I, trichord C-D-E is presented as an ostinato in va (as in Movement III, in Movement I this trichord plays a central role in the unfolding of the primary whole-tone cycle). By the addition of B♭ in vnII at m. 22, this ostinato (C-D-E) in va at mm. 14ff. is cyclically expanded to Y-10, B♭-C-D-E (vnII and vc at m. 22). At the closing of the exposition (mm. 44ff.), C-D-E is presented as a pedal chord (Ex. 340). Analogously to the cyclic expansion of the C-D-E ostinato to Y-10 (B♭-C-D-E) at m. 22, pedal-chord C-D-E at mm. 44–45 is cyclically expanded at the beginning of the

341   *Fourth String Quartet*, Movement I, mm. 157–60

development section (m. 50) to Y-0 (C-D-E-F♯). Cell Y-10 is thus transposed in terms of its cyclic-interval 2 to Y-0, C-D-E serving as an invariant segment between these two transpositions. Cell Y-0 at mm. 50–51 is then transposed by its cyclic interval to Y-2 at mm. 51–52.[3] At mm. 99ff. in the recapitulation, basic Y-10 returns. The next prominent occurrence of Y (Y-8 at mm. 152–56 of the coda) is the complementary interval-2 transposition of Y-10. (As was shown in Ex. 187, Y-8 occurs as part of the X-9/Y-8 progression, which is an inversion of the basic X-0/Y-10 progression at mm. 10–11 of the exposition.) Cell Y-8 is cyclically expanded at mm. 157–60. In vnI and va (Ex. 341), the succession of interval-4 boundaries of the intervallically expanded X motives outlines the primary whole-tone scale, D-E-F♯-G♯-B♭-C-D, while the canonic answer by vnII and vc outlines the same scale at its tritone transposition, A♭-B♭-C-D-E-F♯-A♭. These two permutations of the primary whole-tone cycle are symmetrically related to the basic trichord C-D-E (sum 4), which served as an axis for the background-level unfolding of Y cells throughout the movement. The complete occurrences of the whole-tone cycle at mm. 157–60 are the ultimate expansions of basic trichord C-D-E, which opened the transition at mm. 14ff. in va.

These culminating manifestations of the complete whole-tone cycle are anticipated earlier in the coda (mm. 145–48). At the end of mm. 145ff., if we consider certain elements in vnII and va to be vertically interchangeable, a strict double canon is revealed between the two upper and two lower instruments (Ex. 342). These interchanges between vnII and va are as follows: in m. 145, the va F♯ can be interchanged with the eighth-note rest in vnII; in m. 146, the va F♯ with C♯ in vnII; and in m. 147, the va F♯ with the A♯-C♯ in vnII. The result of these interchanges is that vc and va (doubling on the fourth beat of m. 145 at interval 2, F♯-G♯) canonically answer vnII and vnI

3 Milton Babbitt, "The String Quartets of Bartók," *Musical Quarterly* 25 (July, 1949): 380–81.

342   *Fourth String Quartet,* Movement I, mm. 145ff.
(hidden strict double canon)

(doubling on the preceding eighth-note, also at interval 2). This canon between the paired voices (vnI/vnII and va/vc) is anticipated in the passage
marked "piano" (mm. 143–45) by two simultaneous linear statements of the
subject, one beginning with F♯ (vc/va), the other with G♯ (vnI/vnII). These
simultaneous statements generate a sequence of vertical interval-2 dyads
(F♯-G♯, A-B, C♯-D♯, F-G, G♯-A♯, B-C♯). This sequence grows out of the
"piano" segments in mm. 135–44, where these vertical whole-tone dyads
are successively added to one another. Beginning at the double canon (m.
145, beat 4), these dyads are paired vertically to produce a sequence of
tetrachords (F♯-G♯-A-B, A-B-C♯-D♯, etc.). The primary interval-couple of
each of these tetrachords is based on interval 2, while the tertiary interval-
couple (intervals 2 and 6) of tetrachord A-B-C♯-D♯ is an expansion of the
tertiary interval-couple (intervals 1 and 5) of tetrachord F♯-G♯-A-B. At the
same time, the secondary interval-couple (A-C♯ and B-D♯) of tetrachord A-
B-C♯-D♯ (based on interval 4) is an expansion of the secondary interval-
couple (F♯-A and G♯-B) of F♯-G♯-A-B (based on interval 3). These two types
of tetrachordal collections alternate in the remainder of the canon. The expanded tetrachords are Y cells, the entire expansion procedure culminating
in Y-8 (A♭-B♭-C-D) at m. 152.

Throughout this passage the intervallic expansion to whole tones is set
in an arithmetically expanding rhythmic context. In the opening passage of
the coda (mm. 134–48), the "forte" segments, which are based on the X motive, appear in an irregularly contracting pattern. The "piano" segments,
conversely, expand in a regular arithmetic progression initiated at the end of
m. 135 through m. 136 by a single quarter-note. At mm. 137 and 138, two
quarter-notes are presented twice. From m. 139 to m. 144 the progression
arithmetically expands from three to six notes, followed at m. 145 by the
final contraction of the "forte" X-motive. At mm. 145–48, the expanded six-
note "piano" segment becomes the subject of the double canon. At mm.

149–51, another canon based on an arithmetically expanding progression (see Ex. 140) leads to the prominent X-9/Y-8 statements (m. 152), which represent a return to the barline.

At the opening of the middle section of Movement V (mm. 156–81), the thematic material, which is first stated in vnI and va, is related to the Y/Z constructions that were shown in Example 334. In mm. 156–59, the thematic material in vnI combines Y-6 (Gb-Ab-Bb-C) and Y-11 (B-C♯-D♯-F). The tritone ranges of these two Y cells form Z-6/0 (Gb-C/B-F). This is shown in Example 343 as part of a large progression of Y/Z constructions that are the bases of the linear thematic statements at mm. 156–81. In the va counterpoint at mm. 156–60, Y-1 (Db-Eb-F-G) is joined with Y-6 (Gb-Ab-Bb-C), their tritone ranges outlining Z-1/7 (Db-G/Gb-C). Then, in mm. 166–69, va repeats the latter Y/Z construction, while Y-8 (Ab-Bb-C-D) is joined with Y-1 (Db-Eb-F-G) in vnI to outline Z-8/2 (Ab-D/Db-G). In the final statements of this thematic material (mm. 175–77), vnII repeats the construction based on Z-8/2, while in va, at mm. 175–79, Y-8 (Ab-Bb-C-D) is joined with Y-3 (Eb-F-G-A) to outline Z-3/9 (Eb-A/Ab-D). Thus, this succession of Y/Z constructions simultaneously unfolds both whole-tone cycles. Each of these linear thematic statements ends with an X cell partitioned into its complementary whole-tone components (secondary interval-couple).

Cell Z is also basic to the generation of the interval-5/7 cycle throughout the quartet. The cycle is divided into two complementary partitions gen-

343 *Fourth String Quartet*, Movement V, mm. 156–81

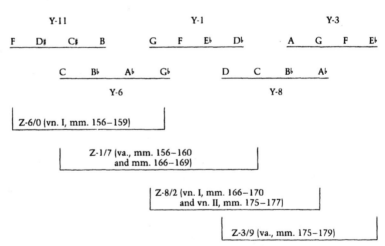

344 *Fourth String Quartet*, Movement V, mm. 15–18

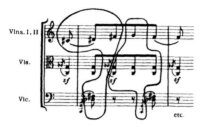

erated, respectively, from the two interval-5/7s of Z, which are separated by
the tritone. This generation occurs most explicitly and systematically in
Movement V, where both partitions of the cycle are unfolded through expanding interval-5/7 segments. The beginning (mm. 1–42) of the first large
section of the movement is pervaded by Z-1/7, D♭-F♯-G-C (in enharmonic
spelling, C♯-F♯-G-C).[4] In the opening chordal passage (mm. 1–11), vc adds F
to C-G of Z-1/7 to begin a cyclic expansion of one of the partitions. In mm.
12ff., the grace-note A♭ (in enharmonic spelling, G♯) is added in va to begin
a cyclic expansion of the other partition based on C♯-F♯ of Z-1/7 in vc, giving us the interval-5/7 segment F♯-C♯-G♯. To this segment the theme in vnI
and vnII at mm. 15–18 adds one new tone, D♯ (Ex. 344). Thus, the entire
pitch collection in the theme and accompaniment (mm. 12ff.) consists of the
interval-5/7 segments C-G and the expanded F♯-C♯-G♯-D♯. At mm. 37–40,
the grace-note A♭ (i.e., G♯) of va at mm. 11ff. becomes part of a modified
linear thematic statement in vnI and vc. This statement now includes the
expanded F♯-C♯-G♯-D♯ with G from the other 5/7 partition. On the last
chord of va and vc at m. 43, C-G of Z-1/7 is expanded to pentachord C-G-D-
A-E (Ex. 345a). Then, at mm. 44ff., F is added as a grace-note in the ostinato
of vc. This expands the interval-5/7 partition in vc and va to F-C-G-D-A-E.
In vnI and vnII at mm. 44–45, Z-1/7 is shifted to its interval-3 transposition,
Z-10/4 (B♭-E♭-E-A) (Ex. 345b). In the ostinati of vc and va (mm. 44ff.),
the interval-5/7 segment F-C-G-D-A-E is a cyclic extension of one of the
interval-5/7s (E-A) of Z-10/4. Thus, this expanded partition (F-C-G-D-A-
E), which initially stems from C-G of Z-1/7, cyclically connects the two
interval-5/7s (E♭-B♭ and A-E) of Z-10/4 (see Ex. 345b). On the last eighth-
note of vc in m. 68, B is added to the partition (F-C-G-D-A-E) in the ostinato
of vc, expanding the cycle to F-C-G-D-A-E-B. (At mm. 75ff., C-G and then
F♯-C♯ of Z-1/7 return.)

4 In an earlier draft of this movement, Z-1/7 is presented in the latter spelling (C♯-F♯-G-
C)—perhaps originally intended by Bartók to adhere to the cyclic implications in cell Z.

345 *Fourth String Quartet*, Movement V, mm. 43ff.

(a) Expanded interval-5/7 partition (mm. 44ff., vc and va)

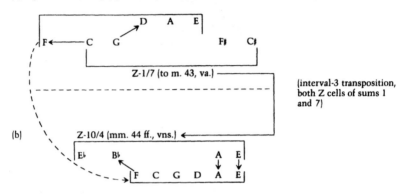

(interval-3 transposition, both Z cells of sums 1 and 7)

(b)

346 *Fourth String Quartet*, Movement V, mm. 66–68

The linear thematic material at mm. 47–74 begins an unfolding of two complementary partitions generated from the 5/7 dyads (G-C and C♯-F♯) of Z-1/7. At mm. 49ff., the two sustained tones (C♯ and D♯) lead to an expanded segment, C♯-(-)-D♯-A♯ (mm. 67–75 in the ostinati of va, vnI, and vnII). At m. 67, this segment is joined to G-D-A-E (Ex. 346), which has been unfolding in vc since m. 58. At mm. 76–89, the two interval-5/7s (C-G and F♯-C♯) of Z-1/7 in vc are the first dyads of the two complementary partitions, C-G-D-A-E-B and F♯-C♯-G♯-D♯-A♯-E♯, which unfold in all the instruments from m. 76 to m. 101. These expansions begin at m. 76 as F♯ is added in vnII to the C♯-(-)-D♯-A♯ of vnI and vnII (mm. 67–75). At the same time, the complementary segment (G-D-A-E) in vc at mm. 58–67, which follows C-G-D-A of va (mm. 44–56), is shifted back to the latter tetrachord in va at mm. 75–82. (These are the first occurrences in Movement V of the

interval-5/7 tetrachords of the X/Y-generated system; see Ex. 189.) The partition segments F♯-C♯-(-)-D♯-A♯ and C-G-D-A that begin this passage (mm.
75ff.) are further expanded in the linear thematic statements at mm. 81–85
and 89–98. The paired imitation in mm. 81–85 anticipates the canon that
appears at mm. 89–98 (Ex. 347). The vnI and vnII double at interval 5/7
throughout the canon, and va and vc double at the same interval in the answer. By the addition of G♯ in vnII at m. 89, the collection F♯-C♯-(-)-D♯-A♯,
which preceded the canon (mm. 75ff., vns), is expanded to F♯-C♯-G♯-D♯-
A♯. This segment is then mixed with 5/7 dyads (G-D in vnI and vnII at m. 90
and C-G in va and vc at m. 91) from the complementary partition, C-G-D-A-
E-B. At the cadence at m. 98, dyad A♯-E♯ in the violins completes the six-
note partition stemming from F♯-C♯, while dyad E-B in va and vc completes
the other six-note partition stemming from C-G. These two final 5/7 dyads
(A♯-E♯ and E-B) form the secondary interval-couple of Z-11/5 (B-E-E♯-A♯).
Thus, Z-1/7 (G-C/C♯-F♯) in vc at mm. 76ff. initiates both these complementary 5/7 partitions and Z-11/5 (B-E/E♯-A♯) in m. 98 completes them
(Ex. 348). In this passage (mm. 76–98), the relationship between the secondary interval-couple of Z and the two complementary partitions of the
interval-5/7 cycle is maximal, since these two six-note partitions (F♯-C♯-

347 *Fourth String Quartet*, Movement V, mm. 89–98

348 *Fourth String Quartet,* Movement V, relation of 5/7 cyclic partitions
to cell Z (mm. 76–98)

G♯-D♯-A♯-E♯ and C-G-D-A-E-B) are separated by the tritone (the interval
that separates the two 5/7 dyads of Z).

In the cadential passage at mm. 94–98, metric departure and return to
the regular 2/4-barring contributes to the establishment of these cyclic
completions. The stretto implies overlapping metric patterns of 3/8. At the
cadential point (mm. 99–100), all the instruments return to the explicit 2/4-
barring on the reiteration of the final 5/7 dyad, B-E.

The next passage (mm. 102–20) ends in va with pentachord C-G-D-A-E.
The syncopated chords at mm. 121–32 (Ex. 349) juxtapose the interval-5/7
trichord D♭-A♭-E♭ in the upper three instruments with trichord D-A-E in vc
from the latter pentachord (C-G-D-A-E). At mm. 133–41, E♭-B♭-F in vc is
joined with interval-5/7 trichord D♭-A♭-E♭ to produce the expanded pentachord D♭-A♭-E♭-B♭-F, while the alternate chord (D-A-E) in vc is joined
with C-G-D in the upper instruments to produce the expanded pentachord
C-G-D-A-E. At mm. 145–48, C-G-D of this pentachord (C-G-D-A-E) then
occurs as the basis of the cadence. This cadence, which ends the first large
section (A) of the movement, is based on an expanding arithmetic progression that culminates on the cadential 5/7 segment. At m. 130, a single group
of three sixteenth-notes interrupts the syncopated chords. At mm. 136–37,
this segment is expanded to four sixteenth-notes. At mm. 141–45 sixteenth-
notes are grouped in patterns of 2 × 3, 3 × 3, and 4 × 3.

In the ostinati of vnII and vc at mm. 151ff., which open the middle section (B) of the movement, pentachord C-G-D-A-E is partitioned into the two
tetrachords C-G-D-A and E-A-D-G of the X/Y-generated system (at intervals
7/5 and 5/7; see Ex. 189). It is also significant that pentachord C-G-D-A-E
has axis of symmetry D-D, the same as that of F-C-G-D-A-E-B at mm.
50–51 of Movement III and of the primary whole-tone segment (C-D-E).
Unison and octave D-D, the tonal center of Movement III, is emphasized at
the cadence (mm. 145–47) of section A of Movement V. In Bartók's early
sketch of this cadence, this unison D and its tritone A♭, which together represent the dual axis of the X/Y-generated system and of the central movement, are more important foreground events than they have become in the
final version. The sketch (Ex. 350) ends with A♭ in vnI and then D in va and

349 *Fourth String Quartet*, Movement V, mm. 121–48

349 continued

350 *Fourth String Quartet*, Movement V, mm. 145–48, comparison of early sketch with final version

(a) Early sketch (see Illustration 13)

(b) Final version

vc; the cadential C-G of the final version is not included. This sketch therefore supports the hypothesis that the stages of the X/Y-generated system—in this case, at intervals 5/7 (E-A-D-G), 6/6 (D-Ab), and 7/5 (C-G-D-A)—were the basis of Bartók's thoughts throughout the compositional process. While vc and vnII play tetrachords C-G-D-A and E-A-D-G, vnI and va play linear thematic statements based on a succession of Y/Z constructions.

Each Y/Z construction comprises an eight-note segment of the interval-5/7 cycle (Ex. 351). The entire succession, in turn, progresses by interval 5/7. In the combined ostinati of vc and vnII (mm. 151ff.), pentachord C-G-D-A-E is cyclically expanded (mm. 182–86, 196–205) by the pedal tones (A-E-B) in vnII and va to complete the six-note partition C-G-D-A-E-B.

In the recapitulation and coda (mm. 238–369) pentachord C-G-D-A-E becomes increasingly prominent as it is juxtaposed with complementary cyclic segments stemming from F♯. In the middle of the coda (mm. 357–68), the last explicit appearance of the interval-5/7 cycle occurs in the pedal tones (E-A in vc at mm. 357–59, D-G in vnII at mm. 363–66, and C in va and vnI at mm. 367–69), giving us C-G-D-A-E. At mm. 369–74, this segment expands to the pedal tones G♭-B♭-D, a shift that represents the tetrachordal expansion either from interval 7/5 to 8/4 or interval 4/8 to 5/7 of the X/Y-generated system (see Ex. 189). The syncopated chords near the beginning of the recapitulation (mm. 241–48) initiate the process that leads to pentachord C-G-D-A-E in the coda. In mm. 241–48, C is the highest note and its tritone G♭ (in enharmonic spelling, F♯) is the lowest. The latter note in vc is the first of the interval-5/7 segment G♭-D♭-A♭-E♭. At the same time, F-C-( )-B in the upper three instruments implies an incomplete 5/7 segment, F-C-G-D-A-E-B. In the syncopated chords at mm. 256–60, F-C/B is shortened to C/B, which implies the range of the 5/7 partition C-G-D-A-E-B. G♭-D♭-A♭ remains in vc. At mm. 268–71, the G♭-D♭-A♭ segment is cy-

351 *Fourth String Quartet*, Movement V, mm. 156–79

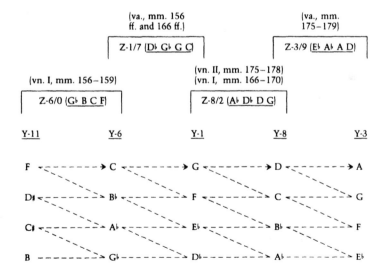

352   *Fourth String Quartet*, Movement V, mm. 265–67

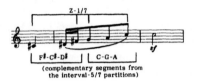

clically expanded by chord E♭-B♭-F-C, while the segment based on C is expanded to C-G-D. The next group of syncopated chords (mm. 281–84) is C-G-D-A. This tetrachord is then expanded, in mm. 296–99, to the basic pentachord C-G-D-A-E. The preliminary sketches significantly demonstrate that the sforzando chords in the remainder of the recapitulation, which ends at m. 331 in the sketch—that is, mm. 332–64 of the final version are omitted—are exclusively based on the other interval-5/7 tetrachord, G-D-A-E, of the X/Y-generated system rather than on the expanded 5/7 chord F-C-G-D-A-E of the final version. Thus, all the sforzando chords at the end of the original recapitulation, from m. 281 through m. 331, are exclusively based on one or the other of the two interval-5/7 chords from the X/Y-generated system, C-G-D-A and G-D-A-E, or the combination of both as pentachord C-G-D-A-E.

The linear thematic material throughout the recapitulation and coda joins segments from the two complementary partitions that stem, respectively, from F♯ and C. From the end of m. 265 through m. 267, two equivalent segments, F♯-C♯-( )-D♯ and C-G-( )-A, from these partitions are joined in the linear statements—both segments, which are separated by the tritone, stem from the secondary interval-couple (C♯-F♯ and G-C) of Z-1/7 (Ex. 352). In mm. 272–80 and 284–95, each of these segments is expanded, to F♯-C♯-( )-D♯-A♯ and F-C-G-D-A-E. At the end of the recapitulation (mm. 320–40), the linear thematic statements contain an expanded F♯-C♯-G♯-D♯-A♯ (and G-D), while the chords consist of the segment F-C-G-D-A-E. Analogously to the thematic statement at mm. 265–67 (see Ex. 352), each of the expanded linear statements in the coda (mm. 365ff.) outlines a transposition of cell Z. The paired linear statements in vnI and va at mm. 365–69 outline Z-1/7 (C♯-F♯-G-C); vnI and va at mm. 369–71, Z-11/5 (B-E-F-B♭); and vnII and vc at mm. 371–72, Z-3/9 (D♯-G♯-A-D)—the succession of which gives us all twelve tones. This foreshadows mm. 375–85, which outlines the same transpositions of Z in the accents and sforzandi (see the analogous passage at mm. 156–60 in Movement I; Ex. 141).

In Movement I, the basic 5/7 tetrachord E-A-D-G first appears in the passage from the fourth eighth-note of m. 37 through the beginning of m. 39. This passage is initiated (m. 37) by a sforzando on a 5/7 dyad, G-D. Then pedal-tones E and A in vnI and vnII, which are simultaneously played with the pedal-tone D in vc and va, cyclically expand the initial 5/7 dyad (G-D) to tetrachord G-D-A-E. In the closing of the exposition (mm. 44ff.), the pedal tones outline the whole-tone trichord C-D-E, a symmetrically related partition of the basic 5/7 pentachord C-G-D-A-E. In the analogous passage at mm. 126–34 (più mosso), the closing of the recapitulation, this whole-tone trichord is replaced by C-( )-D-A in the pedal tones. The latter appears complete (C-G-D-A) in the final pedal-tone passage of the coda, mm. 149–51. Thus, the pedal-tone passages near the end of the exposition (mm. 37–39), recapitulation (mm. 126–34), and coda (mm. 149–51) outline one or the other of the basic interval-5/7 tetrachords (E-A-D-G and C-G-D-A) from the X/Y-generated system. From the end of m. 115 through m. 119, the pedal tones combine these two tetrachords to form the interval-5/7 pentachord C-G-D-A-E.

At m. 31 of Movement II, a diatonic collection (F-G-A-B-C-D-E) is stated as a simultaneity that is also the interval-5/7 segment F-C-G-D-A-E-B. The latter is a symmetrical cyclic expansion of the basic 5/7 pentachord (C-G-D-A-E) that unfolded in the pedals of Movement I. The syncopated chords in vc and va at mm. 34–36 then juxtapose a segment (C-G-D) from this seven-note collection with trichord C♯-G♯-D♯ from the complementary part of the 5/7 cycle. This combination (C-G-D/C♯-G♯-D♯) can be seen as an interval-5/7 expansion of the secondary interval-couple of Z-8/2 (G♯-C♯/D-G) (Ex. 353). Comparison of an early draft of this passage with the final version (Ex. 354) shows that Bartók originally intended to give the entire 5/7 cycle in two complete partitions (F-C-G-D-A-E-B and F♯-C♯-G♯-D♯-A♯). This passage, based on the cyclically expanded 5/7 dyads of Z-8/2, is a focal point for the unfolding of complementary 5/7 segments in the first two thematic statements (mm. 1–16). At mm. 1–7, the first statement of the chromatic theme (in vc and va) spans an interval 5/7, E-B. In vnI and vnII, at mm. 10–16, this theme is transposed by interval 5/7 so that the range is B-F♯. These successive boundaries outline an expanded interval-5/7 segment, E-B-F♯. Measures 1–2 of the initial thematic statement outline a chromatic as-

353 *Fourth String Quartet*, Movement II, mm. 34–36, vc and va

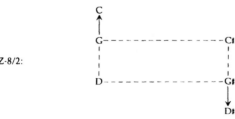

354   *Fourth String Quartet*, Movement II, comparison of early draft
of mm. 31–36 with final version

(a) Early draft (see Illustration 14)

(b) Final version

cent from E to A♯ and mm. 3–4 a chromatic descent from B to E♯; these two
tritones form Z-11/5 (B-F/E-A♯) (Ex. 355a). Analogously, mm. 10–11 of the
second statement of the theme outline a chromatic ascent from B to E♯ and
mm. 12–13 a chromatic descent from F♯ to B♯; these two tritones form
Z-6/0 (F♯-C/B-F). While the combined 5/7 boundaries (E-B-F♯) are cyclically
extended at mm. 34–36 by the foreground-level 5/7 segment C♯-G♯-D♯, the
remaining combined 5/7 components (A♯-E♯-B♯) of the two thematic Z-cell
outlines are cyclically extended at mm. 34–36 by the foreground-level 5/7
segment C-G-D (see Ex. 355a). Measures 189–204 of the recapitulation
again present (in va) Z-11/5 and (in vnI) Z-6/0 in the linear thematic statements, with vnII at mm. 198–201 now adding Z-1/7 (Ex. 355b). The last Z
cell (Z-1/7), an interval-5/7 transposition of Z-6/0, expands the original 5/7
segments (E-B-F♯ and A♯-E♯-B♯) of the combined Z cells (see Ex. 355a) to E-
B-F♯-C♯ and A♯-E♯-B♯-G (see Ex. 355b).
     In the middle of section B (mm. 113–36), the pedal tones outline the

interval-5/7 segment B-E-A-D-G. In vc at mm. 129–36, C appears as the main cadential tone. Together with the pedal tones, it completes the interval-5/7 partition B-E-A-D-G-C (in referential order, C-G-D-A-E-B). At the same time (mm. 113ff.), vnII and va play a stretto based on a succession of ostinato figures, each encompassing a tritone. These tritones in vnII and va (Ex. 356) follow one another at interval 5/7 (see Ex. 147, sequence of Z cells). This progression simultaneously unfolds two interval-5/7 segments (F-B♭-E♭-A♭-D♭ and B-E-A-D-G). At mm. 136–37, the initial tones of the glissando together outline C-D-E-F♯. The tritone range (C-F♯) of this whole-tone

355 *Fourth String Quartet*, Movement II, mm. 1–16 of first section (A)
and mm. 189–201 of the recapitulation (A′)

(a) mm. 1–16 (Z-cell outlines of the first two thematic statements)

(b) mm. 189–201 (Z-cell outlines of three thematic statements)

356 *Fourth String Quartet*, Movement II, mm. 113–37

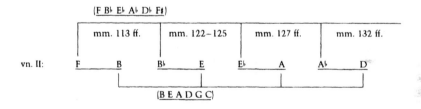

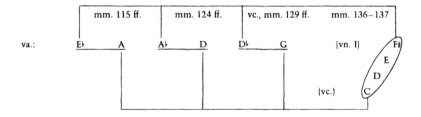

tetrachord cyclically expands the two interval-5/7 segments to F-B♭-E♭-A♭-D♭-F♯ and B-E-A-D-G-C, the same two partitions (C-G-D-A-E-B and F♯-C♯-G♯-D♯-A♯-E♯) that are basic in Movement V (see Ex. 348).

In Movement III, vc at mm. 10–11, each of the three-note figures initiated by a grace-note outlines an interval-5/7 trichord (G-C-F, D-G-C, and B-E-A), giving us the interval-5/7 segment F-C-G-D-A-E-B (Ex. 357a). In the second phrase of the vc solo (mm. 14–21), the succession of three-note figures initiated by the grace-notes (C-G-D at m. 17, G-D-A at m. 18, and D-A-E at m. 19) outlines a segment (C-G-D-A-E) that is symmetrically related to F-C-G-D-A-E-B of the first phrase (Ex. 357b). As was shown in Example 190, va and vnII at mm. 50–51 of the middle section of the movement play the interval-5/7 segment F-C-G-D-A-E-B, expressed as a diatonic scale (C-D-E-F-G-A-B), while vc and vnI play the complementary 5/7 segment G♭-D♭-A♭-E♭-B♭. At the cadential points at mm. 57, 59, and 63 of the free recapitulation, vc and vnI, respectively, present successions of interval-5/7 dyads (A-E, G-D, F-C in vc and C♯-G♯, D♯-G♯, B♭-E♭ in vnI), which give us incomplete forms of the latter two complementary 5/7 segments (F-C-G-D-A-E and C♯-G♯-D♯-A♯).

357 *Fourth String Quartet*, Movement III, mm. 10–11, 17–19

(a) mm. 10–11

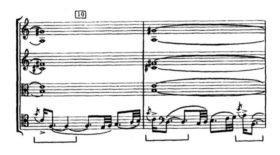

(b) mm. 17–19

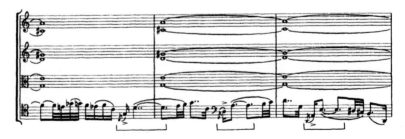

358   *Fourth String Quartet*, Movement IV, mm. 1–13

Movement IV opens (mm. 1–12) with a chordal accompaniment in vnI, vnII, and vc that consists of two interval-5/7 dyads, G-D and A♭-E♭, from complementary parts of the cycle. At the same time, the temporal and registral boundary of the theme in va is the 5/7 dyad beginning on A♭ (m. 6) and ending on E♭ (m. 13). At each successive statement of the theme, the interval-5/7 segment that stems from the opening 5/7 dyad A♭-E♭ is cyclically unfolded. At mm. 13–21 the theme (in vnII) is transposed by interval 5/7 so that it encompasses E♭-B♭. In mm. 20–29 the theme (in vc) is again transposed by interval 5/7 so that it encompasses B♭-F. Thus far, the sequence of thematic statements outlines the interval-5/7 segment A♭-E♭-B♭-F. At m. 27, vnI begins its statement on F, but at m. 28 va answers in stretto on E♭. The latter is transposed back by interval 5/7 to A♭ (vnI and

vnII, m. 37). At mm. 37ff. there are fragmented statements of the theme beginning on the initial A♭. Each of these thematic statements throughout the
first section is metrically defined as a closed structure by the accompanying
arithmetic progression, which departs and returns to the regular barline (Ex.
358).

While dyad A♭-E♭ in the opening chord (D-E♭-G-A♭) initiates the inter-
val-5/7 segment A♭-E♭-B♭-F (outlined in the succession of thematic statements throughout the first large section (A) of the movement, mm. 1–45),
the other 5/7 dyad (G-D) of this chord initiates a complementary segment of
the 5/7 cycle. At the change of chord in the accompaniment at m. 13, the
lower two notes of vc and top note of vnI are A-E. The remaining tones (E♭-
B♭-F) in this chordal accompaniment are explicitly presented in va as an
interval-5/7 trichord. (The latter belongs to the 5/7 segment A♭-E♭-B♭-F,
which, as discussed above, is outlined by the successive transpositions of
the theme.) The two 5/7 tetrachords (A♭-E♭-B♭-F and G-D-A-E) have unfolded in the accompaniment from A♭-E♭ and G-D (Ex. 359). At mm. 21–27,
the 5/7 trichord C-G-D in va cyclically connects these two tetrachords to
give us an expanded nine-note 5/7 segment (A♭-E♭-B♭-F-C-G-D-A-E). This
collection is further expanded in the chordal accompaniment (mm. 29ff.) by
the addition of B in vnII. At m. 37, G♭-D♭-A♭ in the glissando of vc completes the entire cycle from A♭ to A♭ (chordal accompaniment, mm. 1–37)
at the point at which the thematic segments return to the A♭ tonic. Significantly, the basic pentachord C-G-D-A-E is the axis of the larger permutation
of the 5/7 cycle.

Measures 37–41 (near the end of the first large section) are a stretto (Ex.
360) based on fragments of the theme. The vnI and vnII at m. 37 begin on A♭
and are answered in m. 38 by va and vc on E♭. The latter are then answered
in m. 39 by vnI and vnII on B♭. At m. 40, va and vc answer on F. In this
succession the 5/7 segment A♭-E♭-B♭-F is thus outlined once again. In vnI

359 *Fourth String Quartet,* Movement IV, mm. 12–13

360   *Fourth String Quartet,* Movement IV, mm. 37–41

and vnII at m. 40, the interval-5/7 transpositional pattern changes as G♭ begins the next thematic fragment, answered in m. 41 by va and vc on D♭. The last two statements, on G♭ and D♭, complete the 5/7 partition G♭-D♭-A♭-E♭-B♭-F in this stretto. (This partition—in enharmonic spelling, F♯-C♯-G♯-D♯-A♯-E♯—is basic to Movement V; see Ex. 348.)

In the recapitulation (mm. 88ff., vnI and vc) fragments of the theme beginning on A♭ appear in stretto. This is followed at the end of mm. 95ff. by a stretto in vnI and vc, the thematic fragments beginning on G♭. At tempo I (mm. 102ff.), va and vnII now appear in stretto, both beginning on D♭. In m. 106, these statements in stretto are answered by vnI and vnII beginning on G♭. (Thus far in the recapitulation, we have a 5/7 segment G♭-D♭-A♭ of the partition G♭-D♭-A♭-E♭-B♭-F that closed the exposition at mm. 37–41.) At this point (mm. 106ff.), the stretto statements in vnI and vnII (initiated by G♭) are answered at the tritone (C) by inverted stretto statements in vc and va. The vnI at mm. 112–18 and vnII at mm. 115–18 play Y-6, G♭-A♭-B♭-C (the G♭ appears at m. 118). The G♭-C range of this Y cell is the tritone that initiates the inverted canon (end of mm. 106ff.). (At the same time, each of the chords in vc at mm. 112–16 and va at mm. 115–16 implies an incomplete Y cell: D♭-E♭-( )-G at m. 112; D-E-( )-G♯ at m. 113; E♭-F-( )-A at m. 114; E-F♯-( )-A♯ at m. 115; and F-G-( )-B at m. 116. This pattern culminates in the G♭-C range of Y-6 at m. 118.) From m. 120 to m. 122, vc unfolds the interval-5/7 segment C-F-B♭-E♭/A-D-G (or A-D-G-C-F-B♭-E♭). The note C not only initiates this ascending passage in vc but is also the axis of symmetry of this interval-5/7 collection. The range of the final chord is the octave A♭, the basic tone of the movement.

In terms of the interval-5/7 cycle, the middle section (B) of the movement (mm. 45ff.) is complementary to mm. 37–41 at the end of the exposition, which outlines the 5/7 partition G♭-D♭-A♭-E♭-B♭-F, and mm. 88ff. at the opening of the recapitulation, which is based on a segment (G♭-D♭-A♭) of this partition. At mm. 45–54 (Ex. 361a), the pedal chord in vc and va is

361   *Fourth String Quartet*, Movement IV, mm. 45–54, 54ff.

(a) mm. 45–54

A-D boundary

(b) mm. 54ff.

D-G hidden boundary
(chromatic hexachord)

partitioned into two whole-tone trichords (A-B-C♯ and B♭-C-D). Together, these trichords produce chromatic hexachord A-B♭-B-C-C♯-D, which has an interval-5/7 range A-D. At mm. 54ff. (Ex. 361b), this pedal chord is transposed by interval 5/7 to another chromatic hexachord, D-E♭-E-F-F♯-G, which has an interval-5/7 range D-G. The ranges (A-D and D-G) of these inversionally complementary hexachords outline the 5/7 segment A-D-G. At the same time, the linear statements in vnI and vnII (mm. 47–53) are partitioned into two conjunct chromatic trichords (E-F-G♭ in vnII and F♯-G-A♭ in vnI), which produce a chromatic pentachord. At mm. 54–59 this collection is transposed by interval 5/7 to another chromatic pentachord, A-B♭-B-C-D♭. This interval-5/7 transposition in vnI and vnII from the pentachord on E to that on A further expands the 5/7 trichord (A-D-G) of the pedals (vc and va).

In the *Concerto for Orchestra*, the basic symmetrical cells (primarily cell Z) serve as focal points in generation of the interval cycles. Near the opening of the central movement (III),[5] the three upper string instruments together

---

5 The first (in regular sonata form) and second (*Scherzo*) movements mirror the fifth and fourth, respectively, in tempi and formal types.

unfold four complete transpositions of cell Z in stretto, the double basses (mm. 4–9) implying a partial statement (D-G-(∤)-D♭) of a fifth one, Z-2/8 (Ex. 362). While the stretto unfolds these Z cells in ascending minor-second transpositions, the specific linear pairing of Z cells in each instrument produces a secondary, overlapping cell (see dotted brackets in Ex. 362). (The perfect-fourth gap between the minor-second dyads in cell Z, i.e., interval-ratio 5 : 1, is contracted to a major-third gap in the secondary cell, i.e., interval-ratio 4 : 1.) Of the intervals (1, 5, and 6) that form the three interval-couples of Z, only the tritone represents a complete interval cycle, but the combination of these cell-Z statements implies the presence of all six tritone cycles. (At mm. 106–10 the modified recapitulation is exclusively based on Z-11/5, B-E-F-A♯, the tritone property being explicitly manifested by the harmonic structure of the passage, based on one of the tritone partitions, B-F.) At mm. 1off., a new figure, C-E♭-E-G-A♭-B, which exclusively forms the linear and harmonic pitch-content, represents a further intervallic contraction of Z, the minor-second dyads now being separated by a minor third, that is, interval-ratio 3 : 1. This new construction interlocks two complete major-third (or interval-4) cycles, C-E-A♭ and E♭-G-B (Ex. 363), analogous to the two tritone cycles interlocked in each of the Z cells. The secondary cell, 4 : 1 (see Ex.

362 *Concerto for Orchestra,* Movement III, mm. 4–9

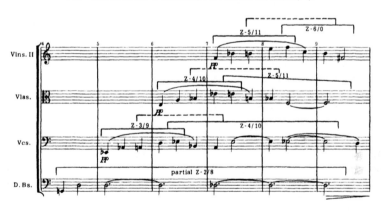

363 *Concerto for Orchestra,* Movement III, mm. 1off.

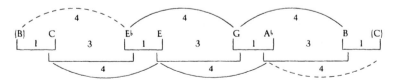

362) in the stretto is transitional in this contraction of cell Z. Thus, two complete types of interval cycles (based on intervals 6 and 4) have unfolded in the opening passages of this movement.

Against the interval-3 : 1 figure (C-Eb-E-G-Ab-B), a lyric oboe theme (mm. 12–18) unfolds a tetrachordal segment of the interval-1 cycle, X-8 (G♯-A-Bb-B). At m. 13, with upbeat, the latter is explicitly partitioned into its interval-2 dyads, Bb-G♯ and A-B, an intermediary stage in the last intervallic contraction from 3 : 1 (C-Eb-E-G-Ab-B) to 1 : 1 (G♯-A-Bb-B). (This connection is supported by the reflection of the oboe melody in the changing uppermost pitch of each successive 3 : 1 arpeggiation.) At mm. 19–22, a rhythmic augmentation of the 3 : 1 arpeggio is introduced by a 2 : 1 segment, C-Db-Eb-E; thus all the interval ratios between 5 : 1 (cell Z) and 1 : 1 (cell X) have been systematically unfolded in the first section of this movement (to m. 33). The main cadential point of this section (m. 33) is based on a partial statement of Z-1/7, Db-Gb-G-( ), which represents a return to the interval-5 : 1 ratio.

The central section of this movement (mm. 34–61), which brings back the introductory theme of Movement I (see m. 30 of Movement I), is based on irregular interlocking relations of intervals 1 and 2, as can be seen in both the theme and the accompanying diatonic scales. The culminating passage of this central section (mm. 54–60) appears to be a focal point for the foregoing intervallic relations, in that it polarizes both the smallest and largest interval-ratios (1 : 1 and 5 : 1): the sixteenth-note figure is exclusively based on X-7, F×-G♯-A-Bb (1 : 1), while the held tritone (F♯-C) and reiterated note (B) in the piccolo together form a partial statement of Z-6/0, F♯-B-C-( ) (5 : 1). The entire pitch-content semitonally fills in the held tritone, F♯-C, which is the largest interval class of cell Z.

At mm. 62ff., a viola theme begins the return phase of the symmetrical arch-form of the movement—that is, whereas the oboe theme that preceded the central section was a culmination of a series of intervallic contractions, the viola theme initiates a series of intervallic expansions. The first va phrase (mm. 62–64) is based on X-10 (A♮-B-B♯-C♯), which, like X-8 of the earlier oboe theme, is marked by whole-tone partitioning, an increasingly prominent characteristic in the successive thematic phrases. The main cadence of this section (m. 99) returns to the 3 : 1 arpeggiation (transposed to G-Bb-B-D-Eb-(F)) of the first section. At m. 101 the coda, a modified recapitulation of the introductory opening, reestablishes interval-ratio 5 : 1 in the arpeggiations of Z-11/5 (B-E-F-A♯) above one of its held tritones, B-F.

All these interval ratios (pairs of interlocking cycles), which unfolded either as complete cycles (5 : 1, interlocking two tritones, and 3 : 1, two major thirds) or partial ones (2 : 1, interlocking two implied minor-third cycles, and 1 : 1, segments of the chromatic scale), are fully developed in the closing scale passages (mm. 482ff.) of Movement V. The vnII (and vc) at mm. 486ff. (Ex. 364a) unfolds two complete interlocking interval-3 cycles (2 : 1 ratio, or

364   *Concerto for Orchestra*

(a) Movement V, mm. 486ff., vnII

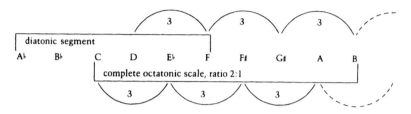

(b) Movement V, mm. 498ff., vnI and vc

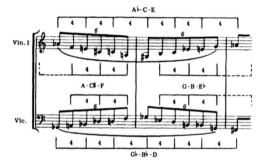

(c) Movement V, mm. 533ff., strings

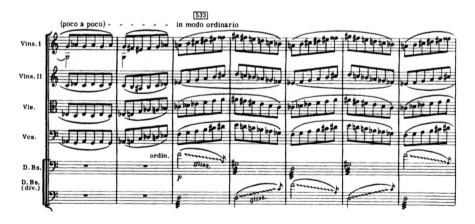

364 continued

(d) Movement V, mm. 573–83, strings and upper winds

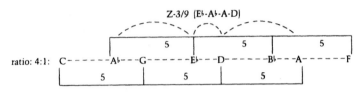

or:

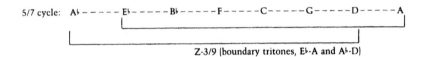

Z-3/9 (boundary tritones, E♭-A and A♭-D)

octatonic scale) in overlap with a diatonic segment.[6] At mm. 498ff. the scales in vnI and vc intervallically expand to ratio 3 : 1, or all four interlocking major-third cycles (Ex. 364b). At mm. 533ff. all the instruments unfold both whole-tone scales, that is, interval-2 cycles (Ex. 364c), which move in parallel pairs of vertically stated tritones: the ascending and descending scales together give us all six tritone cycles. Following some linear mixing of segments from the two mutually exclusive whole-tone cycles, ratio 3 : 1 returns (mm. 556ff.), the latter leading to a D♭-major scale and other traditional modal formations. At mm. 573ff. strings and upper winds unfold an expanded 4 : 1 segment, C-A♭-G-E♭-D-B♭, which is extended by an additional A-F at mm. 579–81. The extended 4 : 1 segment (C-A♭-G-E♭-D-B♭-A-F) interlocks two segments of the cycle of fifths, A♭-E♭-B♭-F and C-G-D-A (Ex. 364d), which together form an eight-note segment, A♭-E♭-B♭-F-C-G-D-A.

This cyclic interpretation is confirmed by the explicit reordering of the 4 : 1 segment G-E♭-D-B♭ (mm. 582–83) into two perfect fifths, B♭-E♭/D-G (mm. 585–86). The two segments are linearly connected by two overlapping Z cells, Z-5/11 (F-B♭-B-E) and Z-4/10 (E-A-B♭-E♭) (Ex. 365). The two Z cells together give us three of the six tritone cycles, F-B, E-B♭, and E♭-A, the flute figures at mm. 587–91 bounded by D-G♯, G-D♭, and C-F♯.) The significance of these two foreground cell-Z statements (Z-5/11 and Z-4/10) is two-

---

6 Such diatonic-octatonic overlappings are anticipated in Movement IV in the famous viola theme that begins the Calmo, or trio section. Also see Example 281, the va theme in Movement IV of the *Fourth String Quartet*.

fold: they represent an expansion from the interval-ratio 4 : 1 (C-A♭-G-E♭-D-B♭-A-F) to 5 : 1; and they serve as foreground-level focal points for the implied structural presence (see Ex. 364d) of Z-3/9, E♭-A♭-A-D, in the 4 : 1 scalar segment. This series of Z cells (Z-3/9, Z-4/10, and Z-5/11), which are separated by semitones, is the same as that which opened Movement III (mm. 5–6; see Ex. 362). Thus, cell Z serves both as a focal point and as a basic structural formation in generation of the interval cycles.

The main theme of Movement I (mm. 76ff.) is a focal point for generation of the interval cycles throughout the introduction. The theme is based on two motives (Ex. 366), each of which is an interlocking of certain cyclic segments. Motive a forms octatonic segment F-G-A♭-B♭-B (interval-ratio 2 : 1), and motive b forms pentatonic segment C-F-E♭-A♭ (two perfect fourths intersecting at a whole tone). Thus, the whole-tone (interval-2) property is common to both motives, where it is systematically integrated with intervals 1 and 5, respectively. In the opening phrases of the introduction, segments of these interval cycles are distinguished by means of contrasting figurations and textures. At mm. 6–10 the upper strings symmetrically unfold an expanding and contracting pattern around an axis of symmetry, C-C, the entire pitch content of this tremolo passage giving us all the chromatic tones between A♭ and E. The expanding and contracting phases of this symmetry are partitioned into mutually exclusive segments of the two whole-tone cycles (A♭-B♭-C-D-E and A-B-D♭-E♭) (Ex. 367). At mm. 1–6, the series of perfect-fourth segments in the celli and basses, which together form a partially ordered five-note segment of the 5/7 cycle (C♯-F♯-B-E-A), linearly contains two whole-tone dyads, B-A and E-F♯. Whereas the tremolo passage is based on a whole-tone partitioning of an interval-1 cyclic segment, this opening phrase is based on a whole-tone partitioning of an interval-5/7 cyclic segment. Therefore the whole tone, a common property of the contrast-

365 *Concerto for Orchestra*, Movement V, mm. 583–86

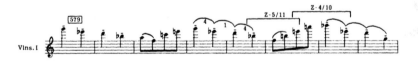

366 *Concerto for Orchestra*, Movement I, main theme, mm. 76ff.

367 *Concerto for Orchestra*, Movement I, mm. 1–10

ing configurations of the opening two phrases, serves as a link between the intervals-5/7 and 1/11 cycles, foreshadowing the cyclic interactions in the main theme (see Ex. 366).

At mm. 16–20, the second statement of the tremolo passage is transposed up a perfect fourth to a new axis of symmetry, F-F, the pitch content now having all the chromatic tones between Db and A. The expanding and contracting phases of this transposed passage reverse the previous whole-tone partitions: the symmetrically expanding segment (Ab-Bb-C-D-E) of the original passage is cyclically completed by D-E-Gb-Ab, while the symmetrically contracting segment (A-B-Db-Eb) of the original passage is cyclically completed by Db-Eb-F-G-A. At mm. 12–16, the original, partially ordered 5/7 segment in the celli and basses (C♯-F♯-B-E-A) is cyclically expanded to a partially ordered six-note segment (C♯-F♯-B-E-A-D) which, at the stringendo (mm. 22ff.), expressly appears in its cyclic ordering. In the remainder of the passage, this six-note segment is cyclically expanded to a partially ordered ten-note interval-5/7 collection (D♯-G♯-C♯-F♯-B-E-A-D-G-C) that leads into the main introductory flute theme (m. 30), the pitch content of which, in contrast to the 5/7 collection, is primarily based on semitones. (The chromatic accompaniment to this theme supplies all but two of the remaining twelve tones.) These contrasting passages, which are formed from partially ordered cyclic segments (interval-5/7 and interval-1/11, respectively), commonly contain whole-tone partitions (brackets, Ex. 368). Thus, while the successive passages that open the introduction expand the interval-1/11, 2/10, and 5/7 cycles, the whole-tone cyclic segments are established as a significant intervallic link between the 1/11 and 5/7 cycles.

The remainder of the introduction (to m. 75) further develops these cyclic interactions in which interval-2/10 cyclic segments appear as partitions in either the 5/7 or 1/11 cycle. At m. 35, an arpeggiated figure that appears to be a rhythmic diminution of the earlier 5/7 passages in the lower strings is also an adumbration of the b motive of theme 1 (brackets, Ex. 369). The figure consists of two ascending perfect-fourth trichords, E-A-D and C-F-B♭, that intersect at a whole tone (D-C). At m. 36, an inverted statement (C-G-D/E-B-F♯) transposes the initial one (m. 35) by a whole tone, so that these ascending and descending phases together unfold larger interlocking segments of the interval-5/7 and interval-2/10 cycles (Ex. 370). The mirror relations of the interval-5/7 trichords in this symmetrical pattern (B♭-F-C/C-G-D and D-A-E/E-B-F♯) jointly form a nine-note 5/7 segment, B♭-F-C-G-D-A-E-B-F♯, like the earlier symmetrical passages (mm. 6–10 and 16–20) based on nine-note 1/11 formations (A♭-A-B♭-B-C-D♭-D-E♭-E and D♭-D-E♭-E-F-G♭-G-A♭-A). The present 5/7 configurations (mm. 35ff.) are also as-

368 *Concerto for Orchestra*, Movement I, mm. 22–34

369 *Concerto for Orchestra*, Movement I, mm. 35–36

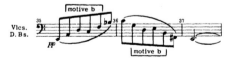

370 *Concerto for Orchestra*, Movement I, mm. 35–36

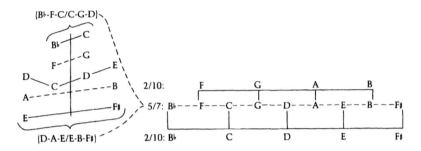

sociated with the earlier tremolo passages, in that they imply the presence of two complementary whole-tone formations, B♭-C-D-E-F♯ and F-G-A-B, similarly of five and four notes. From the end of m. 38 through m. 50, the original 5/7 trichords are dissolved in the inverted stretto of eighth-note figures.

At the return of the main introductory theme (m. 51), a tritone (A♭-D) for the first time appears as a prominent thematic element, serving as the boundary interval of the initial chromatic phrase in vnI (mm. 51–52) and also prominently placed in vnII (Ex. 371). The descending segment in vnI (A♭-G-F♯-E-D), in which tritone A♭-D encompasses elided interval-1 and interval-2 partitions (A♭-G-F♯/F♯-E-D), foreshadows (mm. 58–75) the ostinato eighth-note figure at the conclusion of the introduction and the inverted figure (m. 79) that initiates the second phrase of theme 1. The tritone boundary (E♭-A) of the ostinato figure moves up a whole tone (m. 76) to the tritone boundary (F-B) of motive a, the latter then being transposed down a semitone to the tritone (E-B♭) of the inverted statement of motive a. Thus, at these prominent points in the sonata form (end of the introduction and beginning of the exposition) a succession of three tritone cycles (E♭-A, F-B, and E-B♭) are separated by interval 2 and interval 1, respectively, a reflection of the intervallic alternations in motive a of the theme.

At the modified return of the theme (mm. 123ff., winds), all three of these tritones appear as boundaries of the successive motive-a statements. The two original motive-a tritones (F-B and E-B♭) imply the presence of Z-5/11 (F-B♭-B-E) in the thematic structure, while the third boundary tritone (E♭-A), at m. 127, winds, is now expressly established in the linear statement of the violins (mm. 126–28) as part of Z-3/9 (E♭-A♭-A-D) (Ex. 372). These pairs of tritones form part of a larger series of vertically stated tritones (mm. 117ff., with upbeat, vns and upper winds) that serve as basic structural elements in the generation of a complex of interlocking interval cycles (Ex. 373). The successive pairs of tritones that overlap the barlines (upbeat to m. 117 through m. 121, vns) unfold all three even-numbered Z cells. At the same time, the successive pairs of tritones in each measure unfold all three interval-3 cycles (F-A♭-B-D, G-B♭-C♯-E, and A-C-E♭-G♭). In addition, the series of tritones formed by the successive downbeats in the violins outlines one of the whole-tone cycles, the upper winds explicitly confirming this by doubling the latter with two parallel Y cells (Y-7 and Y-1);

371 *Concerto for Orchestra,* Movement I, mm. 51–52, vns

372 *Concerto for Orchestra,* Movement I, mm. 122–28

373 *Concerto for Orchestra*, Movement I, mm. 117–21

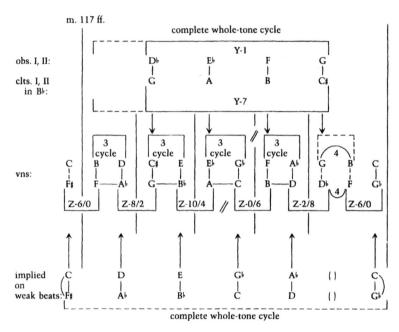

these two Y cells (G-A-B-C♯ and D♭-E♭-F-G) together form the complete whole-tone cycle. The tritones on the successive weak beats in the violins together imply the other complete whole-tone cycle. At m. 125, oboe (see Ex. 372), the tritone boundary (C♭-F) of the inverted a-motive is explicitly established in the violins (mm. 122–24) as the boundary of Y-11 (C♭-D♭-E♭-F), the latter continuing the whole-tone cycle of the upper winds, mm. 118–21 (see Ex. 373). (This statement of Y-11, a slight modification of the inverted a-motive—the motive, C♭-(C)-D♭-E♭-F, contains one chromatic note, C—establishes the whole-tone cyclic property implied within the latter.) Thus, this passage interlocks complete sets of interval cycles—the chromatic (interval-1/11) continuum is partitioned into two cycles of interval 2, three of interval 3, and six of interval 6—the last type of interval cycle (tritone, or interval-6) of which also generates the succession of Z cells (even-numbered, in this case) and serves as the basic structural element in this complex of cycles.

Just as the tritone property, which encompasses motive a, is basic in this generation of four sets of interval cycles (1/11, 2/10, 3/9, and 6/6), the intervallic properties of motive b (see Ex. 366) are basic in generating interlocking partitions of the interval-5/7 and interval-2/10 cycles in the bridge passage (mm. 134–48) between the first- and second-theme groups. The intermediary trombone theme, a transformation of motive b, cyclically extends one of the perfect fourths, E-B, to E-B-F♯-C♯ (mm. 138–44).[7] Furthermore, the pitch content of this C♯-Aeolian trombone theme forms a partially ordered seven-note segment of the 5/7 cycle (A-E-B-F♯-C♯-G♯-D♯), a smaller partition of the latter forming (at m. 137) a whole-tone segment (B-C♯-D♯). Theme 2 (mm. 155ff., oboe), which fuses characteristics of motives a and b of theme 1,[8] further develops these interlocking cyclic segments. The most prominent component of the theme is its initial whole tone, E-F♯. The accompanying strings and horns support the latter with a held 5/7 dyad, B-F♯, the two intervals together forming an interlocking segment of the 5/7 cycle (E-B-F♯); at mm. 175ff. this three-note figure explicitly appears as an ostinato pattern in the harp accompaniment.

In the development section (mm. 231ff.), both motives of theme 1 are primarily developed by cyclical extension of their intervallic properties. The section opens with motive a, bounded by tritone D♭-G, which is transposed up a semitone in the following stretto based on linear statements of motive a, each bounded by tritone D-G♯. The two tritones (D♭-G and D-G♯) together imply the presence of Z-2/8 (D-G-G♯-D♭). At mm. 237–41, the inverted form of the motive moves up again by a semitone, now with tritone boundary E♭-A. The two tritones (D-G♯ and E♭-A) that encompass the linearly adjacent prime and inverted forms of the motive together imply the presence of a second Z cell, Z-3/9 (E♭-G♯-A-D), an interval-1 transposition of the first (Z-2/8). Thus far, the prime and inverted statements of the motive have outlined three tritones (D♭-G, D-G♯, and E♭-A) a semitone apart (see the analogous tritone relations shown in Exx. 362, 365, 372). In an inverted stretto based on motive a (Ex. 374: mm. 242–47), the semitone relation of successive tritones is expanded to a whole tone in the strings (supported by the horns). Tritone E♭-A initiates a series of whole-tone transpositions that culminates (m. 247, violins) at tritone C♯-G, the entire series outlining a complete whole-tone cycle, E♭-F-G-A-B-C♯ (or A-B-C♯-D♯-E♯-G). (While some of the inverted motive-a statements in the winds appear modified, the succession of initial tones also outlines this whole-tone cycle.)

A significant cyclic relationship between motives a and b is found (mm. 248ff., strings) in a canon based on motive b, which follows the motive-a stretto. As was mentioned earlier in this chapter, the prime form of motive

---

7 This interval-5/7 segment is a retrograde of the opening measures of the movement, so this trombone theme serves as a link between the introductory 5/7 passage and motive b of theme 1.

8 This theme is based on the rhythm of motive b and also slightly varies the intervallic structure of motive a, F♯-E-D♯-D-C (mm. 165–67, oboe).

374   *Concerto for Orchestra*, Movement I, mm. 242–47

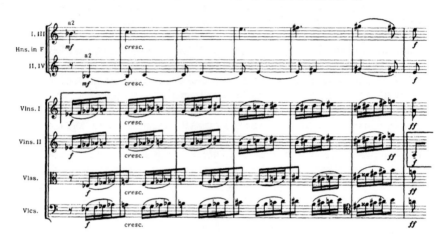

375   *Concerto for Orchestra*, Movement I, mm. 258ff.

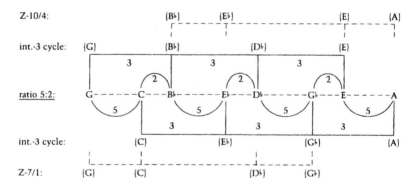

a, which is based on an interval-ratio of 2 : 1 (or two interlocking interval-3 cyclic segments), outlines a partial octatonic scale. At mm. 258ff., a sequential extension of motive b in each of the canonic voices gives us an interval-ratio 5 : 2 ordering, G-C-Bb-Eb-Db-Gb-E-A, of a complete octatonic scale (G-A-Bb-C-Db-Eb-E-Gb), a reinterpretation of the 2 : 1 ordering of motive a. The ratio-5 : 2 ordering (Ex. 375), like the 2 : 1 ordering, is based on two interlocking interval-3 cycles (G-Bb-Db-E and C-Eb-Gb-A). (At mm. 263–64, vnI, a mutation produces an octatonic transposition giving a partial segment, F-Ab-Cb, of the remaining interval-3 cycle.) In addition, the two Z-cell structures, Z-7/1 (G-C/Db-Gb) and Z-10/4 (Bb-Eb/E-A), that form this octatonic collection (see Ex. 375), are partitioned according to their 5/7 rather than their 1/11 interval-couples. The development section ends (mm. 316–85) with a lengthy fugato based on the intermediary trombone theme, the successive interval-5/7 entries (F-B♭-F-B♭/C-G-C-G/F) being separated at two points by interval 2/10 (B♭-C and G-F). The last entry, on F (m. 363), initiates a close stretto, the tail end of each linear statement (mm. 377ff.) of which is exclusively based on a 5/7 segment, D♭-A♭-E♭-B♭. The pitch content of the latter segment is a local 5/7 cyclic extension of the more background-level pitch content (B♭-F-C-G) collectively implied by the entry pitches of the fugato. The two segments combine to form a larger seven-note segment (D♭-A♭-E♭-B♭-F-C-G) of the cycle of fifths. Thus, the development section moves from the cyclic intervallic properties of motive a to those of motive b, these properties having been cyclically generated ever since the opening of the work.

CHAPTER IX

Conclusion

The equalization of the twelve pitch-classes in Bartók's music and the widespread effects this had on his compositional development appear to be relevant to a larger body of post-tonal music. While certain basic assumptions of the equal-division system had been arrived at around the same time by several post-tonal composers, there are several divergent points of origin in the evolution toward the new principles. Of these origins, two extremes are seen in the ultra-chromaticism of German late Romantic music, on the one hand, and the pentatonic-diatonic modality of peasant music, on the other.

Several composers in the late nineteenth and early twentieth centuries turned, as Bartók did, to the modalities of their native folk music as the basis for composition, but it was he who most thoroughly and extensively transformed these modes into the materials of a new musical language. Art music has always been influenced to varying degrees by folk music, but only in the nineteenth century did such nationalistic composers as Liszt (*Hungarian Rhapsodies*), Brahms (*Hungarian Dances*, numerous arrangements of German folk songs, and folk-like settings), Chopin (*Polonaises* and *Mazurkas*), and Dvořák (*Slavonic Dances*) so consciously and systematically incorporate folk elements and styles into their works.[1] However, even these composers had at best little profound understanding, at worst, no knowledge at all of the genuine peasant music of their native lands, and, as in the instances of Liszt and Brahms, their "Hungarian" works were actually

1 *Béla Bartók Essays*, ed. Benjamin Suchoff (New York: St. Martin's Press, 1976), p. 340. The original publication is given in n. 6 of Chapter II.

based on the gypsy instrumental music of the cafés. Folk elements had often become so thoroughly filtered by their incorporation into the sentimental or romantic idioms of the European art-music composers that the folk essence was either totally distorted or lost altogether. In Bartók's opinion,

> The effects of peasant music cannot be deep or permanent unless this music is studied in the country as part of a life shared with the peasants. It is not enough to study it as it is stored up in the museums. It is the character of peasant music, indescribable in words, that must find its way into our music. It must be pervaded by the very atmosphere of peasant culture. Peasant motives (or imitations of such motives) will only lend our music some new ornaments; nothing more.[2]

According to Bartók, Mussorgsky was "the only composer among the latter to yield completely and exclusively to the influence of peasant music."[3] While Mussorgsky captured the essence of his Russian peasant music through pervasive modal coloring and folk-inspired rhythms, he was to remain within the limits of traditional tonality and harmonic construction. His musical idiom, with all its leanings toward folk music, therefore, essentially belongs well within the Western European art-music tradition. The pentatonic and modal characteristics that Debussy acquired, largely through the influences of the Russian nationalists, are the basis of a more significant tendency toward the breakdown of the traditional tonal system and the formation of a new one based on equal or symmetrical divisions of the octave. While Mussorgsky and Debussy played important roles in the evolution toward a new system of pitch relations, each represents only a part of that multifaceted development that is entirely encompassed by Bartók's compositional evolution. Mussorgsky never transcended, on the large-scale level of a work, the traditional concepts of tertian harmonic construction and tonality, but he did prominently employ folk-music elements. Debussy, who was only indirectly influenced by folk music—it remained for him an "exoticism"—went beyond the precepts of tradition in his extensive employment of symmetrical (e.g., whole-tone and pentatonic) constructions. Thus, it was only with Kodály and, especially, Bartók (in Hungary, Rumania, and elsewhere), and, to a lesser degree, with Janáček (in Czechoslovakia) in the early part of the present century that the first extensive scientific investigations of folk music were exploited for the purpose of profoundly altering the foundations of the traditional major-minor scale system.

Bartók's transformational processes covering the broad expanse from the pentatonic and diatonic folk modes to the new constructions of a contemporary musical language are most closely approached in certain works of Stravinsky. Although Stravinsky himself stated that he could never share Bartók's lifelong gusto for his native folklore, and, in fact, that he deplored it in

2 Ibid., p. 341. See ibid. for original publication.
3 Ibid., p. 340. See ibid. for original publication.

Bartók,[4] at least his *Le sacre du printemps, Pribaoutki*, and *Les noces* appear to be direct outgrowths of Russian folk music. Bartók cites *Pribaoutki* as a typical example:

> The vocal part consists of motives which . . . throughout are imitations of Russian folk music motives. The characteristic brevity of these motives, all of them taken into consideration separately, is absolutely tonal, a circumstance that makes possible a kind of instrumental accompaniment composed of a sequence of underlying, more or less atonal tone-patches very characteristic of the temper of the motives.
>
> Even the obstinate clinging to a tone or group of tones borrowed from folk motives seems to be a precious foothold: it offers a solid framework for the compositions of this transition period and prevents wandering about at random.[5]

Even more significantly than in its derivation of melodic "groups of tones" or "intervallic pitch-cells" from folk sources as the basis for establishing the linear surface layers in such works, *Le sacre* perhaps represents the epitome of transformational processes from the folk modes to the abstract symmetrical and cyclic pitch-formations of the equal-division system. The opening folk-song figure of the bassoon solo[6] (to No. 1) unfolds six of the seven notes of the "white key" diatonic collection, the modal permutation (A-B-C-D-E-( )-G) being suggested by the priority of A at each of the local cadential points in this thematic statement. The prominent modal character (either in A-Aeolian or A-Dorian) and the rhythmic qualities of the tune clearly establish the folk mood as a basic stylistic premise at the outset, while structural properties of the tune itself contain the seeds for modal transformation into the interval cycles. The registral boundary of the tune is the minor seventh, E-D, the low note (E) placed as the fifth note of the triplet grouping and the high note (D) analogously placed as the fifth note of the eighth-note grouping (Ex. 376). These boundary tones together symmetrically encompass the modal tonic, A, by forming perfect fourths below and above it, respectively (E-A-D). This background-level interval-5/7 structure lends support to the interpretation that the "white key" content of the tune can be understood as an unordered six-note segment of the 5/7 cycle, C-G-D-A-E-B, generated from C—this note prominently initiates each of the four rhythmic cells of the tune.

At m. 2, a major-minor conflict is introduced by the entry of the horn on C♯, the major third of the A mode. At the same time, pitch-class C♯ foreshadows the unfolding of the complementary six-note partition of the 5/7 cycle (F♯-C♯-G♯-D♯-A♯-E♯), based almost exclusively on the "black key"

4 See Igor Stravinsky and Robert Craft, *Conversations with Igor Stravinsky* (Berkeley and Los Angeles: University of California Press, 1980), p. 74.

5 *Bartók Essays*, p. 318. The original publication is "Der Einfluss der Volksmusik auf die heutige Kunstmusik" ("The Influence of Folk Music on the Art Music of Today"), *Melos* (Berlin) 1/17 (October, 1920): 384–86; No. 2 (February, 1930): 66–67.

6 This rhapsodic tune is originally from Lithuania; see Anton Juszkiewicz, *Litauische Volks-Weisen* (Cracow, 1900), No. 157.

376   Stravinsky, *Le sacre du printemps*, m. 1 through No. 3, m. 5

collection. The single entry pitch (C♯) of the horn, of which the second note, D, is simply an upper-neighbor, represents the first disruptive element outside the "white-key" collection (C-G-D-A-E-B). At No. 1, the C♯, now in the first clarinet, is joined with its interval 5/7, A♭ (in enharmonic spelling, G♯), introducing the first cyclic expansion of the complementary "black key" partition—C♯-G♯ initiates and ends a pair of parallel descending interval-1 cycles. At No. 2, a countertheme is introduced in the English horn, the pitch content of which expands the "black key" partition to a four-note segment (F♯-C♯-G♯-D♯) of the 5/7 cycle. The latter is further cyclically expanded at No. 4f. Thus, while the pitch content of each of these interval-5/7 partitions (C-G-D-A-E-B and F♯-C♯-G♯-D♯-A♯-E♯) is registrally contained within a one-octave range, so that a diatonic thematic contour is expressly outlined in each case, the juxtaposition of the two mutually exclusive six-note collections gives us all twelve tones.[7]

The tritone separation of these two equivalent cyclic partitions, which are respectively generated from C and F♯, is locally reflected in the structure of the theme. At the bassoon cadence (No. 1, m. 2), G♭ and C together form a new, chromatic boundary that is a symmetrical contraction of the original one (E-D). Both these boundaries maintain the modal-tonic A as the structural axis of the tune (E-A-D and G♭-A-C). This chromatic registral contraction to tritone G♭-C is a fundamental step in the transformation of the structure of the folk tune into other cyclic formations as well.[8] Within the

7 For further discussion of the relations in *Le sacre* between diatonic collections and the interval-5/7 cycle, see George Perle, "Berg's Master Array of the Interval Cycles," *Musical Quarterly* 63/1 (January, 1977): 10–11.

8 See ibid., pp. 11–13.

first fifteen measures of the Introduction the bassoon solo unfolds four varied statements of the folk tune, structurally outlined by minor thirds and tritones. The initial statement is a diatonic embellishment of the prominently placed modal tonic (A) and minor third (C), the thematic contour establishing a background-level descent from C to A. At No. 1, mm. 1–2, this descent is now chromatically filled in and occurs within a shorter temporal span. In turn, the tonic, A, descends at the cadence to the minor third below to give us an important foreground statement of A-G♭, or cyclic-interval 3. The cadential tritone, G♭-C, is thus symmetrically partitioned into its two interval-3 components (G♭-A-C) as a prominent foreground event. In the final thematic variant (No. 3, m. 3), the structural descent is further extended to complete the entire cycle, C-A-F♯-D♯ (Ex. 377). While the cadence at No. 1, m. 2, establishes the priority of tritone G♭-C, the chromatic descent of the last statement establishes the other tritone (A-D♯) of this interval-3 cycle as a basic background-level thematic structure.

A significant link between the "black key" diatonic countertheme in the English horn (No. 2f.) and the bassoon cadence (at No. 3, m. 3) on the minor third, F♯-D♯, is established by a special symmetrical relationship between them: the countertheme is exclusively based on the interval-5/7 segment F♯-C♯-G♯-D♯, which is precisely encompassed by the cadential interval-3 segment of the bassoon, F♯-D♯. Furthermore, both the interval-5/7 cyclic partitions, C-G-D-A-E-B and F♯-C♯-G♯-D♯-()-() (i.e., "white key" and "black key" diatonic collections), that have thematically unfolded thus far are symmetrically defined by the background-level interval-3 cycle, C-A-F♯-D♯ (Ex. 378). Thus, at the outset of the Introduction, a transformation of the folk material into the interval cycles begins by means of registral, durational, and temporal emphases on significant structural tones.

The cyclic properties that are either implied or embedded in the opening

377 Stravinsky, *Le sacre du printemps*, No. 3, mm. 1–3

378 Stravinsky, *Le sacre du printemps*, m. 1 through No. 3, m. 3: Segmental Relation between the Ten-Note Interval-5/7 Cyclic Segment and the Basic Interval-3 Cycle

379 Stravinsky, *Le sacre du printemps*, No. 42

octatonic: B♭-C-D♭-E♭-E-F♯-G-A

folk-tune statements are further abstracted and developed as more foreground events in subsequent sections of the work. One instance is the "Jeu
du rapt" (Nos. 45–46), where all three interval-3 cycles (C-A-F♯-D♯, A♭-F-
D-B, and D♭-B♭-G-E) simultaneously appear in descending order against a
5/7 cyclic segment, A-E-B-F♯-C♯-G♯-D♯-A♯-F.[9] Prior to this passage, the
pitch content (Nos. 42–43) is based on an interlocking of two of the three
interval-3 cycles (B♭-D♭-E-G and C-E♭-F♯-A) to give us one of the symmetrical octatonic collections, B♭-C-D♭-E♭-E-F♯-G-A (Ex. 379).[10] At No. 44,
a new combination of two interval-3 cycles, A-C-E♭-G♭ and B-D-F-A♭, gives
us a second octatonic collection, A-B-C-D-E♭-F-G♭-A♭, just prior to the linear statements (at No. 45) of all three interval-3 cycles. The invariant segment to both these octatonic collections (B♭-C-D♭-E♭-E-F♯-G-A and A-

9 Ibid., p. 12.
10 See Arthur Berger, "Problems of Pitch Organization in Stravinsky," *Perspectives of
New Music* (Fall–Winter, 1963): 27–28. This excerpt, given by Berger, demonstrates that the
octatonic collection is also formed here, as one instance, in the lower strings, by a linear interlocking of traditional triads, thereby maintaining a link between the octatonic and diatonic
spectra. The nonsymmetrical triadic partitioning of the octatonic scale will be further discussed below in connection with diatonic/octatonic interactions in the *Symphony of Psalms*.

380 Stravinsky, *Le sacre du printemps*, Nos. 42–45

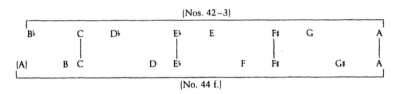

(Nos. 42–3)

| B♭ | | C | D♭ | | E♭ | E | | F♯ | G | | A |
| (A) | B | C | | D | E♭ | | F | F♯ | | G♯ | A |

(No. 44 f.)

B-C-D-E♭-F-G♭-A♭) is the interval-3 cycle C-A-F♯-D♯, which, if only by coincidence, is the basic structure of the opening thematic statements of the bassoon solo. Example 380 illustrates this link between the two octatonic collections. At No. 44, mm. 4–5, this invariant 3/9 cycle is isolated in the oboes and English horns as a prominent foreground event. This is foreshadowed (see Ex. 379) by the roots of the arpeggiated pizzicato triads (No. 42f.) that outline this basic interval-3 cycle.

Interactions of traditional and nontraditional pitch collections in *Le sacre* have also been explored in terms of equivalent partitions of the octatonic scale with both diatonic and octatonic significance.[11] The octatonic significance of the diatonic minor-tetrachord ("0-2-3-5") on the global level is supported by specific instances that confirm the essentially octatonic quality of this tetrachord. As one instance, in the "Danses des adolescents" at No. 13, the upper (0-2-3-5) incomplete minor tetrachord, B♭-( )-D♭-E♭, which also linearly unfolds at No. 14 in the English horn, is given octatonic significance by the opposing lower E. This hypothesis is partially supported by the C-major pitch-content of the bassoon at No. 14, in which the incomplete tetrachord, B♭-( )-D♭-E♭, together with the major triad, C-E-G, give us B♭-C-D♭-E♭-E-( )-G. In the "Jeux des cités rivales" (at No. 64), the upper G-F-E-D minor tetrachord is similarly given octatonic significance by the lower G♯. Many other examples can be cited in which a shared (0-2-3-5) tetrachord serves as the principal connecting link in a primarily octatonic context ("inferred singly or with reference to some form of octatonic-diatonic interpenetration").[12] Ultimately, the basic diatonic premise for this "interpenetration" lies in the symmetrical Dorian mode (e.g., D-E-F-G-A-B-C-D), whose two equivalent minor tetrachords (D-E-F-G and A-B-C-D) allow for two possibilities of octatonic penetration (D-E-F-G-A♭-B♭-B-C♯ or E♭-F-G♭-A♭-A-B-C-D), coming often by way of a tritone or major-seventh "intrusion."[13]

11 Such interactions are discussed in depth by Pieter C. van Den Toorn, "Some Characteristics of Stravinsky's Diatonic Music (II)," *Perspectives of New Music* (Spring–Summer, 1977): 61.
12 Ibid.
13 See the references to Perle, Berger, and van Den Toorn in notes 7–12 of this chapter. Also see my discussion of Bartók's *First Improvisation* in Chapter VII, pp. 220–22, one instance of these relations in Bartók's works.

The primary, though not exclusive, focus of our theoretical discussion has been on the symmetrical partitioning of the octatonic collection (either into a pair of equivalent interval-3 cycles or a pair of minor tetrachords). Certain works of Stravinsky's Neoclassical period, however, are importantly based on nonsymmetrical (diatonic) tertian partitions of the octatonic scale. Although Stravinsky became opposed to the folk-music orientation after he composed *Les noces* (1917–1923), his exploitation of traditional modal (diatonic) properties in the diatonic-octatonic context of the *Symphony of Psalms* (1930) is closely related to procedures (the use of invariant segments as a means of progression between divergent pitch sets) in the music of many post-tonal composers. In the *Symphony of Psalms*, the upper winds at No. 5f. (Ex. 381) unfold a descending octatonic scale (A♭-G-F-E-D-C♯-B-B♭)

381 Stravinsky, *Symphony of Psalms*, Movement I, No. 4, m. 7,
Through No. 5, m. 4

in alternating minor thirds. The opening of the movement (mm. 1–4) anticipates the pitch content of this octatonic set with three diatonic tertian constructions: an E-minor triad (E-G-B), Bb-dominant-seventh (Bb-D-F-Ab), and a first-inversion G-dominant-seventh (B-D-F-G). These chords, which are completely dissociated here from any traditional concept of harmonic progression—the suggested tonics (Eb and C) of the two respective dominant-seventh chords have relevance only as background-level tonal centers—function merely as local diatonic pitch-cells. The total pitch-content of these three diatonic constructions exclusively foreshadows that of the octatonic scale (Ex. 382). Thus, the three tertian chords together give us seven of the eight octatonic tones, Ab-G-F-E-D-( )-B-Bb. This hypothesis is supported by the local unfolding at No. 5, m. 3, in the bassoons of both dominant-sevenths, G-F-D-B and Bb-Ab-F-D (see Ex. 381). The strings, based on the former (G-B-D-F), support the entire passage.

Another diatonic-octatonic link occurs in the introductory passage leading to the alto entry at No. 4. At No. 2, mm. 1–5, the piano unfolds the E-Phrygian mode; the initial two notes of the mode (E-F) then form the basis of the alto chant (Nos. 4–5). The alto E-F shifts (at No. 5f.) to a new semitone, G-Ab, to give us a four-note symmetrical segment (E-F-G-Ab) of the octatonic scale of the winds. The octatonic reinterpretation of the original Phrygian dyad, E-F, is anticipated at No. 2, mm. 5–6, by the chromatic shift in the pianos from the Phrygian-dyad G-A to the octatonic G-Ab. At No. 9, the octatonic material returns to the E-Phrygian mode.

In the late nineteenth and early twentieth centuries, the (symmetrical) whole-tone scale began to appear with increasing prominence as a construction importantly derived from art-music sources. Near the end of Debussy's *La mer*, a melodic statement of the whole-tone scale appears in conjunction with a triadic harmonic basis (Ex. 383), the latter of which, however, is not founded on the precepts of traditional dominant and subdominant voice-

382 Stravinsky, *Symphony of Psalms*, Movement I, No. 5f.

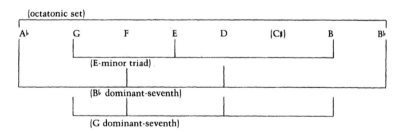

383 Debussy, *La mer* (No. 62, m. 4, horns and trumpets)

384 Schoenberg, *Harmonielehre*, ex. 318

leading properties.[14] Rather, the key of D♭ is established earlier in the movement and at the cadential point of this excerpt is simply asserted by the D♭ tonic-triad.

According to Schoenberg, the conscious use of the whole-tone scale has two forerunners.[15] In the first case (Ex. 384), the melodic projection of the augmented triad results in whole-tone segments by splitting any one of the projected major thirds of the triad into two whole tones by way of passing tones. All these symmetrically divided major thirds taken together result in the complete whole-tone scale. In the second case (Ex. 385), the melodic projection of major thirds from a dominant-seventh chord with its fifth degree either augmented or omitted will result in melodic whole-tone segments by the same usage of passing tones. The latter case is similar to the first, since the altered seventh-chord can be understood as an augmented triad with added seventh. Such an altered dominant-seventh chord gives us four of the six tones of the whole-tone scale, G-()-B-()-D♯-F. Schoenberg also points out that if the latter is further expanded into a ninth chord, G-B-D♯-F-A, five of the six whole tones will result. (Contained within the latter is the "French Augmented-Sixth" chord, B-D♯-F-A, a significant traditional construction that lies exclusively within the whole-tone spectrum.) An additional example is given by Schoenberg to illustrate a "traditional" resolution of a six-note whole-tone chord to a C-major triad (Ex. 386). This six-tone chord results from the simultaneous raising and lowering of the fifth degree: G-B-(D)-F-A to G-B-(C♯-D♯)-F-A. The significance of the transformations of these traditional tertian constructions into the symmetrical whole-tone scale has been summarized by Schoenberg:

14 Arnold Whittall, "Tonality and the Whole-Tone Scale in the Music of Debussy," *Music Review* 36/4 (November, 1975): 261.

15 Arnold Schoenberg, *Theory of Harmony*, trans. Roy E. Carter (Berkeley and Los Angeles: University of California Press, 1978), p. 391.

The whole-tone chords, regarded as vagrant chords, have at least the same possibilities for connection as the augmented triad. Depending on the degrees to which they are referred, they can be used for modulations and modulatory episodes.[16]

The chromatic alterations of such tertian harmonic constructions in extremely chromatic contexts are prominently found in, among others, the

385   Schoenberg, *Harmonielehre*, exx. 319–20

386   Schoenberg, *Harmonielehre*, exx. 321–23

16 Ibid., p. 397.

works of the German late Romantic composers and in Schoenberg's own works.

The ultimate consequences of these developments have their roots in the early part of the nineteenth century. In the chromatic tonal system, use of a major-minor modal mixture has contributed to the development of a new means of subdividing the octave, the resulting harmonic progressions often being perceived less in terms of mixture than as a subdivision of the octave into equal intervals. The ultimate tonal orientation of such passages is established by the cadential focus of such progressions on dominant-tonic relations. A prominent example is found in the "Sanctus" of Schubert's *Mass in E-Flat*,[17] in which the initial E♭ tonic moves to the dominant at the end of the excerpt through a series of descending major thirds, E♭-C♭ (B)-G-E♭ (i.e., interval-4 cycle) (Ex. 387). Furthermore, by means of passing whole tones within the major thirds, a complete whole-tone scale (i.e., interval-2 cycle) is outlined in the bass. In Chopin's *Mazurka*, Op. 50, No. 3,[18] a similar chromatic progression unfolds, in which the initial D-major chord begins a series of ascending minor thirds in the bass, D-F-G♯-B-D (i.e., interval-3 cycle) (Ex. 388). (Each of these cyclic tones is microtonicized by its applied

387   Graphic reduction of a passage in the "Sanctus" from Schubert's *Mass in E-Flat* (Salzer and Schachter, ex. 7–71a)

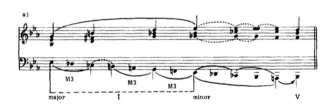

388   Graphic reduction of a passage in Chopin's *Mazurka*, Op. 50, No. 3 (Salzer and Schachter, ex. 7–72a)

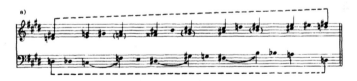

17 The equal divisions of the octave in chromatic tonal music of the nineteenth century are discussed in some detail by Felix Salzer and Carl Schachter in *Counterpoint in Composition: The Study of Voice Leading* (New York: McGraw-Hill, 1969), pp. 215–21. This graphic reduction is taken from ex. 7–71a. See the actual musical excerpt in ex. 7–71.

18 Ibid.; see ex. 7–72 for the musical excerpt.

389   Liszt, *Sonnetto 104 del Petrarca* from the second book of
Années de pèlerinage

390   Berlioz, *Francs-Juges* overture

dominant.) Simultaneously, the upper line structurally unfolds another series of minor thirds, F♯-A-B♯-D♯-F♯, which together form an octatonic
scale. Liszt's *Sonnetto 104 del Petrarca* from the second book of *Années de
pèlerinage* (Ex. 389)[19] contains a series of traditional chords, either dimin-
ished- or dominant-sevenths, that prolong a motion to the tonic E-major at
the molto espress. These chords linearly unfold an octatonic collection, B♯-
C♯-D♯-E-F♯-G-A-B♭, which can be understood as a combination of the two
diminished-seventh chords, B♯-D♯-F♯-A and C♯-E-G-B♭.

There are, of course, other nineteenth-century examples of traditional
chromatic progressions that result in equal divisions of the octave,[20] more
specifically, linear voice-leading properties that outline single or compounded cyclic constructions (i.e., whole-tone scales and their augmented-
triad partitions, or octatonic scales and their diminished-seventh partitions).

19 See Paul Lansky and George Perle, "Atonality, " *The New Grove Dictionary of Music
and Musicians,* ed. Stanley Sadie (6th ed., London: Macmillan, 1980), pp. 669-70.

20 See Gregory Proctor, "Technical Bases of Nineteenth-Century Chromatic Tonality: A
Study in Chromaticism" (Ph.D. diss., Princeton University, 1977).

Certain more unusual adumbrations of the complex of interval cycles may be observed in such works as the *Francs-Juges* overture (1827) and *Les Troyens* (1856–1859) of Berlioz.[21] Such a progression is given in Example 390, where two chromatic scales (interval-1 cycles) ascend in parallel minor-thirds against both whole-tone scales (interval-2 cycles) that descend in parallel minor-thirds. The harmonic result is a series based on reiterations of the three diminished-seventh chords (interval-3 cycles), the progression of which prevents any sense of unambiguous tonal orientation. This example significantly foreshadows passages in the music of Mussorgsky, Bartók, and Berg.

The broad theoretical implications of the basic premises of the equal-division system as it evolved from the chromatic progressions of nineteenth-century music and from the modal bases of Eastern European folk music are manifested in the twentieth century most comprehensively in the music of Bartók[22] and, to a lesser extent, in that of Stravinsky. While Schoenberg also plays a primary role in the development of chromaticism beyond the limits of traditional tonality, it must be emphasized that Schoenberg and his followers made a complete break with the folk-song/diatonic connections. It is in Bartók, above all, that we see these connections. While Stravinsky departs from the folk-music tradition in his Neoclassical works, that tradition was basic to his musical language throughout Bartók's career. The radically new approach to the equal-division concept in a large body of post-tonal music and the ultimate consequences of these developments that began in the late nineteenth and early twentieth centuries have been expressed by George Perle in the final paragraphs of *Twelve-Tone Tonality*:

> The early years of the present century bring us, in consequence of the disappearance of conventional normative elements in the atonal music of Schoenberg and his school, to "an ultimate expansion of possible relations to include the

21 Philip Friedheim, "Radical Harmonic Procedures in Berlioz," *Music Review* 21/4 (November, 1960): 286.

22 The Hungarian scholar Ernő Lendvai, in *Béla Bartók: An Analysis of His Music* (London: Kahn and Averill, 1971), pp. 1–15, offers in his Bartók analyses a theoretical approach establishing a direct connection between traditional tonal functions (i.e., tonic, dominant, and subdominant) and the system based on the equal subdivisions of the octave. He suggests that such key schemes as C-E-A♭-C in, e.g., the *Sonata for Two Pianos and Percussion*, Movement I, represent (through tone substitution) the traditional harmonic relationships of tonic-dominant-subdominant-tonic. According to Lendvai, the upper third (E) may function as a substitute for the dominant—this concept is based on the traditional relative-key substitutes in terms of harmonic root function—the lower third (A♭), for the subdominant. By symmetrically subdividing the cycle of fifths into these three harmonic areas, as illustrated in his "polar-axis" system (see ibid., p. 15), he is clearly suggesting that the tonic C, dominant E, and subdominant A♭ have the same functions as their tritone equivalents and minor thirds. Hence, each of these three functions has four poles, represented in his graphs by the three interval-3 cycles. While this theory is controversial, Lendvai's concept of formal proportions in certain works (based on the ratio of the Golden Section or Fibonacci series) is, to my mind, an important contribution to Bartók studies.

whole range of combinations contained in the semitonal scale" [Perle, *Serial Composition and Atonality*, p. 1]. We have shown how the convergence of the concepts of the interval cycle and (through the twelve-tone system) of strict inversional complementation leads to a comprehensive *system* of tone relations that permits us to define and classify every one of these combinations in terms of its sums and intervals, and consequently to establish differentiations, associations, and progressions between and among all these combinations.

Their sum and interval content are the sole objective basis for whatever connections one may wish to establish between pitch collections, and what else is it to "compose" except to establish such connections? Schoenberg's use of the "augmented triad" in Opus 11, No. 1, and Opus 46 [ibid., pp. 14f and 93]; . . . the symmetrical formations in the works of Bartók and Berg; the whole-tone collections in *Wozzeck*; invariant set segments in the later works of Scriabin [ibid., pp. 41ff.] and in the mature twelve-tone works of Schoenberg, Berg, and Webern; Webern's use of "cognate" sets in the Symphony and elsewhere, . . .—the structural functions of all of these are explicable only in terms of sum and interval content and ordering. They may be objectively defined, generalized, and integrated with one another. Collectively they imply a natural system of twelve-tone tonality.[23]

Bartók himself was keenly aware that he was composing within the equal-division system. He expressed the need for a new notational system in which all the chromatic tones would be given equal value, since traditional notational symbols implied hierarchical tonal functions that were no longer relevant to his music. Perhaps the use of neutral symbolization (numerical signs) for pitch classes, transpositions of pitch sets, interval classes, and sums of complementation in the present study could be seen as a fulfillment of Bartók's desire to reflect the true meaning of his musical language.[24] Several years ago, George Perle worked out what seems to be a consistent and simple terminology for cycles and cyclic collections. The need for such a terminology corresponds to the evolution to another kind of music, in which everything that happens is explicable in terms of cyclic intervals and sums. From the foregoing study of symmetrical pitch-relations in the music of Bartók and other post-tonal composers, it is obvious that the structural *functions* of the diverse melodic and harmonic formations are given meaning primarily by the immediate musical context within which they occur. However, in their structural *properties*, these formations are integrally related above and beyond any connections that are made between or among them in the compositional working out of the material. The special precompositionally determined properties in the broad spectrum of these pitch-class constructions are derived from their cyclic partitioning of the chromatic continuum (see Ex. 70, containing the total complex of interval cycles). The following outline of the new terminology is quoted from Perle's study of pitch organization in *Lulu*:

23 George Perle, *Twelve-Tone Tonality* (Berkeley and Los Angeles: University of California Press, 1977), pp. 171–72.
24 See *Bartók Essays*, p. 459. The original publication is given in n. 6 of the Preface.

Let the letter "C" followed by an interval-class number (0 through 6) designate the cycle. (If, for some special reason, we must distinguish between descending and ascending semitonal scales, or between cycles of "perfect fifths" and cycles of "perfect fourths," there is nothing to prevent the use of complementary interval numbers, 11 as well as 1, 7 as well as 5, etc.) Thus, "C1" represents the semitonal scale, "C2" the whole-tone scale, etc. But there are *two* whole-tone scales. What if we wish to distinguish between them? Since the two partitions of C2 are mutually exclusive, either of them may be identified by any one of its pitches. Let us represent these by pitch-class numbers, 0 for *c*, 1 for *c♯*, etc. The pitch-class numbers of the one whole-tone scale are 0, 2, 4, 6, 8, 10, and those of the other are 1, 3, 5, 7, 9, 11. In general we will specify the partition by employing its lowest pitch-class number as a subscript. In Volume I, pp. 155–159, I discuss the important role of the two whole-tone scales in *Wozzeck*[a] and show how one of these is given significant priority over the other in the course of the work. That "principal whole-tone scale" is $C2_1$. The "subordinate whole-tone scale," which only comes into its own in the final symphonic interlude, is $C2_0$. If for some special reason we should feel that we must specify a particular octave ambitus for a whole-tone scale, there is nothing to prevent our using any other of the pitch-class numbers as subscripts. The three C3 partitions may be analogously represented as $C3_0$, $C3_1$, and $C3_2$, and the four C4 partitions as $C4_0$, $C4_1$, $C4_2$, and $C4_3$. The "augmented triad" that serves as the "pivotal harmonic center" of Act II, Scene 1, of *Wozzeck* (see Volume I, pp. 145ff.) is $C4_1$. Since C5, like C1, does not fall into partitions, it requires no subscript. Finally, the tritone, C6, may be represented in its six non-equivalent pitch levels by subscripts 0 through 5. As for the four-note collection that has been called "Basic Cell I" in reference to *Lulu*,[b] "Cell z" in reference to the Fourth Quartet and other works by Bartók, and "Cell y" in reference to Webern's Opus 5, No. 4,[c] since this consists of two tritones we can represent it by appending two subscripts to "C6." The general collection may be represented as $C6_{n,n+1}$ or $C6_{n,n+5}$. Specifically, $C6_{1,2}$ and $C6_{4,5}$ are the two pitch levels of this collection that are of such foundational importance in the first movement of Bartók's Fourth Quartet. In *Lulu*, in the course of the opera as a whole, $C6_{3,4}$ comes to be identified with the Countess Geschwitz,[d] $C6_{1,2}$ with Dr. Schön, and $C6_{5,6}$ with Lulu. The "French Sixth" may be represented as $C6_{n,n+2}$ or $C6_{n,n+4}$. $C6_{0,2}$ is the specific "French Sixth" chord by means of which Berg effects a modulation to a new axis of symmetry in the second movement of the Quartet, Opus 3, mm. 68–71.[e] The "octatonic" scale may be represented as $C3_{n,n+1}$ or $C3_{n,n+2}$. Its three non-equivalent transpositions are $C3_{0,1}$, $C3_{1,2}$, and $C3_{2,3}$, or, if we prefer to imply the alternative interval series, 2,1,2,1,2,1,2, $C3_{0,2}$, $C3_{1,3}$, and $C3_{2,4}$.[25]

---

[a] George Perle, *The Operas of Alban Berg*, Vol. I: *Wozzeck* (Berkeley: University of California Press, 1980).

[b] This term for the four-note figure with which *Lulu* commences and which is the principal motive of the opera as a whole was introduced in Perle, "The Music of *Lulu*: A New Analysis," *Journal of the American Musicological Society* XII (1959).

[c] See Perle, *Serial Composition and Atonality*, 5th ed. (Berkeley: University of California Press, 1981), vii–ix, xvi–xviii.

[d] Douglas Jarman, "Countess Geschwitz Series: A Controversy Resolved?" *Proceedings of the Royal Musical Association* 107 (1980–1981).

[e] See Perle, *Twelve-Tone Tonality* (Berkeley: University of California Press, 1977), 13.

25 George Perle, *The Operas of Alban Berg*. Vol. II: *Lulu* (Berkeley and Los Angeles: University of California Press, 1984), Chap. 4.

if we want to specify a given interval series *and* permutation of an octatonic collection, we should not preclude the more particularized label of, say, $C3_{4,5}$ for E-F-G-G♯-A♯-B-C♯-D, which is a permutation of $C3_{1,2}$ (C♯-D-E-F-G-G♯-A♯-B). For purposes of this sort, we may depart from the general designation, in which cyclic partitions are represented by the "lowest" number. This particularization would also then take care of certain remaining combined partitions. For example, while two combined interval-4 cycles that form an interval-ratio 1 : 3 series (e.g., C-C♯-E-F-G♯-A, interlocking C-E-G♯ and C♯-F-A) present no problems in being designated as $C4_{0,1}$, the interlocking of two segments of the cycle of fourths or fifths ($C5$) suggests a terminological inconsistency. In the discussion of interlocking 5/7 cyclic segments in the *Concerto for Orchestra* (see Ex. 364d), which illustrates a scale described as interval-ratio 1 : 4 (C-A♭-G-E♭-D-B♭-A-F, interlocking C-G-D-A and A♭-E♭-B♭-F), a problem arises in the general attempt to distinguish between segments of the cycle of fifths. How does one specify $C5_{n,n+i}$, given that $C5$ always suggests $C5_0$ (i.e., the note C is always present in the partition, since there is only one cycle of fifths)? In this special case, we simply label the present combined partition (C-A♭-G-E♭-D-B♭-A-F) as $C5_{n,n\pm4}$, or, more specifically, $C5_{0,8}$, since we are talking about parallel perfect-fourth or fifth cyclic segments separated by a major third.

This terminology permits us to point in a simple, uniform, and objective manner to the properties and relationships of pitch collections of the equal-division system. While it is ideal to employ such symbolization in a study of a large body of post-tonal music, it is just as well, and even advantageous, to have kept the old terminology throughout the present study and only to have presented the new terms briefly at this concluding point. The evolution from an archaic, more diversified terminology to the newer, more uniform one suggests a significance that goes beyond the terminology itself, for it is reflective of and directly connected to the evolution in Bartók's musical language to the more abstract concepts themselves. Thus, one can underscore this musical evolution by making the explicit connection between the older and newer terminologies within a single study.

Chronological List of Cited Bartók Compositions

Twenty Hungarian Folksongs for voice and piano (December, 1906; revised 1938)

Eight Hungarian Folksongs for voice and piano (1907–1917)

Fourteen Bagatelles for Piano, Op. 6 (May, 1908)

String Quartet No. 1, Op. 7 (January 27, 1909)

Four Dirges for piano, Op. 9a (Quatre nénies) (1910)

Duke Bluebeard's Castle, Op. 11 (September, 1911)

String Quartet No. 2, Op. 17 (1915–October, 1917)

Eight Improvisations on Hungarian Peasant Songs for piano, Op. 20, (1920)

Sonata No. 1 for violin and piano (October–December, 1921)

Sonata No. 2 for violin and piano (July–November, 1922)

Mikrokosmos, 153 progressive pieces for piano (1926–1939)

Sonata for piano (June, 1926)

String Quartet No. 3 (September, 1927)

String Quartet No. 4 (July–September, 1928)

Cantata Profana: The Nine Enchanted Stags (September 8, 1930)

String Quartet No. 5 (August 6–September 6, 1934)

Music for Strings, Percussion, and Celesta (September, 1936)

String Quartet No. 6 (August–November, 1939)

Concerto for Orchestra (August 15–October 8, 1943)

Concerto No. 3, for piano and orchestra (1945, unfinished)

Works Cited

Antokoletz, Elliott. "Principles of Pitch Organization in Bartók's *Fourth String Quartet*." Ph.D. dissertation, City University of New York, 1975.
———. "Principles of Pitch Organization in Bartók's *Fourth String Quartet*." *In Theory Only* 3/6 (September, 1977): 3–22.
———. "The Musical Language of Bartók's *14 Bagatelles* for Piano." *Tempo* 137 (June, 1981): 8–16.
Archibald, Bruce. "Some Thoughts on Symmetry in Early Webern; Op. 5, No. 2." *Perspectives of New Music* 10/2 (Spring-Summer, 1972): 159–63.
Babbitt, Milton. "The String Quartets of Bartók." *Musical Quarterly* 25 (July, 1949): 377–85.
Barna, István. "Bartók II. vonósnégyesének módosított metrónóm jelzései" [The altered Metronome Indications in Bartók's Second Quartet]. *Zenei Szemle* (Budapest, 1948).
Bartók, Béla. "Strauss: Elektra." *A Zene* (Budapest) 2/4 (April, 1910): 57–58.

———. "Das Problem der neuen Musik." *Melos* (Berlin) 1/5 (April, 1920): 107–10.
———. "Der Einfluss der Volksmusik auf die heutige Kunstmusik" ("The Influence of Folk Music on the Art Music of Today"). *Melos* (Berlin) 1/17 (October, 1920): 384–86.
———. "Arnold Schönbergs Musik in Ungarn." *Musikblätter des Anbruch* (Vienna) 2/20 (December, 1920): 647–48.
———. "Selbstbiographie." *Musikblätter des Anbruch* (Vienna) 3/5 (March, 1921): 87–90. See also: *Magyar Írás* (Budapest) 1/2 (May, 1921): 33–36; *Az Est Hármaskönyve* (Az Est Lapkiadó RT Kiadása, Budapest, 1923), cols. 77–84; *Sovremennya Muzyka* (Moscow) 2/7 (1925): 1–6; and *Színházi Élet* (Budapest) 17/51 (December, 1927): 49–51.
———. "The Relation of Folk Song to the Development of the Art Music of Our Time." *The Sackbut* (London) 2/1 (June, 1921): 5–11.

———. "La musique populaire hongroise." *Revue Musicale* 2/1 (November, 1921): 8–22.

———. "The Folk Songs of Hungary." *Pro Musica* (1928): 28–35.

———. "A parasztzene hatása az újabb műzenére" ("The Influence of Peasant Music on Modern Music"). *Új Idők (Budapest)* 37/23 (May, 1931): 718–19.

———. "Hungarian Peasant Music." *Musical Quarterly* 19 (July 1933): 267–89.

———. "Aufbau der Musik für Saiteninstrumente" ("Structure of Music for String Instruments"). Preface to the score. (Vienna: Universal Edition, 1937): ii–iii (in German, English, and French).

———. "Témoignage (sur Ravel)." *Revue Musicale* 19/2 (December, 1938): 436.

———. "Harvard Lectures" (extracts of the MSS), *Journal of the American Musicological Society* 19/2 (Summer, 1966): 232–43.

———. *Rumanian Folk Music*, Vol. IV. Ed. Benjamin Suchoff, trans. E. C. Teodorescu et al. The Hague: Martinus Nijhoff, 1975.

———. *The Hungarian Folk Song*. Ed. Benjamin Suchoff, trans. M. D. Calvocoressi. Albany: State University of New York Press, 1981.

Berger, Arthur. "Problems of Pitch Organization in Stravinsky." *Perspectives of New Music* 2/1 (Fall-Winter, 1963): 11–42.

Boulez, Pierre. "Stravinsky Remains." Pp. 72f. in *Notes of an Apprenticeship*, trans. Herbert Weinstock. New York: Alfred A. Knopf, 1968.

Brewer, Linda. "Progressions among Non-Twelve-Tone Sets in Kodály's *Sonata for Violoncello and Piano*, Op. 4." D.M.A. treatise, University of Texas at Austin, 1978.

Cross, Anthony. "Debussy and Bartók." *Musical Times* 108 (1967): 125–30.

Demény, János, ed. *Béla Bartók Letters*.

Trans. Péter Balabán and István Farkas, rev. Elizabeth West and Colin Mason. London: Faber and Faber; Budapest: Corvina Press, 1971.

Friedheim, Philip. "Radical Harmonic Procedures in Berlioz." *Music Review* 21/4 (November, 1960): 282–96.

Gaburo, Kenneth Louis. "Studies in Pitch Symmetry in Twentieth Century Music." Ph.D. diss., University of Illinois, 1962.

Gow, David. "Tonality and Structure in Bartók's First Two String Quartets." *Music Review* 34 (August–November, 1973): 259–71.

Jarman, Douglas. "Dr. Schön's Five-Strophe Aria: Some Notes on Tonality and Pitch Association in Berg's *Lulu*." *Perspectives of New Music* 8/2 (Spring-Summer, 1970): 23–48.

———. *The Music of Alban Berg*. Berkeley and Los Angeles: University of California Press, 1979.

———. "Countess Geschwitz Series: A Controversy Resolved?" *Proceedings of the Royal Musical Association* 107 (1980–1981).

Juszkiewicz, Anton. *Litauische Volks-Weisen*. Cracow, 1900. No. 157.

Lansky, Paul, and George Perle. "Atonality." In *The New Grove Dictionary of Music and Musicians*, ed. Stanley Sadie. 6th edition, London: Macmillan, 1980.

Lendvai, Ernő. "Einführung in die Formen und Harmoniewelt Bartóks." Pp. 1–15 in *Béla Bartók, Weg und Werk, Schriften und Briefe*, ed. Bence Szabolcsi. Budapest: Corvina-Verlag, 1957. (See the English translation, *Béla Bartók: An Analysis of His Music*. London: Kahn and Averill, 1971.)

Maxwell, Judith Shepherd. "An Investigation of Axis-Based Symmetrical Structures in Two Compositions of Béla Bartók." D.M.Ed. thesis,

University of Oklahoma, 1975.

Menuhin, Yehudi. *Unfinished Journey.* New York: Alfred A. Knopf, 1977.

Perle, George. "Symmetrical Formations in the String Quartets of Béla Bartók." *Music Review* 16 (November, 1955): 300–312.

———. "The String Quartets of Béla Bartók." *Béla Bartók.* Program notes for the recordings performed by the Tátrai String Quartet. New York: Dover, 1967. Reprinted in *A Musical Offering: Essays in Honor of Martin Bernstein.* New York: Pendragon Press, 1977.

———. "Berg's Master Array of the Interval Cycles." *Musical Quarterly* 63/1 (January, 1977): 1–30.

———. *Twelve-Tone Tonality.* Berkeley and Los Angeles: University of California Press, 1977.

———. *The Operas of Alban Berg,* Vol. I. *Wozzeck.* Berkeley and Los Angeles: University of California Press, 1980.

———. *Serial Composition and Atonality.* 5th edition, revised, Berkeley and Los Angeles: University of California Press, 1981.

———. *The Operas of Alban Berg,* Vol. II. *Lulu.* Berkeley and Los Angeles: University of California Press, 1984. Chapter 4.

Perle, George, and Paul Lansky. "Twelve-Note Composition." In *New Grove Dictionary of Music and Musicians,* ed. Stanley Sadie. 6th edition, London: Macmillan, 1980.

Proctor, Gregory. "Technical Bases of Nineteenth-Century Chromatic Tonality: A Study in Chromaticism." Ph.D. diss., Princeton University, 1977.

Rimsky-Korsakov, Nikolai. *My Musical Life.* Ed. Carl Van Vechten, trans. Judah A. Joffe. New York: Alfred A. Knopf, 1923.

Salzer, Felix, and Carl Schachter. *Counterpoint in Composition: The Study of Voice Leading.* New York: McGraw-Hill, 1969.

Schoenberg, Arnold. *Harmonielehre.* Vienna: Universal-Edition, 1922. (See the English translation by Roy E. Carter, *Theory of Harmony.* Berkeley and Los Angeles: University of California Press, 1978.)

Smith, Robert. "Béla Bartók's *Music for Strings, Percussion, and Celesta.*" *Music Review* 20/3, 4 (August–November, 1959): 264–76.

Somfai, László. *Cantata Profana,* preface to the score. Vienna: Universal Edition, 1934. New York: Boosey and Hawkes, 1955.

Stevens, Halsey. *The Life and Music of Béla Bartók.* New York: Oxford University Press, 1953; revised 1964.

Stravinsky, Igor, and Robert Craft. *Conversations with Igor Stravinsky.* Berkeley and Los Angeles: University of California Press, 1980.

Suchoff, Benjamin, ed. *Béla Bartók Essays.* New York: St. Martin's Press, 1976.

Szőllősy, András, ed. *Bartók Béla összegyűjtott írásai.* Budapest: Zeneműkiadó Vállalat, 1966.

Treitler, Leo. "Harmonic Procedure in the *Fourth Quartet* of Béla Bartók." *Journal of Music Theory* 3/2 (November, 1959): 292–97.

Van den Toorn, Pieter C. "Some Characteristics of Stravinsky's Diatonic Music (II)." *Perspectives of New Music* 15 (Spring-Summer, 1977): 58–95.

Veress, Sandor. "Bluebeard's Castle." Pp. 36–53 in *Béla Bartók: A Memorial Review.* New York: Boosey and Hawkes, 1950.

Westergaard, Peter. "Webern and 'Total Organization.'" *Perspectives of New Music* (Spring, 1963): 107–20.

Whittall, Arnold. "Bartók's Second String Quartet." *Music Review* 32/3 (August, 1971): 265–70.

———. "Tonality and the Whole-Tone Scale in the Music of Debussy." *Music Review* 36/4 (November, 1975): 261–71.

Index to Basic Terms, Definitions, and Concepts

Index to Compositions

This index includes all music mentioned in the text. The page numbers in italics indicate the main analyses of a given composition.

General Index

CPSIA information can be obtained at www.ICGtesting.com
Printed in the USA
BVOW041217141211

278325BV00001B/97/A